Land!

Number 92

The Centennial Series

of the Association of

Former Students,

Texas A&M University

Graham Davis

Land!

Irish Pioneers in Mexican

and Revolutionary Texas

Texas A&M University Press College Station

Davis, Graham.

Land! : Irish pioneers in Mexican and Revolutionary Texas /
Graham Davis — 1st ed.

p. cm. — (Centennial series of the Association of Former Students,
Texas A & M University ; no. 92)

Includes bibliographical references (p.   ) and index.

ISBN 1-58544-189-9 (cloth : alk. paper)

1. Irish Americans—Texas—History—19th century. 2. Pioneers—
Texas—History—19th century. 3. Businessmen—Texas—History—
19th century. 4. Frontier and pioneer life—Texas. 5. Land
settlement—Texas—History—19th century. 6. Texas—History—
Revolution, 1835–1836. 7. Texas—History—To 1846. 8. San Patricio
County (Tex.)—History—19th century. 9. Refugio County (Tex.)—
History—19th century. 10. Texas—Biography. I. Title. II. Series.
F395.16 D38   2002
976.4′0049162—DC21

2001008478

Land is the only thing in the world that

is worth working for, worth fighting for,

worth dying for because land is the only

thing that lasts.

—*Margaret Mitchell,* Gone with the Wind

Contents

Illustrations

Tables

Acknowledgments

It rains a lot in the west of Ireland. One wet day in the spring of 1992, I was on a coach tour of Connemara, organized by the American Conference for Irish Studies, and our guide was struggling to point out the historic landscape which was shrouded in mist. So I turned to the woman sitting next to me and introduced myself. Her name was Eugenia Landes, an anthropologist from Houston, Texas. She told me that if I was really interested in Irish emigration, there was a great story in Texas. "Come visit", she said, "and I will show you around". She was very persuasive, so I went to Texas and began a seven-year adventure that led to the writing of this book. In an old Mercedes, Gene took me around to libraries, archives, the historic sites of Irish settlement, to the Alamo in San Antonio, and to meet descendants of Irish pioneer settlers in Refugio. After three weeks, I was persuaded there was a story that deserved a fresh look and a wider audience, and became convinced that the Irish in Texas was a significant example of prefamine emigration from Ireland. Gene and I subsequently disagreed over the direction of the project and what began as a joint venture, combining disciplines, continued as a singular, historical study.

In 1993 a research grant obtained from the Nuffield Foundation in the U.K. kick-started the research project with three months gathering information in Texas, and for most summers subsequently I went in search of more material. While enjoying the teaching of Irish studies in England, it was frustrating to be five thousand miles from my sources, but this was compensated for by the warm hospitality and invaluable advice given by many friends made in Texas. At Texas A&M University at Corpus Christi these included administrator Tom Kreppel, who made all kinds of things possible, and archivist Tom Kreneck, who pointed me in the right direction in identifying people and material. Mary K. Whitmire, the president of the Irish Society in Corpus Christi, and Maxine Riley of Refugio Museum were very helpful. In Austin and at Victoria I received much assistance and enjoyed many hours sharing an enthusiasm for Texas history with Louise O'Connor and Margaret Eakin. Margaret, Malcolm, and John Mclean gave me sound advice in drawing on their considerable knowledge.

Bob and Catherine Slobod generously put me up for weeks on end in Austin and listened patiently to all the stories that came up. They all know how much I am indebted to them.

Specialist librarians and archivists are essential to the progress of historical research, and I thank the following who have generously shared their specialist knowledge: Tom Shelton at the Library of the Institute of Texan Cultures in San Antonio; in Austin, Don Carleton and his staff at the Center for American History, Neil Foley of the history department at the University of Texas, Michael Green at the Texas State Library and Archives, Galen Greaser at the General Land Office, and Kinga Perzynska at the Catholic Archives. I am also grateful to researcher Mary White, who located vital information on passenger lists, cholera deaths, and newspaper reports, in New Orleans. Equally, help has been on hand on visits to public libraries in Refugio, Corpus Christi, Victoria, at the Library of the Daughters of the Republic at the Alamo, San Antonio and at the university libraries of Boston College, Massachusetts, and at Carbondale in Southern Illinois. In Ireland, staff at the National Library and Public Archives in Dublin, Kieran Burke at Cork City Library, and Patricia McCarthy at the Cork Archives proved most helpful in guiding me to tithe records, newspapers, and collections of letters that offered insights into the wider emigrant experience. Last, I thank the hard-pressed staff of the Newton Park Library at Bath Spa University College who, through the facility of interlibrary loans, brought me a wealth of articles and books published in Ireland and the United States.

Periodically, over a seven-year research project, it is helpful to put thoughts together and to publish articles in academic journals. Assisting the publication of work in progress were Neil Sammells and Paul Hyland, coeditors of the journal *Irish Studies Review*, which included two articles on the Irish in Texas (1993, 1995), one written jointly with Eugenia Landes. George Ward, the editor of the *Southwestern Historical Quarterly*, in Austin, Texas, also encouraged me to write a piece on models of migration related to the Irish in Texas, which was published in the journal in 1996. Finally, Sylvia Hilton, an authority on Spanish America at the Universidad Complutense, Madrid, suggested the writing of a piece on the Irish in the Texas Revolution for the journal *Revista Española de Estudios Norteamericanos*, which appeared in 1997.

Contacts with others interested in the field of Irish migration studies have sustained my own enthusiasm for the project. Papers given at conferences and public lectures in the United States, Ireland, and Britain have helped to test the water and assist the incorporation of fresh insights. Discussions with a network of scholars, including many leading authorities, have been enormously beneficial in shaping my own thoughts and setting the direction of this study. My thanks go to Donald Akenson, Ruth-Ann Harris, David Fitzpatrick, Patrick McKenna, Kerby Miller, Ed O'Day, Patrick O'Farrell, and Blanche Touhill. For many hours of productive discussion and argument over the years, I make particular mention of Patrick O'Sullivan who not only edited his own six-volume series, *The Irish World Wide*, but also continues through his own Irish diaspora studies network to reach out to interested scholars around the world.

My colleague John Robb provided invaluable help with map production. Jill Palmer, secretary in the faculty of humanities at Bath Spa University College, has shown patience beyond measure in incorporating changes to the text prompted by excellent advice given in readers' reports. As ever, my wife, Beth, deserves more than my gratitude for coping with the disruptions that she has endured with my time spent away researching the book.

As one should never underestimate the importance of serendipity in the writing of books, I am tempted to hand responsibility for this book to the rain in the west of Ireland or, in Irish fashion, to leave it to fate and destiny. Nevertheless what appears in print is down to me.

Land!

Introduction

There is no denying the romance of Texas history. Few states of the Union can boast of a past that includes such a legacy of powerful images: the Spanish heritage of Catholic missions and the distinctive layout of town plazas, the frontier life of the early pioneer settlers from the United States and Europe, the symbolic heroism of the Alamo and the Texas Revolution, and the great wealth of individual cattle ranchers and oil magnates. These popular images incorporate a mix of diverse people and stirring events that played their part in the making of Texas.

Place-names on a modern map of Texas testify to the variety of peoples that contributed to the state's history. Tejas, Waco, and Wichita are names derived from Native American tribes in Texas. Gonzalez, Laredo, Seguín, and San Antonio represent just a few of the Spanish names for Texan cities, and forty-one counties owe their titles to Spanish origins. La Salle County honors a French explorer. Fredericksburg and New Braunfels owe their names to the arrival of German settlers in the 1840s. San Patricio County and McMullen County denote an Irish settlement established in 1829. The counties are named after Saint Patrick of Ireland and John McMullen, one of the two Irish empresarios who introduced Irish settlers to Texas. Austin and Houston are named after two of the most illustrious American founders of the Republic of Texas, Stephen F. Austin and Sam Houston.

Despite the presence and contribution of so many peoples in Texas, its history has been written with little recognition accorded to cultural diversity. In recent years, historians have begun to branch out into new directions, and the Institute of Texan Cultures has, through its exhibitions and publications, celebrated the role of all its people. Yet Texas history has been for a long time interpreted and remains firmly rooted in the popular mind in terms of a dominant culture and written in a spirit of triumphalism and with a sense of Manifest Destiny.

No history is written in a cultural vacuum. Each written history represents a set of values and principles, and has, traditionally served the interests of powerful sections of society or of dominant cultural or ethnic groups. National histories have usually been driven by the need to proclaim the virtues, and gloss over the vices, of a country's past. Where matters of war and conquest are concerned, the history that endures is invariably written by the winners. Traditionally, this has been presented as the story of great men: statesmen and generals, men who, by their actions, changed the course of history by creating nations or winning decisive battles. Until quite recently, the lives of women, ethnic minorities, and the common people were rarely investigated or understood. The writing of history was the art of making heroes, and these served as our models to hand down to the next generation. Although people may be in need of heroes as much as they ever were, looking back on the world stage reveals as many figures to despise as to admire. And while "heroic" history has gone out of favor, the other groups, previously ignored, have sought to fill the vacuum with their own story. This carries with it the danger of replacing one narrow and selective view for another; each group competing for status accorded to victims within a model of "oppression" history or, alternatively and sometimes by extension, claiming exclusive honors in a form of "contribution" history, which becomes as self-serving as histories written to justify conquest.

The story of the Irish empresarios and the Irish colonies of San Patricio and Refugio in Texas has been told in the work of two leading authorities. Yet it is not well known outside the locality of Refugio in which they both lived and worked. Hobart Huson wrote *A Comprehensive History of Refugio County*, published in two volumes in 1953 and 1955. William H. Oberste covered the history of both colonies in his study *Texas Irish Empresarios and Their Colonies*, published in 1953. Both are now out of print and difficult to obtain, having become valuable collector's items. Everyone who follows in their wake owes them a considerable debt of gratitude for extensive research conducted over many years. John Brendan Flannery wrote a well-illustrated and broader study in *The Irish Texans*, published by the Institute of Texan Cultures in 1980, and this contains additional material on the Irish in other communities, such as Victoria, San Antonio, and Corpus Christi. The following year Rachel Bluntzer Hébert published an interesting but idiosyncratic book, which included some creative writing, entitled *The Forgotten Colony: San Patricio de Hibernia*, and Richard Roche published a slim booklet entitled *The Texas Connection: The Story of the Wexford Colony in Refugio* in 1989.

Although different in style and focus, they were all written as local histories, either of Refugio or San Patricio, or as an extension of Wexford history, in following the Irish who emigrated to Texas in 1834. More important, they all presented the story of the Irish colonists in the romantic tradition of the struggle for national freedom, transplanted to Texas. The familiar plot depicts the Irish fleeing from poverty and oppression in Ireland, overcoming adversity in the form of cholera and shipwreck on the Texas coast, struggling to survive against hostile Indians in frontier conditions, and enduring property loss and death through the ravages of war in the Texas Revolution.

It is, however, a selective history, driven by a wish to celebrate the durable qualities of the Irish and to communicate to others the valuable contribution the Irish pioneers made in the creation of the Republic of Texas. It combines both oppression history and contribution history. The history presented in this book attempts to overcome these traps. The story of the Irish pioneer settlers in Texas is dramatic as a narrative. It has no need of added color or partisan storytelling. The approach adopted may be described as "inclusive" history, incorporating the lived experience of men, women, and children, irrespective of race, color, or creed. Although the focus is on the Irish settlers, their outlook was clearly shaped by the legacy of the American Revolution in 1776, and some had spent time in the United States before moving to Texas. All of them became colonists alongside a mixed group of Mexicans, Americans, and other Europeans, and after Texas Independence in 1836, the Irish inherited a Hispanic ranching tradition. The argument employed points to a greater acceptance of the polyglot cultures that shaped the formation of Texas, and a crucial blending of cultures that sustained the development of a ranching system in the Coastal Bend.

Primarily, it is a Texas story, but to understand it fully requires a recognition of a wider world. As a frontier province of Mexico, Texas posed problems of population and settlement in the face of American expansionism. Chapter 1 shows how American and European travelers came to explore the wild frontier and described it as a paradise, a garden of Eden, nature unspoilt and untamed. This was how it was sold to would-be migrants in the high-flown language of the day. On a more practical level, the Mexican government offered immensely generous land grants under the empresario system in the 1820s and early 1830s. The chance to acquire land sparked "Texas fever," which attracted men of broken fortune, malefactors, and land speculators from the American South and Europeans who dreamt of a better life in the New World. The dilemma facing the Mexican government was that to populate the province of Texas required accepting American immigrants, many of whom had no land titles, but American settlers could not be relied on to be loyal Mexican citizens. So an attempt was made to attract European migrants, chief among them Irish Catholics, to act as a buffer against the potential aggression of the United States. In the event, Mexico's colonization policy floundered on a lack of manpower, insufficient financial resources, and the political factions in Mexico City that neglected its northern province.

Chapter 2 begins with a discussion of some of the issues currently being debated in Irish migration studies and focuses on the context of Irish emigration in the prefamine period, 1815 to 1845. This includes a discussion of the previous histories of the Irish in Texas, firmly set in the tradition of oppression and contribution history, and questions the perceived wisdom about why the Irish left Ireland to settle in Texas in 1834. Far from being poor victims among a starving people, the would-be colonists appear to have made rational choices about the risks and prospects involved in choosing a pioneer life in Texas. They had to have the means to pay for the trip plus a year's provisions, and they came from one of the most affluent areas of Ireland.

Further reassessment is made in chapter 3, which offers a fresh interpretation of the role of the four Irish empresarios, John McMullen, James McGloin, James Power, and James Hewetson, who between them in the period 1829 to 1834 settled the two Irish colonies of San Patricio and Refugio in south Texas. They are presented as merchants and entrepreneurs who saw in the development of Texas the opportunity to capitalize on their Mexican contacts and experience through land speculation. In many respects, they were men of vision who had become largely Mexicanized through marriage, commercial contacts, and as Spanish speakers. They were the only Europeans who had any success as empresarios; nevertheless it was a highly risky venture, and as the story relates, they faced innumerable obstacles to achieving successful recruitment and settlement of the two colonies. Surviving letters of the Irish colonists point to the ill feeling back in Ireland over the deaths of so many en route to Texas and of the ill feeling between some of the colonists and the empresarios both in San Patricio and in Refugio.

In chapter 4 the role of the Irish in the Texas Revolution of 1835–36 is discussed. It features not only the heroic struggles and sufferings associated with bloody battles and massacres, and the defiant declarations of independence and resistance against the Mexican "invasion" that have been much trumpeted in previous histories but also an explanation of the loyalty of some of the Irish colonists to the Mexican government to whom in law they owed allegiance as Mexican citizens and to whom they were obligated for the land grants bestowed upon them. Two contrasting wars are examined: a war of political rhetoric by the politicians at odds with each other and a war that was far from a foregone conclusion as it see-sawed from one side to the other. Great heroism was displayed and ultimate glory achieved for the Texan cause, but throughout it was mostly a chaotic and uncertain conflict. The Irish colonies suffered disproportionately in being located in the heart of the war zone. Irishmen played their part not only in the military engagements but also in providing the military with intelligence and supplies, and they were in the vanguard of the movement for Texan independence.

Chapter 5 offers a picture of the pioneer life experienced by the colonists who had survived cholera, shipwreck, and death in trying to reach Texas. Drawing on the wealth of contemporary accounts, I reconstruct the early struggles of the colonists; the building of primitive huts from poles and palmetto grass; encounters with Indians who could prove to be friendly or hostile; the ever-present threat of sickness and disease; and the attempts to build communities, churches, and schools. The chapter begins and ends with an assessment of the influence of the frontier on the Irish colonists. Did the harsh environment of a wilderness destroy the cultural baggage they brought with them from Europe, or did they retain certain features of it and maintain their own sense of identity? What contribution did the early settlers make to their communities and to the growth of towns like Victoria, San Antonio, and Corpus Christi?

Chapter 6 concludes the story of the Irish pioneers in Texas. After all the trials and tribulations the colonists suffered over a twenty-year period into the 1850s – when the Indians were finally cleared out of Texas and the border of the Rio Grande was established at the Treaty of Guadalupe-Hidalgo – a triumph over adversity took place that was of major importance to the development of Texas. The Irish colonists who had settled alongside Mexican neighbors acquired the skills and know-how of cattle ranching in a semitropical climate. These had been developed by the Spanish since the early eighteenth century in Texas and were continued by their Mexican successors. A cultural transfer took place among coreligionists that enabled Irish ranchers to thrive on the opportunities thrown up by the market conditions that followed the annexation of Texas to the United States. New Orleans and later Chicago were to become important markets for Texas beef, first by ship, then on the long cattle drives, and finally by rail to the stockyards.

Throughout the general discussion of the cultural inputs into cattle ranching by Texan, Anglo, or Hispanic is the fascinating story of Thomas O'Connor and the making of a great ranching empire. It is a story published for the first time. And it was made possible only by unrestricted access to the O'Connor family papers, previously closed to public scrutiny, and the freedom to interpret the evidence without restraint. The story begins with a seventeen-year-old boy, a nephew of the empresario James Power, who arrived in Texas in 1834, acquired a land grant of 4,428 acres, and assiduously built a mighty estate of 500,000 acres and 100,000 head of cattle by the time of his death in 1887. His life is pieced together from letters, deeds, folk memory, and even grocery lists. (Orthographical inconsistencies are, of course, prevalent in such sources. Unless the usage seems open to misinterpretation, I have reproduced the original spelling without comment.) The story tells not only how a ranching empire was built but also why Thomas O'Connor relentlessly pursued a policy of land accumulation all his life. Being deprived of the family farm in Ireland, the need to build a security for his family against the many uncertainties of frontier life, and the personal and tragic relationship with his eldest son, Dennis, all contributed to his determination to keep on acquiring land. Through surviving letters, we can also reconstruct the cultural legacy brought from Ireland and passed on to the next generation, and the identification that came from fighting for Texas and from the restored American Union after the Civil War.

Essentially, the whole story of the Irish pioneers in Texas is a story about land: not only the land hunger that prompted the colonists to leave Ireland in search of the prospect of owning vast tracts of land in Texas, a journey of 5,000 miles, but also the imaginative leap that allowed them to go from renting 50 acres to owning 4,000 acres. They were caught up in "Texas fever" as land grants became available to Americans, Mexicans, Europeans, and Irish under the empresario system. The war of the Texas Revolution was fought over the untapped potential territory of the province of Texas. Although many lost out to the depredations of the war, they returned to reclaim their land some years later and had to struggle to keep it. Out of this devastation emerged the figure of Thomas O'Connor and the building of a great, ranching estate on a scale that must have been unimaginable to the original colonists.

The Province of Texas in Newly Independent Mexico

1

It is because we get our information of new countries from those who have an interest in bringing their lands into notice that they are invariably represented as flowing with milk and honey.

— Texas in 1837: An Anonymous Contemporary Narrative

TRAVELERS' TALES AND EARLY HISTORIES

More than likely the Irish pioneers who arrived in Texas in the years before the Texas Revolution (1835–36) had come across examples of travel writing designed to attract settlers to the province. They may not have believed everything they read, but it cannot be coincidence that the language encountered in the travel literature and early histories finds an echo in the descriptions employed by the Irish who settled and wrote about their experiences in Texas. Most often, the testimony was written much later than the time of early settlement, by which time the culture and values of pioneering life had become firmly rooted. The rationalization of the emigrant experience must have been shaped by the events of Texan independence and subsequent annexation to the United States. Nevertheless, it is still revealing of the hopes and dreams that Irish migrants took with them that they were compelled to see Texas in terms of a paradise, a garden of Eden.

John J. Linn, one of the earliest Irish settlers, who arrived before the availability of land grants from the Mexican government and became established as a merchant in Victoria, recalled in his old age that, "Texas was then a terrestrial paradise. Health, Plenty and Good-Will teemed throughout the land."[1] This image of paradise occurs frequently in the literature of the time. Indeed, if ever there looked to be a crock of gold at the end of the rainbow it was the province of Texas in newly independent Mexico. Foreign travelers' accounts conjured up images of El Dorado, from early European ideas of the New World and depicted Texas as a kind of paradise. The Scotsman, David Edward, writing in 1836, was lyrical in its praise:

> The province of Texas in general, for native beauty, and the lower division in particular for exuberant fecundity, is excelled by no other country I have ever known; except perhaps in the *first* by Scotland, and it may be in the *last* by Demerera, South America. And although it is as yet but partially cultivated, still it yields its hundreds and its thousands, not only of those things needful for man and beast, but of those which may be termed the superfluities of their existence.
>
> Yea, its spontaneous productions meet the astonished traveler at every step, in such abundance, as can scarcely be believed by one who has not had an opportunity of seeing and judging for himself. Were a man to explore these regions, particularly in the spring months, he would find such a variety of useful and ornamental plants, as would exercise all the powers which he might possess of delineation and description; as he would find the earth covered with their expanding blossoms; the air perfumed with their aromatic fragrance; both combined so as to enchant the sensitive mind into elysian ideas — confirmed by the gratified eye, until every feeling becomes immersed into poetic inspirations; unfolding the curtain of conjecture, and laying open to the delighted view, those fabled dreams of the Elysian fields.[2]

Drawing on similar influences, an anonymous account written by a "citizen of Ohio" in 1838–39, while giving practical advice to potential migrants about life in Texas, "a more suitable arena for those who have everything to make and nothing to lose than (for) the man of capital or family" was unable to resist writing in a heightened romantic style:

> The summer nights of Texas are proverbial for their beauty. The sky is seldom otherwise than very clear, and the moon and stars, shining with a silver luster, throw a mellow light over the earth that, from some mysterious sympathy in our nature, awakens feelings of calm much akin to melancholy. I have traveled at the hour of midnight over the plains to avoid the heat of the sun at a time when the silence of nature was perfect, and as I looked over the beautiful garden of the earth,

spread out before me like a rosebed, and there surveyed the heavens, lit up with their million lamps, I could scarce resist the impression that I had wandered off to the land of the fairies and that Oberon and his train were laughing at me from every flower and dancing around me in very moonbeam.[3]

Both descriptions are clearly influenced by dreams of a blissful arcadia, of a vision of nature untamed in all its glorious creation. The reference to Shakespeare's character Oberon in the play *A Midsummer-Night's Dream*, written in 1594–95, records a precise image for the source of the description of Texas in 1837.[4] Shakespeare himself was writing in the Elizabethan age, a time when the New World was opening up to English explorers like Sir Walter Raleigh and the scourge of the Spanish, *El Draco*, Sir Francis Drake. These explorer-adventurers needed to paint a glowing picture of beauty and potential wealth to win the support of the parsimonious Queen Bess, who despite her own brand of grandiloquent patriotism was notoriously short of money. More than two centuries later, Protestant English settlers in the young American republic retained their English culture and values, which were articulated at the time of Elizabeth's successor by the King James version of the Bible and the works of William Shakespeare.

From the evidence of their own memoirs, the Irish pioneers who settled in two communities, San Patricio and Refugio in south Texas, were familiar with the notion of paradise and accepted it as part of the explanation of their mental and physical migration to the New World. One of the Irish colonists, Annie Fagan Teal, on seeing the location of her frontier home on the banks of the San Antonio River for the first time, described it in equally glowing terms: "O, it was Paradise! such a beautiful country, green grass and trees in mid-winter, horses running and playing over the vast prairies, deer grazing quietly or peeping curiously through the bushes, while birds were so numerous, the very air seemed alive with them."[5] Rosalie Hart Priour was similarly entranced with the prospect of her first home in Papalote Creek about thirty-five miles from Mission Refugio: "The situation is one of the finest in Texas. The house was built on the bank of the creek and shaded by live-oaks with tops in the shape of umbrellas. The wild grapevines covered the trees and formed a nice, cool arbor the sun could never penetrate. Wild flowers of every variety and in the greatest profusion covered the plains as far as the eye could reach. To me it seemed like a miniature paradise."[6] Officials in

Rosalie Hart Priour, who came to Texas as a child in 1836 and later wrote a memoir of her sea voyage and life in the Refugio colony. *Courtesy Corpus Christi Public Library*

Mexico employed the same language. The Committee on Foreign Relations reported to the Mexican government that the province of Texas was "so fertile, of such benign climate, so rich in metals and natural resources that when descriptions of it by geographers were read out, instantly one came to believe that they were talking of Paradise."[7]

This concept of Texas as a paradise offers an insight into the thinking at the time when its population grew rapidly through a process of foreign immigration and settlement. Other contemporary histories were also in the business of promoting Texas as a fertile land where immigrants could expect to prosper. Of course, Irish migration to Texas was part of a wider process of European migration to the New World and of the largely American movement across the border into Mexican territory. The political uncertainty arising from the United States' relations with its neighbor, Mexico, and over the question of Texas independence, inevitably featured in the travel writing of the 1830s and 1840s. Not content with minimizing the political difficulties confronting Texas as citizens of a province of Mexico before 1836, travel writers assured potential migrants that after independence the uncertain future of the new republic would be resolved through annexation to the United States.

Contemporary explanations of the conflict between the United States, including the Anglo-American settlers in Texas and Mexico, focused primarily on the cultural differences between the two peoples. Drawing on historic prejudices inherited from Protestant English antipathy to Catholic Spain and passed on by Anglo-Americans to the Mexican population within Texas, the events of the 1830s and 1840s were interpreted as part of the grand scheme of Manifest Destiny in the conquest of the American continent. Set alongside what was understood as the inevitable tide of history were the policies of Mexican governments in the period 1821 to 1835 in seeking to populate the northern frontier province of Texas. At the heart of Mexican colonization policy was a tension between the obvious need to populate Texas, through immigration, and a deep-seated fear of foreigners, especially *norteamericanos*. Mexican officials had a clear vision of how Texas could be developed but were constantly frustrated by political conflicts at home in Mexico City and by the shortage of financial and military resources needed to protect their frontier territory.

The historian is faced with the problem of how to arbitrate between an American view of a powerful sense of destiny in conquest and a Mexican view that sees a conspiracy of aggression and deceit in the loss of Texas. I suggest that neither government, American or Mexican, ultimately determined the events that led to war. Most of the movement was unplanned and illegal, and consisted not only of heroic frontiersmen, the stuff of popular legend, but also of refugees from debt and criminal records. Even among the government-sponsored empresario land grants, which included the two settlements of San Patricio and Refugio, the terms of the contract were not fully met, and the eventual land grantees were a more mixed group than has been fully recognized. Mexicans and Hispanics — some recruited from Spanish settlements in Louisiana, others who were from substantial ranchero families — formed an important minority of settlers. This suggests that limiting discussion to the usual American-Mexican conflict is oversimplistic. A focus on the background of the Irish empresarios also reveals the extent of entrepreneurial vision that was present in Catholic and Mexican backgrounds, supposedly bereft of such allegedly Protestant virtues. Details of the reports of the Mexican officials

Terán and Almonte also demonstrate how underdeveloped Texas was on the eve of the conflict with Mexico and how vulnerable it remained in the face of a concerted attack by the Mexican army.[8] Far from history unfolding along predetermined lines within a grand master plan, events proceeded amid uncertainty, frustration, and chaos.

In addition to foreign travelers' celebration of an unspoilt paradise, other contemporary histories were also undoubted exercises in promotion. Two well-known examples of promotional history are Mary Austin Holley's *Texas* (1833) and William Kennedy's *Texas: The Rise, Progress, and Prospects of the Republic of Texas* (1841).[9] As the cousin of Stephen F. Austin, who brought in American colonists to settle in the Austin colony, Mary Austin Holley had a clear interest in encouraging new recruits. Kennedy, an English diplomatic secretary and journalist, warmed to Texas and its people and agreed to work for English recognition of the republic. He wrote fulsome descriptions of "a rich and magnificent prairie," and "sparkling water": "The shores of Matagorda, Aransaso, Espiritus Santo, and Nueces Bays, are higher than the margins of the bays lying farther eastwards, and the rivers which there discharge their waters into the gulf invite the stranger in search of a fertile settlement to journey inland, where he is certain to obtain the fulfillment of his hopes and wishes."[10] The overriding impression given was of a promised land that offered the possibility for immigrants to prosper.

Although the colorful descriptions used to promote Texas to would-be settlers evoked notions of an ancient state of nature, travel writers were not averse to appealing to the contemporary yearning for the romantic adventure of frontier life. Alongside the mundane details of the practical needs of immigrants in setting up homes in Texas, the commentary of their own travels was enriched by encounters with Indians, stories of duels, storms at sea, or anecdotes filled with exotic characters and amusing incidents. All too often such tales had little to do with Texas history but reflected the style of writing in demand at the time. A bloodcurdling account on the fierce Karankawa Indians who inhabited the coastal region where the Irish settled provides an example of the kind of vicarious excitement offered: "As they jump around they approach the victim and cut a piece of flesh off of his body, going to the fire and half roasting it in sight of the victim they eat it with great relish, and so they go on cutting off pieces and quartering him until they take off all the flesh and he dies."[11]

This example of a comic fight provides both adventure and entertainment:

The man who had been slapped adjudged himself sorely aggrieved and on the next day, to mend the matter, sent his adversary a challenge. This was accepted. After preliminaries were settled, the parties met at the edge of town, quite to the delight of a large number of the citizens who crowded around to witness what really appeared to them an amusing spectacle. Firing at the distance of ten paces, both parties missed. The challenger was not yet satisfied. A second round was fired, and the challenger having received his adversary's shot in his wooden leg (I beg pardon of the reader for not informing him sooner that he had but one sound one) came to the conclusion that a bullet in a wooden leg was quite a sufficient apology for a slapped cheek and expressed his entire satisfaction. Thus ended this "honorable" affair.[12]

Such anecdotal and, most likely, invented stories added spice to the economic benefits on offer to would-be migrants. In appealing to young settlers, Texas travel writers purveyed a heightened sense of bravado as part of the package. As Stephen Stagner has expressed it in a memorable phrase: "The storm was a celestial shoot-out, so to speak, and Texas history was born between squeezes of the trigger."[13]

The legitimacy of the Texan rebellion against Mexico was justified on the grounds of the cultural superiority of Anglo-Americans over their Mexican neighbors. Unlike today, when confident assertions about racial characteristics are out of favor or, indeed, illegal if thought to incite racial hatred, nineteenth-century writers held clear views about what may be described as the "hierarchy" of races.[14] Such views held their own rationale in the self-evident triumph of American expansion. The increasing domination by the white man of the American continent was a sign to Protestant Anglo-Americans that the tradition of freedom inherited from an English birthright and celebrated in the successful American Revolutionary War would always triumph over barbarism, despotism, and corruption. Texas history was understood as part of a great tide of history, the working out of a great providential plan.

American negative stereotypes of Mexicans derived less from direct observations than from the inherited prejudices held by their Protestant English ancestors against Catholic Spain. Long memories of atrocities committed against Protestants or dissidents drew on the bloodstained record of the Spanish Inquisition and the Saint Bartholomew's Day Massacre, and those dark deeds became immortalized in such fundamental Protestant texts as John Foxe's *Book of Martyrs*.[15] Traditional English fear of Catholicism was compounded by the despotic power and New World–wealth that in the sixteenth century raised imperial Spain to be the dominant power in Europe. The attempted invasion of Elizabethan England by the Spanish Armada in 1588, if successful, would have not only restored Catholicism but also overthrown cherished English liberties. English colonists in North America carried with them twin beliefs in Protestantism and freedom and regarded Spanish rule in Latin America as "authoritarian, corrupt and decadent and that Spaniards were bigoted, cruel, greedy, tyrannical, fanatical, treacherous, and lazy." [16]

What Spanish historians have dubbed the Black Legend drew on anti-Catholic and anti-Spanish beliefs in Europe but was transferred to the New World and given fresh impetus with the evil reputation of the Spanish conquistadores. Unlike the English colonial settlers who came, ostensibly, to the Americas in search of freedom and a better life for their families, the Spanish imperialists were cast as greedy adventurers in search of gold and silver who oppressed and enslaved the native peoples. Despite winning their own freedom from Spain and establishing an independent Mexico in 1821, the Mexican people were regarded as the descendants of the conquistadores. "We [Anglo-Americans] transferred some of our ingrained antipathy toward Catholic Spain to her American heirs." [17]

Another feature that gave rise to Anglo-American hostility to the Mexicans was that of mixed blood. Commonly described as dark skinned or "swarthy," the Mexican mestizos were generally thought to have combined the worst qualities of Spaniards and Indians. Chief among these was the charge of idleness, which not only associated the Mexicans with the despised Spaniards but also served to explain the relative economic backwardness of the frontier provinces. [18] In fact, the harsh realities of nineteenth-century frontier life meant that for the Mexicans to have survived in the province of Texas, they almost certainly would have had to work harder than their compatriots in the more developed parts of central Mexico or the eastern parts of the United States. They could not rely on native Indian labor and had to work with their own hands. With few exceptions, they lacked the support of towns and markets and had to be self-sufficient in nearly all the necessities of life. They, along with Irish and Anglo-American settlers, also faced the added hazard of defending themselves and their families from attacks by hostile Indians.

So how do we explain the persistence and strength of the belief in the laziness of Mexicans? As David Weber has suggested, it is partly the long ancestry and endurance of the Black Legend, the deeply held beliefs and supporting values of Protestant Englishmen who settled in the seventeenth and eighteenth centuries as American colonists. Their presence and prosperity in the New World reaffirmed, through their own experiences, a sense of destiny as God's chosen people and confirmed their hostility to the autocracy, wickedness, and corruption of Catholic Spain and its dependent Mexico.

Second, there were fears of moral contamination or dilution in the mixing of races. Anglo-Americans generally regarded nonwhite people as lazy. This, of course, strayed beyond a logical position, not merely because of the dependence on black slavery but also because it was not always clear who could safely be included as white. At one time or another in the nineteenth century, Irish, Italians, and Greeks were classed as nonwhite in the United States, although this was a temporary condition that was subsequently altered. In northeastern cities, especially, poor Irish immigrants who found themselves doing "Negro work" were for a time, classed as black.[19]

Third, as Weber has pointed out in discussing the work of psychologists on racial stereotyping, "ethnic hostility is a projection of unacceptable inner strivings onto a minority group."[20] In other words, the ethnic group becomes an alter ego. Does this explanation reveal something of the desire of many Americans to escape from the treadmill of the nineteenth-century work ethic? Were the Anglo-American settlers in Texas quick to despise the Mexicans as lazy because they secretly aspired to a life of idleness built on the backs of the black slaves they brought with them from the southern states? Such a theory is also capable of extension into incorporating what was admired in the observed behavior of Mexican relations between the sexes. The sensuous beauty of Mexican women was much admired by American travelers. The easy familiarity between men and women was a source of ambivalent comment, seen from a more puritanical, American culture. It is not difficult to detect secret physical longings that needed to be suppressed. Tempting sexual liaisons and, even worse, marriage and fathering children of mixed American Mexican blood, would have undermined the cultural identity and sense of superiority Americans derived from a European, Protestant background.

In describing the Mexican character, based on observations of the people of San Antonio de Béxar, an anonymous American writer was able to claim with engaging certitude that despite considerable advances having been made in recent years, the Mexican nation "lagged behind other nations in every essential which constitutes the security and happiness of a people." Texas with 60,000 people had successfully resisted the 9 million people of Mexico, and "when the issue was made upon the field of battle, it was no contest at all."[21] In other words, the Texan victory of San Jacinto in April, 1836, could be put down to the inferiority of the Mexican people. Physical appearance was cited as evidence. "The Mexican of San Antonio, of a dark eye and hair and a thin, bronzed complexion, is inferior in stature and physical development in every particular to the Anglo-Saxon." They speak Spanish but it is "so adulterated and corrupted that it grates like harsh thunder upon the chaste ear of the polished Castilian."[22]

Continuing with a litany of faults, the author alleged that Mexicans were too easily influenced by their Catholic priests, and they were summarily dismissed as "cowardly," "cruel," and by turns, "humble" and "sycophantic," full of "deceit," possessing "excessive pride," and noted for a spirit of "revenge." We are informed that Mexicans enjoyed a life of indolence and ease and most were satisfied with a bare living: "The small quantity of corn which he requires demands but little labor, owing to the amount that may be produced from a little piece of ground, and his animal food is easily procured, there is no necessity for much bodily exertion."[23] These negative characteristics attached to the Mexicans on the part of Anglo-Americans are exactly mirrored by the same kind of comments that English travel writers made about the "lazy" and "morally degenerate" Irish peasantry who were commonly blamed for the disaster of the Great Famine in the 1840s.[24] In the light of the subsequent history of Irish migration to Texas, settling in communities alongside Mexican neighbors, it is obvious that these allegedly racial characteristics ascribed to other peoples were a social construct that revealed more about the values of the more powerful group than of those they criticized.

However, the picture was not entirely negative. Just as the English saw particular virtues in the Irish people, so there were a few Mexican traits that could be depicted as virtues. Mexicans loved to talk, were light-hearted in spirit, and were easier in their relations between the sexes than was the case in the more reserved social climate that existed in the United States. In fact, there was a discernible touch of envy in the way the man from Ohio was entranced by the free-spirited way the Mexican ladies danced the fandango, although when he was made to feel clumsy and foolish in attempting to join in, he felt compelled to scorn the fandango as a "poor concern." But there was nothing equivocal in identifying the impressive Mexican skills in horsemanship: "No people are equal to the Mexicans in the management of their animals when wild and apparently ungovernable. They feel no hesitation in mounting the mustang as soon as caught and it is not long until it becomes perfectly tractable under their rigid government." Yet the overall verdict was that "the inhabitants of San Antonio are yet a primitive people in their whole mode of life."[25] The dramatic events of Texas history, the republic born of sudden and violent change, made it easier to apply an explanation based on cultural conflict and the "moral superiority" of Anglo-Americans over Mexicans. But what shaped the moral explanation of history drew on centuries of old beliefs both in the Americas and in Europe.

MEXICAN POLICY TOWARD TEXAS

If Texas was regarded by contemporary writers as a paradise, it was a sparsely populated paradise. After a bloody war of independence, the young republic of Mexico inherited an enormous territory from imperial Spain, stretching from Oregon to Guatemala, yet Mexico possessed a population of only 6.2 million. The hemorrhage of war had severely drained both the Mexican workforce and the numbers of men capable of bearing arms. The recruitment of foreign migrants who could bring their skills, enterprise, and capital to this land might help to restore the country and populate the northern territories. A successful model of immigration and economic growth was suggested in the neighboring United States of America, where the population had more than doubled, from 4 to 9.6 million, in the period 1790 to 1820.[26]

Coahuila y Texas was the most vulnerable of Mexico's northern states. Following the decline of the Spanish missions, defense was needed from the depredations of *los indios barbaros* (Lipan Apaches and Comanches), but anxiety also existed among Mexican officials about the potential expansion of the United States into Mexican territory. With the acquisition of Louisiana by the United States in 1803, Texas acted as a buffer province against further American aggression. Yet Anglo-Americans were an obvious source of local migrants who had already been crossing into eastern Texas from Louisiana and were outnumbering the Mexican population. Moses Austin, as a Spanish citizen, had contracted the settlement of

Catholic families from Louisiana into land near the Colorado River. His son, Stephen F. Austin, was able to inherit and complete the contract in establishing the Austin colony.

While the Mexican government wanted to exercise control of land grants and settlement to strengthen defense and to further trade, local officials connived at illegal immigration from land squatters or worse. One reason for the American desire to acquire Texas was that it was fast becoming a place of escape for debtors, desperadoes, malefactors, and runaway slaves. The Mexican government looked to European migrants to populate Texas to establish a safeguard against further "Americanization" for the province. An early task for the new Mexican governor Augustin Iturbide in 1821 was to populate the northern province by encouraging the settlement of Mexicans, Europeans, and Anglo-Americans. The primary reason for settling the province was to strengthen defense against Indians and the threat of foreign powers. With no fixed border recognized between Texas and the United States, since the agreement between Spain and the United States in the Treaty of 1819 had not been endorsed, Texas was vulnerable to invasion from Americans.

It was not long since the attempted invasion of Texas in 1812 by Guitiérrez de Lara, who received support from U.S. officials. In the spring of 1813 he had captured San Antonio and proclaimed Texas to be an independent state deriving its political authority from the people, but this mercenary army, weakened by internal quarrels, was defeated by the royalist force under the command of José Joaquin Arredondo. After recapturing the province, Arredondo executed 327 rebels in San Antonio and embarked on a further purge of republican suspects in east Texas. As a result, many Tejanos (Mexican Texans) fled to Louisiana, leaving Texas devastated, deprived of food and cattle, and drained of population. Further abortive invasions by American mercenaries took place in 1819 and 1821, only adding to the ruin and destruction of the province in the last years of Spanish rule.

The loss of wealthy Spaniards after the independence of Mexico left a shortage of capital and entrepreneurial skills as well as a scarcity of manpower and of fighting men to defend the garrison towns of Texas. The policy of inviting foreigners to settle in Mexico represented a shift away from the policy Spain had adopted in its American empire. A suspicion of foreigners meant that Spain relied on its own small population who would "civilize" the indigenous, native people and convert them into loyal subjects. The Spanish presence was considered vital to the success of the policy, and the endurance of the Spanish legacy in the postindependence era bears witness to the success of the policy throughout Latin and South America. However, the idea of keeping foreigners out did not fully apply everywhere. The exceptions to this general rule were the northern provinces of Texas and California, where a shortage of population remained a problem despite attempts to promote internal migration. Inducements in the form of free transportation, seeds, tools, land offers, and exemptions from taxes failed to increase the populations of the frontier provinces. Even the government settlement of soldiers, convicts, and orphans made little difference. By 1821 the population of Texas was a mere 2,500.

The precedent for settling Texas with foreigners, against the policy in place elsewhere, was made with the Spanish acquisition from France of Louisiana in 1762. Frenchmen and Anglo-Americans already lived there, and they were allowed to remain. Furthermore, in 1788 Louisiana was opened to foreign settlers who pledged loyalty to the crown and allegiance to the Catholic church. The intention was to increase the population of Louisiana, but the results were not as beneficial as expected. Spanish officials found the *norteamericanos* unwilling to adapt to Spanish customs and regarded them as potentially troublesome. So the policy allowing foreign settlers was limited to Louisiana, where it was difficult to reverse, but officially Americans were not allowed to settle beyond the boundary of the province. However, an important difference existed between what was official and what was actually happening. From the 1790s on Americans began drifting across the Louisiana border into east Texas, where they settled illegally with the connivance of local officials who welcomed settlers of any kind.

Following the transfer of Louisiana to France in 1800 and its purchase by the United States in 1803, the new buffer between the United States and Mexico was the province of Texas. Relations between the governments of Spain and the United States were strained by the American claim that the Louisiana purchase included the province of Texas. So the imperial Spanish policy allowed some foreigners, but not Americans, to enter Texas, whereas local officials turned a blind eye and welcomed any immigrants, including Americans, who were willing to increase the frontier population.

After the United States gave up its claim to Texas in 1819, a change occurred in Spanish policy toward U.S. immigrants. It began with a land grant in 1821 to Moses Austin, a Spanish subject from Louisiana, to settle an initial three hundred Catholic families on the Brazos River in Texas.

This was to have momentous consequences for the settlement and, ultimately, the destiny of the province. This was not only the beginning of the Austin colony, developed by Moses' son, Stephen F. Austin, after his father's death, but also opened the gates to a much broader influx of American and other foreign settlers. A bill was approved by the Spanish Cortes, supported by Texas governor Antonio Martinez, allowing foreigners to settle public lands of Mexico's northern territory from California to Texas. Although special vigilance was to be kept with regard to Anglo-Americans, the practice was established. In effect, Spain anticipated the policy that was adopted by newly independent Mexico.

In looking to populate the northern frontier territories, the new Mexican government of Augustin Iturbide proposed a colonization plan that would offer incentives for both foreign and Mexican settlers. The government commission accepted the need for more people to defend the north of the country, identifying European and Anglo-Americans as most appropriate for the vulnerable province of Texas. In October, 1821, a group of American filibusters seized the town of Goliad before Mexican troops captured them and, in desperation over the threat from U. S. expansion, prompted a policy of population before it was too late. By February, 1823, Iturbide had a colonization law ready to implement, but within a month his government had fallen from power and the law was annulled.

Compounding the vulnerability of the frontier province of Texas was the instability of politics in Mexico City. The new government, however, did manage to pass a colonization law in 1824 that remained in force as long as Mexico controlled the frontier with the Mexican southwest. This colonization law had very generous provisions for settlers. It guaranteed land, security, and an exemption from taxes for four years to foreign settlers. Foreigners were not legally able to acquire property within twenty leagues of the national border or within ten leagues of the coasts and a limit of eleven leagues was placed on individual ownership. Under the terms of the law, Mexicans would be given preference in the granting of land. A further law in 1828 made Mexican citizenship obligatory for those with two years' residence.

The contradiction at the heart of Mexican policy was that in order to defend the frontier against American invasion, it was thought to be wise and necessary to encourage Americans to settle. In fact, it was a recognition of the reality in the frontier settlements. By 1823 some three thousand Americans lived illegally on the Mexican frontier. With a mere two hundred Mexican troops available, there was no effective control of entry or prospect of repatriation across an ill-defined and inadequately policed border. The modern parallels with illegal migrants crossing the Mexican border into Texas are obvious. In both cases, the geographical extent of the frontier is guaranteed to defeat government policy. In the early 1800s, it was considered better to legalize the status of illegal settlers and, by giving them a stake in the land, encourage loyalty to their new country.

The federal 1824 colonization law was implemented through state law in Coahuila y Texas in the same year. While official fears were expressed about the loyalty of Anglo-Americans, the colonization law of 1825 permitted them to settle but with preference to be given to Mexicans. The terms were decidedly generous. The head of a family would obtain a *sitio*, a square league of grazing land (4,428 acres) and a *labor* of farming land (177 acres). Only modest fees were payable over six years, and no payment was due until the fourth year. The law also specified that foreign colonists should be Christian, industrious, and of good character, and should become Mexican citizens. Additional land was obtained by foreigners marrying Mexican women. The size of the land grants, increased at the last minute from 640 acres to 4,428 acres, encouraged potential colonists but also stimulated speculation in the increased value of land. The terms laid down in the colonization law of 1824 affected only a small minority of settlers in the province of Texas. The majority of American immigrants, who mostly settled in east Texas, were ignorant of the law and of the Spanish language and they remained as illegal squatters on land that lay within twenty leagues of the border or ten leagues of the Gulf of Mexico. At the time of Texas independence in 1836, they occupied land to which they had no title.

Those settlers who were able to secure land titles usually came under the contracts of empresarios, or agents of the Mexican government, who recruited colonists, administered the allocation of lands, and enforced state regulations. In return, they could expect to receive up to five *sitios* of grazing land and five *labores* of farming land for every hundred families that settled in their colonies. Between 1823 and 1835 twenty-seven different parties concluded forty-one empresario agreements with the Mexican government. Most of them were signed by Anglo-Americans. Only a few Mexicans held contracts as empresarios. Successful completion meant fulfilling the contracts within a specified period. The potential number of settlers was 13,091 families or possibly 65,455 individuals. The shortfall in the numbers of settlers may be gauged by the actual population of Texas in 1835, which was only 24,700.[27]

Before 1830 only three empresarios had achieved success in bringing significant numbers of colonists into Texas. The most successful was Stephen F. Austin, who took over his father's Spanish grant in 1821. When the Mexican government recognized his grant, he was able to benefit from the colonization law of 1823, bringing three hundred families into Texas by 1825. Austin was equally successful in meeting the terms of three more contracts from the state government for bringing another nine hundred families to Texas. The Austin colony covered a huge expanse of territory centered on San Felipe de Austin on the Brazos River. To the west of the Austin colony, Green De Witt's colony was situated along the Guadalupe and Lavaca Rivers. Founded in 1825 and centered on the town of Gonzalez, only a third of the four hundred families contracted had gained land titles by 1832. Consequently, De Witt's empresario grant was annulled and the land reverted to the public domain. Adjoining the De Witt and Austin colonies was the only colony that had a majority of Mexican settlers. It was founded by a rancher from the Mexican province of Tamaulipas and centered on what became known as the town of Victoria. It was originally named in 1824 after President Guadalupe Victoria. The De León grant antedated the federal colonization law of 1824 and was issued by the provincial deputation at San Antonio de Béxar. It remained a small colony, with slightly more than a hundred titles issued by 1835. Although De León's boundaries remained a matter of dispute with his Irish empresario neighbors, a number of Irish settled in the De León colony and were important figures in the development of Victoria. One of its most famous citizens, John J. Linn, an Irish merchant and Texas pioneer, also secured a land title in the Power-Hewetson colony at Refugio.[28] Juan Linn Street in Victoria is named after him.

The flow of migrants over the border from the United States to Texas gathered momentum in the 1820s, regardless of colonization laws or empresario contracts. Attracted by the prospect of cheap land and easy terms of payment, Americans were also looking to escape from unwelcome pressures at home. The people who migrated from the American South to Texas were regarded as frontiersmen and pioneers, and they became part of the mythology of the American West.

John J. Linn was a Power-
Hewetson colonist, Victoria
merchant, and quartermaster
in the Texan Army.
*Courtesy Center for
American History—UT Austin*

There is an extensive literature on the American frontiersman that forms part of an heroic tradition. The idea that the American character was embodied in the pioneering, frontier experience where qualities of perseverance and practicality, inventiveness and improvisation were essential to survival, has had a long and enduring influence.[29] At a popular level, the image of the frontiersman fits the legends of Daniel Boone, Davy Crockett, and Jim Bowie. These men have been cast as heroes undaunted by the task of taming a wilderness to receive the blessings of American civilization. In challenging that romantic image, Mark E. Nackman has argued effectively that American migrants to the western frontier and those who moved southwest to Texas were not, for the most part, the stuff of legends but quite ordinary men.[30] They were not utopian pioneers with a high-minded vision of American values but men driven out by discontent and difficult circumstances. Indeed, a good many willing to go had little to lose, having failed in their own communities. They were as likely to be dislocated drifters and fugitives from justice as potential empire builders.

During the first generation of Anglo-American settlement in Texas, most of the migrants were nonslaveholding backwoodsmen and farmers from the hill country of the trans-Appalachian West. Donald W. Meinig has identified the variety of classic types of the southern frontier: "the half-Indian hunter and trader, the restless and the shiftless, the earnest colonist and the crass speculator, the whisky peddler and the itinerant preacher."[31] The frontier population represented a polyglot mixture of all kinds and conditions detached from the more structured societies of the older states of the union who migrated in a headlong rush to the relative freedom of Texas.

What pushed them out was largely the economic pressures encountered in states east of the Mississippi. What pulled them to settle in Texas was the prospect of acquiring abundant, cheap land. In 1819 a financial crisis brought hard times to the American republic, especially in the Ohio and Mississippi Valleys. The closure of a number of banks restricted credit and meant the loss of people's savings. The United States Land Act of 1820 lowered the price of public land from $2.00 to $1.25 per acre and removed the credit allowances for prospective settlers looking to obtain land in the public domain. The economic depression at home coincided with the news that with the blessing of the new Mexican republic in 1821, an American empresario, Stephen F. Austin, was offering titles on hundreds of acres of land in Texas. Thus began the official American migration across the border into Mexico. American settlement in east Texas in Mexican territory north of the Nueces River was not hindered by the claims of the Indian tribes or by the presence of the Mexican population largely concentrated in towns like Béxar, Goliad and Nacogdoches. The government grants of land virtually ignored Indian rights from prior occupancy and the Mexican population in Texas was to become increasingly outnumbered by American settlers.

During the 1820s some ten thousand Americans migrated to Texas, many of them burdened by debt and looking to escape their financial obligations and the penalties of the law. G.T.T. (gone to Texas) became infamous letters when left on the doors of abandoned homes by delinquents wishing to avoid the debt collector and the sheriff in the southern states. The continuation of economic difficulties in the south during the 1820s and 1830s served to swell the tide of migration to Texas. By 1836 the American population had risen to more than thirty thousand, with the major concentration in east Texas representing a continuation of a planter and farming culture that was closer to that of the southern United States than to the rest of Mexico. Largely isolated in eastern and central Texas, Anglo-American settlers not only outnumbered Mexicans but also remained in relative independence from the predominantly Mexican settlements of Béxar and Goliad. While this failure to integrate American settlers concerned the Mexican government, there was little they could do to stop the flow of migrants across the border. Government orders issued to restrict the numbers of Americans entering Texas, as in 1826, had little effect without the means to police the border.

Warning signs of trouble stored up for the future came in the December, 1826, revolt when the empresario Haden Edwards, irritated by conflicts over land titles, rashly proclaimed the independence of Texas under the title of the Fredonia Republic. The revolt collapsed within a month under threat from Mexican troops stationed in Béxar. Fellow empresarios Stephen F. Austin and Green De Witt failed to support Edwards, proclaiming instead their loyalty to the Mexican authorities. The incident demonstrated the potential danger to Mexico from the American presence in Texas. It also illustrated that several interests were behind the further settlement of Mexico's northern frontier territory, with or without government approval. At this point, the availability of cheap land in Texas under Mexican colonization laws was more attractive to Stephen F. Austin than the prospect of annexation to the United States, which would have ended the policy. Mexican officials, following the Haden Edwards affair, were also anxious not to turn away American settlers who benefited trade in frontier communities. The Mexican government, however, was most concerned about security. Consequently, in 1828 General Mier y Terán, a high-ranking former minister and experienced engineer, was sent to review the situation in Texas and recommend improvements for its defense. His reports to Mexico were alarming. Writing from Nacogdoches, he noted that as he had journeyed from Béxar, the Mexican influence diminished to almost nothing, and he was fearful about the "unceasing" stream of Americans.[32]

What I perceive in all this is that certainly in Nacodoches [sic], at least, more government action is needed in the town, since it is a frontier [outpost] with which the Republic should maintain closer contact. By law, the general government possesses vast tracts of land in this country, and in order to distribute them wisely, it is necessary to pay attention to the economy no less than to politics and national security. The total population is a mixture of such strange or incoherent elements that no other like it exists in our entire federation: tribes of savages, numerous and peaceful but armed and always ready for war, whose

progress toward civilization surely will be achieved through close vigilance by a zealous and well-educated political authority, and colonists
who have come from another, more advanced society, better educated
but also more malicious and mistrustful than are the Mexicans. Among
the foreigners there are all kinds: fugitive criminals, honorable farmers, vagabonds and ne'er-do-wells, laborers, etc. They all go about with
their constitution in their pocket, demanding their rights and the authorities and functionaries that [their constitution] provides. Most of
them hold slaves who, now having perceived the favorable intent of
Mexican law with regard to their tragic state, are becoming restless to
throw off their yoke, while their masters believe they can keep them by
making [the yoke] heavier. They commit the barbarities on their slaves
that are so common where men live in a relationship so contradictory
to their nature: they pull their teeth, they set dogs upon them to tear
them apart, and the mildest of them will whip the slaves until they are
flayed.[33]

He noted that Americans, as the majority, would not assimilate with
a population of poor Mexicans whom they regarded as inferior. Moreover, American complaints about the inadequate system of justice and
the political disorganization of the frontier were justified. As a remedy,
he, at first, advocated the reform of frontier institutions before a situation developed in which Texas "will pull down the entire federation."[34]
In 1829, when Mier y Terán assumed military command of the eastern
interior provinces, which included Coahuila y Texas, he exercised a powerful influence on government policy. By this time, he had become more
convinced of the dangers posed by the presence of American colonists in
Texas and more aware of the expansionist plans of the United States. His
sensible recommendations were enacted by the Mexican government.

He wanted new military garrisons and existing presidios strengthened.
He emphasized the need to develop the coastal trade between Texas and
the Mexican ports to improve commercial ties with the rest of the country. Finally, he advocated the need to introduce European and Mexican
colonists into Texas as a way of combating the American presence. It was
an urgent message that unless Texas was occupied by the government, it
would be lost. What followed was a law enacted in April, 1830. This, in
fact, went beyond Mier y Terán's recommendations. Instead of adopting
the policy of European and Mexican colonization, the law prohibited fur-

ther immigration from the United States and rescinded all empresario contracts that had not met the terms of settlement. More provocatively, the law expressly prohibited the introduction of slaves into Texas. This overturned the exemption of Texas in 1829 to the emancipation of slaves in Mexico enacted by President Vicente Guerrero. If it could be presented as a humanitarian move, it was also intended as a means of slowing down in-migration by dissuading slave-owning Americans from moving into Texas.

The 1830 law was a serious step, taken in an atmosphere of alarm at the prospect of Mexico's losing its frontier province of Texas. The American acquisition of Louisiana and Florida were cited as examples of the remorseless expansionism of Mexico's northern neighbor. The arrival in 1829 of Anthony Butler, Pres. Andrew Jackson's representative in Mexico, with an offer of $5 million for the purchase of Texas, convinced Mexican officials of the very real threat posed by American settlers. Enacting policy, however, was one thing; implementing it was quite another. Mexico did appoint a succession of able men as directors of colonization in Texas. Mier y Terán held the office until July, 1832, under the conservative government of Anastasio Bustamente. In August, 1833, Mier y Terán was replaced by Tadeo Ortiz de Ayala, under the liberal government of Valentín Gómez Farías. Ortiz may have lacked the political and military experience of his predecessor but he was an intelligent and much-traveled writer on colonization projects. He fully understood Mexico's awkward relationship with the United States. As early as 1821 he had warned about foreign threats to frontier provinces, especially to Texas, which he saw as the key to a unified plan of defense and progressive development. In 1830 he wrote a report to the vice president that pointed to the dangerous presence of substantial numbers of Anglo-American settlers living in frontier conditions beyond the jurisdiction of Mexico's federal government and remote from the provincial government in Saltillo:

If the independent Mexican government, Excellent Sir, wishes to transmit to posterity with a strong hand the integrity of its possessions, it must not forget for an instant, that as soon as the intrepid descendants of the English gained their independence and consolidated their institutions, they began to reflect upon the meager resources which a mediocre and undeveloped land had furnished them. To fulfil their destiny and to acquire a political preponderance in the new world . . .

they justly aspired to national aggrandisement and to an extension of their limits toward the south and west and encroached upon lands that were more fertile and a climate [that] was more favourable.[35]

The loss of the Floridas and of Louisiana, allied to the increasing American presence over the U.S. border into Texas, gave strength to the Mexican suspicion of foreigners and to the fear of American aggrandizement. Against a background of weak provincial administration, Ortiz warned, "those foreigners – the greater part of them adventurers – that both their special and general laws have been evaded or opposed under slight pretext through the cunning and power of certain men, who secretly despising the nation and accustomed to cunning manipulation and intrigues, will be on the lookout for a favourable moment to consummate their treason."[36] Ortiz argued that further American influence had to be checked with "stubborn firmness" and that the Mexican government needed to "adopt an equally strong system of population and fortifications."[37] Instead of allowing more Americans to settle, Ortiz recommended recruiting European migrants, "establishing a certain number of foreign families on an equal basis with the Mexican families defraying their transportation, providing them with utensils and maintenance for one year."[38]

The population growth would need to be matched by agricultural development, commerce, and industry. In the past, Ortiz contended, too much reliance had been placed on the product of mines. It was a source of wealth that was elusive, unstable, and never likely to have the positive value of the cultivation of fertile lands. He proposed that each district, beginning at the Sabine River, should have its own model farm dedicated to cultivating flax, hemp, mulberries, olives, and grapes, and establishing beehives. Seeds and plants would be provided free to the colonists. Government rewards would be conditional on the progress made. Agricultural produce also had to be turned to commercial advantage through the better use of navigable rivers and ports.[39] Furthermore, in order to develop industry and trade, colonization companies should be found in Europe and offered the exclusive privilege, for a specified period, of hunting for fur-bearing animals, such as the otter, the bear, and the deer. Free ports would be established in the new settlements that would so increase the volume of trade they would in a few years more than compensate for a temporary loss of customs revenue. Tadeo Ortiz made a list of proposals that today appear modern and farsighted. In fact, they were too farsighted for the Mexican government, which lacked the resources and perhaps the collective will to implement them. An insufficient military presence, a policy of benign neglect with regard to the administration of the settlements in Texas, and a lack of commercial enterprise that needed to be harnessed to a vigorous and consistent colonization policy promised problems for the near future.

The law of 1830 introduced two responsibilities for the director of colonization in Texas — to restrict Anglo-American immigration and to facilitate Mexican and European settlement. Experience told Mier y Terán and Ortiz that the policy of keeping Americans out of Texas was simply impracticable. Attempts to enforce the policy would not only upset the American settlers already there but also encourage moves toward independence. In practice, the law, while unable to prevent undesirables from illegal settlement, tended to deter the honest and industrious migrants. Texas preserved its unenviable reputation as a haven for debtors and refugees from justice.

Mier y Terán made plans for five thousand Mexicans to be drawn from every state of the republic in a bid to colonize Texas from the Mexican interior. With state officials unwilling to make a sacrifice of their local populations to settle the frontier province, the scheme failed. Similarly, the idea of sending convicts and their families to the frontier never produced the new levels of settlement required. Some modest success was achieved in the policy of strengthening military garrisons at Béxar, Nacogdoches, and Goliad and building six forts in a circle around the Anglo-American colonists. An increased military presence was designed to cut down on smuggling and illegal immigration. Three posts were strategically placed on key rivers: Lipantitlán on the Nueces, overlooking San Patricio, the Irish settlement; Terán on the Neches; and Lavaca on the Lavaca River. These military posts were intended to be focal points for the growth of colonies, but it was an expensive measure that was unlikely to work without an influx of Mexican farmers and artisans.

The reluctance of Mexicans to move to the frontier territory was compounded by the political instability in Mexico City. The political crisis in the capital led to the withdrawal of troops, leaving the garrisons sparsely occupied. After a period of intense frustration, Mier y Terán, in an atmosphere of internal political strife, despaired of holding on to Texas. In July, 1832, his despair caused him to commit suicide. His successor as director of colonization, Tadeo Ortiz, put greater faith in the recruitment of European settlers, and there is no doubt that, for a brief period, foreigners were offered exceptionally generous terms to settle on the frontier. The primary attraction was an abundance of cheap land and what appeared to be the absence of political interference or conflict. In the 1830s two pairs of Irish-born empresarios were successful in founding settlements in Texas. John McMullen and James McGloin established the town of San Patricio de Hibernia in 1830 on the Nueces River. In 1834 James Power and James Hewetson founded Refugio on the site of the Spanish mission Nuestra Señora del Refugio, a few miles in from the port of Copano. Usually described as Irish colonies, they were, in fact, a mix of Irish and Mexican, with small numbers of American and other Europeans included among the list of land grantees.[40] The full story of the Irish empresarios and of the settlements of San Patricio and Refugio is told in chapter 3. What is significant at this point is the thinking behind the Mexican government's approval of Irish settlers.

Attracting European migrants to Texas was seen as a safeguard against further Americanization of the province. From a Mexican perspective, the Irish, among all European peoples, were identified as the most desirable of settlers. They were regarded as loyal Catholics, having suffered cruel persecutions in defense of their faith. They possessed outstanding moral virtues and were known to be highly industrious. Finally, they were thought to be not too friendly to England or to the United States, so that in case of war, Mexico could rely on brave soldiers, famous in previous centuries for their military valor in fighting for imperial Spain to defend its borders.[41]

While Mexicans were reluctant to migrate to the northern frontier, at least a few Europeans were willing to take a chance on a pioneer life with the prospect of land that was denied to them in their own country. However, an extensive program of European settlement in Texas was simply beyond the financial means of the Mexican government. Ortiz never saw the results of his policy. He died in the summer of 1833, in Vera Cruz, struck down in a cholera epidemic similar to the one that killed many Irish immigrants in New Orleans in 1834. Following the death of Ortiz, the Mexican Senate revoked the anti-immigration laws of April, 1830. The change of policy was brought about under pressure from leading Mexican figures Lorenzo de Zavala and José Antonio Mexía, who had financial interests in the settlement of land in Texas. Meanwhile, the Mexican government remained anxious about the situation in Texas and in January, 1834, sent Juan Nepomuceno Almonte, an educated man and a former member of the governor's staff, to make a full report. Like Ortiz and Mier y Terán before him, Almonte identified the need for more troops to defend the frontier and advocated a policy of further colonization with Mexicans in Texas. Almonte expected to be appointed director of colonization after his report was received in Mexico City, but political events within Mexico intervened. In the spring of 1834 the government of Gómez Farías was overthrown by Santa Anna, who instituted a highly centralized policy that provoked rebellion within several states in Mexico, including the province of Texas. When Almonte returned to Texas in 1836, it was as part of a military force and in time of war.

In one important sense, neither the legislation enacted by the Mexican government nor the opposition of local officials to its implementation was of more than symbolic importance. Increasingly, Anglo-American migration into Texas grew from a steady trickle into an irresistible flood. While a few still entered legally after 1830 as Austin and De Witt colonists, under the liberal administration of Mier y Terán, the great majority of immigrants came illegally. Between 1830 and 1834, when officially it was not permissible to enter Texas, the number of Anglo-Americans doubled to more than 20,700.[42] When legal restrictions were lifted in May, 1834, an estimated 1,000 Americans a month were crossing the Brazos River into Texas. By mid-1836, just after Texas had won a precarious independence, the number of Americans and their slaves had risen to 35,000. As a result, the American presence in Texas was probably in the order of ten times that of the Tejano population, and with a few thousand "civilized" tribes of Indians, the total population, as computed by Almonte, reached 40,000 by 1836.[43]

The full significance of the Americanization of Texas emerged in the conflict that broke out in 1835–36 between Texas and Mexico (see chapter 4). But what happened in Texas through a process of migration, principally from the United States, did not occur as a result of government policy from either Mexico or the United States. Thousands of individuals acted in their own interest in fleeing from debt or criminal sentences in the American South and looking to the prospect of obtaining cheap land in Mexican Texas. They came either as settlers with legal title or, in the majority of cases, as adventurers, without it.

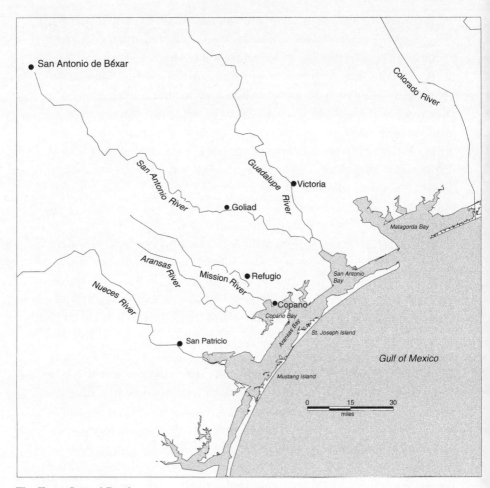

The Texas Coastal Bend

THE CONDITION OF TEXAS

To comprehend the scale of the human adventure that awaited U.S. migrants and Irish and Mexican colonists and the conditions that had to be
endured, I turn to accounts by Juan Nepomuceno Almonte, the Mexican
official who made detailed reports on the state of Texas in 1834.

In January, 1834, Almonte was dispatched to Texas by the Mexican
government to undertake an inspection of the province. His purpose was
to assess the condition of Texas, review the grievances of the inhabitants,
and try to guess whether a revolt was likely and a military invasion would
prove necessary. After spending several months in Nacogdoches and San

Felipe, he reported to the state and federal governments that Texans were not preparing to revolt and that reforms were necessary to address the grievances of the colonists. In his statistical report, published in February, 1835, he provided a clear message to the Mexican government that Texas, which was so rich in potential, had been hitherto neglected. Furthermore, he advocated the migration and settlement of Mexicans to share in its prosperity despite the apparent remoteness from Mexico. Although the tone of the report was optimistic in painting a bright future for Texas, there was an underlying fear that unless greater attention was paid to pursuing a more vigorous colonization policy and to the needs of the colonists, there was a very real danger of Mexico losing out on the benefits of the province:

> What it will be it is not difficult to predict; if the immense development which industry has enjoyed there is considered; and if its advantageous geographic position, its ports, its navigable rivers, the variety of its products, the fertility of its soil, its climate etc., are taken into account, one must admit that Texas is soon destined to be the most flourishing section of this republic. It is not difficult to perceive the reason for such prosperity, if it is remembered that there, with very few exceptions, nothing is thought of excepting the planting of sugar-cane, of cotton, of corn, of wheat, of tobacco; the raising of cattle, the opening of roads, the improvement of rivers; and that the effects of our political disturbances are seldom felt, and often are not even heard of unless it be by mere chance.[44]

Almonte's account had the upbeat quality of a modern business presentation to a prospective client. It was intended to encourage Mexicans to move to Texas where, freed from civil wars and political upheaval, they would surely see their industry rewarded and the value of their land increase. The glowing descriptions proclaiming the fertility of the land, the benign climate, and the abundance of water, in fact, represented only a partial truth. With little of the land under cultivation and very small populations, mostly situated in and around urban centers, the land was underdeveloped but had great potential in both agriculture and industry. What the land needed was capital investment, an increase in population, and a market for its goods. To assist in developing and reaching markets, better communications and better roads were needed; rivers had to be made navigable; and restrictions on coastwise trade between the colonies in Texas and the ports of Matamoros, Tampico, and Vera Cruz needed to be lifted. Almonte was correct in saying that Texas offered enormous potential to whoever would develop it. He was also sensitive to the dangers of ignoring the grievances of the American colonists. Most pertinently, he saw the vital necessity of defending the province of Texas on Mexico's northern frontier and developing a successful policy of colonization. But he was too optimistic about the likelihood of persuading Mexican citizens to settle in Texas and, quite naturally, played down the primitive conditions pioneer settlers had to endure in making a new life out of a frontier wilderness. Looking back on the period of Mexican rule over the province of Coahuila y Texas from 1821 to 1835, it is clear that the repeated efforts of the central government to populate Texas with Mexicans, Europeans, and Americans in ways that would protect Mexican interests from the encroachment of the United States were undermined by vested interests in the frontier communities.

The leading Tejano families could see only benefits from an increased presence of American settlers: they added to security against hostile Indians; they brought an economic gain in trade with American ports; and the imported slaves who worked the cotton fields reduced the shortage of field labor that threatened to ruin the frontier economy. There was opposition to the emancipation of slaves in Mexico in 1829 as a means of discouraging American settlement. The law of 1830 that closed the border to further American immigration was opposed in 1832 by the *ayuntamiento* of Béxar and supported by the *ayuntamientos* of Goliad and Nacogdoches. The petition from Béxar's leading families, including the signatories, Antonio de la Garza, Angel Navarro, and Juan Angel Seguín, argued against the restrictive terms of the law of 1830 because of the benefits of American settlement.[45]

The Mexican government's policy — based on a need to populate and govern the northern, frontier territory of Texas — was fraught with difficulty, and indeed, contained the inherent danger of backfiring by allowing into the frontier a sizable American presence of questionable loyalty in the long run. How much of the political context and danger to peace was understood by individual migrants is impossible to know, but it is likely that individual circumstances weighed heavier than those of governments. The advice given to would-be Texas immigrants, while extolling the virtues of frontier life, was mindful of its hazards: "Nevertheless, those persons who are established in comfort and competency, with an ordinary portion of domestic happiness; who have never been far from home, and are excessively attached to personal ease; who shrink from

Table 1. Population of Mexican Texas in 1834

Department	Area (square leagues)	Major Towns		Indians
Bejar	6,400	Béxar	2,400	9,900
		Goliad	700	
		Victoria	300	
		San Patricio	600	
		Total	**4,000**	
Nacogdoches	5,600	Nacogdoches	3,500	4,500
		San Augustin	2,500	
		Liberty	1,000	
		Johnsburg	2,000	
		Total	**10,600**	
Brazos	5,400	San Felipe	2,500	900
		Columbia	2,100	
		Matagorda	1,400	
		Gonzalez	900	
		Total	**10,100**	

Source: Juan N. Almonte, "Statistical Report on Texas, 1835," trans. C. E. Casteñeda, *Southwestern Historical Quarterly* 38, no. 3 (January, 1925).

Note: Totals for departments include smaller settlements as well as the major towns Almonte listed individually. Therefore, the sum of town populations shown does not equal the total for two of the departments. Indians were not included in the counts.

hardship and danger; and those, being accustomed to a regular routine of prescribed employment in a city, know not how to act on emergencies, or adapt themselves to all kinds of circumstances, *had better stay where they are.*"[46] Yet:

He whose hopes of rising independence in life, by honorable exertion, have been blasted by disappointment; whose ambition has been thwarted by untoward circumstances; who longs only for some ample field on which to lay out his strength; who does not hanker after society, nor sigh for the vanished illusions of life; who has a fund of resources within himself, and a heart to trust in God and his own exertions; who is not peculiarly sensitive to petty inconveniences, but can bear privations and make sacrifices of personal comfort; such a person will do well to settle accounts at home, and begin life anew in Texas. He will find there abundant exercise for all his faculties, a new stimulant to his exertions, and a new current for his affections. He may be obliged to labor hard, but riches are a very certain reward of his exertions and cares. He may be generous without fear of ruin. He will find society in nature, and repose in solitude; health in exertion, and happiness in virtuous occupation; and if he has a just view of ambition, he will glow with generous pride, while he is marking out an untrodden path; acting in an unhackneyed sphere, and founding for himself, and his children after him, a permanent and noble independence.[47]

Stripped of the evangelical, Scottish Presbyterian tone, Edward's advice was practical and sound. More pertinently, it was prophetic in relation to the Irish emigrants who became pioneer settlers under the empresario system. They had experienced frustrations at home or looked to retrieve their personal fortunes. They longed to be free from the payment of rents, taxes, and tithes in Ireland. Above all, they looked to acquire the ownership of land. The colonists were sold the prospect of an earthly paradise in Texas and the potential to become wealthy beyond any expectation they could have had in Ireland. How much they knew of the privations to come in their life on the frontier is not known, but the opportunity to secure a permanent independence for themselves and their families was a prospect to savor.

The Context of Emigration: Prefamine Ireland

Unless a change took place in the management of the land in Ireland, he could only anticipate an increase in poverty and misery; and that such change cannot take place unless something was done to remove the people. The prospect of tranquility and security in Ireland would only be achieved through the introduction of emigration on a large scale.
— The Reverend Thomas Malthus, Select Committee on Emigration from the United Kingdom

THE IRISH DIASPORA

In the popular memory there remains an inextricable association between Irish emigration, the years of the potato blight, and the trauma of the Great Famine (1845–52). Certainly, this was the period of the most dramatic and frenetic exodus from Ireland, but the story of Irish emigration is about more than just the famine years, when about 1 million people died and perhaps 1.8 million emigrated. In the region of 1 million Irish emigrants, twice the number of the preceding two hundred years, sailed to North America in the period 1815 to 1845. From 1852 to 1910 Ireland experienced a population loss of a further 5 million people through a continuous process of emigration that has become almost a permanent feature of Irish life. The sheer scale of Irish emigration can be highlighted with a single statistic: almost as many people left Ireland between 1815 and 1914 as Ireland's peak population total of just under 8.2 million in 1841. During the nineteenth century, something on the order of three-quarters of Irish emigrants went to the United States.[1]

Another way of gauging the level of migration in the prefamine period is to compare figures of the annual outflow from Ireland.[2] From the peace that concluded the American Revolution in 1783 through 1814, perhaps 100,000 to 150,000 left Ireland for the New World. This represented an annual outflow of around 5,000 people; some years it was less, owing to the restrictions imposed on shipping by the European wars. With peace concluded in 1815, some 20,000 Irish, mostly from Ulster, sailed in 1815–16 to British North America and to the United States. In both 1831 and 1832 a record figure of 65,000 emigrated mostly to British North America, a movement prompted by the removal of government restrictions, cheaper fares, prosperity abroad, and economic depression at home. This signaled the onset of a process of mass migration from Ireland that was to endure until the 1920s. Between 1828 and 1837 a total of nearly 400,000 Irish went to North America, and while more Catholics, artisans, and laborers from all parts of Ireland were increasingly represented in the emigrant population, most Catholic emigrants were drawn from the ranks of small to middling farmers, not from the laboring poor. By 1842 a record 93,000 emigrants left Ireland and began to face employment difficulties in Canadian and American port cities. In 1851, during the famine, the all-time peak figure of 245,000 left Ireland and settled overwhelmingly in the United States. Although the above figures are only estimates, a comparison between total population growth, the level of annual emigration, and total emigration from Ireland shows an unmistakable trend of increased emigration preceding the famine, a trend that would continue throughout the rest of the century.

Emigration was not a random process. It might best be understood in the broader context of the global activity of the British, and to a lesser extent, the Spanish empire. Donald Akenson, a leading authority on the Irish diaspora, asserts that although Irish emigration was exceptional in terms of degree and duration compared with other European migrations to the New World, it nevertheless formed part of a still greater movement from the British Isles to the far-flung colonies and former colonies of the British Empire. Between 1815 and 1914 an estimated 20-million-plus people sailed from the British Isles to destinations beyond Europe, 13 million of these to America, roughly 4 million to Canada, and approximately 4.5 million to Australia and New Zealand. The Irish did not go in significant numbers anywhere the British had not gone first. From the eighteenth century onward the Irish mingled with the British flow. Frequently they were on the same ships. They passed through the same foreign ports and went on to settlements in the same new worlds. It is no accident that the overwhelming bulk of the Irish diaspora went to points in the English-speaking world.[3]

The global reach of imperial armies and navies, and the trading routes between European ports and the colonies provided the distribution network for the flow of migrants from Britain and Ireland. For instance, prominent among applicants for assisted passage to British North America in the 1820s were Irishmen who had served abroad in the British army and navy.[4] Evidently their experience of foreign travel and the awareness of wider opportunities gave them a taste for settlement overseas, especially if it could be financed by the British government.

Moreover, a long history links Ireland with Spain: through the church of medieval Christendom, the estimated 50,000 "wild geese" who fled Ireland to serve in the imperial Spanish armies in the seventeenth century, and the Irish who married into elite Spanish families who then served as administrators, soldiers, or merchants in the dominions of Spanish America. Patrick McKenna, an authority on the Irish in Argentina, has claimed that the first Irishmen to set foot on what was to become Argentina were three Galwaymen who formed part of Magellan's crew in 1520. The first Irish settlers in Argentina, the Farel brothers from San Lucas de Barrameda in Spain, were part of a pioneering expedition led by Pedro Mendoza in 1536. On board his fourteen ships, he took cattle, sheep, horses, and pigs that were among the earliest of such animals to reach the American continent. McKenna has also found Irish names among the troops on board British ships captured by the Spanish off the coast of Argentina in the 1760s and 1770s that contributed to early Irish settlement in New Spain. Later, he identified the importation of a hundred Irish butchers and tanners brought into Buenos Aires in 1785, which was to lead to the foundation of the Argentine meat industry.

Of specific relevance to the Irish migration to Texas was the earlier settlement of Irish soldiers who became farmers and laborers in the river Plate area of Argentina. A shortage of manpower in 1823 led to the recruitment from Ireland of 200 skilled laborers employed on public works and the new town of Belgrano to accommodate them. A growing number of Irish migrants, mostly from Westmeath and south Longford, found their way to Argentina in the 1820s. A smaller group also left from the Forth and Bargy area of Wexford in Ireland. They were encouraged by Patrick Browne, who had been sent to Buenos Aires as manager of a Liverpool bank in 1826. When he turned from banking to start his own salt meat business, he sent home to Ireland for workers from his native Wexford; this group represented some 15 percent of the total Irish migration to Argentina.[5] The timing was significant. The personal knowledge of such a movement from County Wexford to Argentina in 1826, and through the intermediary of a local man, would have made the migration from Wexford to Texas, via James Power in 1833–34, all the more acceptable.

The opening up of trading and investment opportunities between the port of Liverpool and the city of London and newly independent countries in South America was also paralleled with increased trade between the Mexican ports of Vera Cruz, Tampico, and Matamoros, and the Louisiana port of New Orleans. A regular trade in cotton between New Orleans and Liverpool was matched by an increasing return of industrial goods and the human cargo of European migrants, including the Irish. Notable among the European merchant communities in these ports were Irishmen who made considerable fortunes from trade and speculation in mining and other enterprises. It was in these commercial circles that the future Irish empresarios Power and Hewetson and McMullen and McGloin developed their business acumen, established their contacts in New Orleans and Mexico, and learned of the exciting prospects for land speculation in Texas, in newly independent Mexico.[6]

To understand fully the dynamics of the Irish diaspora, it is as well to recognize the interconnectedness of the Irish migrants to different parts of the world. The Irish rarely moved from Ireland to one destination and then settled there permanently. A large proportion of the Irish who sailed to America did so from British ports, and Ruth-Ann Harris has argued that seasonal or temporary residence in Britain often preceded immigration to the United States.[7] Second- and third-stage migration was common, prompted by news of better economic prospects elsewhere. For instance, a second-stage migration from Canada into the northern United States was undertaken by thousands of Irish migrants during the nineteenth century. Emigrant letters provided a news information service from Ireland to other relatives abroad not only of conditions back home but also of the success of family members in other countries.[8] Letters maintained an essential contact as families were dispersed worldwide.

In exploring the issues surrounding Irish emigration, one of the key things to investigate and assess is the conditions in Ireland that prompted people to leave the country of their birth. As my particular concern is with emigration in the decades immediately before the famine – specifically, with the emigration from County Wexford and other parts of south-

ern Ireland to the province of Texas in the republic of Mexico — I focus on
the population pressures, economic conditions, and regional variations in
Ireland during the period between Napoleon's defeat in 1815 and the eve
of the famine in 1845. I discuss patterns of emigration in relation to the
situation of the tenant farmers who left southeastern Ireland in search of
a new life as pioneer settlers in Texas. First, however, I explore how their
emigration has been understood to date and explained in previous work
on the subject.[9]

PREVIOUS HISTORIES

In all the published studies of the Irish in Texas, the explanations of
why the colonists left Ireland for the New World emphasize the oppression of the Irish people. It is possible to reconstruct how that consensus
view came about. The evidence for it is in the words of some of the
colonists themselves and this is reinforced in the correspondence of one
of the major historians who has written on the story of the Irish colonies
in Texas. Monsignor W. H. Oberste quoted the Power-Hewetson colonist
William St. John who in later life declared: "We were too much oppressed
in Ireland. We could not live there."[10] An important source of Oberste's
information on "oppression" in County Wexford, in particular, and in Ireland, in general, at the time of James Power's recruiting visit in 1833 was
his fellow Catholic priest, Owen Kavanagh of Ballygarrett. Oberste corresponded regularly with Kavanagh during the 1940s and 1950s in preparation for writing his book published in 1953.[11]

In replying to Oberste's repeated enquiries about Power's family in Ireland, Kavanagh invariably said that little was known about them. This
disclaimer was usually accompanied by a passionate tirade unleashed
against the iniquities of English rule in Ireland. Kavanagh always referred
to the atrocities that followed the Irish Rebellion of 1798 in which Wexford featured prominently; to the persecution of Catholics; to the oppression of Protestant landlords; and to English misrule:

The church at Ballygarrett was burned by the yoemanry — January 1799
and all the parochial records destroyed, after the rebellion of 1798,
when Wexford rose against the British army of occupation. I may re-
mark that the Yoeman as they were called, were recruited from the descendants of the Cromwellian Planters, to support the British army of
occupation. These Planters were of course Protestants and when the

rebellion was suppressed, a persecution of the Catholic population followed in which the cowardly yeomen were the leaders under the protection and connivance of the British Government. This will also explain how easy it was for James Power to collect such a large number to emigrate in 1834 for anyone who could get away, fled the country.[12]

For good measure, Kavanagh also linked with Catholic emigration the terrible suffering of the Great Famine that began in 1845 and the evictions by rapacious landlords in Cullentra in 1853. The point has to be made that Kavanagh's explanation extends to an unusually elastic sense of chronology. In explaining why a particular group of migrants left Ireland in 1834, he included events as far back as the mid-seventeenth century (the Cromwellian Planters) and the rebellion of 1798, which occurred before some of them were born, and even to events (the Great Famine and the evictions) that had not yet occurred. Yet Oberste generally accepted his interpretation and described the topography of Wexford in terms that bore all the marks of an oppressed people: "The landscape in all directions is broken by ancient hedgerows, of irregular patterns and sizes. These once marked, and do so now, the boundaries of individual land holdings. They were originally built by a people in bondage to mark off the small acreage assigned to the despised tenants by the all powerful and demanding Planters, the English landlords, during those centuries when no Irishman could own property."[13]

It is important to note that all landlords were assumed to be English and Protestant and that the reference to "no Irishman could own property" meant no Catholic Irishman. While it is true that the majority of landowners in Ireland were Anglicans of English descent, many regarded themselves by the 1790s as patriotic Protestant Irish nationalists. Politically, they represented every shade of opinion, from High Toryism to the Radicalism of Daniel O'Connell, the self-styled "liberator" and architect of Catholic emancipation in 1829, and who was himself a Catholic landlord in County Kerry. Given the wide range of estate holdings in Ireland, landowners cannot be recognized as a homogeneous group. They were also highly mobile, doubling in number throughout the eighteenth and early nineteenth centuries, and increasingly open to entry from successful Catholic farmers, merchants, and industrialists eager to improve their social status. Increasingly, the Ireland of 1834 had Catholic landowners who were buying up the land of improvident Protestant landowners. Alexis de Tocqueville quotes Monsignor Kinseley, the bishop of Kilkenny, whom he interviewed when traveling around Ireland in 1835: "Everyday we see the rich Catholics of the towns lend money to Protestants, and these latter end by being obliged to break entail and sell their lands. In this way many of the estates pass gradually into the hands of the Catholics. We have seen lately in this county two Catholics, Messrs. X and Y, buy two estates, one for 20,000, the other for 30,000 pounds sterling."[14]

Kevin Whelan, a modern authority on County Wexford, has identified how the Catholic gentry had managed to retain their estates during the eighteenth century, despite the penal laws, and how Catholic maltsters in the port of Wexford grew prosperous in dominating the lucrative trade in supplying the brewing industry in Dublin.[15] Also, Anglo-Irish landowners commonly regarded themselves as Irish, and there were a few landlords in County Wexford in particular who were proud of their Norman ancestry, as the survival of French surnames such as Power (originally Poer), Roche, and Devereux testifies. Interestingly, these surnames were present among the Power-Hewetson land grantees who settled in Texas. Neighboring County Waterford, which also sent Irish colonists to Texas in 1834, had seen less seventeenth-century settlement but had also been densely settled by Anglo-Norman families in the Middle Ages. More than 58 percent of all landowning families in County Waterford in 1851 were described as Gaelic-Irish or of old English origin.[16]

The importance of the 1798 rebellion as an explanation of Irish emigration in 1834 was also endorsed by John Brendan Flannery: "It was bloodily put down by the English with the aid of Hessian mercenaries. The brutal reprisals thereafter visited upon a helpless citizenry increased the stream of emigration."[17] What is conveniently ignored here is the brutal sectarian violence between Irish Protestants and Irish Catholics that was a feature of the events in Wexford in 1798. The collaboration of Catholics and Protestants in the movement of the United Irishmen, led by the Protestant lawyer Wolfe Tone, ultimately disintegrated into a sectarian war. Kevin Whelan has also commented on the scale of sectarian violence in County Wexford, which reestablishes the importance of religion in the 1798 rebellion. He made a number of key points that provide a very different context to the subsequent emigration of James Power's colonists to Texas in 1834. First, he pointed to the density of the eighteenth-century Protestant presence in the north of the county, "especially in the baronies of Scarawalsh and Gorey, the storm centers of the rebellion, focusing on a quadrangle between Enniscorthy, Bunclody, Arklow and Kilmuckridge." This Protestant colony owed its existence to the plantation of the 1620s, which was reinforced by subsequent migration, and unlike Protestants in much of southern Ireland, they were strongly established in the countryside among the farming and laboring classes. Catholic townlands were also present in the same area of northern Wexford, so creating a pattern of alternating Protestant and Catholic townlands.[18]

Second, both Catholics and Protestants were well organized in conflicting political camps. Protestant landlords fought against Catholic grievances, opposed the admission of Catholics into the Volunteers in the 1780s, and resisted the Catholic Relief Acts in the 1790s. Whelan contends that the presence of Catholic Defenders and Protestant Orange Orders in County Wexford, and the spread of millenarian rumors of religious massacres and an apocalyptic triumph of the Catholic faith prophesied, help to explain the butchery in the form of chapel burnings and killings committed by both sides in 1798.

Third, one consequence of the violence and bad blood of the rebellion was that many Protestant families either converted to Catholicism for safety or emigrated to the New World. In the prefamine period, Whelan noted, "there was a sizeable out-migration of north Wexford Protestants, for example, to Ontario. . . . In the decade after 1798, Protestant society in Wexford became defensive, introspective and suspicious."[19] So far from the oppression model that depicts Catholics as the sole victims of the 1798 rebellion, in the case of north Wexford, the area from where Power's party were to emigrate to Texas, it appears that emigration was more likely among Protestants than among Catholics.

Yet for Flannery and other historians of the Irish in Texas, English oppression provided a useful explanatory tool in accounting for the Irish leaving Ireland: "The Irish were robbed of their ancestral lands, denied education, prohibited from holding office or having political representation. They were persecuted for their religion and forbidden their age-old culture and legal system. They were reduced to that state so aptly described by an English Lord Chancellor of the 18th century. No such person as an Irish Catholic is presumed to exist under English law."[20]

By the 1830s some of these restrictions had been lifted. Far from being denied to Catholics, education was more advanced in Ireland than in the rest of Europe, and Catholic tenant farmers exercised a vote in the British Parliament where their charismatic champion Daniel O'Connell called for the repeal of the union with Great Britain, supported by a sophisticated organization of popular pressure through the Catholic Association in Ireland. Religious persecution was at an end, and the reality that faced the British government was a recognition that the Catholic church was a formidable force in Irish affairs. This was endorsed in the legislation introduced in 1829 with the Catholic Emancipation Act. However, Flannery argued that, even when the infamous penal laws had fallen into disuse and legal recognition was given to Irish Catholics, "the new legal provisions found little reflection in the practicalities of daily life. Irish tenants were still at the mercy of landlords, English mercantilist policy still bled Ireland economically, and the Catholic and Presbyterian Irish were still required by the tithing laws to give financial support to a church to which they did not belong."[21]

Furthermore, the compelling sense of oppression suffered by the Irish under English rule tends to portray emigration as an involuntary act, as a form of enforced exile. Other accounts, however, depict emigrants as masters of their own destiny, as active agents making a courageous life-choice to leave Ireland and better themselves abroad. Donald Akenson is a leading exponent of emigration as a positive and life-enhancing movement: "In my view," he writes, "they [the men, women and children of the Irish Diaspora, and especially those of the migrant generation] were heroes. They were not passive jetsam, but rather were individuals who collected information, weighed alternatives, and then took journeys to various New Worlds that were as far away from their previous experience as colonies on the moon would be for someone of our own age. They willed and survived, and ultimately their descendants prospered."[22] It is reasonable to assume that the prospects held out for them in the New World were just as important in the decision to emigrate as the restrictions facing them at home. Certainly, the evidence of surviving letters from Irish pioneer settlers in Texas points in that direction.

From a Texan perspective on Irish emigration, Hobart Huson, the historian of Refugio, quoted the journal of Rosalie Hart Priour, one of the original settlers who went as a child to Texas with James Power in 1834: "Their object in coming to America was to secure lands of their own, my recollection being that under the law in force in Ireland at that time no Catholic was permitted to own land, with only a few exceptions, most of the lands in that country being also entailed and not subject to be sold or divided."[23] For Martin Power, the nephew of the empresario James Power, it was clearly *economic* pressure that persuaded him to leave Ireland, and despite all the misfortunes he experienced in Texas, it was again *economic* benefit that prevented him from returning home, despite strong family pressures to do so:

> the only thing that ever caused me to leave was the dulness of the times and fearing not with standing all my brothers off duty and hard labors to add to little stores — that they would be at least tore to-pieces by making two farms of one. I have thought deeply for the past two years I spent there you know we were getting mity [*sic*] little better and we all doing everything that was in our power.
>
> I have for my time at least 80 pound a year since the day I left Ballinhash to present date. . . . I know that you would not at this time insist on me to go home . . . and not only that but see the door open *to make an independent fortune in a short time.*[24]

Can it be argued that the difficult conditions in Ireland provided a breeding ground for pioneer settlers in the New World? Richard Roche has argued that religious discrimination against Catholics in Ireland helped to produce the strength and resilience required of pioneer settlers: "The anti-Catholic Penal Laws, imposed in the late 17th early 18th centuries, were not removed from the Statute Book until 1829 — a mere four years before the Ballygarrett migration and well within the life-time of most of those who left for Texas in 1833 – 34. From such an historical and social background then, it was but to be expected that a tough, self-reliant, independent-minded people would emerge."[25]

It is a curious argument that oppression, which is normally associated with subservience, bred qualities of self-reliance and independence. Such qualities were more likely to flourish where people were able to exercise a measure of control over their lives, and that was only possible with the availability of some capital and freedom from want. In the prefamine period, overwhelmingly, only those who had some means above the plight of the poorest in society, were able to afford the Atlantic passage. The most oppressed class of poor cottiers and laborers were the least able to leave unless they were supported financially by enlightened landlords or by the British government.

Further evidence from the testimony of William St. John, earlier cited as evidence of oppression, records his reply to the question asked of him in 1892, "What induced your father and mother to leave Ireland with you and to come to America?" He recalled, at the age of seventy-six, that he was born in County Tipperary where his father was a farmer and replied: "Just to better our situation and get more land." And on an earlier occasion, he testified: "The people had plenty of means but were oppressed in Ireland. They were coming to Texas to get land."[26]

THE CONDITION OF PREFAMINE IRELAND

Just as there appear to be conflicting interpretations to explain why the Irish pioneers left to settle in Texas, so an objective assessment of the conditions that existed in Ireland in the decades preceding the famine is not merely a matter of description, despite the numerous descriptive accounts that survive. Prominent among these were the voluminous writings of contemporary travelers who journeyed from Britain and Europe to Ireland in the early nineteenth century. Two principal themes emerge from the great body of travel writing: the outstanding beauty of the landscape in Ireland and the thoroughly wretched condition of the Irish peasantry. The power of these images served to distort the true condition of prefamine Ireland.

Two examples, the first by William Makepeace Thackeray from the southeast and the second by J. C. Curwen from the northwest of Ireland, represent these contrasting themes of beauty and poverty and pose the question of interpretation to the reader. First, a lyrical tribute:

The aspect of the country [along the road to Glendalough in County Wicklow] is wild, and beautiful of course; but why try to describe it? I think the Irish scenery [is] just like the Irish melodies — sweet, wild and sad even in the sunshine. You can neither represent one nor the other by words; but I am sure if one could translate "The Meeting of the Waters" into form and colours, it would fall into the exact shape of a tender Irish landscape. So, take and play that tune upon your fiddle, and shut your eyes, and muse a little, and you have the whole scene before you.

Second, a moral condemnation:

The appearance of the cabins by the side of the road, [a few miles outside Ballybofey in County Donegal] and the state of the potato grounds bespoke the absence of industry; while the looks of the children, nearly in a state of nakedness, left nothing to conjecture as to the wretchedness in which the parents existed. I made some enquiries of a little boy, which he answered in Gaelic; this furnished me with a pretence for following him home. His mother was employed in the cabin, by attending

The Thirty-two Counties of Ireland

to four other children. In this miserable hut there was no division of apartments; the cattle occupied one end, the family the other, near the fire was a bed, which apparently served for the repose of all the human beings. . . . The most extreme poverty and wretchedness were manifestly apparent, with the absence of what we had everywhere else constantly found, kindness and hospitality.[27]

The constant repetition of these images of physical beauty and human squalor claim our attention and also require an explanation. William Makepeace Thackeray, the English novelist, was certainly guilty of that common English habit of romanticizing Ireland. While he recoiled from the street beggars and rural poverty he witnessed, he remained enchanted by the picturesque scenery of Ireland's mountains and lakes. To him, the landscape took on a mythical and magical quality, symbolic of links with ancient songs and legends from the early Christian period. Equally John Curwen was struck not only by the poor condition of the peasantry, but in common with the dominant orthodoxy of the time, equated the physical condition with a moral condemnation of the poor. He assumed a lack of peasant industry, deplored the use of a "primitive" foreign tongue that he could not understand, and earlier in the piece, condemned the illegal manufacture of poteen whiskey. So, contemporary descriptions were colored over with a framework either of an imaginative fantasy or with imported moral values.

In addition to the work of travel writers, a great deal is known of pre-famine Ireland from the many reports and investigations dealing with the daunting problems that faced the country. Official reports pointed to the fundamental effects of overpopulation: thousands of people eking out a bare subsistence living on a few acres in one-roomed rural hovels; squatter settlements situated on the edge of towns, and hosts of beggars infesting the central streets. Chronic underemployment, with the availability of wage labor averaging only seventy days a year in the poorest areas of Ireland, meant that any scheme of public works attracted an abundant supply of laborers. Emigration was one of the proposed remedies advocated by Irish and English commentators but was nevertheless considered a social evil. Not only were there obvious moral and physical dangers to those who went, but there was the damage caused to the country, with the loss of the most enterprising people. The necessity for emigration, while being recognized was, nevertheless, resented and, in these circumstances,

Table 2. Distribution of Irish Farmland, circa 1841

Class	Average Size of Farm (in acres)	Number of Farms	Total Land (in millions of acres)	% held
Landlords	–	10,000	3.5	17.5
Wealthy farmers	80	50,000	4.0	20.0
"Strong" farmers	50	100,000	5.0	25.0
Family farmers	20	250,000	5.0	25.0
Peasant farmers	5	300,000	1.5	7.5
Laborers, etc.	1	1,000,000	1.0	5.0

Source: Cormac O'Grada, "Poverty, Population, and Agriculture, 1801–1845," in *A New History of Ireland: V. Ireland Under the Union, I. 1801–1870*, ed. W. E. Vaughan (Oxford: Clarendon Press, 1989), 114.

it was difficult to applaud the courage of emigrants while simultaneously mourning their loss.

Contemporary reports presented a virtually unanimous picture of poverty in Ireland. The squalid conditions of Irish cabins, the ragged appearance of the peasantry, and the unwanted pressure from street beggars in the towns commanded the most attention. Personal impressions were also supported by statistical evidence. The 1841 census of Ireland recorded that more than two-fifths of all families lived in one-room cabins or tenements without adequate furniture or bedding.[28]

Housing conditions were merely a symptom of the depth of poverty in Ireland. The distribution of land can be identified in the farm sizes recorded. To place the Irish emigrants to Texas in context, they would have been among the more fortunate tenant farmers, occupying farms of twenty or more acres. The Irish economic historian Cormac O'Grada has constructed a table that provides an approximate picture of the structure of Irish agriculture in the prefamine period (see table 2).[29] This was not only a hugely unequal distribution of land but also a structure that had become more unequal since 1815, benefiting the comfortable farmers at the expense of the poor peasants and laborers who were dependent on mere subsistence or even survival at the base of Irish society.

Nobody doubted that the majority of holdings were too small to be economically viable or provide families with a living. The report of the Devon Commission, which investigated the system of Irish agriculture in 1843, approached the problem by identifying the size holding that was necessary to support a family without alternative income and counting those that fell below the standard required. On the assumption that 6.5 to 10.5 acres, varying according to the knowledge and skill of the small-holders, were needed to support a family of five people, it was calculated that 326,000 occupiers were below the minimum standard.[30] Taking into account an estimate of total family members that figure represented a "surplus" population of about 1.5 million people.[31]

The proposed remedies in the Devon Commission report pointed to the extent of wasteland, bog, and unimproved land that could be made into remunerative farmland by draining, use of fertilizer, and increased grazing for cattle on upland areas. By adding in this way to the available stock of holdings, as many as 500,000 poor laborers could receive suffi-cient parcels of land to support themselves. It could be argued that it was entirely sensible on the part of the British government to examine ways to improve and modernize Irish agriculture, given the great population pressure on the land, the shortage of employment, and the endemic pov-erty at the base of Irish society. However, the subsequent actions of Brit-ish governments during the famine period remain open to criticism, even when a conspiracy theory now commands little academic support.

The central question that was raised by the Reverend Thomas Malthus in 1827, as a witness before a government commission on emigration, was that of overpopulation. T. W. Freeman raised the same question in an es-say written in 1989: "was Ireland overpopulated? and the answer is an emphatic 'yes,' given that overpopulation is assessed in relation to the de-velopment of resources at any given time." He concluded that the prob-lems of Ireland in the 1840s were similar to those in modern India, and it should be remembered that conditions have changed beyond what could have been envisaged in the 1840s. In "areas now having perhaps a dozen farms and fifty or sixty people to the square mile, there might be sixty or more farms and 300 (or even more) [people] to the square mile."[32]

The pressure on the land came from too many poor families in Ireland dependent on agriculture at a time when alternative forms of employment were diminishing through a process of deindustrialization, especially in textiles. A sizable part, perhaps 2 million people out of 8.2 million in 1841, lived in a state of endemic poverty. Only farmers with holdings of twenty to thirty acres or more were exempt from being sucked down into poverty, and even they faced the uncertainty of their tenure, received no compen-sation from landlords for improvements they made, and might well have to subdivide the land to provide for dependents in the family. If they chose to hire the land on the conacre system, the price charged could be cripplingly high and depended on the return from a good crop.[33] Landlords looked on with dismay at the extent of subdivision on their estates. Some recommended emigration as a means of clearing people off impossibly small plots; a few even financed their own emigration schemes and encouraged the amalgamation of holdings to facilitate more productive methods in agriculture. In other respects, prefamine Ireland appeared to be relatively backward. Compared with its powerful neighbor Britain it was a predominantly rural country. Little urbanized, with industry in retreat in most parts of Ireland, the population looked to be too dependent on the monoculture of the potato and was being pressed on to the cultivation of poor land.

Yet despite the bleak uniformity of contemporary accounts, there is no consensus among historians interpreting the economic and social conditions of prefamine Ireland. Recent writing has qualified the picture presented by contemporary travel writers. Even the poor of Ireland were comparatively well heated with access to peat as fuel and enjoyed a more nutritious, if monotonous, diet than agricultural laborers in England. The dependence on the potato diet, with an adult male consumption averaging twelve pounds per day, meant that famine struck when there was a crop failure, but excess deaths were caused by disease rather than directly by starvation. Smallpox, cholera, and puerperal fever were killer diseases. Starvation, although endured especially during the summer months between crops, claimed few deaths in the official record. Sir William Wilde, in his report of 1841, listed a mere 117 deaths from starvation in the previous ten years compared with 7,702 deaths from drowning, 1,239 from intemperance, and 792 deaths from suicide over the same period.[34] Comparative rates put the Irish experience in perspective. Life expectancy in Ireland at thirty-eight years was only marginally below that of England (forty years) and was comparable with the rates in France or Germany and better than those found in southern Europe.[35] Infant mortality rates, the most sensitive barometers of family health, were to become lower in Ireland than in England, possibly due to a higher level of breast feeding and a superior diet in Ireland.[36]

The poor landless laborers, able to earn a family income of perhaps fifteen to twenty pounds a year, in cash and kind, were the most vulnerable to the ravages of famine, and suffered in the decades before 1845 with the decline in employment opportunities. Poor laborers were also the least likely to emigrate to America because they could not afford the passage money, which represented the equivalent of three or four years' gross income. This predicament was overcome to an extent with the provision of remittances sent back in the form of prepaid tickets, a phenomenon that can be documented in the 1820s and that took off during the later years of the famine period, to provide the overwhelming financial support for emigration to the United States.[37]

Prefamine Ireland was, in many respects, like a modern Third World country in terms of its levels of inequality. Above the ranks of the poor laborers and cottiers were the smallholders, renting 5 to 20 acres, who were vulnerable to shifts in prices of agricultural produce, the availability of domestic textile work, and the insecurity of tenure on their holdings. Smallholders with more than 20 acres could at least contemplate the possibility of emigration as an alternative by selling the lease on their land, selling all their stock, and investing in the passage money for a new life in America or Canada. For instance, a farm of 30 acres or more in the eastern counties of Ireland might expect to have thirteen cattle, a good number of sheep, horses, pigs, and poultry as part of the farm stock. The value of the cattle alone at £6 10s. per head would amount to a figure of £84 10s., sufficient to finance family emigration to America in the prefamine period.[38] Farmers on holdings of 20 acres or more were comfortable, and those occupying 50 to 80 acres, "strong farmers," enjoyed good standards of living. They ate well, lived in better-class housing, and could afford, along with the professional and mercantile classes, to grant dowries worth several hundred pounds to their daughters. These farmers remained aloof from the ravages of the great famine in the late 1840s and even prospered from the high prices and the amalgamation of holdings that were characteristic of the famine years.

Undoubtedly, the industrial revolution in Britain was a major influence affecting the Irish economy. It meant an expanding urban market for Irish agricultural produce but also dealt a blow to much of the Irish textile industry. Irish farmers on medium to large holdings, the most specialized producers, gained most from increased food exports to Britain and other ancillary trades, flour millers, bacon curers, and butter manufacturers, also benefited from supplying the British market. The concentration of cotton manufacturing in Lancashire in the northwest of England, centered in Manchester, and the focus of the woolen cloth industry across the Pennines in Yorkshire, located in Leeds and Bradford, had a devastating effect on the largely domestic textile production of southern Ireland. From the 1820s a process of deindustrialization took place that threw thousands of textile workers out of work and pushed them either back into the overcrowded agricultural labor market or prompted them to transfer their skills to alternative textile centers in Scotland, northern England, or Massachusetts in the United States. Other regions of Britain, such as East Anglia and the West Country, suffered comparable loss of industrial employment in textiles, and the same centripetal economic forces were at work there as in Ireland. As part of the same process of industrial concentration already evident in the first half of the century, the Belfast region was becoming the major center of linen production in Britain.[39] Belfast grew by attracting labor from its rural hinterland, which undermined domestic production in the north midland counties and prompted an exodus of Irish textile workers to Scotland.[40]

REGIONAL DIFFERENCES

Regional differences within Ireland were of such magnitude that generalizations about the condition of prefamine Ireland, as a uniform entity, are difficult to sustain. For instance, as Cormac O'Grada has shown, farms of £100 value per annum were common in Ireland's home counties near Dublin, while there were few in Mayo, Kerry, or even in Ulster, and there were none at all in Connemara.[41] In terms of farm size, the east-west divide was most pronounced. The proportion of holdings of 5 acres or fewer by county show the western counties of Mayo registering 73 percent, Roscommon 64 percent, Galway 62 percent, and Sligo 61 percent. While no county in Ireland had less than a quarter of its farms under 5 acres, the lowest figures were represented by the southeastern counties of Wicklow (28 percent) and Wexford (29 percent). In broad terms, the line from Derry in the north to Cork in the south of Ireland divided the poorer western counties from the more advanced eastern counties of Ireland. Yet this crude division concealed areas of prosperity such as the Limerick lowlands where dairy cattle were a successful specialization and ignored areas of distress in south Ulster or in the Wicklow mountains.[42]

Regional differences are highlighted in a comparison of two areas: Gorey Union in County Wexford, which sent Irish colonists to Texas, and Gort Union in County Galway, situated in the poorer west of Ireland. While Gorey had four thousand fewer in population than Gort, it had about a third more in acreage. So the size of holdings was larger in Gorey than in Gort; 54.9 percent of the holdings in Gorey did not exceed 20 acres, but the equivalent figure in Gort was 80.5 percent. In Gorey, 28.5 percent of

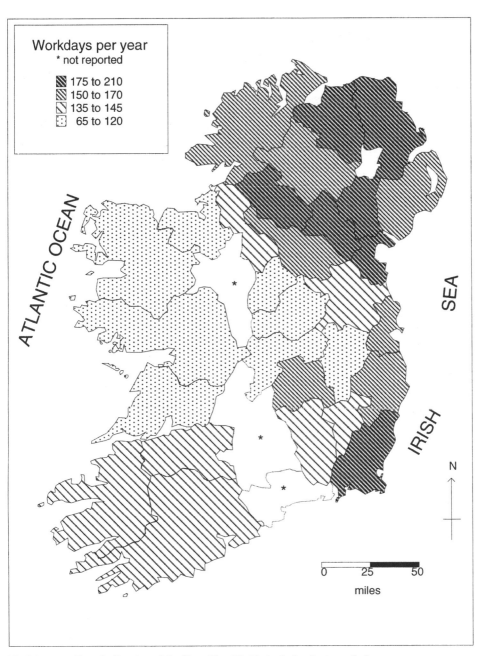

Workdays per Year, Indicative of the East-West Divide in Ireland, circa 1836

holdings were in the critical range of 20 to 50 acres, which would have in-volved the provision of stock and some capital, compared with only 15.4 percent in Gort. With holdings of more than 50 acres the contrast was even starker; Gorey had 730 such holdings, more than three times the 231 in Gort. A further indication of the relative backwardness of Gort's agriculture was the huge difference in acreage held in common: 34,415 acres or 32.2 percent of the total acreage compared with the equivalent figures of 1,710 acres or 1.3 percent of the total acreage in Gorey.

A series of indicators point to the unmistakable conclusion that County Wexford, from where many of the Irish recruited by James Power left for Texas, was one of the most affluent areas of Ireland. In terms of the proportion of arable to uncultivated land, Wexford was listed fifth among the 32 counties of Ireland, possessing 88.5 percent arable and 7.8 percent uncultivated land compared with the national average of 64.7 percent and 30.3 percent respectively. The counties of Wicklow and Wexford in southeast Ireland had proportionately twice as many boot- and shoemakers and three times as many carpenters as Mayo or Kerry.[43] Regional inequality compounded social inequality. Regional poverty, as recorded in 1841, was also a good predictor of the distribution of above-average mortality in the years 1846–49. Inequality appears to have in-creased between 1801 and 1845: while the income of landlords and farm-ers paying less than a full economic rent rose, the condition of the poor worsened. Joel Mokyr shows a decline in the welfare of the poor in every county after 1815, with the exception of Wexford and Wicklow. Replies by magistrates and clergymen and other informants to the Poor Inquiry of 1835–36 show that Wexford was the only county in Ireland registering an improvement in living standards.[44] Ruth-Ann Harris has compiled a table on county rankings in Ireland in 1841, including a whole range of vari-ables; the valuation of land, the level of wages, days worked per year, the literacy level, quality of housing, and the numbers employed in agricul-ture, trade, and industry. For rental valuation per acre, County Wexford comes out at the top of Ireland's thirty-two counties, and it is in the top ten for wages, days worked per year, a high percentage of arable land, lit-eracy, high quality of housing, and the percentage employed in trade and manufacturing.[45]

The trend of greater inequality and worsening conditions among the poor placed greater burdens on farmers who were taxed in order to support distressed laborers. Middle-class complaints were made against higher taxes on commodities, tea, sugar, tobacco, and malt, and in the

1830s and 1840s the main burden of tithes and poor rates fell on those with property. The tenant farmers of County Wexford who chose to follow James Power to Texas in 1834 may well have felt themselves facing the prospect of increasing economic burdens at the same time as looking to improve their own financial outlook in the New World. So the argument that the poverty and oppression in Ireland led to increased emigration in the 1830s takes on a fresh interpretation. Those small to medium farmers who still had capital decided to free themselves from the growing burden of maintaining the swelling numbers of poor cottiers and laborers who lacked the means to leave the country.

The relative good fortune of the area from which many tenants left with James Power is evoked in this description of Kilmuckridge in Lewis's topographical description of Ireland:

> KILMUCKRIDGE, a parish, in the union of Gorey, barony of Ballaghkeen, county of Wexford, and province of Leinster, 4 miles (E.S.E.) from Oulart; on St. George's Channel, and on the old coast-road from Wexford to Dublin; containing 1,602 inhabitants. It comprises 3,898¾ statute acres, principally under tillage: the soil is a rich loam, resting on a substratum of marl, which forms the chief manure; it is peculiarly adapted for tillage, and the state of agriculture has in consequence been highly improved. There is little bog, but coal is occasionally landed at Morris Castle.[46]

Regional differences were also present in population trends. The national rate of population growth had been rapid since the late eighteenth century, but the rate of increase was slowing down before 1845 and a marked contrast remained between the east and west of Ireland.

Population growth was twice as high in the relatively poorer provinces of Munster and Connacht compared with the more commercially advanced areas of Dublin, Derry, Athlone, and Waterford. A generally lower age of marriage in western counties encouraged by the greater availability of marginal land facilitated higher fertility. In part, the slowing down of population growth can be attributed to emigration after 1815, when it increased dramatically, and also to a rise in the marriage age in eastern Ireland. Between 1811 and 1841 the age at marriage increased by 1.5 years, and the birth rate between 1821 and 1841 fell almost 10 percent from 42 to 38 per thousand. The mean age of marriage for women was 23 in rural Connacht and 24.5 in Leinster. As O'Grada has noted, ironically, eastern Ireland at least was moving toward the kind of moral restraint involved in family limitation advocated by the Reverend Thomas Malthus. This did not prevent criticism being made during the famine years that the problems of Ireland could be put down to a lack of such restraint and forethought by an impoverished peasantry.[47]

Part of the regional imbalance in population was attributable to differential emigration rates. From 1801 to 1841 more than 1.5 million people left Ireland, with 900,000 going to the United States or Canada (British North America) and the remainder going mostly to Britain. By the early 1840s emigration was removing one-half or more of the natural increase, and with a high proportion of young adult male emigrants the effect was to reduce the prospects for marriage and birth rates in the future. Other discernible patterns in the tide of prefamine emigration included higher levels of movement from the east and north of Ireland, the predominance of family migration, and an increase in the numbers of proletarian Irish able to leave. By the 1820s and 1830s more than two-thirds of those who sailed to New York or Boston were laborers or displaced textile workers. Only a sixth were described as artisans.[48] It was from this particular prefamine emigrant group that McMullen and McGloin recruited when they journeyed from Mexico to New York in 1829 to interview newly arrived Irish who might be induced to settle in Texas. Folk memory records that those who acquired their land grants in San Patricio colony were regarded as lower in social status than those who went directly from Ireland to settle in Refugio.[49] Many of those who decided to stay in New York and Boston often experienced a tough time, being compelled to undertake rough, laboring work and to live in poor, overcrowded slum conditions.[50]

Structural changes in agriculture and industrial employment have been linked to high levels of emigration from Ulster and the north midland counties, but the southern counties of Wexford, Cork, and Waterford also suffered as mills closed down and thousands left Ireland in search of employment in Britain, Canada, and the United States. A dependence on converted cargo ships for emigrant passage tied the overseas movement of people to the established trade routes. The logistics of trade in timber, cotton, and imported flax seed determined the regions of primary settlement in the Americas. As Cecil J. Houston and W. J. Smyth have argued, "What the emigration regions of Ulster, the major metropolitan ports, and the southeastern counties had in common, apart from overseas links, were complex and changing regional economies. Collectively they represented the most advanced sectors of the contemporary Irish economy and their established merchant and shipping links with the British colonies across the Atlantic provided not only the logistics but also the mentality for emigration."[51]

We cannot interview those who were contemplating emigration from Ireland in the 1830s or even reconstruct precisely the hopes and fears of the Irish who went to Texas, but we do have the detailed comments recorded in 1835, taken by witnesses in a cross section of Irish counties that record the reasons for the levels of emigration over the preceding few years. The informants, some fifteen hundred people from all over Ireland – landlords, magistrates, and clergy of all denominations – represented a valuable body of local knowledge. While these comments reveal regional and district variations in the level of emigration from Ireland, there are consistent patterns of explanation that represent the mental landscape of the time.

An analysis of the statements reveals that the incidence of emigration overseas (not including to Great Britain) was widespread throughout Ireland, occurring in areas of great social and economic contrast, from Mayo in the west to Carlow in the east, and also varied within counties where an area recorded as experiencing no emigration was found alongside one that recorded many emigrants. The distribution of emigration was not concentrated entirely in areas of poverty or even of prosperity, but was a general feature of Irish rural life. The movement of people took place largely above the ranks of the poorest. It was overwhelmingly self-financed (landlord-sponsored emigration being a rarity); emigrants included men, women, and children, and all religious denominations were represented, including Protestants from the southeast and Catholics from Ulster.[52]

It seems highly likely that the Irish who went via the United States with McMullen and McGloin to Texas in the 1820s or went directly from County Tipperary to San Patricio and with James Power in the 1830s to Refugio would have shared a similar outlook to those revealed in the following selection of recorded contemporary comments.

Emigration has been very considerable among all classes of late years: many persons possessed of capital have gone after the expiration of old leases of farms held by them at a low rent, and of which they could not expect a renewal on the same profitable terms. (Barony of Mohill, Co. Leitrim)

I am convinced that one-third of the entire population of my parish would start immediately if they had a free passage offered to them. (Rev. Geraghty, P.P.)

Most of those who departed were persons possessing small capital, hardly any destitute persons, inasmuch as they had no profitable mode of investing their capital, which they found continually diminishing of late years, especially since the decline of the linen trade. (Mr. McDonnell, Barony of Murrisk, Co. Mayo)

For some years the emigration of laborers and small farmers has been considerable, but, unfortunately for Ireland, they have generally been the most industrious, well behaved, and in most cases the most monied of their class, thus leaving the worst, and all the riff-raff, as an increased burden on the country. They have emigrated, some from want of employment, or other means of subsistence, at home; others from the hope of considerably improving their condition, excited by the success of their relatives and friends who had emigrated a few years before and who had, in many cases, assisted them to join them by paying their passage out. (Barony of Balrothery, Co. Dublin)

Emigration has not been very considerable during the last five years; not so considerable as during the previous five years, chiefly from want of means. The principal emigration has taken place among small farmers, who were led to emigrate more generally by distress occasioned by high rents and low prices, and some few from having been ejected. Some of the gentlemen and Protestant farmers stated that one of the great causes of emigration among Protestants had been the disturbed state of the country, and the violence of the Roman Catholic population; but the Roman Catholics denied this, and said that the country was perfectly quiet at the time of their emigration, and that it was the badness of the times which induced the Protestant, as well as the Roman Catholic farmers to emigrate. The high rents have not yet had the effect of forcing the substantial farmers from the country, but many of them find themselves sinking so fast in the world from high rents, and the present low prices of agricultural produce, that they are now seriously contemplating emigration. (Barony of Talbotstown Upper, Co. Wicklow)

[In the case of emigration from County Tipperary, evidence suggests that the news of the bad experiences of some who went to Texas may have affected the level of subsequent emigration.] In 1834 a considerable number emigrated. In the present year there were not so many, principally because some vessels were lost last year [a possible reference to the shipwreck of the Irish colonists off the Texas coast]. The greater number were merely able to pay their passage, but there were several who took considerable property with them. The object of these emigrants was simply to better their condition. (Mr. Scully, Barony of Middlethird, Co. Tipperary)

Mr. Duckett says, "A landlord here paid the expenses of emigration to America of many of his labourers and small farmers and none refused." (Barony of Middlethird, Co. Tipperary)

Since the spinning trade has failed, within the last 12 years, many girls have gone, and by all accounts have done well; servant girls get six or eight dollars a month in Quebec, Montreal, and St. John's. (Mr. Black, Barony of Fews Lower, Co. Armagh) [53]

From these comments, the decisive push and pull factors affecting small to middling farmers can be discerned. What was pushing them toward the contemplation of emigration was the economic circumstances of high rents and low prices that was eroding their incomes. The decline in textiles also limited the possibilities of obtaining alternative household income outside agriculture. Moreover, what capital they possessed could not be invested profitably outside the farm, and farm improvements themselves were not subject to compensation by the landowners. Finally, when leases on farms expired and came up for renewal, the new rents demanded were expected to be set at higher levels. To farmers hemmed in by restrictions and the absence of opportunities in Ireland, emigration must have appeared as a viable, albeit risky alternative. It was made possible by the selling of farm stock and leases to finance the Atlantic passage.

What was pulling them to take that alternative in the New World was the hope of bettering their condition, especially in the long run and for the benefit of the next generation. The most compelling pressure to leave came in the form of emigrant letters conveying news of the economic success of relatives and friends. Letters provided exciting details, for instance, of the wages of servant girls, sufficient in many cases to pay for remittances back to Ireland to cover the cost of passage to America for other family members. Other letters provided a personal endorsement of the opportunities for acquiring land in Canada and America and sought to allay fears of wild beasts and savage Indians in frontier societies. A compelling sense of well-being, abundant food, plentiful land, and genuine reward for the industrious emigrant lay tantalizingly across the Atlantic ocean.

The partial potato failure in 1831 and the cholera epidemic of 1832 may have been added inducements for Irish colonists deciding in the summer of 1833 to go to Texas the following year, but the colonists' departure was not so much driven by a sense of hopelessness about a depressed economy as by the limited opportunities arising from structural change and restricted growth in Ireland. They were not "motivated by abject poverty but rather by a perception of diminished opportunities for themselves and future generations, and the critical perception that emigration offered a solution to their dilemma."[54]

There are parallels between the Irish who went to Texas and the Irish families, studied by Bruce S. Elliott, who left Tipperary for Canada. Elliott argues that economic difficulties provided a reason but not a paramount reason to move. Betterment of self was a factor but less important than providing a secure start in life for the rising generation. Migration was a strategy of heirship and kinship, and these ties also influenced the choice of destination.[55] The family worked as a functional socioeconomic unit. The parallels have more substance because the St. Johns of Tipperary who came to North Tipperary in 1709, as German Palatine refugees from religious and political conflict, also went with James Power in a second migration to Texas in 1834. The growing willingness of people to emigrate from southern Ireland is further indicated by the number of applications made to Peter Robinson for his schemes of assisted emigration to Upper Canada in 1825–27. Printed circulars announced:

> To all who may be disposed to emigrate from the South of Ireland and who may be accepted by the Superintendent, the Government will afford a passage to Canada and will convey them to their lands free of expence – Provisions will be found them and they will be furnished with medical assistance, upon their arrival at the tract destined for their settlement. Every male emigrant above the age of 18 years and under 45 will receive a location ticket for 70 acres of land; the utensils necessary for a new settler, will be furnished them at the public expence, and they will receive provisions for one year after they shall have taken possession of their lands.[56]

Of the 50,000 applicants, only 1,615 families could be accommodated within the terms of the parliamentary grant of thirty thousand pounds available to finance the scheme. Throughout southern Ireland, information on the scheme raised awareness and expectations of the possibility of emigration. By the standards of the day, it was a generous scheme but was much less attractive than the prospect that was held out to potential colonists in Texas.

Given the willingness of many people to leave Ireland, why did the British government not devise a national scheme of emigration? The laissez-faire doctrine that included the law of supply and demand as an immutable part of the laws of nature also assumed that the scope for government intervention was limited by the free play of the market. A report of the Select Committee on Emigration from the United Kingdom in 1827 claimed that the "extreme wretchedness of a great portion of the peasantry in many parts of Ireland" was caused by an "excess of labour, as compared with any permanent demand for it, which has reduced and must keep down the labourer at the lowest possible amount of subsistence." Furthermore, the report asserted that the insecurity of property arising from the state of the population effectively discouraged capital investment in Ireland; "that is to say, no person will be disposed to establish large manufactures, or to make great agricultural improvements, in a country which has been, and may again be the scene of insurrectionary movements." The remedy for Ireland's ills was seen as emigration, which would restore the equilibrium in Malthusian terms between people and resources: "The question of Emigration as connected with Ireland, has already been decided by the population itself." It was up to the legislature to decide whether it should be directed to the improvement of the North American colonies (in Canada) or whether they should "deluge Great Britain with poverty and wretchedness."[57]

The Reverend Thomas Malthus was an important witness and his opinions were clearly accepted by the committee. He stated that unless a change took place in the management of the land in Ireland, he could only anticipate an increase in poverty and misery, and such change could not take place unless something was done to remove the people. The prospect of tranquility and security in Ireland would only be achieved through the introduction of emigration on a large scale. "My opinion is, that it has very great possibilities, that it might be a very rich and very prosperous country. . . . I think that a judicious system of emigration is one of the most powerful means to accomplish that object."[58]

The British government toyed with the idea of a mass system of state-assisted emigration from Ireland to British North America, following the example of Peter Robinson's scheme in the 1820s. Landowners in Ireland and agents in Canada were asked to give evidence on the level and quality of voluntary emigration and the likely effects of introducing a system of loans to finance a state scheme. Witnesses before the committee indicated that there was a large untapped demand in Ireland for emigration on such terms, with the loans to be paid back over a period of years. Unlike the Robinson emigrants, who were carefully selected from the distressed peasantry of Munster, voluntary emigrants generally had some property. Those who sailed from Derry to Quebec, for instance, with their families, possessed from £30 to £50, and a few took £500 with them.[59] One reason for the British government's reluctance to invest in such schemes on a larger scale was the fear that a state-sponsored plan would stem the flow of voluntary emigration and therefore become self-defeating. Also, with the border between Canada and the United States easy to cross, many emigrants to Canada were moving south in search of employment in the northeastern United States. While the emigrants themselves looked to prosper through such secondary migration, this undermined the potential return on the government investment in the British colonial settlement in Canada.

In looking at the wider diaspora, it can be argued that the Irish who went to Texas were part of a stream of tens of thousands who were lured to the New World by the exciting prospects detailed in emigrant letters, newspaper reports, and the propaganda of emigration agents. The added attraction provided by the empresario James Power was the personal appeal of a charismatic personality, colorful stories of his own adventures among the native Indians, and not least, the unique opportunity for the emigrants to own thousands of acres of land in Texas. They went primarily in family groups in line with the general pattern of migration from Ireland before the famine. As late as the 1830s family migration was the most common form of movement overseas.

The economics of family migration meant that the cost of the Atlantic passage was prohibitive for the poorest and most oppressed sections of Irish society. James Power advised his would-be colonists to take farming implements for a large farm and provisions for a year, as well as all the personal belongings people required to start a new life on the frontier. Many families took their furniture and their own textile looms with them. That would have meant an addition to the passage money that had to be found in advance. Each passenger had to pay $30.00 (approximately £7.50) for the passage from Liverpool to New Orleans. The two-week stay in Liverpool and provisions for the six-week voyage itself would have required further outlays. Then there was the cost of the passage from New Orleans to the Texas coast and some capital to fund the early period of settlement in Texas before they could grow their own crops and become self-sufficient. It seems likely that the cost of the whole journey for a family of five people, including the cost of provisions and storage and the expense of lodgings in Liverpool, would have been in the region of $240.00 (£60), very much in line with the estimated cost of the state financing of emigrants to Canada and the equivalent of four times the annual wage of a Wexford laborer at the time.[60]

Little is known of the precise economic status of the Irish colonists. They were described overwhelmingly as tenant farmers, probably renting between 20 and 60 acres (an average of 30 acres) in southeastern Ireland. The evidence of the Tithe Applotment Books, which listed landholders for the purposes of assessing tithes paid to the established church, should not be read at face value. Richard Roche, on examining them, concluded that "many of the farms were under 10 acres" and that with rents at more than £1 per acre, "the average total annual income of most of the small-holders was between £9 and £10.5 per head." Nevertheless, he conceded that the lands in the Macamores (the name given to the region) were highly rated and very productive.[61] The Tithe Applotment Books recorded the situation in December, 1834, which was after the emigrants had left for Texas. Those who had sold their leases to raise the fare would not show up in the records. Then only about a third of farms were assessed for tithe, which explains why many of the names of families that went to Texas are not recorded. Also it is possible that land was held by the same family in different townlands, thus making it difficult to establish the full size of the family holding. We should also recognize that an Irish acre was equivalent to 1.6 English acres. To confuse the two is the modern equivalent of equating English pounds sterling with American dollars, a fact that will be fully understood by American tourists in Britain. It is possible to find some evidence for larger-sized holdings by comparing the same names in the Tithe Applotment Books (TAB) for 1834 with the Griffith Land Valuation in 1841. For instance, Martin Redmond had 2 acres in the former and 9 acres in the latter. The equivalent figures for John Roche were 19 acres in TAB and 27 acres in Griffith and for John McGrath 35 and 55 acres.[62] So Roche's view that the farms rarely exceeded 20 acres might be amended by the realization that, in practice, they were more commonly 20 to 30 acres, and some of those who went were from families with larger holdings.

It is also important to consider the practicalities of families being able to finance the cost of emigration. In the province of Leinster in 1841 the value of livestock on a farm of 15 to 30 acres was reckoned at £48.7 and above 30 acres at £161.2. Selling off livestock may have contributed but would not have met all the costs of emigration. The evidence of a Wexford landowner, Charles Walker, given before the Devon Commission in 1844 suggests that the sale of a tenant-right could also have yielded a useful source of capital to finance family emigration.

Have any instances of the sale of the tenant-right come under your own observation?—Yes, A farmer held eight acres at £2 an acre. There were sixteen years of his lease remaining. He had built his house and offices, which probably cost him £60. I should say the land is not first class land, and he sold his interest about a year ago for £180. I know of another more remarkable instance. A man held thirty Irish acres. His rent was 14s. an acre. The land, by bad management and by hiring it out to these usurers, is reduced at this moment about to a state of barrenness. There are eight years of the lease to come, and a life which is an old one. He is in arrears three years rent: his house is a perfect ruin, and his interest was purchased subject to all these arrears for £160. I may mention generally that the tenant-right sells very high in this country.[63]

Even allowing for landlord bias and exaggeration, it was clearly feasible for some tenant farmers to find the means to meet the costs involved in emigration to the New World.

Only a few went to Texas as indentured servants dependent on other families. James Power's relatives the O'Briens were described as doing very well in Ireland and were only persuaded to leave by the prospect of doing "a great deal better in Texas."[64] Thomas O'Connor, Power's nephew, was from a family of tenants of the Mill Farm, Kilmuckridge, who probably occupied about 80 acres of land, as well as possessing a secondary income from the mill. In the Tithe Applotment Books a Thomas Connors is listed as being assessed for 8 acres of bog land at 5s. per acre and 59 acres of third-class land at 12s. 6d. per acre. Also a James Connors had 48 acres of first-class land assessed at 19s. per acre and 17 acres of bog at 5s. per acre.[65] The Hart family had lost the sum of $25,000 (£6,250) in the bank in Wexford through the foolish generosity of Rosalie's father and had nothing left except the 50-acre family farm.[66] They were a family of broken fortune who hoped to recoup what they had lost by acquiring land in Texas and were also attracted by the prospect of a warmer climate that was important for Rosalie's health.

Other contemporary evidence, exemplified by the report in a national newspaper printed in the summer of 1833 that may well have been read by some of those contemplating the move to Texas, suggests that these Irish migrants formed part of the same exodus that took many relatively prosperous Irish farming families to North America.

> During the present season, twenty vessels left Londonderry for the U.S. with 2,774 passengers and twenty vessels for British America [Canada] with 3,780 passengers. . . . A large portion of the emigrants to the States were respectable farmers, and that fully three-fourths of the whole number are Protestants. Some, we know took with them considerable sums of money . . . many of course very little . . . but, supposing the average to have been only 10l [£10] each, the sum of 70,000l [£70,000] is abstracted from a district of about forty miles square – no inconsiderable amount to this impoverished country. We are at a loss to know whether we should congratulate those who have gone away or lament for those that remain, for the loss of such a valuable class of the community. From all we can learn, double the number are preparing to leave next season, despairing of better times here.[67]

Kerby Miller has provided further insights and evidence regarding the impact of changing inheritance and marriage patterns in stimulating emigration among farmers' sons and daughters. The practice of impartible inheritance, passing the undivided farm to the eldest son, which was more common in the eastern counties of Ireland, left the noninheriting siblings emigrating to the New World, supported by the favored brothers or the family as a form of compensation.

> Increasingly, after 1814 farmers' superfluous offspring faced the alternatives of an aimless, celibate life under the parental roof, reckless marriage accompanied by probable destitution and degradation to the ranks of cottiers or laborers, and emigration in search of the "independence" denied at home. No wonder contemporaries frequently re-

ported that "the unmarried of both sexes [were] the most inclined to emigrate." . . . Often the expressed willingness of farmers' children to emigrate stemmed more from status anxiety than from actual want. Many farmers' sons were like William Carleton: "a fine well-dressed young fellow . . . from whom great things were expected," and who vowed accordingly that he would "walk over the country, mile for mile, from one end of it to the other" before he would "degrade [him]-self to the condition of a day labourer." . . . all hoped that emigration to the New World would somehow transform them from "poverty to Independence."[68]

Frustration at home prompted an ambition to succeed abroad. Kerby Miller quotes the census commissioners in 1841 who noted that emigration did "not appear to be the first step in the march of improvement. It is when a man has already begun to move upwards that he seeks a more advantageous field than his native country affords."[69]

Emigration remained controversial in Ireland. The case for emigration pointed to the scale of voluntary movement that suggested there must have been an overall gain for those who went and for those who remained. The case against lamented the high quality of the emigrants that must have represented a loss of human capital in brains, skill, bone, and sinew. As ready-made adults, the cost of their upbringing fell on those who remained at home and possibly added up to a loss of national income of between 1 and 2 percent.[70] While a few landlords in Ireland financed emigration schemes and some poor law unions sent mostly female paupers out of Ireland to Canada, the United States, and later to Australia, the overwhelming majority of Irish migrants were self-financing or had their passage paid by remittances from other family members. Politicians, clergymen, and newspaper editors in Ireland might have railed against the evils of emigration: the betrayal of the nation, the dangers of a loss of faith, or even worse, a conversion to Protestantism, and the inevitable loss of capital and inhabitants to the country. The warnings given to would-be emigrants stressed the perils of the Atlantic crossing, the poverty and hardship suffered by Irish settlers in American cities, and the inevitable longings they experienced for the familiarity of convivial life back in Ireland. Yet what is striking about the sheer numbers of self-financing migrants is that collectively they represented a popular movement on a truly massive scale. Most people ignored the advice of their political and religious leaders and took their chances as part of a migrant flow in a bid to better themselves and their children.

If the information drawn from passenger lists points to the occupational structure of the emigrants being similar to that of the country as a whole, there is no available measure of personal characteristics such as temperament, ambition, resilience, or the willingness to take risks, but one might reasonably assume those willing to emigrate would have been more likely to have possessed such qualities. There is also the regional dimension that suggests that with more emigrants leaving the more advanced parts of Ireland, they were more likely to have been literate and English-speaking, to have been better informed, and to have more resources than the mass of the peasantry doomed to stay in poor western counties.

Where previous histories have fostered an image of oppressed victims driven into exile from their native land, I argue that emigrants were able and willing to make their own choices, weighing up future prospects against their own situation. These emigrants were predominantly small farmers from some of the most affluent parts of Ireland and possessed sufficient capital to finance the trip and buy provisions for a year. Surviving letters point to their belief that they would do better in acquiring several thousand acres in Texas than renting a few acres in Ireland, if not for themselves, then certainly for the next generation. They may not have fully understood all the risks involved in setting out on their adventure, but they sensed a great opportunity was being offered to them.

3

Irish Recruitment and the Settlements of San Patricio and Refugio

It is a troublesome business and requires much more perseverance and patience than anyone can imagine who has not tried it.
— The Austin Papers

THE IRISH EMPRESARIOS

Stephen F. Austin, the most successful of all the empresarios, was well qualified to comment on the difficulties encountered by foreigners who looked to settle people in Mexican Texas. The first obstacle was to gain the trust and confidence of Mexican government officials and to secure the contract in the face of a powerful suspicion of all foreigners. The second involved the recruitment of would-be colonists who had to be persuaded to settle in a wilderness, and third, there was the frustrating business of the allocation of land grants. This process could be delayed by the failure of the Mexican government to appoint commissioners or further held up when boundaries were contested by other empresarios or officials jealously guarding their own claims on territory. In the event, all the attempts made by European empresarios ended in failure, with the exception of two pairs of Irishmen who were partially successful in founding colonies in south Texas.

This chapter examines the importance of the Irish empresarios, their attempts to recruit settlers, and the establishment of the colonies of San Patricio and Refugio. In the process, a fresh assessment is made of what shaped and determined their actions. In previous accounts, the Irish origin of the empresarios has always been given prominence and the Irish presence among the settlers has equally dominated the history of the colonies. Yet it can be argued that it was almost incidental that the four successful empresarios shared the common birthplace of Ireland. Two were born in the northwest of Ireland: John McMullen in east Donegal county in 1785 and James McGloin in Castleregal, County Sligo, in 1801. Two were born in the south of Ireland: James Power, in Cullentra, County Wexford in 1788 or 1789 and James Hewetson in 1797 or 1798 in Thomastown, County Kilkenny.[1] Although the accident of birth gave them a common Irish ancestry, none of them, as far as we know, had met in Ireland, and all of them left their native country as young men. Their Irish identity was important in persuading the Mexican government that Irish migrants would make good settlers and act as a buffer against the potential aggression of the United States. But to win the contracts to act as empresarios, they first had to persuade officials of their loyalty to Mexico.

More important in shaping their futures and in the making of their contributions to the destiny of Texas was that they all set out as young men in search of adventure in the New World. McMullen first entered America in Baltimore, Maryland, and settled in Savannah, Georgia, where in 1810 he married Doña Esther Espadas, a widow with two children. In the 1820s he moved to Matamoros, Mexico, on the border of the province of Texas, where he continued to make a living as a merchant. In 1827, according to family legend, McGloin met McMullen in the English port of Liverpool where the younger man was bound for Australia but was persuaded to go with McMullen to Matamoros. McGloin, who was twenty-six when he arrived in Matamoros on board the *Isobella*, was listed as a merchant. Both men learned Spanish and formed part of the merchant community of Europeans in Matamoros. In 1828 McMullen and McGloin were partners in seeking permission from the Mexican government to act as empresarios in introducing Irish colonists to Texas. The partnership was strengthened when McGloin married McMullen's stepdaughter, the widow Eliza Cummings Watson.

James Hewetson emigrated to Philadelphia in the United States, possibly as early as 1807, and became qualified in medicine. He met Stephen F. Austin at Saint Louis, Missouri, accompanied him to New Orleans, and was a member of Austin's party at Béxar, before moving on and settling in Saltillo and Monclova in Mexico. There he was engaged in mercantile, manufacturing, and mining enterprises and became an influential figure in government circles in the province of Coahuila y Texas, of which

Saltillo was the capital. In 1826 he established a partnership with James Power to found a colony in Texas. In 1827 Hewetson became a Mexican citizen, and in 1833 he married a wealthy widow, Josepha Guajardo.

James Power immigrated to Philadelphia at the age of twenty or twenty-one, in 1809. A year later, he had moved to New Orleans, made the acquaintance of immigrants from all over the world — Irish, German, English, West Indian, Spanish, and Portuguese — all looking for greater opportunities in the bustling port city, and become part of a thriving merchant community. During his time in New Orleans he became acquainted with Stephen F. Austin and procured letters of introduction from him to officials in Mexico. Twelve years later, in 1822, James Power moved to Saltillo, Mexico. In 1823 he spent time in Matamoros and New Orleans and had opened a general merchandise business dealing in mining equipment. At this time Power met Hewetson, whose similar interests in merchandise and mining took him between Saltillo and Monclova.

It was at Matamoros in 1824 that James Power met Felipe Roque de la Portilla, a native of Spain and retired soldier in the imperial army, who had been rewarded for his service to his country with a town lot in the villa de San Marcos and twelve leagues of land near the town of Gonzalez in Texas. After repeated depredations from Indians, he was forced to abandon his ranch and return with other colonists to the Rio Grande, on the border between the province of Texas and the rest of Mexico. In July, 1832, James Power married Dolores Portilla, the daughter of Captain Portilla, in San Patricio.[2] Portilla himself became a Power-Hewetson colonist, receiving a league of land in 1834.

All four Irish empresarios were merchants and men of enterprise. All had experience in their early manhood as men of business, merchants trading between the United States and Mexico or speculating in the high-risk enterprise of dealing in mining equipment in Mexico. Having accumulated some capital and having made useful contacts in business and government circles, all four entered into the hazardous and expensive activity of colonization in Texas. Speculation in land continued alongside the adjunct of merchant activity. Important influences that shaped their outlooks and provided opportunities were the time spent among the European merchant communities in New Orleans and Matamoros, the association of both Power and Hewetson with one of the fathers of Texas, Stephen F. Austin, and the family alliance between Don Felipe Roque de la Portilla, colonizer and rancher. Furthermore, it is surely not a coincidence that both Power and Hewetson married into high-ranking Mexican families. This was not only politically astute in recommending them-selves to government officials in Mexico but also represented something of greater significance: Santiago Power and Santiago Hewetson, as they styled themselves, spoke Spanish, and became Mexican citizens. McMullen was fluent in Spanish and translated for the provisional government of Texas. Indeed, all four empresarios were able to speak Spanish, had become fa-miliar with Mexican ways, and were content to include local Mexican fam-ilies as settlers in their colonies of San Patricio and Refugio. Hewetson left Power to organize the new colony of Refugio, where he made his sub-stantial fortune. He lived most of his life in Mexico. McMullen sold his empresario grant to his partner McGloin, and left him to establish the colony of San Patricio. For his part, he made a new life, buying and sell-ing land and becoming active in the politics of the predominantly Mexi-can town of Béxar, where he served as alderman from 1840 to 1844. Through marriage, political association, and language ties, the Irish em-presarios were incorporated into the rich Hispanic culture of Mexico.

The period from 1800 to 1821 was a time of political fluidity in the his-tory of the southern United States and of New Spain and Mexico. Florida and Louisiana had belonged to the Spanish and French empires, and Mexico achieved its independence from Spain in 1821. In the same pe-riod, land speculation was a driving force behind territorial expansion in the United States, and successful colonization, if it could be achieved, held out a dazzling prospect of accumulating great personal fortunes. Talk of land speculation was rife among merchants trading between New Or-leans and Mexico, and under the empresario system, established by the Mexican government for the colonization of Texas, allowed those who se-cured empresario grants the prospect of amassing huge tracts of land.[3]

James Power and John McMullen, both of whom became leading fig-ures in their colonies, possessed a remarkable vision of the future devel-opment of Texas. Power had ambitions to build a port on the Aransas to exploit the potential growth in trade between the southern states and Mexico.[4] McMullen had visions of developing trade along the Rio Grande and of turning San Antonio into an industrial center.[5] Both men were also active in the early state government of Texas and in their local commu-nities, and they worked with influential figures such as Sam Houston and Mirabeau Lamar to establish the republic of Texas. McMullen was in-volved only marginally in looking after the colony at San Patricio, spend-ing little time there and falling out with the settlers. Hewetson, was even less involved in the affairs of the colony at Refugio. He stayed in Mexico where he built up a very considerable fortune in land and manufacturing. Acquiring the empresario contracts was only part of the wider economic activity of men who remained merchants and commercial adventurers.

EMPRESARIO CONTRACTS

In 1827 John McMullen and James McGloin, residents and merchants of Matamoros, made their first application to the state of Coahuila y Texas for an empresario contract. The territory chosen for colonization was located in east Texas between Galveston Bay and the Sabine River. The application was rejected because the same territory had already been the subject of an earlier petition by Joseph Velhein and David G. Burnet. Undaunted by this failure, McMullen and McGloin petitioned once more, in January, 1828, for a concession on any other territory that was available for colonization. They offered to settle five hundred families under the terms and conditions stipulated by the colonization law of 1825, but once again their application was unsuccessful. However, McMullen and McGloin got better news on hearing that the contract of the American empresarios John Purnell and Benjamin Drake Lovell was about to be surrendered. The original intention may have been to establish a socialist colony, but as with so many utopian communities, misfortune dogged the enterprise. Purnell was drowned at Matamoros, and Lovell's petition in 1826 to extend the limits of the colony to include the ten littoral leagues beyond the mouth of the Nueces River was not granted. Lovell asked to be relieved of his contract.

McMullen and McGloin took advantage of the new opportunity, went in person to Leona Vicario (the renamed capital, Saltillo), and presented their petition to colonize the same territory granted to Purnell and Lovell. Stretching from the Nueces to the Medina, near San Antonio de Béxar, it represented a sizable land grant. Their opportunism was rewarded. Within two days the application was granted. The terms of the contract included the following conditions that were to prove important in the subsequent unfolding of events:

Article 4. All lands belonging to private individuals, or communities, within the limits of the above described territory, shall remain free and unmolested, as well as the Mission of Refugio and the lands appertaining thereto.

Article 5. In conformity with the aforesaid Colonization law, the Empresarios John McMullen and James McGloin are bound to introduce the Two hundred families they offer, within the term of six years from this date, under the penalty of forfeiting the rights and privileges granted to them by said law.

Article 6. The families who are to compose this Colony, besides being Apostolic Roman Catholics, as they offer in their petition, must be of good moral habits, accrediting the same by certificate from the authorities of the places from which they emigrate. . . .

Article 8. For this purpose, and for the security of the persons and property of the new Colonists, against the incursions of Indians, or other enemy, the National Militia, shall be organized, in conformity with the regulations provided by law.[6]

Other important details specified in the contract were that the empresarios and the new colonists would hold themselves subject to the constitution and general laws of the nation and of the state that they adopt for their country (article 10); that once one hundred families had been introduced, the government should be notified, so that a commissioner could be dispatched to give the colonists possession of their lands and to furnish the town with law (article 9); and that all official communication and public documents had to be written in Spanish (article 11). Stripped of the legal terminology, these articles contained portents of the problems that faced the empresarios in fulfilling the terms of the contract and in the obligations of loyalty to which the colonists would have to agree in accepting their land grants. It was a matter of coincidence and contention that the two colonies of San Patricio and Refugio were situated adjacent to each other. Although the ten littoral leagues occupied by the Power-Hewetson colony were officially excluded from the McMullen-McGloin grant, the boundary between the two territories remained confused, which was to be the cause of future dispute.

The story of the Power-Hewetson empresario contract was more affected by hazards than that of McMullen-McGloin. In September, 1826, James Hewetson, in partnership with James Power, applied for permission to settle four hundred families—half of them Mexican and half native Irish—and to colonize the ten littoral leagues located between the Nueces River and Lavaca Creek and between the Trinity and the Sabine Rivers, plus the twenty leagues adjoining the border with the United States. It was a hugely ambitious request that, if granted, would have extended along a major part of the Texas coast. It also ran counter to the General Colonization Law of Mexico that forbade the colonization of border territories without the approval of the general supreme executive power.[7] With the exception of Austin's first colony, situated between the Lavaca and the Trinity, none of the littoral leagues had hitherto been approved for colonization. Clearly, the Mexican government was fearful of American expansionism and believed that the settlement and control of the coast was crucial to the development of Texas. Nevertheless, what appealed to government officials was the idea of a colony of Catholic settlers, Mexican and Irish, who it was thought would make loyal citizens of the new republic.

While Don Santiago Hewetson, as he styled himself, resident of Monclova and a Mexican citizen, took the lead in the petition and could recommend himself as a friend to Vice Governor Victor Blanco, opposition came from powerful figures who challenged the petition. Stephen F. Austin tried to preempt the application by staking his own claim to add further territories from the littoral leagues to his existing colonies.[8] Another rival for the same territory was the Mexican empresario Martín de León, whose colonization territory was centered on the town of Victoria, which projected into the littoral leagues. Self-interest and a deep hostility to foreign colonization of Texas determined his opposition to the Power-Hewetson colony.

The Power-Hewetson application, accompanied by the report of the state authorities, was passed on to the supreme executive power. Not until April 22, 1828, was it approved, and then only relating to the littoral leagues between the Lavaca and the Nueces. When the matter was referred back to the state authorities, a more restrictive area was designated for colonization. The contract agreed to on June 11, 1828, between Governor José María Viesca, for the State of Coahuila y Texas, and James Power and James Hewetson represented by their agent Victor Blanco limited the territory of the grant to land situated between the Guadalupe and Lavaca Rivers.[9]

Key features of the contract, shaped by the Colonization Law of 1825 and similar in many respects to the McMullen-McGloin contract, included the express condition "that one half of this Colony must be composed of Mexican families and the other half foreigners from Ireland." Article 2: "all possessors with legal titles, which may be found within the limits designated in Article 1st shall be respected by the Colonists, of this Contract, and it is obligatory on the Empresarios to see this duly executed and fulfilled" (article 3). Also included was the freedom of the authorities to build forts, wharves, or warehouses for the defense of the port or other public purpose (article 4), which obviously served the commercial and military interest of the coastal land. In conformity with the law of 1825 the empresarios were bound to introduce and establish two hundred families, within the space of six years, under the penalty of forfeiting their rights.

The area of colonization was not only a severely reduced territory from the original application, the contract also provoked a fierce criticism from powerful figures in Mexican government circles. Following his return from inspection of important sites in Texas in 1828, General Manuel Mier y Terán recommended that Texas be garrisoned with convict-soldiers and new forts be constructed at strategic points such as Lipantitlan, on the Nueces, La Bahía, Victoria, and at Aranzazu, on Live Oak Point. This change of policy prompted the infamous decree of April 6, 1830, by the Mexican Congress that put a stop to foreign immigration. Mier y Terán, in his capacity as *commandante* of the Eastern Internal Province of Mexico (which included Texas), began to establish a greater military presence in Texas, and took a strict line on limiting the extent of colonization. The existing colonies associated with Austin, De Witt, and De León were recognized, but all other contracts were suspended, titles to land were denied to many foreign settlers, and newly arrived migrants from the United States received orders to leave the country.[10]

After a visit to Texas in 1832 Tadeo Ortiz de Ayala reported to the secretary of relaciones in February, 1833, on the state of colonization and the administration of the province. His report questioned the position of the Power-Hewetson colony that he thought had been "agreed upon unwisely and without reflection."[11] He also drew attention to the strategic importance of the extensive coastline from the port of Matagorda to that of Corpus Christi, including at its center the port of Copano. He pointed to the fact that the expiration date on the contract, six years after its agreement in 1828, was almost due. Furthermore, the territorial claims of "these Irishmen" was disputed by the citizens of La Bahía (Goliad) and by the only colony of Mexicans, which was led by Don Martín de León. With public tranquility endangered over disputes involving the Power-Hewetson claim between state and government officials, Ortiz de Ayala advocated the rejection of at least part of the grant. What was, in effect, an antiforeigner stance also extended to the McMullen-McGloin grant. He expressed concern that it formed a very large tract of land, one of the richest parts of Texas, and despite an extension of time there was little prospect of the contract being fulfilled. He remarked, dismissively, that they could count only on "certain lazy, Irish families from the United States."[12] Finally, he questioned whether the empresarios could fulfil their contract because of lack of resources and enterprise and noted that the two Irish colonies were in dispute with each other over land.

In the face of delay and a dispute with De León, Hewetson applied in March, 1829, for an additional grant of land, arguing that the original grant was too small to settle four hundred families. The proposal was for an augmentation to extend the littoral leagues from the Guadalupe to the border of the state of Tamaulipas on the Nueces River. To add weight to the proposal, James Power had become a naturalized Mexican citizen on February 6, 1829. The application was approved on April 2, 1829, but it was still fraught with difficulty. Martín de León remained in dispute with Power and Hewetson because part of his town of Victoria lay within the augmentation. There was also apprehension in the *ayuntamiento* of Goliad that its territorial rights and those of its citizens were being infringed. Similarly, the rights of the claimants to land previously belonging to the missions at Goliad and Refugio appeared to be threatened. Most of the claimants to mission land were Spanish and Mexican, but a few were also Indian families, Karankawas and Cocos.[13]

The right of the empresarios to the mission lands was resolved when the governor adjudicated in the dispute. In April, 1830, Power and Hewetson petitioned in support of their rights on land belonging to the former missions and requested authority to establish the capital of the colony at the site of the mission of Refugio. The petition was approved the same day and endorsed by the state congress the following year. In May, 1831, Governor Letona issued instructions regarding the disposal of mission lands and properties. The families belonging to the Mission Espíritu Santo were to receive the land to which they were entitled under the colonization law of the state. Each family would also receive gratis from Power and Hewetson a yoke of oxen or bulls, with the necessary farming utensils. The empresarios were also obligated to receive as settlers all Mexican families, such as the inhabitants of Goliad who had applied to the government for lands. These would be included within the total number of families under the contract. It was agreed that the point most eligible for the town or city of the colony was the site of the mission of Refugio. Therefore the town property still existing would be sold off to the highest bidder and the proceeds of the sale would be delivered to the judge and paid into the state treasury.

The Indians of the Refugio mission received teams, carts, and farming implements, together with the exclusive possession of a piece of land in the vicinity of Goliad. While the Indians appeared content with the arrangement, it only added to strained relations between the empresarios and the *ayuntamiento* of Goliad. Most of the claims of the local Spanish and Mexican settlers were quickly settled. They exercised their rights to become colonists and obtain their land grants through the colonial commissioner. Some purchased land directly from the state and a few were able to obtain larger tracts of land through buying in addition to their grant entitlement.

The opposition of Martín de León remained the most formidable obstacle to colonization. De León opposed the Power-Hewetson contract of 1828, petitioning the governor to declare the contract null and void and the land to be distributed to the citizens of Goliad or for the benefit of De León.[14] His own prior claim of a contract with the revolutionary government of Béxar in 1812 was discounted by the governor but gave the hint of legitimacy that could influence officials who shared his antiforeigner views. With the augmentation of the Power-Hewetson grant approved, De León supported by Ramón Músquiz, the *jefe político* at Béxar, took his case directly to the federal executive. Músquiz had his own claim on six leagues of land on the Lavaca River and shared with De León a hostility to foreign settlement. The matter was referred to General Manuel Mier y Terán who adjudicated in favor of Martín de León. He decided that the law of April 6, 1830, effectively annulled the Power-Hewetson contract and discounted Power's argument that the law related only to American colonists and not to the Irish or to Mexicans. Terán ordered Power not to survey any of the ground within his concession and to wait on a final report on the dispute.

The report was issued by the vice president on December 23, 1831, and confirmed by the state government on March 10, 1832. However, a compromise was agreed upon through the efforts of the *jefe político* at Béxar, who went in person to Victoria to confer with De León on the boundary between the two colonies and then went to Refugio where he obtained the agreement of James Power. With the dispute resolved, the last major obstacle to colonization appeared to be removed. De León died in the cholera epidemic of 1833, but further delays were caused by the change of Mexican government policy and by the competing claims of empresarios. Local inhabitants and officials were looking to secure their own political and economic interests. This meant that time was running out on the six-year period within which the contracts had to be met.

John McMullen and James McGloin were fortunate in not facing delays over their contracts and were able to proceed with the business of organizing the recruitment of colonists. As things turned out they were less fortunate when it came to the conferment of land grant titles to their settlers. They sold their mercantile interests in Matamoros and in the summer of 1829 sailed to New York in search of newly arrived Irish migrants who might be persuaded to move to Texas. In New York, through newspaper advertisements and in interviews with prospective settlers, they presented a dazzling prospect: the soil was highly fertile; the land was perfect for grazing purposes; and the chosen site was alongside a sparkling river that was navigable to the Gulf of Mexico. Their salesmanship reaped its reward. Some thirty-five Irish families, mostly from New York, but some from Kentucky and New Orleans, agreed to a second-phase migration and the prospect of a new life in Texas.

A somewhat jaundiced view of McMullen and McGloin's recruiting was recorded in letters written by Thomas Gunning in 1832 to Major O'Hara in Sligo, Ireland, on his return to New York, in which he described his experiences as a would-be colonist in San Patricio:

Kitty & I left New York coaxed but I must say totally led astray by a notorious pair of scoundrels, by name [McMullen and] McGloin from Cloonacool. The younger was in Mexico often before this, the older in New Orleans, they held out such extravagant expectations & promises, being men of practical experience & apparently very comfortable besides my wife's namesake that under the circumstances I couldn't hesitate going along in fact we never could think for a moment they w'd practice any deception in our behalf but it soon turned out otherwise. The father-in-law of the younger McGloin, McMullen, had a schooner supposed to be his own & chartered a Brig in this port to take out passengers by scheming & placcard advertisements they succedding [in] recruiting about 32 families of whom accidentally & otherwise 34 died in the short period of 13 months, some drowned, some shot & etc—

however after a voyage of 5 weeks we reached our destination the province of Texas about 15 hundred miles west of the City of Mexico.[15]

It is clear from his letters that Gunning was unsuited to the rigors of pioneer life, and his negative reaction to his Texan adventure may have been influenced by the death of his wife on the return journey, thirty miles from New Orleans. "Had I remained in New York," he wrote, "which is the Garden yes the Emporium of all America, we could be very happy & well off today." [16]

The would-be colonists set sail from New York to Copano aboard two chartered boats, the brig *New Packet* and the schooner *Albion*. In October, 1829, they reached the coast of Texas. The *Albion* was blown off course and Capt. Thomas Duehart mistook the landmarks along the shore and landed at Matagorda Bay instead of at the port of Copano. Led by empresario McGloin, the passengers made their way to Mesquite Landing on the Guadalupe, and then marched inland some twenty miles to Mission Refugio, the nearest settlement. McMullen and the thirty-five colonists aboard the *New Packet* arrived at Copano and also marched to Refugio, intending to pick up provisions before heading on to their destination, San Patricio, on the Nueces River.

Notice of the safe arrival of the Irish colonists was sent to the customs officials in Goliad; they in turn informed the departments of the Mexican government. Attached to the report was the manifest listing the families aboard the *New Packet*, which arrived from New York under Capt. Jonan Haris, and information on the tools for farming and for various trades to establish their homes, a thousand feet of lumber together with windows and locks they brought with them.[17] A further report, with the manifest list, was received by officials in Mexico City from the captain at the port of Matagorda confirming the arrival of the two ships, and this report was then forwarded to the governor of the State of Coahuila y Texas. A note in the margin alerted the state authorities to check that the new colonists were truly of Irish origin and not "North Americans." Interestingly, among the list of passengers aboard the *Albion* and the *New Packet* were Spanish or Mexican families who were most probably recruited from Louisiana.[18] It was imperative for McMullen and McGloin to make up the numbers and to meet the terms of the contract. Their ability to speak Spanish was no doubt of great value in providing assurances to would-be Hispanic colonists.

Having survived the voyage and the trek through the flat coastal strip, the settlers encountered the first of many hazards that lay in wait for them in their adopted country. Their presence had been observed by the native Indians, and it was not long before they received a visit from a party of Lipans who came to Refugio to demand gifts from them. McMullen, described as "fearless, impatient, not even tempered like his partner, McGloin," was not one to compromise or negotiate.[19] He refused their demands and ordered Captain Kelly to organize the men into a civil militia and to fire the cannon to frighten the Indians away. McMullen's resolve had the desired effect on the Lipans, but at the expense of creating alarm about their possible return. Given the danger from hostile Indians, many of the settlers now wanted to stay at Refugio with the protection of a stone church rather than risk the move to San Patricio.

A third party of McMullen and McGloin colonists arrived in Copano in December, 1829. They were greeted at Refugio by confusion and growing discontent. Power and Hewetson, on hearing of the news in Saltillo that a group of Irish colonists had arrived in Texas and were staying in Copano and at the Refugio mission, complained in November, 1829, to Governor Viesca. They demanded that McMullen and McGloin move their people to their own colony on the Nueces River.[20] Various layers of authority were then brought into play involving officials in San Antonio (de Béxar), Goliad, and at San Felipe de Austin. Prompted by Viesca, Román Músquiz, the *jefe político* in San Antonio, investigated the situation. He learned from Mariano Cosio, the customs officer at Goliad, that when the first McMullen and McGloin colonists arrived at Refugio they were sick and short of supplies. They asked if they could remain for a few days to recover. McMullen then applied for permission from the alcalde of Goliad to remain at the mission. Permission was granted on condition that they subject themselves entirely to the orders of the superior authority. Armed with this local knowledge, Músquiz reported the problem to Commissioner General Antonio Padilla, who revealed that he had already approved the transfer of the McMullen and McGloin colonists to Refugio on December 7. However, they had to leave unsettled the ten littoral leagues and the lands of the Refugio mission.

With his colonists more eager to stay in Refugio than to risk moving to a new location, McMullen demanded the right to remain at Refugio, petitioned for use of the stone of the ruined mission, and contested the rights of Power and Hewetson to the mission lands. The Mexican officials were faced with a conflict of interest between two neighboring Irish colonies. With crops planted and permanent buildings about to be constructed at Refugio, a more entrenched position would soon develop. Músquiz ordered the alcalde at Goliad to summon McMullen to his court and insist that he vacate the lands occupied at Refugio and transfer to the place designated for colonization. Only those who had planted grain could remain until their crop was harvested.[21] The withdrawal of authority to stay in Refugio forced McMullen and McGloin to transfer the colonists to the Nueces. However, discontent and some personal animosity toward McMullen among the settlers had strengthened resistance to follow the empresarios' lead. Father Doyle, the Irish priest, advised Aldrete, the alcalde of Goliad, that only sixteen families were prepared to leave Refugio for a new colony. There was great dissatisfaction among the other families and several individuals had requested passports for New Orleans.[22]

In the meantime, in July, 1830, McGloin had explored the territory assigned to the colonists and had chosen a suitable site on the Nueces River. Toward the end of August, McGloin notified Aldrete that twenty-five families had left to occupy land on the selected site. This began the gradual process of relocation that took place between August and November, 1830. In the process, an unknown number of would-be McMullen-McGloin colonists chose not to settle there. Another brush with a band of the much-feared Comanche Indians, prior to an attack on their enemies the Karankawas, added fear to disenchantment and prompted some to return to the more settled conditions of the United States. Others who had squatted at Copano and Refugio refused to move, and when the Power-Hewetson colonists arrived at Mission Refugio in May, 1834, a number of McMullen-McGloin colonists were still there.[23] Taking that into account, it is probable that more left Texas than followed McMullen and McGloin to the Nueces.

Against a continuing background of insecurity and discontent, McMullen and McGloin petitioned the government on December 18, 1830, to appoint a land commissioner to establish the colony and place the colonists in possession of their lands.[24] On January 29, 1831, José Antonio Saucedo was appointed as commissioner of the new colony, but it was to be many months before he visited the site. While they waited, the colonists familiarized themselves with their territory, each family chose allotted lands on which they wished to secure title, and they agreed to establish a town to be called San Patricio de Hibernia, in commemoration of the patron saint of Ireland.

Saucedo arrived in October, 1831. The town site was established and the lands surveyed by one of the leading colonists, William O'Docherty. However, the frustration and discontent was to continue over the issue of land grants, not merely for a few months but for the next four years. Only a dozen titles were granted, which allowed the building of picket cabins, leaving the other families in a state of uncertainty over their future. The colonists, after the high expectations and promises held out to them, had experienced nothing but obstacles and delays since they had arrived in Texas in 1829. They had thrown up primitive *jacales* as shelter, but enforced idleness in cultivating their land had a demoralizing effect. Father Doyle, who had built a picket church dedicated to Saint Patrick, was soon succeeded by Father T. J. Molloy. In June, 1832, a Dominican priest and two nuns arrived from Ireland, wishing to establish themselves at San Patricio; they had to be housed in the abandoned chapel at the Refugio mission, for want of suitable accommodation, and they stayed for only a short period. The fleeting presence of a Catholic ministry could only have added to the sense of impermanence among the settlers in San Patricio.

The delay in granting further land titles was driven partly by the change in policy introduced by the law of April 6, 1830, prohibiting further immigration from the United States. The alcalde of Goliad was uncertain about the status of foreigners who had resided in the United States. Saucedo also waited on clarification of the law before recognizing new colonists. Further delay arose with the death of Saucedo in 1832 and the appointment of his successor, J. María Balmaceda, in March, 1833. In turn, Balmaceda busied himself with internal politics in Monclova, managing only to extend the deadline for the fulfilment of the empresario contract from August, 1834, to 1838. In March, 1834, he granted land titles to four or five Mexican rancheros, and in April the *ayuntamiento* of San Patricio was established. William O'Docherty became alcalde, and Thomas Adams, Francisco de León, Francisco Leal, and Patrick Boyle became *regidores*. The *ayuntamiento* thus had an equal representation of Irish and Mexican settlers.

Exasperation over the delays in securing titles led to a loss of San Patricio colonists, who joined Power's colony in Refugio. There they were readily accepted by the empresario James Power and found that the commissioner, Vidaurri, was issuing titles very promptly from August until December, 1834.[25] During the summer of 1834 a new group of recruits from County Tipperary in Ireland under contract from the Mexican government arrived safely at Copano and transferred all their belongings and

James McGloin's residence at Round Lake near San Patricio was restored as the last surviving Irish empresario home. *Courtesy UT Institute of Texan Cultures at San Antonio*

two years' provisions on to lighters to get ashore. The government sent some soldiers to protect the colonists and some carts to assist them in transporting their goods inland. All their miscellaneous belongings were discharged unsorted on the beach and, in very hot weather, children were protected under awnings while preparations were made to move everything a mile inland to pitch their first camp in open prairie. The soldiers lived on the provisions of the colonists and appeared reluctant to face danger when Indian raids seemed imminent. A paste made of cactus root for axle grease was used to keep axles of the old, rickety, screeching carts from igniting and being consumed by fire.[26] This ill-assorted party left their camp and settled in and around San Patricio.

Finally, in the summer of 1835, Commissioner Balmaceda came, at last, to San Patricio and issued the colonists their land grants. A total of 70 headright grants, 6 special grants, and 106 town lots were sold for the sum of $408.00. The sites of municipal and ecclesiastical buildings were also allocated at the same time. Under the terms of the McMullen and McGloin contract, some 60 land grants were issued to Irish-born settlers and 23 to Mexican settlers.[27]

The recruitment and settlement of the San Patricio colonists had extended over a period of six years from 1829 and 1835. Those years were marked by uncertainty and delay over the location of their site, either to stay in Refugio or to move on to the Nueces River. The colonists themselves arrived at various times: the first ones were led from New York in 1829 by McMullen and McGloin; a few others came with McGloin in 1833; a third group arrived on their own initiative from the United States. Finally, in 1834 a party arrived from Tipperary to swell the numbers of settlers and to compensate for some of the original party who decided to stay at Refugio, joined the Power-Hewetson colony in 1834, or rejected the pioneering life and returned to the United States. Although invariably described as an Irish colony, it was in reality a mixed settlement that included Anglo-Americans, Spanish Americans, local Spanish rancheros, and native Mexicans, as well as Irish Americans and natives of Ireland. The specification in the contract that half the families should be Mexican and half Irish was not strictly met, nor was the proviso that all should practice the Catholic religion.[28]

Recruitment to the Power-Hewetson colony in Refugio was undertaken under the severe pressure of the deadline for the fulfillment of the contract, due to expire in June, 1834. It was, therefore, more concentrated and dramatic, and it was to be marked by tragedy on an epic scale. Having faced a number of delays since the empresario contract was first agreed in 1828 and then augmented in 1829, James Power and James Hewetson also encountered frustration in attempts to recruit colonists directly from Ireland through the offices of an English agent, Archibald Roberts. He had acted for Power and Hewetson without success since 1828.[29] It was decided that James Power would make the journey himself to Ireland to recruit colonists and so meet the terms of the contract.

According to family legend, recalled by Dolores Welder, Power's daughter, his departure posed an agonizing decision for the empresario. When the ship was ready to leave Port Aransas on April 17, 1833, a man was spotted on shore frantically trying to attract the attention of those on board. He turned out to be Francisco Portilla, James Power's brother-in-law, with the news that Power's wife, Dolores, had just given birth to a son and wanted him to return home. The captain refused to postpone the sailing, leaving Power with the choice of abandoning his wife and newborn son or forsaking his empresario project.[30] He chose the path of ambition and destiny, proceeding on his way but with what private regret can only be imagined.

Power was to set out for Ireland from Philadelphia on October 14, and it is likely that between April and October he was renewing old acquaintances and looking for new recruits in New Orleans and Philadelphia, as well as possibly returning home to visit his wife in Texas.[31] According to one account, Power found several of his emigrants in Philadelphia and started them off immediately for Texas.[32] He reached Ireland around the end of May and, after an absence of more than twenty years, was reacquainted with his family and friends in Ballygarrett, County Wexford. Amid great rejoicing, he was met by his sister Elizabeth, who had married Thomas O'Brien. Other members of the welcoming party were his brother-in-law Thomas O'Connor, the husband of Power's deceased sister, and O'Connor's son Thomas. Among his family and friends James Power possessed a legendary reputation. With many a story to tell of his adventures among Mexicans and Indians in the New World, he was a charismatic and persuasive figure to potential colonists.

Handbills were soon posted throughout Ireland to advertise the benefits of life in the province of Texas. Meetings were held in his sister's house in County Waterford, and he made speeches to large gatherings of people who came from as far afield as Carlow, Wicklow, Kilkenny, Tipperary, and Sligo. As recalled by one of the colonists, Rosalie Hart Priour, Power claimed Texas to be one of the "richest countries in the world" with "a most delightful climate. Gold was so plentiful, according to his account, you could pick it up under the trees. A great many believed him. As proof of what he told, he was going to take his only surviving sister and her family with him. And he told them that as she was happy and prosperous at home, he would never advise her to go to a new country if he was not certain she would do a great deal better in Texas."[33]

Potential recruits were informed of the generous land grants under the provisions of the State Colonization Law. The opportunity to own thousands of acres of land was the most substantial of the benefits available to those who wished to emigrate to Texas. What may not have been apparent to small farmers in Ireland was the very large acreage needed to make a living from ranching in Texas. However, James Power was so persuasive that some 250 families signed up for the expedition. Power's sister, her husband, and their five children all went. James Power's nephew, Martin Power, who walked with a stick, also agreed to follow his uncle to Texas.

Each family agreed to pay thirty dollars for the voyage, payable at Liverpool, and a fee for their lands (177 acres of tillage and 4,428 acres of pasture). They were required to take farming implements for a large farm and provisions for a full year. These conditions meant that the families had to possess some means above that of the poorest in Ireland. This is confirmed by Rosalie Hart Priour who recalled that the "colonists were all farmers with the exception of four or five who came out as hired men and servants. They all sold everything they owned but all seemed to have more or less money."[34] Thomas O'Connor, who was seventeen on his arrival in Texas, was the younger son living at the Mill farm at Kilmuckridge in County Wexford, which was to be passed on to his brother, Dennis. As compensation for not having any part of the family farm, he was probably staked by his parents to try his luck in the New World and entrusted to the care of his uncle, the empresario James Power. (The remarkable story of Thomas O'Connor is told in chapter 6.) It also seems likely that Power continued to ship smaller numbers at every opportunity until he himself embarked from Liverpool with around a hundred souls in the *Heroine* en route to New Orleans where they were due to meet the passengers of the *Prudence*, which had gone ahead.

THE VOYAGE

The adventures of the would-be colonists began when they sailed from Wexford to Liverpool in December, 1833. There they spent a couple of weeks visiting relatives and "hurrying from store to store buying all that was needed to endure the dreaded sickness 'le mal de mer' and the rigors of the voyage to come."[35] Their ship, the *Prudence*, left Liverpool on December 26 but had to return to port three days later as a result of stormy weather. While the colonists remained in port waiting for the weather to clear, the Liverpool newspapers published details of shipwrecks at sea. If the emigrants read these accounts, any sense of foreboding they had about the voyage and the significance of their decision to emigrate could only have been reinforced. Normally, emigrant sailings took place between the spring and autumn when the weather for the Atlantic crossing was less hazardous. This was suspended in the panic atmosphere of the famine years when a reckless disregard of safety led to more winter sailings.

In the meantime, Power had recruited a further eight families in Liverpool and beginning early in 1834 the whole party embarked for New Orleans on two ships, the *Prudence* and the *Heroine*. There is some confusion in surviving accounts about the dates of the respective voyages of the two vessels, with conflicting versions drawn from official records and the statements and memoirs of the passengers themselves. Part of the confusion stems from the two voyages made by the *Prudence;* the first voyage began on January 8, 1834, and the second probably began in early March, 1834. The *Prudence* was the older of the two ships, built at Saint John's Newfoundland in 1802, a sailing vessel of 281 tons, with two masts, a single deck, and a square stern. Each family had their own quarters on board ship with space provided for their own cooking. Facilities were limited in what was most probably a converted cargo ship, crowded with passengers to make the voyage financially viable. Power's contacts in New Orleans enabled him to arrange a charter deal with Thomas Elmes for bringing passengers on the return journey from Liverpool after sending cargo from New Orleans on the outward journey.[36] James Power, his relatives the O'Briens, and his nephews Martin Power and Thomas O'Connor, were passengers on board the *Heroine*, a large sailing vessel of 340 tons. The *Heroine* arrived in New Orleans on May 7, 1834. A total of seventy-one adults were recorded on the passenger list, but there is no record of the children on board.[37]

Most accounts of emigrant voyages have dwelt on the appalling conditions on board ship and the heavy mortality from disease, and have emphasized the suffering of passengers in cramped conditions.[38] Rosalie Hart Priour's description of the voyage aboard the *Heroine* contains a surprising degree of playfulness as she recalled her childhood experience, but also a mixture of joy and sorrow, all confined within a secure belief in the infinite wisdom of the Almighty: "Everything went on perfectly until we entered the Bay of Biscay. There even at the best of times, it is very rough, but we had the misfortune to encounter a storm. One by one, the passengers were compelled to go to their berths, and before long even the sailors could not walk the deck."[39] When the captain ordered that the hatches be closed, Rosalie found a small hiding place that was inviting to a child wanting to watch the storm rather than be confined to the cabin below:

> I could sit there and watch the play of the elements in all their grand display and the waves dashing over the ship as if the angry waters would swallow everything that came their way. I was in my element — I knew no fear. I was young and innocent, and when spoken to about death, I always answered, "We have to die once and we may as well die now as at any other time. God can protect us from danger, if it is His will to do so. If not, it is our place to submit."[40]

Nor did Captain Russell fit the cruel and heartless stereotype, and he was evidently fond of children. He invited young Peter Burns and Elizabeth Hart, Rosalie's sister, to spend time on deck with him.

When an order was to be given, he would take them and make them speak the order after him, and as both of the children were too young to pronounce the words correctly, it caused a great deal of merriment. Everyday at eleven o'clock, he would order a waiter full of raisins, almonds, cake, and other things to be brought on deck, and tell sister Elizabeth and Peter Burns to invite the other children to their party. He always made them play host and hostess to their guests. Everything went on splendidly, and nothing occurred to disturb the equanimity of the passengers for about six weeks.[41]

A sighting of what was feared to be a pirate ship caused a brief alarm but it turned out to be a merchant ship that had been tacking about for forty-eight hours to avoid what was perceived as danger from the *Heroine*. A passenger who had slipped away and made his wife and daughter hide him between two feather beds, in fear of his life, was not allowed to forget the incident for the rest of the voyage.

The captain, unacquainted with the Florida coast, chose to make the tour of the island of Cuba. Rosalie's young sister, Elizabeth, could not be kept from going on deck in the middle of the day. "She said she had to be there to give orders, that the Captain could not do without her. One day, while on deck, she was sun struck and after lingering two days in the most dreadful suffering, her spirit took its flight to join her angel sisters in heaven. The Captain mourned for her as if she were his own child. . . . . She had to be sewn in some new canvas, with weights to sink her, and with love and sorrow, lowered into her last home on earth."[42] The passengers on board the first journey of the *Prudence* arrived safely in New Orleans and there waited for the other would-be colonists to leave Ireland. Some may have gone ahead to Texas where they were looked after by early settlers, John Dunn and Power's relatives the Portillas.[43]

The second journey of the *Prudence* brought eighty-one passengers from Liverpool, as recorded in the abstract passenger list, arriving on the Louisiana coast on April 20, 1834.[44] The *Louisiana Courier* (New Orleans) reported the arrival of the British ship *Prudence* at anchor outside the bar with a cargo of salt and seventy-five passengers.[45] This time there was a tragic loss of life when they came ashore at New Orleans, which was gripped by a cholera epidemic that had ravaged the city for the past two years. Judging by the cholera cases reported in the charity hospital, the disease continued to claim its victims.[46] Some had already died and others were in hospital. Rosalie Hart recalled: "There was very little to make us feel satisfied, we arrived at a time when the cholera was raging in New Orleans and people there were dying so fast that it was impossible to dig graves and the dead were being buried in trenches." Forbidden to eat vegetables or fruit for fear of catching the disease, those who disobeyed were the few to escape it, and after eight or ten days they were ready to leave "that hothouse of pestilence and death."[47] Only a few of the passengers aboard the *Prudence* have been identified as cholera victims in New Orleans, but this is not surprising given the circumstances of the time. Dr. Theodore Clapp , a clergyman resident in the city who ministered to cholera patients in 1832 and 1833, recorded that within the space of twelve months at least ten thousand died from two episodes of yellow fever and Asiatic cholera:

> A great number of bodies, with bricks and stones tied to the feet were thrown in the river. Many were privately interred in gardens and enclosures, on the grounds where they expired, whose names were not recorded in the bills of mortality. . . . Large trenches were dug, into which these uncoffined corpses were thrown indiscriminately. . . . The same day, a private hospital was found deserted; the physicians, nurses, and attendants were all dead, or had run away. Not a living person was in it. The wards were filled with putrid bodies, which, by order of the mayor, were piled in an adjacent yard, and burned, and their ashes scattered to the winds.[48]

Before they departed New Orleans, Rosalie's father, Tom Hart, met a Mr. Griffith, a relative by marriage, on board a steamer and he explained that he had come out as an emigrant under the Mexican government's agreement with Colonel Powers. "Oh, Tom!" he said, "For God's sake do not take your family to Texas. It is inhabited by savages, and no society, and I will give you any situation on the steamer you wish; if you do not want to stay with me, I will find a plantation for you, between here and St. Louis, where you will be much happier than in the wild, savage country you intend to go to." Despite Griffith's pleading, Tom Hart could not be persuaded. He had given his word to James Power and would not break a promise.[49] This promise was to cost him his life.

From New Orleans, the colonists were transported on the last leg of their journey to the Texas coast in two chartered schooners, the *Wildcat* and the *Sea Lion*. The *Wildcat* made the trip in twenty-four hours only to be wrecked on arrival at Saint Joseph's Island, one of the barrier islands along the coast. Stormy weather compounded the natural hazards associated with sand bars and shallow waters. John J. Linn, Victoria merchant and Irish colonist, recorded the scene aboard the *Wildcat*: "As our little schooner reached the bar a rough sea broke on her and a heavy swell threw her from the channel, and she became unmanageable. The consequence was that she struck heavily on the bar in about five feet of water where she remained fast aground. . . . Another heavy sea struck her and completely washed her decks. Those upon deck only saving themselves by clinging desperately to the ropes."[50] Rosalie Hart's family were on board the other schooner, the *Sea Lion*, which took forty-eight hours to make the trip to Aransas Pass, twice as long as the *Wild Cat*. They could see that the *Wild Cat* had run ashore and Rosalie recalled that "Col. Power ordered the Captain of our schooner, in my hearing, at the point of his pistol, to change his course and avoid running his vessel aground. After casting anchor for the night, the captain of our schooner weighed anchor and in the night, also ran our schooner ashore. . . . Luckily no lives were lost by the grounding of the two schooners. The remainder of the colonists were transferred by lighter to Copano, where the Mexican Customs house then stood."[51]

Then real tragedy struck the party. Cholera broke out among them and the passengers were compelled to stay for two weeks on the wrecked schooner. "My recollection," Rosalie continued, "is that about 250 persons died and that many were buried at sea. A child of Mr. St. John's brother, Mr. Wm. St. John, now at the Mission, died and through sympathy for the grief stricken parents and their horror of burying their child at sea, I remember seeing my father and Mr. Paul Keogh, take the child in a little boat to St. Joseph's Island where they buried it. After burying the child, Mr. Paul Keogh fell sick with the cholera and died on St. Joseph's Island and was buried there also by my father who remained with him to his death."[52] The deaths occurred so quickly that survivors struggled to throw the bodies overboard as fast as they died. To relieve those dying on the shore, Tom Hart dug down four or five feet into the uninhabited Saint Joseph's Island in search of freshwater, and his wife, Elizabeth Hart, comforted them until death.

Having gone forty-eight hours without any kind of nourishment, Tom Hart himself became sick. His wife provided warm drinks and applied warm salt, working all night to relieve him. By the next morning, he was free of cramps but complained of a lump in his stomach. Tom Hart was lowered on a feather bed into a boat and compelled to keep his damp clothes on until the boat was unloaded. Then the Hart family were landed on a sand beach where there was no shelter from the fierce sun. Elizabeth made a crude tent from bedclothes to protect her sick husband, but in the middle of May, it was "so hot that the ground would burn the feet in the middle of the day, if you happened to have on shoes with thin soles."[53] There he died quietly, and without any other materials to hand, the family buried him wrapped in a blanket.

At this point, Rosalie Hart's account reveals the first break in a stoical resignation to God's will. Writing much later in life, she tried to imagine how her mother endured the loss of her husband on arrival in a hostile land: "We were in a strange country, thousands of miles from our friends and relations, on a sand beach exposed to the burning heat of summer or drenched by rain through day and at night surrounded by wild animals, not knowing the minute we would be drowned. Then there were thousands of naked savages even more to be dreaded than wild beasts, and a company of Mexican soldiers on guard for the purpose of preventing us from moving from that place under two weeks time, for fear we would spread the cholera."[54] At last they were allowed to travel twelve miles inland to the mission at Refugio where they found, apart from the Mexicans, that only four huts were occupied. Two of the houses, including James Power's house, belonged to Irishmen. They were primitive *jacales* with poles to form the walls, and roofs covered with coarse grass. They had an earth floor, no windows, and even the doors were made of poles. By contrast, the Catholic mission that had been built by the Spanish and was made of rock two feet thick contained two rooms for the use of the priest. It made a lasting impression on Rosalie Hart: "The inside was the richest I have ever seen in my travels. The railing in front of the altar had a band of silver all along the bannisters and the altar itself was profusely ornamented with gold and silver. The pulpit was very much decayed, but splendidly carved. . . . Between the pulpit and the door was a statue of the blessed Virgin with the infant Jesus in her arms and I think it was all gold."[55] Showing less than expected reverence, their actions dictated by necessity, the Mexicans had filled the church with corn.

James Power was a sick man during the period of the colonists' landing, but he lost no time in seeking help from the chief of the department, Ramón Músquiz. He announced the arrival "on the beaches of Aransas some one hundred and fifty persons from Ireland, and they are enduring a great deal of hardship because the captains abandoned two endangered ships, losing most of the household goods, and forges; and having left some seventy people in the hospitals of New Orleans who are to come as soon as they improve and a considerable number dead as the result of a new outbreak of cholera there."[56] Of the 100 passengers aboard Power's chartered brig from New Orleans, under the command of Captain Ramsdale, a good sailor but an unprincipled man, 50 or 60 died, including James Power's sister and two of his nieces. According to the testimony of William St. John, "probably one third of the people who started with me from Ireland to America died of cholera, I don't think as many as one half died. . . . there were some who returned to Ireland, approximately eight."[57] From an initial total of between 250 and 350 emigrants who set out from Ireland, between 80 and 120 never arrived alive in Texas.

Músquiz replied promptly to Power, sympathized with the tragic experiences of the colonists, and ordered the *ayuntamiento* at Goliad to give them every assistance: "It is unfortunate to have arrived to this country with such suffering and to have been in want by the abandonment of the vessels at the shore by which were lost their furniture and tools for carpentering, weaving and farming which they had brought and most of all it is regretted that in this country there is no facility to restore the loss of such necessary utensils."[58] He also requested from the government the early appointment of a commissioner to issue land grant titles.

ESTABLISHING THE POWER-HEWETSON COLONY

A new commissioner, José Jesús Vidaurri y Borrego, was appointed on June 19, 1834, and dispatched to the Power-Hewetson colony with instructions to proceed according to the colonization law of March 24, 1825. The articles contained within the act specified that a new town containing two hundred inhabitants should elect an *ayuntamiento*, if there was no other within eight leagues. The principal lines of the town should run north and south, east and west, with a square designated to measure 120 varas on each side, exclusive of streets, to be called the principal or constitutional square. This should form the central point from which streets should run forming blocks according to plan. On the east side of the principal square, the church, curate's dwelling, and other ecclesiastical buildings would be sited, and on the west side, the town hall and municipal buildings. Suitable sites should also be found for a market square, a jail, a school, and other buildings for public instruction, and outside the town limits, a burial ground. The streets were to be laid straight, twenty yards wide, for the salubrity of the town. Mechanics who presented themselves to settle in the town would be eligible for a town lot, with no expense except for the cost of the stamped paper used for issuing titles, and a subsequent tax of a dollar per annum for building a church. The empresario would have the choice of two lots, and the others would be distributed randomly.

Armed with his instructions Commissioner José Jesús Vidaurri, accompanied by his brothers, Santiago and Lazaro Serna, and by James Hewetson, arrived in Refugio within a few weeks of his appointment. Vidaurri established the *ayuntamiento* of Refugio in July, 1834. John Dunn was the first *alcalde;* the other town officials were Joshua Davis, James Brown, John James, and Martin Power. A local militia was formed, and James Power became its leader and lieutenant colonel. Vidaurri immediately set about defining the four square leagues for the town of Refugio, employing James Bray as surveyor and Michael Fox, John Kelly, and Timothy Hart as chain bearers to survey the four leagues and measure the streets and lots. Subsequently, he employed S. A. White to make a fresh survey to eradicate some of the inaccuracies over undulating ground in Bray's survey.

Some exceptions were allowed for the Refugio town site. The streets were thirty varas wide, instead of twenty; only half a block was dedicated to the church and municipal buildings. The presence of the old mission obviated the need for a church and municipal center, and the half-block on the east side was used for school purposes. Once the streets and town lots were laid out, homesites were auctioned at public sale. These took place between August 4 and December 18, and totaled seventy purchases.[59] In 1835 James Power bought the mission site from John Shelly, the original petitioner, and donated the lot and buildings to the church in 1840. To facilitate the award of land grants to the colonists, Vidaurri employed S. A. White to define the boundaries of the Power-Hewetson territory. Instructed to follow a line ten leagues up the Guadalupe river and ten leagues up the Nueces, connecting the upper points to form a north boundary of the ten littoral leagues, White completed the survey by October, 1834.

The first land titles were issued on August 4 in the presence of the two empresarios, James Power and James Hewetson. The process of seeking out desirable lands on the Nueces, Aransas, and Mission Rivers took the colonists several months, from September to December, and more titles were issued during that period, a total of 219¾ leagues to 210 grantees. Closely related families like the O'Connors and the O'Briens took adjoining plots. A number of travelers who were passing through Refugio in search of suitable coastal land were also persuaded by Power and Hewetson to stay and settle in the colony. The problem was that they were from nationalities outside the provisions of the contract. The Refugio colonists petitioned Vidaurri to allow non-Mexican and non-Irish to be admitted in place of the number that originally came from Ireland.[60] Governor Vidaurri agreed to the request, only stipulating that the new settlers would meet the qualifications demanded by law. The result was that the original notion of a colony settled by Irish and Mexicans exclusively was changed to include natives from the United States, England, Scotland, Canada, Germany, Italy, and Greece.

The granting of land involved a formal ceremony. Each prospective settler had to submit a testimonial of good conduct and morals and to profess an allegiance to the Catholic faith. In turn, the empresarios had to indicate their willingness to admit the applicant to the colony. A certificate of title that contained a description of the land in question was then issued by the commissioner. The grantee received a copy; another was retained for inclusion in the leather-bound Libro Becerro; and a complete record of all the transactions was then submitted to the government.

For each league of pasture land, a grantee paid $30.00 – $3.50 for each *labor* (177 acres) of irrigable land and $2.50 for nonirrigable land. A generous provision allowed the deferment of payments for the first four years, with equal installments to be paid within the following two years. The commissioners also received payments of $15.00 for every league of grazing land and $2.00 to $2.50 for each *labor* depending on the quality of the land. Surveyors were awarded $8.00 per league, $3.00 per *labor*, and 12 reals (Mexican currency) for each town lot.

A colonist acquired a grant for a league of land, 4,428 acres, for less than one hundred dollars (£25). For most colonists this was a unique opportunity to become owners rather than tenant-occupiers of property. In Ireland, ownership of land was possible for only a small minority of Catholics. In terms of the cash exchange for land, it was the bargain of the century, but other transaction costs have to be included in the equation. Expenditures for the journey, the farm implements, and provisions for a year must be considered, and many of the colonists lost their belongings before they landed. Others paid a very heavy price, beyond any monetary value, in loss of life incurred through cholera and shipwreck during the voyage from New Orleans to Texas. As the author of *Texas in 1837* observed: "If the emigrant has no other object in going to Texas than to secure this gratuity of land, it is a matter of great doubt whether it will ever prove he can expect to find himself comfortably situated in the country."[61]

This tragic start was only to be the beginning of much suffering and many further hardships that had to be endured as the colonists sought to establish themselves in their new homeland. Surviving letters of the Power family from the 1830s point to the bad feeling that existed between some of the colonists and the empresarios when news reached Ireland of cholera, shipwreck, and severe loss of life among family members. James Power became the target of much of the criticism that stemmed from a sense of betrayal. Even his brother, Dan Power, in writing to his own son, Martin Power, in August, 1835, expressed the pain caused by a reputation that was now badly damaged: "Let your Uncle know there never was such grievous callamity in this country as there has been since accounts came from Texas and the blame chiefly to him. I am sorry to the heart to have him accused with deception as being my Brother and always considered him a person of good principles, however the case may be, tell him (that I ask one favour) to use his utmost endeavours to advance the [illegible] few is living from this country as there came a few favourable letters from some of them and he being the instrument that caused them to go there."[62] On the back of the letter, in a note to his brother, Dan Power asked him to give instructions to Martin to send home "those three immegrants money as I shewed him letter to their Parents." To his son, Martin, he also made a direct appeal: "I have shown your letter to the friends of said boys [Paul Kehoe, Richard Roche, and William Monahon], so I expect you will be as good as your word and loose no time in sending they money with a correct account of each mans share, this will be a satisfaction to us, and prevent a deal of sinsure and backbiting in this neibourhood."[63]

The tone of disapproval was merely a prelude to some heavy emotional blackmail intended to induce Martin to abandon his disastrous move to Texas and return to his family in Ireland.

Thanks be to the allmighty we are in good health as you left us and hope in god these lines will meet you also, and more capable of giving a more plain explanation how you are situated in that country. I should have written to your uncle but as I think you will show him this short information he will excuse me — I am much troubled for my Sister and

Brother relations, and friends Death that has died on their passage and in Texas, the Lord have mercy on their souls. Dear Martin I have been in middle health for a few days after parting you and my brother, I got very sick and I remained so untill last May. I then recovered and was finely till August & cannot say whether it is the old complaint, or the bad accounts coming to many people through this country contrary to my expectations — My child I am not capable of expressing the sorrow I felt since parting with you. I did not conceive the satisfaction your person afforded untill your absence occurred. Dear Martin I believe you will not accuse me with flaterry [the letter is torn here] always loved more than I could let known and at present I think your person would give immediate relief or if God pleased to call me out of this world (were you here) I think I would die contented, this is written in presence of your Mother and James and our wishes are you would come home if possible.[64]

The letter ends with the conventional compliments to friends and concludes, rather pointedly, "from your affectionate parent at present," Dan Power.

The family pressure must have been kept up for some time because Martin Power was still responding to it four years later in 1839: "I havent true suffered a good deal in hanging on to thy country but to me it was all novel the worst of times I contented myself with thinking that these moments would answer for a fireside chat when united to you all but dear parents I hope I have experienced all the bitters of a new country and I know that you would not at this time insist on me to come home when I begin to taste of some of thy secrets (sweets)."[65] In an earlier letter written in April, 1836, by the empresario James Power, reference was made to the dark cloud of the war with Mexico hanging over Texas and the burning of the colonists' houses in Refugio, all events outside his control along with the cholera epidemic and shipwrecks. Power's own resentment against some of the Irish colonists was quite forcibly expressed:

I regret to see so much bad feelings amongst people who I once loved, and who I thought I had done everything in my power to advance their views, I have given them all, and much more than I promise them, I have been their servant, night and day and at my own expense, they say I am the cause of their misfortunes, that I have deceived them, when you come encourage no person from Ireland with you leave them to do

Reading of the Texas Declaration of Independence by Charles and Fanny Norman shows James Power *(front left)* seated next to Sam Houston, who is wearing buckskins. *From the collection of the Joe Fultz Estate, Navasota, Texas. Courtesy of the Star of the Republic Museum*

the best they can for themselves, several who came with me, were and are excelant people and regret to say many more of them became idle, I have been acused of them getting the cholera, my relation Martin Cullin, have given me more trouble, and injures the colonist in his bad counsel more than he can do good, he is here, it is to be regreted, he ever saw Texas.[66]

Further evidence of discontent and personal conflicts between the colonists involved Power's partner, James Hewetson, who also had a painful run-in with Cullen as early as September, 1834. Hewetson charged Cullen before the alcalde in Refugio at the time when the land grants were being awarded:

Santiago Hewetson, Empresario of this Colony before your Honor and lodges certain protests regarding which he states: That on the night of the second day of the present month of September my person was attacked in the house of the Comissioner Santiago Reily by citizen

Mordocaio Cullen who gave me serious facial blows on the hair (gray hair) and head which could have caused death or damage to my senses, for the reason that he found me under the influence of liquor which I had taken with some friends and on account of his hidden resentment because as an empresario I did not concede to his ambitious demands. To this injury there is to be added the defamation which he caused on this same occasion imputing (to me) the crime of defrauding the colonists and the government; bringing to the first (named) discord and discontent and a belief in such calumnies with offense to our honor.

Nor are these the only offenses of the citizen Cullen. He publicly threatened one of the Regidores because he would not accede to his many individual demands: and on various occasions he has stirred the town with the purpose to oppose the empresarios, so that these transgressions became serious to that office (of *empresario*). Without a doubt your Honor should know the seriousness of these (things), and for which reason I accuse (him) before your Honor in due form under oath.[67]

Possibly disillusioned by his experiences with the colonists, James Hewetson soon left Refugio for Saltillo, Mexico, where he was to build up a considerable estate. Hewetson corresponded with Power and continued to take an interest in his land grants in Texas, but this interest was always secondary to his main activities in Mexico. Writing in 1845 he told Power that he had a factory in Saltillo turning out "1500 pieces of first quality Manta [cotton sheeting] yearly of 10 lbs and 10 oz of each piece; it is equal to Apple manta and the best in the country."[68] At the time of the U.S.-Mexico War, he stood aside from the conflict, commenting with characteristic humor: "I consider it rather an unpleasant task to oblige myself to undertake the breaking of other men's sculls when at the same time I risk my *own* in the attempt."[69] At his death in 1870 he owned 145 leagues of land (642,000 acres), and had long since given up his empresario lands in Texas.[70] One other reason for his move to Mexico may have been that he had killed a man in Texas.

James Power, who had done the most to recruit settlers to the Refugio colony and who was to be its undisputed leader during the Texas Revolution, did not live to profit from his investment, nor did he see his vision fulfilled of a port city at Aransas. He was to be dogged for the rest of his life by litigation from Gov. Henry Smith and his nephew Joseph B. Smith over title to coastal land. Smith's challenge was made on the basis that coastal land purchased by Power and Hewetson was invalid because it fell outside their title to empresario land. Power's lawyers argued that no distinction existed under the colonization law of 1824 between land purchased and lands obtained as empresarios within the ten littoral leagues. While the dispute raged on in the 1840s, unscrupulous land speculators took certificates on land situated on Copano and Aransas Bays, irrespective of Power's claim to the land. In 1845 the Republic of Texas, in an attempt to restrict endless litigation, required the owners of land in Refugio and San Patricio counties to have their boundaries designated and marked. Proper surveys were to be conducted and forwarded to the General Land Office.

However, the Irish of Refugio and San Patricio refused to incur the expense of having the surveys done. Power could only argue that the original surveys had been lost during the upheaval of war. Smith's attack on their land rights exasperated the people of Refugio and San Patricio. At a protest meeting held in Refugio on October 10, 1853, they resolved to prevent any survey being made on their lands granted to them by the former government and pledged to "oppose and repel by force of arms" anyone disposed to make such a survey.[71] Smith's answer to these resolutions was characteristically intemperate. He claimed that the terms of the empresario contract had not been fulfilled, only seventy colonists had been settled instead of two hundred, and titles had been awarded illegally, some to persons in Ireland and in Mexico.[72] In an added note, he accused half the Irish of being traitors to the revolution. The citizens of Refugio refuted the charge by referring to the Irish presence in Dimitt's Company of Texas Volunteers, the roster at Lipantitlán, the Alamo, Goliad, and at San Jacinto.[73] The eventual verdict came from the Supreme Court of Texas in 1855. The colonists themselves secured their land grant titles, but Power and Hewetson, on a legal technicality, lost the coastal land claimed by Smith and also the ownership of other purchased lands amounting to 190,000 acres.

James Power died on August 15, 1852, at sixty-three years of age. His grave is an imposing monument in Mount Calvary Cemetery in Refugio. The inscription celebrates his career as an empresario, soldier, and statesman. He was survived by his seven children, three from his first marriage and four from his second marriage. The marriage alliance between the Power and Portilla families, Irish and Mexican, was followed in the next generation by marriage between Dolores Power and John Welder, a native of Germany. This fusion of cultures culminated in the Welder family's becoming successful cattle ranchers in south Texas.

John McMullen's career as an empresario formed only part of his business activities. His new base in San Antonio from 1836 provided a network of contacts and opportunities. He resumed his old merchant activity, bought up town property to let, and became a land baron, buying and selling on a large scale. Most of his land leagues (46,698 acres) in San Patricio were sold in 1844 for five thousand dollars to his son-in-law James McGloin. He then acquired 18,892 acres near San Antonio. As early as 1833 he had bought eleven leagues of land on the Medina for eleven thousand dollars. Ten years later, he was to sell the land to a group of Alsatian immigrants led by Henri Castro. The town of Castroville lies on part of the McMullen land. He also bought and sold land in the King William District of San Antonio. It was later to become a fashionable center for wealthy German settlers who built some grand houses in the district.

All of a piece with his business enterprise, McMullen was active in local politics and the law, where his interests were interwoven with land and trade transactions. He was elected to the council three times in the early 1840s, and his financial acumen gave him a key role in council affairs. He was also elected as chief justice of Bexar County in 1844, having served as justice of the peace and acting judge of the probate court. John McMullen died a violent death. He was killed on the night of January 2, 1853, in San Antonio in his two-story house on Commerce Street (where the public library stands today). The unknown assassin gagged him and stabbed him in the throat. It was thought the motive was plunder, as the place was ransacked.[74] His estate was divided between his heirs in Pennsylvania and the grandchildren of his deceased wife, the five children of James McGloin. In recognition of his service to the state of Texas, John McMullen has a county and a street in San Antonio named after him.

McMullen's fellow empresario, James McGloin, also left San Patricio sometime in 1836 and moved to San Antonio for a few years. Like his father-in-law, McGloin engaged in business and was active in pursuing the claims of the empresarios and the colonists over title to their lands granted by the Mexican government. He was also involved with McMullen in litigation over land in Medina County. In 1844 his wife died, leaving him with the responsibility of raising five children. In 1846 he returned to San Patricio and welcomed returning colonists and some new settlers.

Among these were J. B. Murphy and his wife, Margaret Mary Healy, who came to San Patricio in 1850. In 1853 McGloin married Murphy's aunt, Mary Murphy. Two years later he built the first frame house at Round Lake, a mile west of San Patricio. This restored house remains as a monument to his role as an empresario and leader of the San Patricio colony. James McGloin died in 1856. His will was contested by Mary Murphy, and following disputes over the inheritance and subsequent political and financial problems, the estate was run down.

The empresarios were entrepreneurs, men of vision, who had an eye for a business opportunity. They proved to be determined, as they had to be to overcome the obstacles posed by Mexican officials and fellow empresarios. They succeeded, in part, through becoming Mexicanized, speaking Spanish, establishing contacts in the Mexican government, and marrying into Mexican families. What have been commonly described as Irish colonies were, in reality, formed from a mix of Irish, Mexican, American, and other European settlers. The Mexicans and the Irish had much in common: a shared Catholic religion and mind-set, the trials involved in establishing title to their lands, and tough conditions in founding a frontier settlement. These common bonds were to be severely tested in the months that lay ahead as the war clouds gathered.

Up to 1835 the would-be colonists who had left the United States or Ireland to seek a new life in Mexican Texas had suffered a catalog of bad luck, and all too many families had experienced a disastrous loss of life. To those migrants who had survived the journey and the landing, the prospect of a paradise in Texas was soon to be threatened by the need to defend their newly acquired land in the conflict known as the Texas Revolution.

The Irish and the Texas Revolution, 1835–36

Ah! there was no glare and glitter in those life-and-death struggles of the Texas pioneers. . . . Some were for independence; some for the constitution of 1824; and some for anything, just so it was a row. But we were all ready to fight.

—Noah Smithwick, *The Evolution of a State, or, Recollections of Old Texas Days*

Traditionally, the story of the Texas Revolution has been understood in terms of the freedom of Anglo-American settlers in a war of independence fought against a despotic Mexican government.[1] At the birth of a republic, fashioned by bitter struggle, massacre, and military victory, a triumphalist rhetoric is to be expected. The blood sacrifice of the war, especially the symbolism of the Alamo and Goliad, have become defining moments in the "glorious" history of Texas. Significantly, the language of the participants has become incorporated into a broader American ideology of freedom to be employed against tyranny in any form and located in any part of the world.[2] However, more recent studies have emphasized the complexities and sheer chaos of the revolutionary period from October, 1835, through April, 1836, and some attempt has been made to understand not merely an Anglo-American version of events but also the perspective of all the participants in the conflict. That includes the difficulties faced by the Mexican Texans, the privations of the citizen-soldiers and civilians driven off their land, and the sufferings of the conscripted troops led by President Santa Anna and General Urrea who crossed the Rio Grande to suppress the Texas rebellion.[3]

To date, written history has concentrated on the military and political leaders of the revolutionary period. The men who displayed outstanding courage and vision at a time of potential disaster have been installed in the hall of fame, cast in the role as the founders of the republic of Texas. It is the embodiment of heroic history, a school of thought that places great men as the shapers of the destiny of peoples and nations. The mural devoted to the Texas Revolution at the State Archives in Austin remains a powerful visual monument to the importance of Stephen F. Austin, William Barret Travis, and Sam Houston, who receive star billing in the panorama of the Texas story.

In a similar vein, the published histories of the Irish colonists' involvement in the Texas Revolution, although not fully integrated into the mainstream, have been written in the unmistakable tradition of contribution history. Flannery strikes the characteristic note with his bold claim: "In terms of lives sacrificed, property lost, and land despoiled, none gave more to Texas independence than the Irish colonists of San Patricio, Refugio, and Victoria. When they espoused the Texas cause, they knew they would bear the brunt of the conflict. Their colonial area was a crossroads of battle."[4] The story relates, at a local level, how the Irish fought nobly, died heroically, suffered disproportionately from loss of life and property, and contributed to the political process of building the infant republic. James Power, Irish empresario, friend of Sam Houston, and leader of the Refugio colony, is thus honored for his stout defense of Texan independence and for raising a volunteer army to stand against the Mexican invasion, as "a loyal son to Texas."[5]

This chapter sets out to review both the political and military history of the Texas Revolution. Through the language of the participants, the shifts of meaning behind the high-flown rhetoric are examined in the context of a time of great peril. The events of 1835–36 are also reconstructed from the perspective of the experience of the citizen-soldiers and civilians who have left accounts for posterity. Throughout the narrative and as a corrective to the dominance of Anglo-American histories, a fuller recognition is given to the experience of the front-line communities of Refugio and San Patricio that were mixed settlements of Irish and Mexican colonists. The role of the Irish settlers during the war years deserves a fuller recognition, not in an exclusive spirit of self-congratulation but in a broader discussion of the issues of citizen participation and divided loy-alties in the changing circumstances of the war period. The importance of the acquisition and retention of land as a central motivation continues the overarching theme of the book.

LAND AND FREEDOM

Daniel W. Cloud, a young Kentucky lawyer who was to become one of the defenders of the Alamo, represented the patriotic courage of an as-piring nationhood in his letters: "Ever since Texas unfurled the banner of freedom and commenced a warfare for 'Liberty or Death' our hearts have been enlisted in her behalf."[6] Cloud's high-flown language conveys the spirit of idealism and heroism in which the events of 1836 have been mostly portrayed. After the final, sensational victory of the war at San Jacinto where revenge was taken for the massacres at the Alamo and at Goliad, and Texan independence was won if not secured, the language of freedom possessed a self-fulfilling quality. But in truth, the revolution started as a civil war between centralists and federalists within Mexico, with the Texans defending the liberal Mexican Constitution of 1824 against the central government of Santa Anna, and ended as a war of independence for Texas. The main participants in the Texan struggle, Anglo-Americans, Tejanos, and Irish settlers, all employed the language of freedom but their meanings varied according to circumstances and cul-tural values.[7]

The Anglo-American settlers wanted to preserve the freedom of virtual self-government that was allowed with the generous provision of land and minimal interference by the Mexican government. The Tejanos also wished to preserve freedom from interference by the central government of Mexico, but they were also concerned about the increasing American-ization of Texas that made them "foreigners in their own land."[8] The Irish, who immigrated on the promise of great tracts of land set in an earthly paradise, found to their consternation that they were obligated to defend their property by force of arms. So the freedom to preserve life and their newly won land grants was a central concern of the Irish colonists.

The young republic of Mexico, which gained its independence from Spain in 1821, remained vulnerable to the threat of American expansion that had followed the Louisiana Purchase in 1803. The neighboring Mexi-can province of Coahuila y Texas was a large, fertile territory coveted by the United States. Several attempts had been made to purchase Texas, but the Mexican government preferred to retain it and populate the country with settlers as a buffer against American expansion. Inevitably, this included Americans who were attracted by the prospect of large tracts of land and, in some cases, by the opportunity to escape from criminal charges in the United States. Thus one authority suggests a high proportion of debtors and malefactors among the adventurers who crossed the border during the heady atmosphere of "Texas fever."[9]

Daniel W. Cloud was one such adventurer who revealed his motives in two remarkable letters:

Our Brothers of Texas were invited by the Mexican government while republican in its form, to come and settle. They have endured all the privations and suffering incident to the settlement of the frontier country and have surrounded themselves with all the comforts and conveniences of life. Now the Mexicans with unblushing effrontery call on them to submit to monarchial, tyrannical despotism at the bare mention of which every true hearted son of Kentucky feels an instinctive horror followed by firm and steady glow of virtuous indignation. The cause of philanthropy, of humanity, of liberty and human happiness throughout the world calls loudly on every man who can aid Texas.[10]

The legitimacy of rebellion by Anglo-American settlers against the Mexican government was sanctioned by the overthrow of the republic and the constitution of 1824. Moreover, by invoking the precedent of earlier rebellions, Cloud gave credence to a sense of historic mission that rationalized the ultimate triumph of the Anglo-Americans in Texas. "Inheriting the old Saxon spirit of 1640 in England [the Parliamentary revolt against King Charles I], 1776 in America, the inhabitants of Texas throw off the chains of Santa Anna, assert their independence, assume a national sovereignty and send a corps of diplomatic agents to the parent state of Washington."[11] Thus the ultimate political goal of belonging to the United States instead of to Mexico was clearly stated. The ultimate personal goal of acquiring untold wealth was thinly concealed beneath the following peroration: "If we succeed the country is ours: it is immense in extent and fertile in its soil and will amply reward our toils. If we fail, death in the cause of liberty and humanity is not cause for shuddering. Our rifles are by our sides and choice guns they are, we know what awaits us and are prepared to meet it."[12]

When the guns were fired in earnest during the desperate defense of the Alamo in February–March, 1836, William Barret Travis, the commander, surrounded by the overwhelming numbers of Santa Anna's Mexican army and perhaps sensing his place in history, sent a message to "the People of Texas and all Americans in the world": "I call on you in the name of liberty, of patriotism and of everything dear to the American character, to come to our aid with all despatch."[13]

Contemporary rhetoric points the way to the political causes of the conflict. The ruling hand of Mexico represented a benign neglect for the citizens of Texas. They had received a generous provision of land but little since 1821 in the way of military protection or government interference. Nevertheless, tensions grew in the 1830s over a number of related issues that coincided with an increasing Anglo-American presence and a desire by the Mexican government to exercise greater control and regulation over its northern frontier province.

Tension arose over the subject of immigration. While the Mexican government needed to populate the province to develop its rich potential, government officials were nervous of the increasing Americanization of Texas as the Mexican population became outnumbered. The independent character of the American settlers added to the nervousness on the Mexican side. They had mostly come from the southern states, and Texas represented a haven for those seeking sanctuary from debts, criminal prosecutions, and the social restraints of settled communities. Legislation enacted in 1830 to restrict the immigration of Americans failed to stem the flow of illegal settlers crossing the border into Texas, and the law was rescinded in 1833. Similarly, Mexican attempts to enforce tariffs and erect customs houses in 1830 were met with determined resistance by the settlers. The lack of means to raise taxes or to develop the coastal trade between Texas and the Mexican ports perpetuated the dependence of settlers on imported goods from New Orleans and other U.S. ports. In effect, Mexico failed to incorporate its northern province into the national body politic and the national economy. A further source of frustration and irritation occurred over the question of judicial reform. The settlers found it irksome to have to make appeals to distant courts. As on other issues, Texans wanted to secure local autonomy and opposed what were perceived to be the encroachments of central government.

A desire for personal freedom from government led inexorably to a demand for the independence of Texas from the state of Coahuila. What emerged as a rallying cry for a cluster of grievances was, in effect, the preservation of land, "the symbol and means of freedom."[14] Alongside the patriotic crusade for freedom and the quest for land (volunteers to the

Texan army were promised entitlement to land upon enlistment), it has been commonly asserted there were key issues of cultural conflict between the Anglo-American settlers and the Mexicans.[15] An editorial in the *Telegraph and Texas Register* early in 1836 asked the question, Shall we declare for independence? The situation of Anglo-American settlers was compared with those of the American colonists in 1776: a rebellion was justified and independence essential because of tyranny, neglect, and a lack of protection from Indians, added to which the Mexican government was seen as more despotic than that of King George III. To add strength to the argument, cultural and racial arguments were included to justify independence on the grounds that there were no ties of blood between the two peoples: Mexicans were depicted as "a people whose inert and idle habits, general ignorance and superstition, prevents the possibility of our ever mingling in the same harmonious family; and if possible, could only be done by self degradation. . . . There is no reason then that influenced the patriots of 1776, that does not, with tenfold force, apply to us, and the only remaining consideration would be, whether, we have an equal prospect of success."[16] It was obviously important to find a constitutional precedent to justify rebellion against the Mexican government, and the reference to the "patriots of 1776" was intended to rouse those settlers who had hitherto shown a reluctance to volunteer for the Texan army. It was also directed to an American audience that was more likely to support Texas if its cause became one of independence as a step toward becoming part of the United States.

The reference to ignorance and superstition was a standard form of anti-Catholicism and posed as a Protestant grievance in a Catholic country. This was again represented on March 12, 1836, when a long catalog of complaints against a despotic government included one that invoked religious freedom: "It denies the right of worshipping the Almighty according to the dictates of our conscience, by the support of a National Religion, calculated to promote the temporal interest of its human functionaries rather than the glory of the true and living God."[17] While some of the complaints that referred to "military acts of oppression and tyranny" had some credence in the wake of the siege of the Alamo, the religious grievance had the aim of pandering to Protestant prejudice rather than possessing genuine substance. The republic of Mexico was a Catholic state, whereas most American settlers were nominally Protestant, if they possessed any religious allegiance at all. In practice, this was less a source of conflict than has been identified because of the lack of enforcement of religious uniformity by the Mexican government, which had allowed the old Spanish frontier missions to lapse into neglect. The presence of a few Anglo missionaries led to the appearance of occasional camp meetings and Sunday schools but was insufficient to establish Protestant churches. Rather more significant was "the absence of piety and morality due to the weakness of formal religion. Conventional minds considered Texas to have a distinctly irreligious climate of opinion."[18] A more consistently dominant cultural trait was the intense individualism of Texans who, if they brought such qualities with them from the United States, found them reinforced by life on the frontier.

Individualism, as Paul D. Lack has argued, was a serious impediment to the growth of a genuinely collective revolutionary spirit and had the effect of undermining the political and military effort required to counter the threat of the Mexican invasion. It was further reinforced by the regional differences that separated the largely Anglo communities from those that retained a Tejano presence within the province of Texas. Donald Meinig has pointed to the geographical divide between the predominantly planter economy of central and east Texas and the ranching culture of southwest Texas.[19] Cultural and ethnic considerations compounded different economic interests and raised the chances of internal divisions. To sustain the plantations, African labor was imported in increasing numbers during the 1830s such that slaves represented about 10 percent of the Texas population. To Anglo planters who continued the strongly racial outlook of the American South, the institution of slavery was essential to the production of the staple cotton crop. This contrasted with the liberal terms of the Mexican Constitution of 1824 that deplored the idea of slavery as a matter of principle. In practice, there was no enforcement imposed against slaveholders, but with a growing restlessness among the black population, it added to the volatility of the situation when in 1834 Juan N. Almonte informed the slaves of their rights to freedom under the law. The few Tejanos in the Austin colony worked primarily as wage laborers and were regarded as quite separate in their manners and habits from the Anglo landowning class.

Yet elsewhere in Texas, Tejano families either held positions of power and status or were sufficiently numerous to dominate communal life. In Nacogdoches, some six hundred Tejanos at least took a share of political power up to 1834. Tensions arose over the failure to secure written titles in the face of new settlers squatting on the land while empresarios contested for control of land claims. In the city of Béxar and on the ranches of that department, Tejanos provided the political and cultural leadership. Understandably, Tejanos were divided in their loyalties. Appalled by the destruction of the constitution and by Santa Anna's use of force, the empresario Lorenzo de Zavala spoke for a number of leading Mexican "traitors," such as José Antonio Navarro and Juan Seguín, in defending the right of Texans to rebel against the central government: "The fundamental compact having been disolved, and all the guarantees of the civil and political rights of citizens having been destroyed, it is incontestable that all the states of the confederation are left at liberty to net for themselves, and to provide for their security and preservation as circumstances require."[20]

Yet as they were outnumbered by the Anglo-Americans and increasingly segregated geographically within Texas, many Tejanos felt their way of life was threatened and certainly did not support the dismembering of their country by means of an independent Texas. By 1835 some twenty thousand Anglo-Americans, many of whom were illegal squatters, had arrived in Texas, exceeding the native Mexicans by a ratio of ten to one. From the Mexican standpoint, the policy of inviting Americans to settle as a buffer against the aggression of the United States and to prevent the depredations of marauding Indians had backfired. The colonists were dependent on trade with America to sustain their communities and on American markets to sell their cotton. They also looked to the United States for moral support and for example in terms of political rights. The Mexican expectation of loyalty from the colonists in return for land grants and exemption from taxation proved to be misplaced.

Paul Lack has also suggested that cultural differences explain the conflicts between Tejano residents who claimed prior occupancy on lands that were granted to the Irish empresarios Power and Hewetson and Mc-Mullen and McGloin in southwestern Texas.[21] Disputes arose between rival empresarios De León and James Power. Yet cultural differences cannot explain the disputes over land between the two so-called Irish colonies and delays in granting titles to the San Patricio colonists prompted some of them to transfer to the Power-Hewetson colony centered on Refugio. More important, the De León colony and both the Power-Hewetson and McMullen-McGloin colonies contained a mix of Mexican and Irish settlers. In practice, the empresarios were only too willing to accept the claims of resident Mexicans, and an assortment of other settlers, Anglo-Americans and Europeans, to fill the quotas in their contracts, especially where so many intending Irish colonists had died en route to

Texas from cholera and shipwreck. The empresarios' entitlement to land depended on the number of colonists who settled, and they happily poached potential colonists from each other.

The position of the Irish colonists in Refugio, San Patricio, and Victoria was more akin to that of the Mexican Texans than their Anglo-American counterparts. Having just acquired their land grants from the Mexican government and settled into communities alongside Mexican neighbors, the Irish colonists in 1835–36 were faced with a terrible dilemma of which side to support in what began as a civil war and only later turned into a war of independence. The Irish enjoyed friendly relations with Mexican settlers in San Patricio. They cooperated in sharing the town government, worshiped at the same Catholic church, and were bonded together by enduring the hardships of pioneer life. Indeed, the Mexicans advised them about the planting of crops, how to predict the weather, and how to singe the cactus for cattle to eat. The Mexicans passed on their local knowledge and skills to equip the Irish to become part of a ranching culture. The presence of the neighboring Mexican garrison at Lipantitlán, with which cordial relations existed between the officers and the colonists, would have added to a natural sympathy toward the Mexican cause in the dispute. So not surprisingly, the initial allegiance of the San Patricio Irish was to the Mexican government that had granted them their land and to which they had sworn an oath of loyalty as Mexican citizens. In October, 1835, Philip Dimitt, the Texan commandant at Goliad, reported with dismay that "the people of San Patricio have joined the military at the Nueces."[22] In November, 1835, the Mexican general Cos described them as *"los fieles Yrlandeses vecinos de San Patricio."*[23] Dimitt's roster of troops stationed at Fort Goliad on January 10, 1836, consisted of eighty-eight men, half of them Refugio colonists, among whom the great majority were Irishmen.[24]

These conflicting loyalties were literally blown apart by the large force under the Mexican commanders Santa Anna and Urrea, which crossed the Rio Grande in February, 1836, and forced the Irish into rebellion by the wanton destruction of lives at the Alamo and at Goliad in March, 1836. The property of the Irish settlers was burned down and their communities at San Patricio and Refugio were destroyed. Uncomfortably situated in the war zone and close to the vital port of Copano, both communities suffered devastation in the fighting between the Texan and Mexican armies. Herds of cattle were driven off the land, and families were forced to evacuate their homes. Most families hurriedly piled children and belongings on to carts and went north; a few San Patricio families sought refuge with friends in Matamoros.

Whereas in the early stages of the war, the San Patricio Irish were more likely to fight alongside the Mexicans, the Refugio Irish, under the leadership of Col. James Power, Nicholas Fagan, and John J. Linn, opted for Texan independence. The tricky question of loyalty was addressed by James Power in a letter to fellow colonist Peter Keogh. Power must have articulated the views of many: "Texas had sworn to support the federal constitution of Mexico and particular that of Coahuila. We received our lands under the federal government. We have kept our oath which ought to be considered a virtue with Sant Anna, it have become a crime [sic]."[25] Clearly, the issue of which side to support was a cause of anguish to men of principle.

Although Power was anxious not to move too far ahead of the cautious political stance taken at San Felipe, Fagan took the lead in the declaration at Goliad in December, 1835, and many of the colonists enlisted in the Texan armies. Personal leadership was an important decider in determining which cause to support. John McMullen spent much time in San Felipe with the provisional government, and in his absence, Susan, wife of the alcalde William O'Docherty who had connections in Matamoros, assumed the leadership of the San Patricio colony. James Power, a friend of Sam Houston, with his merchant contacts in Mexico was able to provide advance intelligence of the Mexican armies. He was also an important player in the coastal trade between New Orleans, Galveston, and the Mexican ports. The local port of Copano was vital for the military supplies needed by both armies, as well as being essential to the survival of the two colonies. Both James Power in Refugio and his fellow merchant John J. Linn in Victoria serviced the Texan army with vital supplies during the conflict.[26] So they had a financial stake in supporting the cause of Texan independence. In the longer term, with economic interests in coastal trade and land, benefits were linked with a future annexation to the United States. Moreover, to secure the financial and military support of American friends in the United States to resist the Mexican invasion of Texas, it was imperative that there eventually be a declaration of the independence of Texas.

As the war progressed the political leadership of Texas was riven with conflicts that threatened the prosecution of any sustained military resistance to the invading Mexican armies. A division between the "war" and "peace" parties was driven by personal differences as much as by arguments about the desirability of Texan self-government within a federal Mexico or the pursuit of outright independence. Those who favored military action were depicted as hot-headed warmongers, boastful and reckless, and motivated by self-interest in terms of tax evasion as merchants or as land speculators. Their more conservative opponents, who wished to avoid violent methods and urged loyalty to Mexico, were branded as Tories who resisted the expected support for the Texan cause. Those who had been settled in Texas for some time and had built up some acceptance of Mexican rule were more likely to support the peace party. Arrivals fresh from the United States were eager for military action.[27]

It has been argued that those loyal to Mexico tended to come from the older, established parts of the United States whereas the rebels had migrated from frontier settlements in the lower South. Older settlers had economic and political gains inherent in their Mexican citizenship. More recent arrivals, who had not secured land grants, faced the prospect of purchasing land from pioneer settlers.[28] The experience of the Irish colonists was more complicated. The San Patricio Irish mostly came to Texas between 1829 and 1833 via established communities in New York, Kentucky, or New Orleans. The Refugio Irish came directly from Ireland in 1834. Even though they arrived later, they obtained their land grants within months rather than over a period of years. The length of time before colonists received their land grants and the quality of relations with their neighbors were probably more important factors in determining loyalties than the time of arrival or even place of origin. All the Irish colonists wanted to protect their property, but the relations with their Mexican neighbors, both individually and collectively, and the influence of local leadership appear to have been the determinants of Irish allegiance. Moreover, pragmatism brought a switch to the Texas cause as circumstances changed.

THE POLITICAL AND MILITARY CONTEXT

Bitterness, recriminations, and taunts of betrayal were reinforced by personal struggles for political leadership. Before 1835 Stephen F. Austin, as the moderate leader of the peace party, had urged conciliation with Mexico, supported by D. C. Barrett. They were opposed by William and John Wharton and Henry Smith, who were the advocates of a war of independence leading to the inclusion of Texas within the Union. Such positions, however, were not set in concrete. To add confusion and complexity to the state of emergency, the mood shifted during the critical months from November, 1835, to March, 1836, when altered circumstances created changes in the way the rebellion was defended. Austin had been arrested in Saltillo for advocating a separate state government for Texas and imprisoned throughout 1834 in Mexico City. He returned from imprisonment in September, 1835, convinced that war was now inevitable. As late as November, 1835, conservatives loyal to Mexico were still predominant while remaining opposed to the threat of Santa Anna's troops.

A further duality is suggested in the language of commentators at the time. It is no exaggeration to claim that there were, in fact, two wars being conducted at the same time. One was a roller coaster and ramshackle affair of sieges, skirmishes, and set-piece battles. The other was a war of words, not only threats of terror matched by ringing declarations of high principle but also the desperate call to arms aimed at volunteers to the Texan cause. This verbal war possessed an air of unreality about it that has sometimes been forgotten with the intoxication of ultimate victory.

The war of words threatened to undermine the military campaign, with effective government virtually paralyzed by the bitter conflict between the General Council and Gov. Henry Smith. Changes in membership by December, 1835, made the council more inclined to support the conservative Austin camp. Most of the members who retired in November were Wharton supporters who were also allied to Governor Smith. They were replaced by pro-Austin men James Kerr, John J. Linn, Randall Jones, and Juan A. Padilla; by the Irish empresario John McMullen; and by James Power's stand-in, John Malone. As a group, they were reluctant to proclaim independence for Texas. Faced with a hostile council, the combative Governor Smith exercised his veto in attempting to rule by dictate, but his moves to bring the volunteer armies under his civil jurisdiction merely served to add the military to the political opposition ranged against him. On December 17, Smith moved against his political opponents, charging Barrett in a secret session of the council with a raft of crimes that included forgery, counterfeiting, and embezzlement, but this only prompted the council to reassert its constitutional power to appoint and rule on the misconduct of officials. At the heart of government in San Felipe, Smith, finding himself politically isolated, became almost unhinged with rage. On January 9, he tried to shock the council into submission with a message of fire and brimstone that was full of intemperate language and personal abuse. He alleged that the scoundrels and traitors on the council were endeavoring to ruin the country. In the interests of the good of the country, his "duty" prompted him to suspend the council and assume command of the army and navy.

Once again, the move proved counterproductive. Two days later, the General Council responded with a vote of impeachment against Governor Smith on charges of violating his oath of office, perjury, slandering members of the council, adopting dictatorial powers, and general misconduct. Smith was thrown by this swift and decisive action, and his effort to apologize and seek a belated compromise with the council came too late. With impeachment proceedings pending, acting-governor Robinson continued the attack on former governor Smith, accusing him of a tyrannical use of power reminiscent of Caesar, Napoleon, and the enemy at the gate, Santa Anna. For his part, Smith rejected impeachment as invalid and refused to hand over executive documents even under pressure from the marshal of Texas and a citizens' posse. Smith clung on to government papers and to his title in the expectation that the March convention would acquit him of the charge of impeachment, but when the council of January 18 failed to secure a quorum, the government of Texas descended from stalemate into anarchy. The war of words continued between Robinson and Smith, focusing on personal attacks and self-justification of the removal of internal enemies. Amazingly, all this division and political chaos was taking place within a month of Santa Anna's crossing into Texas.

The military story of the war of Texas independence against Mexico that was fought between October, 1835, and April, 1836, has a gloriously romantic appeal for Texans. So naturally, it has been told in the most exhilarating style and presented in simple terms of good versus evil, freedom versus despotism, Protestantism versus Catholicism, and courage winning out against cruelty in an Anglo-American triumph. T. R. Fehrenbach's epic *Lone Star: A History of Texas and the Texans* provides a brilliant example of the genre. In a chapter entitled "Blood and Soil" the opening quotations introduce the reader to a compelling narrative of events that set the scene perfectly: "We consider death preferable to disgrace," and "God and Texas, Victory or Death" both attributed to Col. William Barret Travis at the Alamo, and less characteristically, Stephen F. Austin, in his late conversion to the necessity for war: "To suppose that such a cause will fail when defended by Anglo-Saxon blood and by Americans . . . would be a calumny."[29] By contrast, Stephen L. Hardin's *Texian Iliad: A Military History of the Texas Revolution*, representative of the less partisan style of historical writing in recent years, is a balanced, analytical account of the war that offers a sound explanation of why battles were won

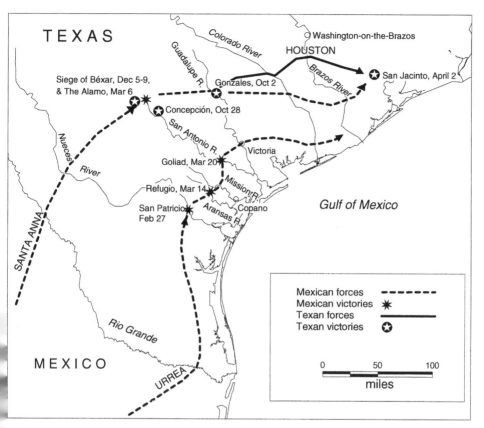

Texas Battles for Independence, 1835–36

and lost by identifying the different military skills and traditions of the two sides. Where the long rifles of the American volunteers could strike the enemy from behind trees or walls, they could have a devastating effect. Where the Mexican cavalry could engage the enemy in open ground, their superior horsemanship outclassed their Texan opponents.[30] Hardin's emphasis on the different strengths of the opposing armies during the battles of the Texas Revolution goes a long way to explain the course of the war. The Texan confidence in the effectiveness of the Kentucky long rifle was justified, provided riflemen had sufficient cover in wooded areas or behind stone walls, but its slow speed in reloading made it powerless on the open prairies when used against Mexican cavalry. The early battles fought in late 1835 support this analysis.

At the Battle of Concepción on October 28, 1835, James Bowie, in command of 91 Texan rebels, took up a defensive position on a tree-lined bend of the San Antonio River. Well protected and concealed behind a high bank, their accurate rifle fire brought devastating losses to General Cos's 500 infantry and cavalry, forcing them to withdraw to Béxar. A similar event took place at Nueces Crossing on November 4, where a party of 70 Mexican dragoons attacked Ira Westover's 40-strong band of Texans. In a well-defended timber grove, Westover's men inflicted severe damage on the Mexican troops under Captain Rodriguez. Unable to match the firepower of the Texas rifles Rodríguez's forces were forced to withdraw. A third example occurred during the Grass Fight on November 26 on the prairie outside Béxar. In open country, the Mexican cavalry, which possessed superior equestrian skills, appeared to have the upper hand over the Texans until the latter dismounted and took up a defensive position from which the Mexican troops were unable to dislodge them. Cos again retreated to the town.

The Texan attack on Béxar provided further evidence of the importance of weaponry and terrain. When the Texan force led by Ben Milam and Frank Johnson stormed the city of Béxar, the "glimpse-and-snipe" street-fighting that lasted from December 5 to 10 gave them a decided advantage. The long rifles of the Texans were highly effective at aimed fire, covering a distance of up to two hundred yards. The old Brown Bess muskets of the Mexican *soldados*, a holdover from the open-field volley fire of the Napoleonic wars, were inferior weapons that wasted much ammunition. The double-barrel shotgun loaded with "buck and ball" also proved deadly in close combat. After five days of house-to-house fighting, and having endured heavy losses, General Cos surrendered the city and took his depleted force back across the Rio Grande.

In assessing the course of the war, Stephen Hardin has argued that strategic errors compounded tactical mistakes. General Cos was at fault in choosing Béxar instead of Goliad. Not only was the open terrain around Goliad better suited for the use of cavalry but also the presidio was much closer to the port of Copano for the provision of supplies. It was an important error that was repeated by his brother-in-law Generalissimo Santa Anna, who after crossing the Rio Grande on February 16, 1836, directed his army to capture Béxar, to avenge Cos's humiliating defeat and surrender. The famous siege and capture of the Alamo proved to be a wasteful digression, of little value in military terms, and it became very costly to the Mexican cause in terms of the casualties sustained and the valuable time lost in pursuit of Sam Houston's retreating army. Whereas the heroic resistance of Travis and his men at the siege of the Alamo, over thirteen days until its fall on March 6, was to assume great symbolic importance for the Texan cause, Béxar, on the western edge of inhabited Texas, was less important strategically than the garrisons along the coastal strip.

Santa Anna was also at fault in splitting his forces. A unified command under General Urrea would have had a greater chance of suppressing the Texan rebellion. Throughout the campaign Urrea was the most successful commander on either side. He crossed the Rio Grande with 1,000 men at Matamoros, swept up the coast, defeated Johnson's Matamoros force near San Patricio on February 27, and on March 2 overwhelmed Grant's rebels at Agua Dulce Creek. He then captured the mission at Refugio on March 14, where King's men were executed on March 20, and Colonel Fannin's army surrendered to him after a bloody fight before the soldiers were executed on March 27 at Goliad.

LIVING IN THE WAR ZONE

The effect of the political impasse and the constant arguments between the self-styled leaders, when viewed from the frontier war zone, was to create frustration and anger. This took its most powerful form in the publication of the Goliad Declaration on December 20, 1835. The volunteers who gathered at the presidio chapel in Goliad signed a declaration that solemnly vowed, at the risk of their own lives, that "the former province and department of Texas is, and of right ought to be, a free, sovereign and independent State." Before the assembled troops in the parade ground of Fort Goliad, Nicholas Fagan raised the Irish flag of independence.[31] The tone of the document sent to San Felipe is worth quoting to convey the sheer exasperation of the Irish, American, and Mexican settlers who signed it:

> They have seen their camp thronged, but too frequently, with those who were more anxious to be served by, than to serve their country — with men more desirous of being honored with command than capable of commanding. They have seen the energies, the prowess, and the achievements of a band worthy to have stood by Washington and receive command, and worthy to participate in the inheritance of the sons of such a Father, frittered, dissipated, and evaporated away for

the want of that energy, union, and decision in council, which, though it must emanate from the many, can only be exercised efficiently when concentrated in a single arm. They have seen the busy aspirants for office running from the field to the council hall, and from this back to the camp, seeking emolument and not service, and swarming like hungry flies around the body polite.

They have seen the deliberations of the council and the volition of the camp distracted and paralyzed, by the interference of an influence antipatriotic in itself, and too intimately interwoven with the paralyzing policy of the past, to admit the hope of relief from its incorporation with that which can alone avert the evils of the present crisis, and place the affairs of the country beyond the reason of an immediate reaction. They have witnessed these evils with bitter regrets, with swollen hearts, and indignant bosoms.

A revulsion is at hand. An army, recently powerless and literally imprisoned, is now emancipated. From a comparatively harmless, passive, and inactive attitude, they have been transferred to one preeminently commanding, active, and imposing.[32]

Clearly such revulsion demonstrated a willful distancing of a citizen-soldiery from politicians regarded as corrupt, vacillating, and self-serving. The rationale for declaring the independence of Texas was both principled and pragmatic. There is an obvious expression of the interests of the Irish colonists, led by Nicholas Fagan, who had obtained their land grants from the Mexican government and now faced the prospect of their lands being forfeited. Refugio's colonists were prominent among those who signed the Goliad Declaration. Among the full list of ninety-one signatures, thirty-one were Refugio colonists, plus five others resident in the Refugio municipality.[33] After the siege of Béxar, the colonists now faced the full force of the Mexican army that threatened to expel them from their lands:

Already, we are denounced, proscribed, outlawed, and exiled from the country. Our lands, peaceably and lawfully acquired, are solemnly pronounced the proper subject of indiscriminate forfeiture, and our estates of confiscation. The laws and guarantees under which we entered the country as colonists, tempted the unbroken silence, sought the dangers of the wilderness, braved the prowling Indian, erected our numerous improvements, and opened and subdued the earth to cultivation, are either abrogated or repealed, and now trampled under the hoofs of the usurper's cavalry. . . .

Why contend for the shadow, when the substance courts our acceptance? The price of each is the same. War — exterminating war — is waged; and we have either to fight or flee.[34]

The document also contained the class views of the soldier-citizens and a slight against the "Creoles of Texas" too easily attached to tyranny, arguing it was up to the North Americans of Texas to set them an example of egalitarianism: "a new, invigorating, and cherishing policy — a policy tendering equal, impartial, and indiscriminate protection to all; to the low and the high, the humble and the well-born, the poor and the rich, the ignorant and the educated, the simple and the shrewd — then, and not before, will they become even useful auxiliaries in the work of political or moral renovation."[35] In practice, no foreign power would respect them or advance them credit without a clear policy of independence. So a virtue should be made of necessity in declaring for a free, sovereign and independent state and a heroic stand made against tyranny. Confidence in the "cooperation of our fellow citizens" and in "the approving smiles" of the Almighty possessed an air of wish-fulfillment about them.[36]

Rhetoric and reality were some distance apart. A state of unpreparedness was in evidence in the most exposed frontier zone on the River Nueces. The people of San Patricio not only were divided in their loyalties but also lacked basic supplies with which to sustain their communities. "We have neither men nor means to withstand any force that may be sent against us, as the people are still devided," John Turner wrote to Captain Dimitt. They feared "the vengeance of the Mexican army will be poured upon us; but there is still a Remnant of patriots who wish to support the constitution, & would prefer death to slavery." The letter requested men and supplies from Dimitt's command at Goliad, "as there is none to be had here at any price, and our men are too few to spare in pursuit of it."[37] The politicians in council, elated by the victory over the Mexican general Cos at Béxar in December, 1835, were nevertheless exercised by the need to move beyond independent military units and augment the regular army in the field. Sweeping statements of alarm came easier than measures of practical help, which were difficult to implement as most energy was devoted to political factions.[38] Any dispassionate assessment of the situation must have concluded that Texas was in great danger; nevertheless, the expectation of glorious victory pervaded many pronouncements. For instance, D. C. Barrett, chairman of the Committee of State and Judiciary, wrote early in January, 1836:

> The enemy is endeavouring to concentrate and bring upon us a large force which must be met and vanquished as soon as possible after he takes the field: munitions of war and supplies of provisions to be landed at or near the port of Copano as circumstances will admit, is all important to our present and contemplated future operations. Whatever can be done by you, in this way, and sending volunteers to the same destination, will aid your adopted country in the struggle for freedom and constitutional rights. A cordon of ports are being established from Béxar by Goliad to San Patricio on the Río Nueces, and government agents will be stationed at each post to receive and provide for volunteers, and take charge of all public stores. Indeed, we hope to extend the line to Matamoros at no very distant time! . . . The rich rewards of our labors and our dangers is ever in view, and immediate possession but awaits the successful termination of the present struggle.[39]

This letter, while acknowledging the threat of invasion and the importance of supplies to the Texan forces through the port of Copano, close to the Irish settlements in the war zone, still conveyed an air of vaunted confidence and the expectation of rich pickings from a Texan expedition to Matamoros. All this was fantasy, as subsequent events proved. It was intended to appeal to American volunteers to support the cause of Texas. The vital necessity of enlisting moral and material support from the United States led inexorably to a shift from a conservative defense of the Mexican Constitution of 1824 to the more revolutionary step of declaring for the independence of Texas.

On January 14, Maj. Gen. Samuel Houston was sent an official communication from J. C. Neill, lieutenant colonel commanding the army at Béxar. It was the third official notification, all of which complained of scarcity of provisions, men, and money:

> The men all under my command, have been in the field for the last 4 months, they are almost naked, and this day they were to have received pay for the first month of their last enlistment, and almost every one of them speak of going home, and not less than 20 will leave tomorrow, and leave here only about 80 efficient men under my command, and there are at Laredo now Three thousand men under the command of Genl. Ramirey, and two other Genls. and as it appears by

a letter received here last night, one thousand of them are destined for this place, and Two Thousand for Matamoros, we are in a torpid defenceless Situation, we have not and cannot get from all the Citizens here, Horses enough since Johnson and Grant left, to send out a patrole or Spy Company.[40]

Neill also referred to the valuable support from some of the local Mexicans, Capt. Salvador Flores and two others who had volunteered to spy out the situation of the enemy's invading force at Laredo, and while little aid was likely from the citizens of the town, as they had no money, Don Gaspar Flores and Luciano Navarro had offered all their goods, groceries, and beefs for the use by the army.

A letter from W. W. Wharton in Nashville, Tennessee, to Governor Smith in February, 1836, made it plain that the ultimate prospect of Texas becoming part of the Union was essential to harness American support: "The question is now sprung in the papers in regard to the annexation of Texas to the United States. . . . As I wrote to you from Velasco, if a belief obtained here, that we were carrying the war beyond the Río Grande, for cupidity, conquest, pillage, plunder or any other motive than to make our enemy acknowledge the independence of Texas, it would drown our cause beneath all depth."[41] A few days later, the same correspondent reported enthusiastically on a meeting of two thousand people where the notion of supporting the Texan cause drew much applause and the view that Tennessee alone would furnish five thousand volunteers. The ladies of Nashville had pledged to arm and equip two hundred men, and money was donated for steamboat passage to convey volunteers to the Texas coast.[42]

Meanwhile, in the war zone hundreds of miles away to the south, the plight of volunteer soldiers was completely exposed to the oncoming Mexican army. Col. James Fannin wrote to the acting governor trying to puncture the complacency among most people in Texas who believed the war was over and deploring the fact that so few citizens had volunteered to serve in the army:

In my last, by Captain Tarleton, I informed you, that I could find but some half dozen citizens of Texas in my ranks, and I regret to say that it is yet the case. There is great complaint, which, though just, I find but little difficulty in assuaging at present; there being a reasonable prospect of *speedy action*. This is life to a volunteer army, and though many, very many are really *naked*, and quite *barefoot*, and, until my arrival here, had eaten no *bread* for some time, (and a prospect of being

out before I could get it from Demit,) I am proud to say that they mani-
fested willingness, nay, an anxiety to meet the foe, and despoil him of
his honours and illustrious deeds, won at Tampico, and more recently
acted out in the unfortunate fall of Zacatecas. They look to the people
of Texas, *en masse*, to embody and march to the rescue. Shall they be
disappointed?[43]

A week later the empresario James McGloin wrote to John Bower, the
elected delegate from San Patricio to the General Council, following the
elevation of John McMullen as president pro tem. McGloin was anxious
to have Colonel Fannin know the desperate and exposed situation of the
colonists in San Patricio, who had supplied significant numbers of men
under arms in the field:

> San Patricio Febr 22d 1836
> Mr. J. Bowers
> Dear Sir:
>   You will do me the favor of representing the Situation of this place
> to Col. Fanning [Fannin] as you pass through Goliad and State to him
> that there is now in the field one hundred of the Colonists belonging
> to this colony both regulars and volunteers that there is sixteen left in
> the place to protect the families and only six days ago the Indians killed
> three person on the other side of the river and had taken all the horses
> from here // at the Same time you will state to Col. Fanning that this
> is one of the most Important Points in all Texas for the defence of the
> Same as being the Grand Pass into it, by so doing you truly oblige your
> Humble Servt.
> James McGloin[44]

Members of the council, who were unable to send supplies or reinforcements to the army even conceded that without troops to protect the
colonists in the war zone, it was difficult to command the loyalty of its
subjects: "With regard to the Setlers on the Nueces, we think, situated as
they are, and have been for some time past, unprotected, and the enemy
close at hand, we believe that great allowance be made for, and much
lenity [sic] shown them by the commander but would advise that those
who have been actively employed, against us, and are proven to be enemies, should be sent to the seat of government to be disposed of as the
government may think proper."[45]

After the fall of the Alamo and the massacre of the prisoners at Goliad in March, 1836, General Houston's army appeared to be in retreat before the advancing forces under Santa Anna, and most of the settlers had fled from their devastated communities at San Patricio and Refugio in the "runaway scrape." There was a distinct air of panic and uncertainty among the political leaders of the provisional government, disappointed by the lack of volunteers joining the Texan army despite the inducements offered in the form of land grants. The failure of men to enlist in the army could provoke exasperation among onlookers who championed the Texan cause from the relative safety of Nashville, Tennessee. Sarah Wharton wrote to former governor Smith perplexed as to whether liberty or land would prove to be the vital motivator: "I cannot conjecture what can be their object. Is it pecuniary? Common sense would teach them that their property, whatever it might consist in, would be worth many times as much under a settled government."[46]

David G. Burnet, the president, reflected the mood of despair just one week before Sam Houston's remarkable victory at San Jacinto. While women and children were being driven from their homes and sheltering in woods, too many citizens were lingering in idleness at home, or ingloriously flying before the enemy. "Is it possible," he asked, "that the free citizens of Texas, the descendants of the heroes of '76, can take panic at the approach of the paltry minions of a despot, who threatens to desolate our beautiful country?"[47]

The sense of exasperation and despair was transformed by the victory at San Jacinto that effectively secured the independence of Texas. A bargain struck with Santa Anna that he would be spared if the Mexican armies withdrew from Texas soil achieved a temporary reprieve from the Mexican presence. The infant republic still lacked the means to pay for a standing army and was, in effect, reliant on financial and military support from American volunteers, but now there were grounds for a return of triumphalist rhetoric. A more cynical note was struck in a letter from William Parker to Ira Ingram in June, 1836, pointing up the irony of an upsurge of volunteers once the victory had been won: "Many who were panic stricken but a short time since, and who alarmed at the reputed numbers of the enemy flew before him, far in advance, as from a desolating pestilence, are now among the first to repair in the field and enroll themselves for duty."[48]

Some sober reflections by participants on the dramatic turn of events qualify the ultimate victory for the Texan cause. President Burnet, writing to officers in the army in September, 1836, recalled how desperate the situation had been at the start of the year. The country was without the means to sustain an army in the field and lacked funds at home and credit abroad. With the army in retreat before the enemy, the news of the fall of the Alamo spread dismay throughout the land, and citizens fled before the approaching desolation. "These, gentlemen, are facts which run through everyone's recollection, and which are painfully impressed upon my memory."[49] Burnet's correspondence also reported some of the recriminations that surrounded the war effort. Some had suffered greatly while others appeared to avoid any commitment to the war but were charged with looking to protect their own interests and speculate on a rise in property values that victory and independence would bring about. Old party factions and regional conflicts resurfaced after the war. In a statement that might have been expressly written on behalf of the Irish colonists of Refugio and San Patricio, he wrote:

> It cannot be disguised that the principal sufferings and losses incident to the war, have been sustained in very unequal proportions, by the citizens of the country. The population of the Colorado and west of it, and of the Brazos, have experienced all the miseries of a successful invasion, by a foe, whose watchword was death, and whose purpose was extermination, while other and populous sections of the country, have been comparatively exempt from molestation or inconvenience – Many citizens have suffered an entire devastation of their personal goods. Others have had their dwellings destroyed by the enemy; others again have seen theirs given to the flames, by their own countrymen, for purposes connected with the public defence.[50]

During the war, Refugio and San Patricio were ravaged, overrun, and virtually depopulated by the armies that marched and countermarched through the frontier war zone. Burnet pressed for compensation to be paid to those who had suffered loss of property, recognition of the colonists' land grants, and a resolution of the uncertainty over title that was being compounded by "unscrupulous speculation in the public domain."[51] The injustice involved in loss of lands vacated during the war had Burnet "regretting instances of individuals taking possession of certain vacated and supposed forfeited lands, doubtless with a view of claiming hereafter to hold them as headrights, bounties, preemptions, or in some other way to secure to themselves by possession and occupancy, a priority of right over their fellow-citizens, in reference to these forfeitures."[52]

Entitlement to land and compensation for its loss remained key issues during the war and its aftermath. At the meeting of the first Congress, in November, 1836, Mr. Wharton was highly sarcastic about the lack of visibility of the rich planters and merchants at the battle of San Jacinto:

After this scrutiny, I was compelled to see and know that the *wealthy* of Texas had but little participation in the victory alluded to. . . . Where were they, God only knows; but one thing is certain; *very, very few* of them indeed were in the battle of San Jacinto. . . . The planter, I suppose, was taking care of his negroes, and the merchant of his goods; at least they were not in the field; many of them, I admit, were necessarily absent on business more serviceable to their country than would have been their service in the field. Many, I grant, were compelled to fly to take care of their families, on account of the sudden and unexpected falling back of our army from the Colorado. But for the absence of many, there is no excuse. I found that the battle of San Jacinto was achieved by the poor men of the country, at least half of whom had never located a headright in Texas, and were as destitute of land as the volunteers themselves. When this was made palpable to my mind, I exclaimed, and I claim again, with all my heart, give to those gallant and conquering heroes their bounty to the uttermost extent of the law.[53]

Wharton advocated that the heroes of San Jacinto should be rewarded with land. In the case of the Irish colonists who served in the army, such as Walter Lambert and Thomas O'Connor, they were able to receive bounty grants of 640 acres for each three months of military service. While some lost their property, others made valuable gains in the form of land grants and contracts with the army.[54]

There was, in truth, a consistent theme running through all the events of the Texas Revolution and among all those who lived through it, whether as soldiers, citizens, or bystanders. It was the central preoccupation with land. The prospect of land generously granted by the Mexican government had brought the settlers in the first place. What was called "Texas fever" was a fever to acquire land. Without colonists settling the land there was no real prospect of developing trade or a likelihood of building ports and merchant fortunes, as James Power planned on the coast of the Gulf of Mexico. So many of the leading politicians and merchants were engaged in some form of land speculation that was dependent for success on an independent Texas, linked to the United States, that one study identifies speculation in increased land values as the leading factor in causing the war with Mexico.[55] A clear example of the culture of land speculation is found in a letter from Joseph E. Plummer, a government official who built a house made of shell and concrete at Copano, not far from fellow Refugio colonists James Power, Walter Lambert, and Patrick Shelly. He wrote to his son, Frances: "I have bought 10,124 acres of land and taken up Government paper to the amt. of 5,000 Dollars with about $8,000 in goods and 2,500 in cash the land I expect to be able to keep till you want it and then it will be worth 5 to $50 per acre I think I have done a much better business than I could have expected by any other occupations or by keeping my negroes and farming as I now feel certain to give my children a pretty start in life — after giving them an education all of which is certainly very gratifying to me and, is all you can reasonably require."[56]

Speculation in land values was not, however, confined to the wealthy. One soldier in the war of 1835–36 calculated he made a profit of $1,968.25 on the value of his land, and this consideration, rather than patriotism, had been his motivation for fighting.[57] Beyond the hopes and dreams of individuals lay the realpolitik of U.S. expansion and the frailty of a newly independent Mexico. While America wanted to annex or buy Texas, the Mexican government desperately wanted to retain its rich, fertile province but lacked the means and sometimes the will to do so. Freedom, like the bloody flag over the battlements of old Goliad, could blow one way or another, but the land remained a fixture for all to contest.

A careful reading of contemporary accounts points to a sober recognition of how the war was experienced by soldiers and civilians. Despite the patriotic and defiant rhetoric of politicians and military commanders, the war was far from uniformly glorious. For instance, not all Texans responded to the call for arms. There was constant indiscipline among the citizen-soldiers and a deep resentment among them of politicians and land speculators. There was a complete lack of coordination of the regular and volunteer armies, and severe problems providing supplies and payment to the troops in the field. For much of the war, before the fall of the Alamo in March, 1836, there was regular disagreement over political objectives. Was it to defend the 1824 Constitution of Mexico or to opt for the independence of Texas?

If there was a war of words as well as fighting in the field, it might equally be argued that the war itself was experienced in different ways, depending on the mere fact of geography. Harbert Davenport, who made an intensive study of the military campaigns, has pointed to the physical separation of settlements in Texas. In the autumn of 1835 when the Texas Revolution began, the American settlements in Texas with a few straggling exceptions were all east of the Guadalupe and south of the historic San Antonio–Nachitoches trail; the region to the north and west of the American settlements was the habitat only of roving, predatory tribes of Indians and was entirely impractical as a field for military operations; and the region between San Antonio and the Rio Grande was likewise a wilderness, with the main roads from San Antonio to Laredo and from San Antonio to Residio Rio Grande (below Eagle Pass) constantly exposed to Indian raids.

The political frontier of Texas was the Nueces River, but the western limits of Anglo-American settlement were at the Guadalupe, with the Irish colonies of Refugio and San Patricio forming outposts to the Southwest. Politically, these Irish colonies were associated with Béxar, and not with Austin's and De Witt's colonists, from whom they were separated, in a sense by Martín de León's Mexican colony around Victoria and the older Mexican settlements that centered on Goliad.[58]

The war, when viewed from a distance in Washington or Nacogdoches, was a cause for concern. For the frontier communities of San Antonio, Goliad, Refugio, and San Patricio, the war was a bitter experience of devastated property and loss of life. Subjected to the damage caused by both armies, the Irish colonists and their Mexican neighbors living in the war zone were compelled to take sides and to suffer the consequences. The confusion of divided loyalty to Mexico or Texas was dispelled by the brutal treatment experienced by the Irish colonists. After the destruction at Refugio and San Patricio and the massacre at Goliad, loyalty to the Texan cause was sealed by the blood of their fallen comrades.

Distance from the political center also made local circumstances important in determining which cause to support. The presence of the Mexican garrison at Lipantitlán, close to San Patricio, and the good relations established with the Irish colonists provided practical reasons for support of the Mexican cause. Friction between the Irish colonists in Refugio and their Mexican neighbors in Goliad inclined them toward supporting the Texan cause. When Ira Westover took a small troop of men to attack the garrison at Lipantitlán in November, 1835, he found that the engagement involved Irishmen on both sides:

Having taken James O'Riley, an Irishman, in the fore part of the evening whom we supposed to be aiding and assisting the enemy, he preferred to go to the Fort and induce them to surrender if we would protect him. We therefore made use of him and the Fort surrendered at 11 o'clock on condition of being met at liberty on parole and not to take up arms against us dureing the war. Twenty one men were in the Fort, four of whom were prisoners, five Irishmen and one Englishman from San Patricia, some from choice and others from compulsion, were assisting in keeping Garrison. There were two pieces of Cannon a four and a two pounder. The former belonged to Messrs McMullen and McGlowen of San Patricia and was taken from them by force.

A few days later an engagement took place by the bank of the river Nueces just outside San Patricio. Westover claimed twenty-eight of the enemy were killed, wounded, or missing, including three of the Irish, the judge, alcalde, and sheriff, while the Texans had but one man injured, Sergeant Bracken, who had three fingers shot off from his right hand and the other fractured with the same ball. The difficulty of obtaining a team to move the 4-pounder in bad weather led Westover to abandon it: "I, together with Capt. Kerr, John J. Linn & James Power who rendered signal service advised the propriety of throwing the Artillery in the river and it was accordingly done. The men all fought bravely and those on the opposite bank of the river were enabled to operate on the flanks below the crossing which they did with fine effect." [59]

Not only were the San Patricio Irish fighting against the Refugio Irish but what may be termed a fluidity of allegiance was evident on both sides, reflecting the gradual shift from a civil war between centralists and federalists to a war of independence. It was also fitting that James Power was authorized to encourage the Mexican General Mexía to join the Texan forces at Béxar. He preferred to go to Copano, join with 200 Mexicans in preparation for an attack on the port of Matamoros. Power reported that Mexía "could not place his military character at stake by accepting a command under the Provisional Government of Texas," but he hoped, "the Governor and Council would place armed vessels to blockade the ports of Vera Cruz and Tampico, and order all vessels bound for said ports to Matamoros, where they can discharge their cargo." As late as February, 1836, a general plan to revolutionize Mexico on behalf of the federalist cause was included in dispatches to General Mexía.[60]

Differences over the objectives of the war remained an obstacle to its successful prosecution, and this was compounded by the lack of authority over the troops in the field. An instance of this occurred among the citizen-soldiers of Goliad in November, 1835. The commander in chief, Stephen F. Austin, had ordered that Capt. Philip Dimitt be replaced by Capt. George Collinsworth. The men's disaffection and disobedience was not simply a loyalty to Dimitt as their chosen commander; it was expressed as a matter of democratic principle for which they had taken up arms — to withstand arbitrary power and despotism. The petition that was sent to Austin, of which more than a third of the signatories were Refugio colonists, was a foretaste of the democratic principles enunciated in the Goliad Declaration of Independence.[61] With the Mexican armies crossing into Texas to subdue the rebellion and with maintaining a sizable Texan army in the field becoming increasingly difficult, it was no longer safe for the women and children in the frontier communities to remain at their homesteads. So began what became known as the "runaway scrape." The evacuation of families from Refugio and San Patricio was led by the young, Irish colonists Thomas O'Connor and his cousin John O'Brien. Many families subsequently lost all their possessions. Surviving petitions for compensation submitted after the war represented the tip of the iceberg. Widow Mary Byrne "had a good comfortable house and 8 head of cattle with a large and valuable lot of household furniture and farming utensils" in Refugio. She was compelled to leave it all in the retreat. Responsible for five young children and dependent on her own exertions, she was still in Victoria in November, 1839, and unable to return to her burned-out home, which had been destroyed by the troops of King and Ward in defending Refugio. She claimed compensation of $500, the value of her property, exclusive of her house and cattle, and asked for an allowance until she could safely return to her abandoned house on the frontier.[62] Thomas Pew and Michael Hely of San Patricio claimed compensation for the loss of two horses taken by the Mexican army on account of Patrick McGloin, also of San Patricio, being in the Texan army. McGloin retreated to La Bahía and also submitted a list of articles that were taken from him by the Mexican army: 72 head of cattle ($570), 2 horses ($100), 50 head of hogs ($100), and furniture to the value of $250.[63]

Mrs. Dilue Harris recalled the pitiful experiences of families who struggled to reach safety ahead of the invading troops:

By the 20th of February the people of San Patricio and other western settlements were fleeing for their lives. Every family in our neighborhood was preparing to go to the United States. Wagons and other vehicles were scarce. Mr. Stafford, with the help of small boys and negroes, began gathering cattle. All the large boys had gone to the army. . . .

Our hardships began at the Trinity. The river was rising and there was a struggle to see who should cross first. Measles, sore eyes, whooping cough, and every other disease that man, woman, or child is heir to, broke out among us. . . .

The horrors of crossing the Trinity are beyond my powers to describe. One of my little sisters was very sick, and the ferryman said those families that had sick children should cross first. When our party got to the boat the water broke over the banks above where we were and ran around us. We were several hours surrounded by water. Our family was the last to get to the boat. We left more than five hundred people on the west bank. Drift wood covered the water as far as we could see. The sick child was in convulsions. It required eight men to manage the boat.[64]

The difficulties that faced the women, children, and Negroes were followed by disaster for the colonists who had remained at Refugio. Lewis Ayers, a member of the General Council of the provisional government and a San Patricio colonist who moved his family to Refugio, described his experiences in trying to remove his family from Refugio in late February ahead of the advancing Mexican armies. He had heard news that fifteen hundred men had reached San Patricio and another seventy-five hundred under the command of Santa Anna had arrived at San Antonio de Béxar. Also a number of the local Mexican rancheros had sworn to assassinate him. He could not procure a team of horses to move his goods, as the Texan army had pressed nearly all that were available to haul provisions. He went to Goliad and procured from Colonel Fannin teams to assist in the removal of his family under the care of Captain King. Ayers himself was appointed as assistant quartermaster general at Goliad. Captain King took it on himself to punish some Mexican rancheros who had been plundering at the mission, but finding the enemy reinforced by many Indians, he retreated to Refugio.

There has been a good deal of plundering during the day by the Mexicans and Indians; feather beds opened and feathers scattered to the winds, for the purpose of ascertaining if there was any money secreted in them. In the morning a party of 7 rancheros came armed to the house for the purpose of plunder, but seeing Mr. Foley, my brother-in-law, A. H. Osborn and myself all well armed, they did not think best to attempt it, and were quite civil. . . .

My family were living about one mile from the village, my goods and furniture on two wagons and carts, my family and teams protected by Capt. King were taken to the Church they were fired at by the enemy on the way but fortunately escaped injury but some of our furniture was well out by balls. After King had gotten all the families remaining in that place in the Church, he sent an express to Col. Fannin for more force to protect them all on rout to Goliad.[65]

Fannin dispatched Lieutenant Colonel Ward with 120 men, including Lewis Ayers, to Refugio. They arrived on the afternoon of March 12, and that evening there was a skirmish with the enemy, who were driven off. During the night a party of about 50 men attacked the enemy, killing some and driving off the remainder of them. Later the next day, Ayers went with a party of 100 men to hunt up the enemy. Captain King took 28 of the men searching out the local ranches, only to find them deserted. On their return to the mission they were surprised to find the Mexican general Urrea with 1,500 men in possession of the town. The colonists and their families were in the church. King's troop, now reduced to 22 men, following the loss of 6 deserters, retreated to the woods that offered a good defensive position. About 100 Mexicans attacked for half an hour then retreated with the loss of about 20 killed and many wounded. An hour later, the Mexicans made a second attack with 200 men in two parties and opened a cross fire. King's men stood firm, suffering 1 man killed and 4 wounded but inflicting heavy losses on the enemy in the hour-long engagement. A third attack toward nightfall failed to dislodge the Texans, who decided to escape under cover of darkness. Having crossed the river at an unguarded point and taking the wounded in a painful ascent of the steep river bank,

> [w]e wandered about all night endeavouring to reach Goliad, but when day dawned on the 14th we found our selves only about 3 miles from the Mission, having lost our way. We hurried on about two miles further, when we were attacked by a party of Mexicans, and were compelled to surrender, our guns being most of them wet, and having no chance to retreat. We were then marched back to the Mission, tied together two by two, the rope at the same time connecting up altogether, after which we were marched about one mile where we found a body

of the enemy drawn up to receive us, we also found a few of our friends, who had been picked up one by one, making in the whole 33 men. The Soldiers loaded their guns to shoot us but in consequence of there being two Germans among the prisoners the execution was postponed at the request of a Col. in the enemy's service who was a German by birth. Our treatment during the next 24 hours was most brutal and barborous.[66]

Lewis Ayers, his family, and the two Germans were spared the cruel fate of the other prisoners at the mission. They endured no more than a severe lecture and eventually escaped to New Orleans. General Urrea was apparently moved by the tears of Ayers's wife and four children to grant them clemency. The rest of the party were unceremoniously taken out, shot, stripped naked, and left on the prairie one mile from the mission.[67]

Even when a Mexican victory was being described, a defiant and confident air of superiority over the enemy was commonly found in eyewitness accounts. Written from hindsight and shaped by the knowledge of ultimate victory at San Jacinto, defiance claimed its own justification. An account written by Sabina Brown, one of the Irish colonists at Refugio whose husband was killed at Goliad, expressed the eagerness of the defenders in wishing to do battle with a numerically superior enemy. "When at supper time they heard that there was a band of the enemy on a ranch ten or twelve miles below the Mission, they said to one another; 'Jolly, now for a fight; maybe they will come tonight,' but morning came and no Mexicans, much to the disappointment of the Texans who were starving for a fight. And then they began clamoring 'if they can't come we can go there'; and away they went."[68]

That was the prelude to Captain King's venture out of the mission before being captured by Mexicans and returned to Refugio to be executed. The Mexican attack on the beleaguered mission church at Refugio, defended by Colonel Ward's Georgian Rattlers was described as an exciting spectacle for the civilian onlookers. "At daylight the fun began for the whole Mexican army tried to take the galant little band of Georgians out of the old church and failed three times in that day. . . . In the gray light of morning they began shooting with their cannon at the old church, this they kept up for two hours and then they came on foot and on horse-back thick as the grass growing out of the ground. When they got within reach of the Georgians' rifles the fight began and the Mexicans began to waver backward and forward and finally ran back to the river leaving the hill south of the church literally strewn with their dead and wounded." In the hardest fight of the day, "the sulphur smoke rose high in the air and the rifles of the Georgians rattled like shot in a gourd, and they whooped for joy when they saw the Mexicans fall."[69]

In the afternoon, there was a call for volunteers to take the cannon from the enemy and about nine or ten came forward: "Out they went over heaps of dead Mexicans while their comrades in the belfry were dropping Mexicans thick and fast around the cannon. They reached it and took it without losing a single man and rolled it into the church and a yell went up that seemed to shake the rafters of the house."[70]

Another witness, E. N. Hill, who was a mile away in the church with his mother, later recalled the massacre at Refugio: "Capt. King and his command (with the exception of one man) . . . were marched out upon the road to Béxar, about one mile from the church, where they were ordered to face about and kneel. They were about to comply when one of the men called out: 'Boys, we are about to be murdered; let us face the cowards, and die like men.' They refused to turn, and were shot down as they stood; and to make sure, each one afterwards had a lance run through his body."[71]

One of the spared, the German Herman Ehrenberg, had volunteered to fight with the Georgian Grays and wrote his own colorful account of what took place at Refugio. "As a few of the victims were still breathing, the soldiers completed their ghastly work by smashing their brains with the butt ends of their muskets."[72]

These accounts are full of examples of raw courage and suffering, rough treatment faced by women and children, and the brutal killing of Texan prisoners. Discrepancies in the details can be partly explained by the propaganda value of alleged Mexican atrocities that not only fired up the Texan population to seek revenge but also helped justify a rebellion against the legally constituted government in the eyes of international opinion, and especially in soliciting aid from the United States. The Mexican colonel Francisco Garay justified the decision on military grounds. His troops were demoralized and suffering from the rigors of the climate. He was threatened by enemy forces at Copano, Goliad, and Victoria, and Ward had escaped with two hundred men. "I yielded to the difficult situation which encompassed me, and gave them permission to shoot about thirty adventurers whom I had made prisoners in the earlier engagements, after I had left camp, at the same time setting at liberty those who were colonists or Mexicans."[73]

A more sympathetic account, written by a Mexican general in a private capacity to his wife, expressed his disgust at the barbarous scenes he witnessed during March, 1836:

> Before I reached Agua Dulce, the dead bodies of foreigners, already mangled by wild beasts, appeared by the way, and in San Patricio I saw the graves of the fallen, both of Americans and Mexicans. On marching to the ruins of the Mission del Refugio, we found the enemy in possession of the church. We commenced our assault at six in the morning, and the action continued until midnight, when they fled. They fought with an enthusiastic valor equal to that of our own men. Several of our troops were shot within four paces of the wall, the enemy being invincible, and their station only known from the voluminous flashes which issued from the building. Our loss that day, in killed and wounded, amounted to 40; and of the enemy 25 out of 30 who fell into our hands, as also some others whom we found in the church. But what an awful scene did the field present when these prisoners were executed, and fell dead in heaps; and what spectator could view it without horror! They were all young, the oldest not more than 30, and of fine florid complexions. When these unfortunate youth were brought to the place of death, their lamentations and the appeals which they uttered to Heaven, in their own language, with extended arms, kneeling or prostrate on the earth, were such as might have caused the very stones to cry out with compassion.[74]

Herman Ehrenberg, the German soldier who escaped the massacre at Refugio, marched south with the Grays to San Patricio hoping to persuade the men of the garrison to return to Goliad. They feared they would be cut off from the Texan army and wished to bring back the artillery. Ehrenberg also confirmed the divided loyalties of the San Patricio colonists. "The settlers in this locality, being almost all fervent Catholics, were rather out of sympathy with our unorthodox beliefs and opinions, and many had fled across the Rio Grande. Not all of them, however, took such drastic steps to avoid coming into contact with the dangerous heretics we were supposed to be and a few even showed as ardent patriotism as we could have wished."[75]

In the neat and well-laid-out hamlet of San Patricio, they found Johnson and Grant occupying empty houses, as most of the colonists had departed. Returning to Goliad, they found Colonel Fannin's men isolated, dwindling in number, and unaware of the enemy's progress in Texas. Then news of two disastrous episodes reached Goliad. First, the massacre of King's men at Refugio, then a report from General Houston on the fall of the Alamo. Goliad looked to be next for the invading Mexican army. Houston's message begged Fannin to lead his troops across the Guadalupe River to unite his troops with the militia. Faced with an occupying army, a shortage of food supplies, and the loss of many of the volunteers, there was little prospect of help in raising a siege by the enemy. Reluctantly, Fannin burned part of the fortification, destroyed large quantities of dried meat and corn, and spiked every cannon that could not be transported. Fannin's party made slow progress en route to Victoria and more stores and baggage were abandoned. Having moved only about eight miles from Goliad, they sighted the enemy.

Abel Morgan, a saddle maker and physician's assistant from North Carolina, who was originally in Capt. Ira Westover's company under Colonel Fannin, later recalled, in the vernacular language of a soldier, what became known as the fight on the prairie. Fannin's army of 360 men was surrounded in open country by a Mexican force of 1,900 men, half of them cavalry. Morgan was instructed to take care of the wounded but without access to water he could do them no further service. A square was formed with oxen and wagons as a defense against the enemy, but a Mexican employed to drive the oxen, as soon as he was ordered to halt, let the wild cattle go and ran off to the Mexican army.

> I walked into the square. I knew we had some new muskets in the ammunition wagon. I selected me one of them and catched up two packs of cartridges and walked out to my wagon again where the balls were whizzing about like bees swarming. About that time after, I had fired eight or ten times, by myself, there come out four men, and we formed a platoon of five, an Irishman by the name of Cash was the head of the platoon. I was next. A Dutchman by the name of Baker next. A young man from Georgia next. The last had a rifle. . . . He was not a soldier but a visitor, and had his horse and gun along. After a few rounds, Cash received a ball in the corner of his head and as he fell he handed me his gun, saying "take this, she won't snap." My gun had got mucky with powder and missed fire, and he had noticed it. I took it and kept it the balance of the day. The ball cut the size of it out of his head but did not kill him. In a short time Baker who stood at my left hand, was shot

down. He had his thigh broken, and before he was carried into the square he got another ball in the body. Then both [Cash and Baker] were carried into the square.[76]

Fannin's men had nine cannon but with many of the regulars killed or wounded and the volunteers unwilling to man them, only five were in constant use. Nevertheless a deadly combination of cannon and rifle fire maintained a continual bombardment throughout the afternoon until sundown. Ehrenberg captures the exhilaration as the battle raged between Mexican cavalry and the firepower of the Texan forces:

When the Mexicans came within five or six hundred paces of us they fired their carbines, but their shooting did not disturb us, for the bullets flew high above our heads. . . . Our army now waited for the approach of its adversaries. But although the latter kept discharging one volley of shot after another, we did not return their fire because they were still beyond the reach of our rifles. Our artillery officers, tall fine-looking Poles, decided likewise to let the enemy's cavalry draw near before opening fire. Finally, when the Mexican horsemen had come close enough to us, our front line moved aside so as to leave free range to our cannon, which poured heavy shot upon our hasty and over-confident assailants. The effect of the artillery fire was immediate and horrible. Frightened by the noise, the horses of the enemy plunged and kicked wildly. Many of the Mexicans were thrown off their saddles, and their riderless horses galloped aimlessly across the field, while wounded men and beasts lying prostrate in the dust were trampled upon by the advancing or retreating cavalry squadrons. . . .

[A renewed attack by Mexican horsemen and infantry brought heavy casualties sustained on both sides. Ehrenberg strikes a modern note in depicting the carnage on the battlefield.] Assailed on every side by the combined forces of our adversary, we fought with the grim endurance of despair. . . . The clear reports of our muskets mingled with the dull roars of the cannon, and the shrill blasts of the Mexican bugles filled the space around us with a deafening noise. More impressive, perhaps, than any sound in this tumult were the booming volleys of artillery, which fell upon the enemy with the rolling sound of thunder. Cowardice is absent from the battlefield during these moments of great intensity, for who has time to think of life or to feel the grip of fear in the fierce exultation of battle? Men forget death in these minutes of supreme selflessness. The senses are benumbed; so is consciousness. Almost no heed can be given to the directions shouted by the officers; the adversary alone engrosses the attention of eyes and ears. Such is my memory of the feelings I experienced while I was fighting. . . . Many of our soldiers lay on the ground dead or seriously wounded; all our gunners save one, a Pole, had perished, and their bodies had fallen in a heap around the field pieces which were now idle and almost useless. . . . Men, horses, rifles, and all kinds of objects lay scattered over the trodden soil of our corner of the prairie, now the abode of death and desolation.[77]

As night fell, it was clear that despite the losses endured by the enemy, perhaps 750 men, Fannin's troops, also decimated by casualties, were in a desperate situation. The Mexicans separated their forces into three divisions, one watching the road to Goliad, another blocking the way to Victoria, and the third located between the other two. Fannin himself was wounded and was mindful of the plight of many others suffering from battle wounds. Irish colonist Andrew Boyle provides an insight into the mood in the Texan camp. "I was shot in the right leg, a little above the ankle about 3 o' clock in the afternoon. After the enemy retreated then commenced our real trouble, the wounded cried for water and we had none to give them, some of our men dug for water, others threw up entrenchments expecting to continue the fight the next day, we had killed our oxen and used them as breast-works during the battle. Col. Fanning was slightly wounded in the thigh, I lay close by him that night and hearing my groans, he kindly offered me his good leg for a pillow."[78]

An attempt to break through the encircling enemy forces would have meant abandoning the wounded to the uncertain mercy of the enemy. There was still an outside chance that his scouts might return with reinforcements from Victoria. According to John J. Linn, who was in Jack Shackelford's company, the men agreed to negotiate for an honorable surrender for the sake of protecting the wounded: "When the matter was first proposed to Colonel Fannin he was for holding out longer, saying: 'We whipped them off yesterday, and we can do so again to-day.'"[79] But on finding that a majority of the troops accepted the necessity of capitulation, he ordered the raising of a white flag. The Mexicans promptly replied with one of their own, and the two parties met midway between the forces. Ehrenberg claimed that Hotzinger, the German, was the only one who could speak English but only in a limited fashion, so the greater part of the transaction was conducted in German and then translated into

Spanish. Linn's account has Captain Dusangue as the interpreter, accompanying Colonel Fannin and Major Wallace. Andrew Boyle also recalled that "two of our officers met two of the Mexican officers and articles of capitulation were agreed on; the first article guaranteed to us our lives and personal property and another article that we should remain as prisoners of war until honorably discharged or sent to the United States, giving our paroles of honor never to return to Texas. Upon our part we agreed to give up all government property in our possession; these articles of capitulation were signed by both parties."[80]

Eventually the terms were agreed on: "the surrender of all our arms as prisoners of war and be treated in a civilized way, with the wounded attended to and taken back to Goliad, we could retain our private property, and were to be sent by ship from Copano or Matamoros to New Orleans. Our freedom was to be granted on a pledge not to fight against the government of Mexico." The terms were reported back to the men by Colonel Fannin and confirmed by Major Wallace and Captain Dusangue. The articles of capitulation were put in writing and signed by the respective commanders. The Mexican colonel Hotzinger, who was superintending the surrender of arms, exclaimed: "Well, gentlemen, in ten days liberty and home!"[81] After the surrender was completed, Colonel Horton's party of scouts returned from Victoria, but too late and with insufficient force to have saved the day.

That afternoon, Fannin's depleted force was marched to the presidio at Goliad and imprisoned in the church. The wounded, Andrew Boyle among them, waited two or three days for Mexican carts to carry them there: "their sufferings were great from the heat of the sun, want of water and medical aid. The wounded upon their arrival in Goliad were put into the hospital."[82] Those not wounded had no water nor a morsel of food to eat, and having waded across the San Antonio river armpit deep, they arrived at the church dripping wet to sit flat down on the stone floor. After enduring severe discomfort in the overcrowded church and bartering belongings for food from the Mexican guards, they were joined by 120 new prisoners from Major Ward's troops who had been captured by the enemy after losing their trail on the prairie. Another 100 prisoners arrived on the seventh day. Captain Miller's volunteers from New York were captured soon after landing at Copano and were lodged outside the fort. At eight o' clock the next morning, some 400 of the prisoners were taken out on the order of Santa Anna and lined up under a 700-strong Mexican guard. They were told that Miller's volunteers, Colonel Fannin, the doctors, and the other wounded prisoners would come to New Orleans later on. Ehrenberg sensed something was wrong:

> The Mexican soldiers, who were as a rule very talkative, were unbearably silent; our men were grave; the atmosphere was hot and close. Everything filled us with anxiety, and our surroundings increased our uneasiness. . . . I glanced at the Mexican escort and noticed for the first time their parade uniforms and lack of baggage. Gloomy reflections assailed my mind. I remembered the events of Tampico, San Patricio, and the Alamo; I thought of the character of our enemies, their treachery, their love of plunder, their lust for blood. . . .
>
> Our leaving the main road unexpectedly and the brisk galloping of a few lancers on our right puzzled us. We noticed for the first time that the Mexicans who marched between us and the hedge had stayed behind. . . . Our perplexity grew; we were unable to understand such a maneuver. A command to halt given in Spanish struck our ears like the voice of doom, for at that very moment we heard the distant rattle of a volley of musketry; almost instinctively we thought of our comrades who had been separated from us and most probably taken in the direction from which the shots came. Bewildered and anxious, we gazed inquiringly now at each other, now at the Mexicans. The Mexican officer shouted to us again and ordered us to kneel; the few of us who understood would not or could not obey this command. Meanwhile the Mexican soldiers hardly three feet away from us held their rifles pointed at our chests.[83]

A second command to kneel was followed by another volley of musketry and a wail of distress from fallen comrades. Ehrenberg felt blood spurting on his clothes from the lieutenant alongside him, and his friends were falling in convulsions around him. He had nothing to lose and everything to gain by charging the bayonet of the Mexican in front of him. Amid the smoke from the muskets, he brushed past the enemy, receiving several sword blows on the way and made for the river and safety.

Back at the fort the wounded were dragged out into the quadrangle and summarily shot. Jack Shackelford, captain of the Alabama Red Rovers, whose son and two nephews were among the victims, learned from the interpreter that Colonel Fannin was the last to die and that he met his fate in a dignified manner. Fannin's request that he should be shot in the breast, not in the head, was not adhered to, despite a solemn promise given. "We were marched into the Fort about 11 o'clock, and ordered to the Hospital.—

Had to pass close by our butchered companions, who were stripped of their clothes, and their naked, mangled bodies thrown in a pile. The wounded were all hauled out in carts that evening; and some brush thrown over the different piles, with a view to burning their bodies. A few days afterwards . . . the flesh had been burned from off the bodies; but many hands and feet were yet unscathed — I could recognize no one — The bones were all still knit together, and the vultures were feeding upon those limbs which, one week before, actively played in battle."[84]

Hobart Huson, who spent many years compiling lists of the Irish colonists involved in the war, accounted for twelve men from Refugio and San Patricio among those who were killed at Goliad. A further nine Irishmen survived, including John J. Linn from Victoria.[85] Shackelford, John J. Linn, and Herman Ehrenberg were not the only ones who escaped the carnage at Goliad. A few prisoners were able to bribe their way out by speaking Spanish, and the doctors were spared to tend to the Mexican wounded. Andrew Boyle was saved by the personal intercession of a Mexican officer. He was taken to the Mexican officers hospital and a couple of hours later was addressed in English by an officer:

> "You make your mind easy Sir, your life is spared." I asked him, "if he would permit me to ask the name of the person to whom I was indebted for my life," he answered me "certainly, my name is General Francisco Garay, second in command of Urrea's division." I then asked him, "how it was that he happened to know my name," he told me that when the division passed through San Patricio "he had quarters at my Brother and sister's house and he was treated with a great deal of kindness by them, that in leaving he was anxious to remunerate for the several little delicacies so acceptable to a soldier on a campaign that were daily placed on his table." My sister refused to accept any remuneration, saying, "that she was most happy to have him there as his presence was a protection to the house," he then asked "if he could do anything for her," she replied, " there is one thing General you can do for me, which I will esteem as a great favor, I have a Brother in the Revolutionary Army and should he through the fortunes of war ever fall into your hands as a prisoner, see that he is well treated."[86]

Garay proved as good as his word. He procured Boyle a passport to go home, and he was duly taken in an oxcart to the mission at Refugio and then on to San Patricio.

Other Irish colonists were also spared by the intercession of their neighbor Capt. Don Carlos. Nicholas and John Fagan, James Byrnes, Anthony and John B. Sidick, and Edward Perry survived the massacre, proof that personal friendships can transcend the bitter divisions of war. The family legend of Nicholas Fagan's escape was recorded by Kathryn Stoner (Mrs. Tom) O'Connor, the wife of Thomas O'Connor's grandson:

> On the day of the Massacre a boy came up to Nicholas Fagan and told him he was ordered to go into a certain orchard and remain until sent for. Mr. Fagan, thinking it a hoax, paid no attention to it. The same message was delivered a second time and was again unheeded. A third message arrived and told Mr. Fagan the authorities ordered him to take a quarter of beef to Miller's orchard and for him to stay there until ordered away. Without understanding the strange command Fagan did as he was told, and had barely reached his designated place when he heard the heart rending cries of his comrades, "Don't shoot! For God's sake don't shoot us." Shot after shot followed in quick succession until the last voice was hushed in eternal silence. But Don Carlos had saved his friends. John Fagan [Nicholas's son] was said to have been out on a foraging expedition getting beef for the army, and so missed the massacre.[87]

While this story reflects the Irish tradition of storytelling, including the familiar image of the message being delivered three times, there is no reason to doubt its authenticity. An estimated 28 prisoners escaped the massacre at Goliad on Palm Sunday, March 27, 1836; 342 were killed.[88] It is also clear that from the Mexican perspective that distinctions were made between the colonists who were still, legally in their eyes, citizens of Mexico and the "adventurers," mostly *norteamericanos* and assorted Europeans who had volunteered to fight for the independence of Texas.

While the Goliad massacre has been commonly depicted as an example of the treachery of the Mexicans, Stephen L. Hardin has correctly pointed to Santa Anna's lost opportunity in not using the prisoners more intelligently for propaganda purposes. If he had returned the defeated volunteers to New Orleans, few would have wanted to see Texas again, and Mexican humanity and Texan neglect would have stemmed the flow of American volunteers. Instead of commanding the moral high ground, Santa Anna was depicted as a barbaric hate-figure. The result of the martyrdom of Fannin's men, together with those who died at the Alamo, at last roused Texan settlers to avenge those who had been sacrificed to the cause of Texan independence.[89] And it was largely Texan volunteers under the command of Sam Houston who secured the great victory at the battle of San Jacinto on April 21, 1836. With the battle cry of "remember the Alamo and remember Goliad," the Texans caught Santa Anna's Mexican army unawares, sweeping all before them when they drove them into the bayou reddened with blood as they were cut to pieces in a furious onslaught. Col. Pedro Delgado, an officer with Santa Anna's army, described the rout of the Mexican army:

> On the left, and about a musket-shot distance from our camp, was a small grove on the bayshore. Our disbanded herd rushed for it, to obtain shelter from the horrid slaughter carried on all over the prairie by the blood-thirsty-usurpers. Unfortunately, we met on our way an obstacle difficult to overcome. It was a bayou, not very wide, but rather deep. The men, on reaching it, would helplessly crowd together, and were shot down by the enemy, who was close enough not to miss his aim. It was there that the greatest carnage took place. . . . The enemy's cavalry surrounded the grove, while his infantry penetrated it, pursuing us with fierce and bloodthirsty feelings. . . . Thence they marched us to their camp. . . . After having kept us sitting in camp about an hour and a half, they marched us into the woods, where we saw an immense fire. . . . I and several of my companions were silly enough to believe that we were about to be burnt alive, in retaliation for those who had been burnt in the Alamo. We should have considered it an act of mercy to be shot first Oh! the bitter and cruel moment! However, we felt considerably relieved when they placed us around the fire to warm ourselves and to dry our wet clothes.[90]

In assessing the military significance of the Texas Revolution, Hardin offers a judgment that awards honor to both sides. A legacy of courage inspired Texan soldiers of later generations, but what he termed "the disorganization, pettiness, and the lust for power that required so much needless sacrifice," should not be forgotten. Nor was courage confined to the Texan army: "the Mexican *soldado* served with distinction, fought with courage, and died with honor," and "Urrea emerged as the most competent general of the war."[91] Major mistakes were made, primarily by Santa Anna, in risking the long drive into unfamiliar territory and, fatally, dividing his forces and being caught unawares by Houston's forces at San Jacinto. Much has been made of Fannin's hesitancy and self-confessed unfitness to command the ill-fated garrison at Goliad, although his bravery in battle and honorable death is not in doubt. However, as Hardin has argued, Fannin's weaknesses should not detract from Urrea's military skills. He learned from his mistakes at Refugio where he sustained severe losses. He took a leaf out of the Texan book, seeking cover at Coleto Creek when Fannin's army was caught exposed in open country and ultimately forcing them to surrender. His overall military strategy was calculated to leave Fannin operating blindly. He seized all the ports along the Texan coast and cut off supplies to the Texan army. He was also well served through the intelligence supplied by local Mexican rancheros who were able to identify Fannin's movements and harass Texan outriders.

On the Texan side less recognition has been accorded to the value of intelligence and supplies provided by the Irish settlers. In reality, this was probably more important in influencing the war than the numbers of Irish colonists who enlisted in the army. James Power and John J. Linn provided valuable advance information on the movement of troops, and in the critical months of February and March, 1836, supplies of food and clothing were given to the Texan armies at Victoria and Goliad. Power provided mules, oxen, and beef cattle for government use in 1835, and in 1836 he supplied clothing for the army at Victoria, including 105 pairs of duck pantaloons and 365 shirts. In October, 1836, Power styled himself as "Commandant Texas Spying Company," confirming his role in supplying military intelligence for the Texan army. John J. Linn supplied corn to Colonel Fannin's army in February, 1836, and in April was responsible for a major consignment of flour, coffee, rice, salt, molasses, and bar lead from Galveston valued at $2,266.86.

Other examples taken from the audited accounts in the army archives confirm the support role of the Irish colonists. Nicholas Fagan supplied corn and beef to Mission Refugio in December, 1835, and February, 1836. James McGloin at San Patricio provided corn and an ox to the army in February, 1836, and in the same month, Thomas O'Connor at Refugio sent an invoice for $120 for hauling goods to Copano and supplying 3 oxen to Goliad. Another Power-Hewetson colonist, Victor Loupy, supplied Fannin's army with a consignment of 206 beefs and 6 oxen valued at $2,420 in the first three months of 1836. A note attached to Loupy's invoice recorded that "without exertion of said Loupey, that Army must have suffered materially for the want of beef." The colonists were all subsequently paid for provisions and the hauling of goods in support of the Texan cause.[92] What records have survived may not indicate the full scale of the contribution made by colonists to support the Texan forces during the war. John J. Linn's importance has received some recognition. Kathryn O'Connor in a speech on the part the Irish had in the settling of Victoria and vicinity quoted his biographer Victor Rose:

> Juan Linn was the first to counsel opposition to the program of centralisation of the Mexican Government by Santa Anna. Consequently we find him urging action on Austin and his advisors long before they found courage to take up arms. His letters to Austin's colonists were largely instrumental in crystalising sentiment there against the encroachments of Santa Anna. . . . He was, we might say, the liaison officer between the Anglo-American colony on the [one] hand and the Mexican and Irish colonies on the other. His previous residence in New York and New Orleans made him familiar with the American temperament, and his Irish nationality affiliating him with his neighbors in the south, while his command of the Spanish language endeared him to the Mexicans and made him peculiarly fitted for this role. . . . He was a member of the Consultation and elected delegate from Victoria to the Convention at Washington-on-the Brazos which declared Texas independent of Mexico. He was quartermaster for the Texas Army and through heroic efforts kept it supplied with necessities at a time when that was almost impossible. He also supplied Fannin with 20 yoke of oxen to remove the army from Bahia, though by doing so he deprived his own people — even his wife and baby — of the means of transportation to flee from the Mexican army.[93]

Linn's final contribution in the war was to act as interpreter between President Burnell and Santa Anna, after his capture. Within nine months of San Jacinto, he had organized a group of Irish colonists to obtain a shipment of building materials in New Orleans to rebuild their shattered communities in south Texas.

The central importance of the logistics of the campaign became even more apparent by April, 1836, when Santa Anna's army went north in pursuit of the provisional government in Harrisburg and looked to engage Sam Houston's retreating army. The farther north the Mexican armies of Santa Anna and Urrea marched, the greater the logistical problems of supply. The winter of 1835–36 was the coldest in memory, with blizzards of ice and snow having proved a formidable trial to Urrea's troops from Yucatán, who were unaccustomed to cold temperatures. Six of them died in a single night from exposure. Increasingly, a shortage of supplies meant the Mexican armies marched on half rations. Once beyond the Colorado River, the terrain favored the Americans, leaving the grassy coastal prairies for the wooded and marshy ground of east Texas. Fewer Tejanos lived in this area, and it was the stronghold of the American settlements. The terrain at the battle of San Jacinto was highly suited to the American style of warfare. Thick oak groves and the marshland alongside the San Jacinto River were unsuitable country for the Mexican cavalry. Even so, what was most critical to the Mexican defeat at San Jacinto was Santa Anna's elementary mistake in pitching his camp in a vulnerable position. While enjoying an afternoon siesta, his army was surprised and overwhelmed in an action that lasted a mere eighteen minutes. All the advantages gained from previous victories were recklessly thrown away. Even after suffering great losses, the Mexican army remained a substantial force but was forced to withdraw for logistical reasons. The capture of Santa Anna provided a useful bargaining counter for Sam Houston in insisting on the removal of Mexican troops from Texan soil.

The final battle of the war, fought on April 21, 1836, did not resolve the political uncertainty over the Texan border with Mexico, which was not decided until the Treaty of Guadalupe Hidalgo in 1848. During the fragile years of the Texas republic, Mexican raids were a constant threat. A persistent cultural legacy was found in the racial bitterness and suspicion that scarred relations between Anglo-Americans and Mexicans. An enduring influence remained in the cultural borrowing of Tejano equestrian skills by Anglos and Irish settlers, expressed in the adoption of the Spanish saddle, the bandana, and spike-roweled spurs. The improvements in horsemanship that followed the Mexican lessons of the war culminated in the legendary prowess of the Texas Rangers as men on horseback, especially in dealing with the Indian problem.[94] It was paralleled by the cultural transfer of a Hispanic ranching tradition in south Texas (see chapter 6).

Previous histories have assiduously made a roll call of Irish names recorded as present in the battles of the war or as volunteers under various commanders, who represented their communities in the provisional government of Texas or signed the Goliad Declaration and the Declaration of Texan independence.[95] Most of these histories make a positive case for the importance of the Irish contribution, in the hour of need, both on the military and the political front. However, Paul Lack has questioned the role of the San Patricio Irish, arguing that very few enlisted in the Texan cause and confirming that at least some of their leaders were regarded as

Tories and even pro-Mexican in their loyalty. This should be placed in the context of Lack's detailed analysis of the army of the Texas Revolution. Of the 3,685 soldiers who served at any time during the war, about 40 percent came as volunteers from the United States, after the fighting had begun. The combined municipalities of Texas produced just over 2,000 soldiers, or 1 in 20 of the Texas population of around 40,000. According to Lack's own figures, 25 men enlisted from Refugio and 29 from San Patricio, which represented about 8.3 and 4.8 percent of their respective populations. In total, this was slightly above the average figure of 5 percent throughout Texas.[96] Yet enlistment in the army was only one measure of the Irish contribution to the war. The debate might profitably be extended to include other means of assessing the contribution of Irish colonists. Some consideration should be given to the level of loss and suffering inflicted on the people and property of Refugio and San Patricio. This might be regarded as a sacrifice that cemented the loyalty of the survivors to the independence of Texas.

Three further arguments should also be considered. Insufficient attention has been paid to the vital importance of providing supplies for the Texan army. It is no exaggeration to claim that without supplies of beef, horses, and corn offered willingly to the garrisons at San Patricio, Goliad, and Refugio, there would have been no effective resistance to the invading army under General Urrea. Irish colonists James Power, John J. Linn, James McGloin, Nicholas Fagan, and Thomas O'Connor, plus other settlers such as Victor Loupy, took the lead in supplying the army, as surviving accounts reveal, and through their trading contacts in Mexico, Power and Linn were able to forward vital information on the advancing Mexican armies. A notable contribution was also made by leading Irish colonists to the politics of Texas independence. The empresario John McMullen was elected as temporary president of the council. James Power, a respected member of the council and close friend of Sam Houston, used his influence to secure the general's election to the convention as the second delegate from Refugio. In turn, this facilitated his assumption of the role of commander in chief before the San Jacinto campaign.

It can also be argued that in the rapidly shifting developments of Texas politics, where personalities, sectional interests, and regional loyalties all played a part, the command of political experience and knowledge of Spanish, possessed by McMullen, Power, and John J. Linn, were important influences in maintaining the support of leading Tejanos, linking the frontier Irish colonies with the American settlements further north, and breaching the gap between the politicians in San Felipe and the citizen-soldiers in the field. The extent of that gap was illustrated by the hostility directed at the politicians by the signatories of the Goliad Declaration on December 20, 1835. Here the political leadership of Nicholas Fagan deserves recognition and the forty-two Irish signatories to the declaration represent an interesting measure of loyalty to Texas. While this pointed the way to the official declaration of independence on March 2, 1836, Goliad assumed an additional symbolic importance in being twinned in courage and sacrifice with the massacre at the Alamo.

Furthermore, the judgment that the Irish in San Patricio should be considered as traitors to the Texan cause is to view the war in partisan terms and misunderstand the circumstances faced by the Irish colonists at the time. What was clearly influential was that Mexican neighbors in San Patricio had been helpful to the Irish settlers, and the Mexican government had been generous in issuing land grants. Irish colonists were on good terms with the local Mexican garrison at Lipantitlán whose officers treated them well. Arguably, it was an honorable position not to take up arms against the country of their adoption that had provided them with the ownership of land and the rights of citizenship. The circumstances were different in Refugio where the Irish had experienced strained relations with their Mexican neighbors in Goliad. Moreover, at an individual level, strong friendships between Irish and Mexican families prevailed against the pressures of war. During the conflict, John J. Linn was helped to escape to New Orleans by the De León family. The Fagans, Andrew Boyle, and others were saved from the massacre at Goliad by the intercession of Mexican friends. Local conditions and personal friendships transcended the divisions created by the war and affected the lives of individual colonists. It is also worth making a distinction between those Irish colonists that lost family members or all their possessions and others who gained through securing bounty land and payment for army contracts. The war did not provide a common experience for all the Irish colonists. It was not merely the difference in allegiance between the San Patricio Irish and the Refugio Irish. The war accelerated the differences between families, extending the bitter experience of earlier deaths from cholera and shipwreck in 1834. By 1836 some families were worse off through death and destruction, others prospered with more land and capital to invest for the future.

Finally, the great suffering endured by the Irish colonists of San Patricio and Refugio during the conflict represented a disproportionate loss of property and loss of life, which was to have a profound effect on their sense of identity. Following the killing of King's men at Refugio, the massacre of Fannin's men at Goliad, and the symbolic power of the heroic deaths of Travis, Bowie, and Crockett at the Alamo, the surviving Irish colonists felt that they had shared in a "blood sacrifice" that strengthened their allegiance to the infant republic of Texas and confirmed their attachment to the land granted to them by the Mexican government. These sentiments were expressed in a letter written with great pride at the time, celebrating the participation of Walter Lambert and Thomas O'Connor in the battle of San Jacinto, and later were enlisted as an argument in defense of the settlers' right to their land.

I have never sold one dollars worth [of property] since but every article of them have been plundered and taken away by the Mexicans last spring when the[y] came on with the intension of ecterminating us or Compelling us to Submit to their new formed despotic Government we being compelled from the perimtory demand made to take one side or the other in case of not complying forfiture of our property we being patriots we clung to the Republican Party and cleared the country of the desolation that threatened on every quarter around us. In doing so I was compelled to abandon every article that was movable [except] the most serviceable of my clothes as they came on surprise. I will at a future period give you all a long verbal history of the present Revolution which I participated in some of the victories won on our side. Thomas O'Connor & Walter Lambert [original Irish colonists] have shared in one of the greatest victories we can read of in the annals of war both have proved themselves worthy the donation our infant Republican Government is generous enough to bestow on each individual that participated in the said Battle of San jacynto which is half a league of land.[97]

The principle of military involvement in the war, advanced by the colonists themselves as a defense of land grants acquired from the Mexican government, may be extended to incorporate the idea of contribution to the war effort in justification of their retention under Texan law. A compelling case can be made in the totality of an Irish contribution made up from the number of the soldiers in Dimitt's command at Goliad, those who died at the Alamo and those who were killed or who escaped from the massacre at Goliad, and from those who fought in the final victory at San Jacinto.[98]

It has been argued that the language of freedom varied with the participants involved and was, at least in part, a cover for the protection of other interests — land and political power — and that the stubborn resistance to the threat of a despotic government by citizen- soldiers did not represent an articulate philosophy of democratic politics but a defense of land acquired and freedom demanded from government interference in frontier life. Significantly, land was confiscated from colonists who surrendered with Colonel Fannin. This reinforces the view that for both sides land was a key issue. If it was claimed as a Protestant victory, nonetheless Catholic Tejanos and Catholic Irish contributed to it. There was no lack of courage, but it was not all found on one side. Texan and Mexican troops were called on to display it in ample measure. Military victories were more often the result of one side enjoying advantages of weaponry or terrain, with the Kentucky long rifle and the Mexican cavalry holding the aces, provided they enjoyed an accommodating setting. Nor was cruelty a uniquely Mexican trait. The executions at Refugio and Goliad, directly ordered by Santa Anna, were deplorable but were condemned by fellow Mexican officers. And they were paralleled by the butchering of the retreating Mexican army before prisoners were taken at San Jacinto.

How far was the war a turning point in history? It was certainly momentous in gaining Texas its independence from Mexico, but the new republic, impoverished and vulnerable to further attack, could only survive as part of the larger union of the United States. The dispute concerning the Texan southern border of the Rio Grande was not settled until the end of the U.S.- Mexico War in 1848. The future of Texas would be as part of the American South, the Confederacy, and after the Civil War, once again part of the United States, but a Mexican presence remained and a cultural legacy long persisted, especially in south Texas.

Those colonists who had survived the war and gradually returned to restore their property were still to face the rigors of a tough, pioneering life in the settlements centered on San Patricio and Refugio that had been abandoned and virtually destroyed.

The Life of Pioneer Settlers in Texas

As an old lady remarked, Texas was "a heaven for men and dogs, but a hell for women and oxen."
—Noah Smithwick, *The Evolution of a State, or, Recollections of Old Texas Days*

THE IDEA OF THE FRONTIER

The experience of the Irish pioneer settlers not only coincided with the epic events of the Texas Revolution but also was shaped by a broader phenomenon—the influence of the frontier. Largely omitted in previous histories, the everyday life of the pioneer settlers is examined within the context of the academic debate on frontier values. In turn, this leads to discussion of the contribution of the early settlers to the development of Texas during the nineteenth century. How can the success of individual Irish-born pioneers in Texas be explained in comparison with the relative hardships of Irish immigrants who settled in East Coast cities such as Boston and New York? How does the Irish experience in Texas fit with the notion of the "culture of exile," which has been offered as an explanation of the difficulties the Catholic rural Irish faced in coming to terms with life in urban America? These issues are explored in this chapter.

The idea of the frontier has exercised an immensely powerful hold over the American imagination and, in turn, images of the frontier have been adopted all around the world.[1] The existence of the frontier and its closure at the end of the last century has been heralded as a defining influence in the modern world. Since Frederick Jackson Turner's seminal essay "The Significance of the Frontier in American History," published in 1893, the academic debate has continued on the role of the frontier in shaping the way America developed. Turner claimed that the frontier experience explained the nature of American democracy and forged the values of American citizens. The availability of "free land" and the frontier influence on the pioneer-hero were seen as central to the development of American institutions:

> The frontier is the line of most rapid and effective Americanisation. The wilderness masters the colonist. It finds him in European dress, industries, tools, modes of travel and thought. It takes him from the railroad car and pits him in the birch canoe. It strips off the garments of civilisation and arrays him in the hunting shirt and the moccasin, it puts him in the log cabin of the Cherokee and Iroquois. . . . In short, at the frontier the environment is at first too strong for the man. He must accept the conditions which it furnishes, or perish. Little by little he transforms the wilderness, but the outcome is not the old Europe, not simply the development of Germanic germs. . . . The fact is, here is a new product that is American. . . . Thus the advance of the frontier has meant a steady movement away from the influence of Europe, a steady growth of independence on American lines.[2]

Expanding on the Turner thesis, the Texas historian Walter Prescott Webb developed the theory of the frontier, defining it as a force for the disintegration of the cultural baggage that Europeans brought with them to the New World. In a characteristic phrase, he argued that "European institutions and practices wore themselves out against the abrasive frontier grindstone."[3] Webb believed that the individual, finding himself alone in the presence of nature,

> could do in this new environment anything he wanted to do and as much of it as he wanted to do without human opposition. For example, if he wanted to cut down trees, kill game, or navigate streams, he could cut, kill, and navigate without seeking a permit or running afoul of a policeman. The hazard that the tree might fall on him, the game tear him to pieces, or the stream drown him was his own lookout, he was neither prohibited nor rescued from his own acts. Nature viewed anything he did with a cold and impersonal, though sometimes a kindly eye. He found his own rewards and his own punishments, a double responsibility which in the first instance developed his boldness, initiative, and aggressiveness, and in the second fostered wariness, caution and circumspection — acknowledged frontier traits. The fact that

this man found his own rewards and punishments, and complete self-responsibility for his fortunes, did things to his psychology. It was natural that he who survives in such a situation would come to think very well of himself. It is true that many did not survive, could not stand the frontier and so they dropped out of the problem, leaving the stage to those who had learned their lines.[4]

Webb's defense of the frontier was driven paradoxically by important influences drawn from European thinkers: a Wordsworthian belief in nature as a benign force for good while at the same time it operated as a theater for a Darwinian survival of the fittest. So the frontier was both egalitarian in shedding Old World obsessions of rank and social hierarchy, and individualistic and competitive in allowing the strongest to come out on top.

By contrast, travel writers, still retaining the prejudices of European civilization, were more prone to emphasize the barbaric rather than the noble features of frontier life. Ray Billington, a leading historian of the American West, has collected examples of the genre that depict the westward-moving pioneers as seizing the opportunity to escape from civilized ways. For instance, the seventeenth-century pioneers of the Swedish settlements on the Delaware River were depicted as "not much better" than savages and given over to fighting, drunkenness, and laziness. In the Carolina backwoods of the eighteenth century, a minister was bluntly dismissed by the settlers who wanted "no D — d Black Gown Sons of Bitches among them" to interfere with their constant "Revelling, Drinking, Singing, Dancing, and Whoring." He went on to report that on the frontier "many hund[reds] do live in Concumbinage, swapping their wives as Cattel, and living in a State of Nature, more irregularly and unchastely than the Indians." If the frontier allowed uninhibited social conduct and looser moral standards, Billington claims it was not "inhabited solely by profane tobacco-spitting, nose-biting, eye-gouging, half-horse-and-half-alligator riproarers." What is argued is that the frontier legend of lawlessness was propagated by a few centers — the Mississippi river towns where the mountain men made their annual rendezvous, the cattle towns, mining camps, and the "hells on wheels" of the railway crews. While the hell-raising of these places was endlessly reported for their sensational newspaper copy, the numbers involved represented only a small proportion of pioneer settlers.[5]

A further distortion by western travelers lay in the description of frontiersmen as fugitives from justice — debtors, delinquents, and malefactors who fled from the laws of civilized society and became illegal squatters on frontier lands. Texas acquired a reputation for attracting more than its fair share of such characters, who abandoned wives and homes and escaped from a run-in with the sheriff when leaving the southern states to settle on cheap land available in Texas. Billington claims that the true pioneers were, in fact, the thousands of small farmers, ranchers, and entrepreneurs who formed the bulk of those who moved west. Unlike their more colorful fellow pioneers, the reprobates or indolent backwoodsmen, these sober and industrious frontiersmen were the founders of a western culture. Moreover, it was a culture that inevitably included much that was imported from the civilized eastern states.

By the 1960s traditional ways of depicting the frontier story came to be regarded by historians as "racist, sexist and imperialist."[6] There was discomfort over the violent conquest of the Indians; the notion of free land on the frontier was discredited; and the archetypal Anglo-Saxon frontiersman was found to be unrepresentative of western settlers. Meanwhile, the appeal of western myths and folklore continued unabated among the American public. What followed was the new western history that not only incorporated the contemporary issues but also returned to one of Turner's key ideas. Turner had argued that the process of invasion, settlement, and community formation repeated itself in a wave of sequential frontiers. So successive frontiers could be studied in a comparative way. Conflict gave way to the formation of new structures and to more stable regions across America.

The general characteristics identified by new western historians are applicable to the Irish pioneers who settled in south Texas. So a broader framework of reference can rescue their experience from the merely parochial and connect it to a fuller version of the American West. Four general characteristics of frontier life are applicable:

1. The frontier, often seen as isolated, was in fact connected to other parts of the world. European economies and merchants (including the Irish empresarios all of whom had merchant backgrounds) were central to the creation of colonies in the New World, and European expansion involved the movement of people looking for new opportunities (including the Irish migrants who settled in Texas).

2. The frontier was a place where displaced migrants brought the familiar world of European values with them and looked to change with the opportunities that opened up for them. Irish and Catholic values were retained but new opportunities to acquire land, to enter professions and the business world, were seized on by Irish settlers in Texas.

3. Frontier communities were peripheral to imperial, metropolitan centers. They were perennially short of labor and capital, and frontier economies were extractive, transferring nonindustrial resources to more populous areas. The Irish settlements in Texas were dependent on New Orleans for trade and for access to capital. With the development of ranching, beefs were exported by sea to New Orleans before the northern markets opened up.

4. The remoteness of frontier life undermined social and political hierarchies. State power was weak; economic activity was poorly regulated; and cultural innovation faced few barriers. A lack of political and economic controls was a factor in the conflict of the Texas Revolution. The coexistence of European and native traditions allowed for a genuine mixture of cultures. This was especially evident in the intermarriage of Irish and Mexican families, the more easily facilitated by the common bond of the Catholic religion.

The isolation of frontier life meant that within the structure of the family it was often the women who maintained some rudiments of civilized standards, and the upholders of civilized values were the group of cultivated people who assumed positions of leadership over the rest of the community. Food, clothing, medicine, care of the children, and the preservation of a form of worship were the natural and enduring concern of women pioneers. Herein lies one of the paradoxes about the reporting of frontier life. What has been celebrated repeatedly is the image of the frontiersman, armed with an ax and a rifle, a rugged individual who tamed a wilderness, subjugated native Indians, and built settled communities. In Texas the pioneer settlers not only were part of what became the American frontier but also took on the sanctified role of archetypal figures who helped establish an independent republic against the tyranny of the Mexican president and generalissimo Santa Anna. The creation of frontier virtues was overwhelmingly depicted as the construction of a male world. Yet most of the surviving contemporary accounts of pioneer life, apart from the reports of military campaigns, that allow us some understanding of the frontier experience in Texas, were written by women.

Clearly, women were the guardians of the family network and the pre-servers of family histories.

Most of these surviving accounts were memoirs, written or dictated in old age. Inevitably, with the lapse of time, some distortion and selectivity are part of the long-remembered past. A greater sense of immediacy was present in letters written at the time, and there was also the possibility of more introspective accounts of pioneer life. Other surviving accounts are the stories and anecdotes handed down the generations within families. These have sometimes been written up in newspaper and magazine articles by journalists with an eye for good copy for the general public. Old Texas tales, especially those that recall the pioneer frontier days, form part of a literary genre that perpetuates popular myths.[7] Taken together, it is possible to reconstruct some practical aspects of the life of the Irish settlers in Texas, but the forms and traditions of such writings have to be recognized and the meanings contained in them require interpretation that is inevitably subjective.

PIONEER LIFE

In acknowledging the situation of the colonists who arrived to obtain their land grants under the auspices of the Mexican government in the period 1829 to 1835, the political figure W. H. Wharton provides a context in an address to the nation in April, 1836:

> The donation of 4428 acres, sounds largely at a distance. Considering, however, the difficulty and danger necessarily encountered in taking possession of those lands it will not be deemed an entire gratuity nor a magnificent bounty. If this territory had been previously pioneered by the enterprise of the Mexican government, and freed from the insecurities which beset a wilderness — trod only by savages — if the government had been deriving an actual revenue from it and if it could have realised a capital from the sale of it — then we admit that the donation would have been unexampled in the history of national liberality. But how lamentably different from all this was the real state of the case. The lands granted were in the occupancy of savages, and situated in a wilderness of which the government had never taken possession, and they were not sufficiently explored to obtain that knowledge of their character and situation necessary to a sale of them. They were shut out from all commercial intercourse with the rest of the world, and inac-

cessible to the commonest comforts of life; nor were they brought into possession and cultivation by the colonists without much toil and privation, and patience and enterprise, and suffering and blood, and loss of lives from Indian hostilities, and other causes. Under the smiles of a benignant heaven, however, the untiring perseverance of the colonists triumphed over all natural obstacles, expelled the savages by whom the country was infested, reduced the forest into cultivation and made the desert smile.[8]

Special pleading apart in defense of the Texan cause, there was a substantive truth in the statement of the conditions faced by the pioneer settlers. Irish families, who had arrived on the Texas coast by sea, made their final trek inland by covered wagon, oxcart, and horseback. While the children slept or played in the back, the mother would often drive while the father went ahead to choose the best road: "At first it is a novelty," one account recalls, "but the weather changes — the rain falls, crossings are filled bank to bank. There is nothing to do but wait. They must camp in the river bottoms until it runs down. Mosquitoes, insects of all kinds, harass them. Poisonous snakes lurk in the driftwood. Panthers, bears, leopard cats infest the woods. But most of all is the fear of stealthy Indians who may come upon them and massacre them all."

Where men delighted in describing the teeming wildlife to be killed at will, women were more sensitive to the dangers of wandering unprotected through a wilderness.

Along with the brave pioneer is the pioneer woman, who shares her part of the burden. She must cook, she must wash, she must watch over her children. If they are sick she must nurse them in a crude way. At last they reach their home. A house must be built; until then, they live in camp. It was generally of logs or pickets covered with palmetto. Made of mud or stones, the chimney was of importance, for here the meals were prepared. The hearth was 18 inches high for convenience. Boiling was done in vessels hanging from a crane; frying, with coals raked out of the fireplace; baking, in a Dutch oven. My mother related that my grandmother, Eliza Sullivan, had a large Dutch oven built in her yard. The hired man fired it Friday night and kept it burning until morning. Saturday, it was cleaned of ashes, and with a long paddle she would put in 20 pies, 10 or 12 loaves of bread, and her cakes and cookies. They would bake perfectly and have a flavor unexcelled. The Pioneer woman arose early and milked eight or ten long-horned cows, that had to be hobbled or tied to a post, to get as much milk as one Jersey cow gives now. She parched and ground her coffee, made her bread, cured her meat, tended her poultry and garden, moulded her candles, made the soap – and with water carried from the well the clothes were kept as white as snow. There were no sewing machines and her family was clothed by the stitch-stitch of her nimble fingers. Her husband's suits rivaled the tailor made. His shirts were ornate, unlike those of to-day. Her own clothes reflected her artistic hand. Her children, likewise, wore clothes adorned by the mother's deft fingers. We marvel that these women had time for church and social duties, and for neighborly kindness. Then there were no nurses and few doctors; consequently, the neighbors helped one another.[9]

While the details of women's work was recalled with accuracy, the sentimental tone of the above account owes something to fond memories of childhood relived in old age. This may also have been an idealized standard of domestic perfection to which most could only aspire.

The first settlement seen by Rosalie Hart Priour on her arrival with her mother at the Mission Refugio in 1834, consisted of "only four houses or rather huts."[10] With the mission church used as a store house for corn by the Mexicans, there was no temporary accommodation to be had for the newly arrived migrants. "We had to camp out. There was no place to shelter even the sick. Mother piled up her trunks and the farming utensils about ten feet from the church and covered overhead with bed clothes, so as to form a tent. It was not very comfortable quarters, but it was the best we could do. No one would build a house for us before they provided for their own families, but promised as soon as that was done to build a house for mother."[11]

Rosalie's father, Tom Hart, had died on the beach soon after their arrival in Texas, and she and her mother had no one to build a house or to fence a field, so a surveyor, Isaac Robinson, taking pity on them, offered to share his large house on Papalote Creek about thirty-five miles from the mission. On the same creek lived Robert Carlisle and his family. These were the only two houses between Refugio and San Patricio. Apparently Robinson told Mrs. Hart that his wife would be too lonesome by herself and the house was large enough for two families. They had a large field already fenced. If the Harts would hire a man to work the field, they could have one half of the crop raised. So Rosalie Hart and her mother went to live with the Robinson family in Papalote Creek. The first sighting of the house and its location made a lasting impression on the young child:

> The situation is one of the finest in Texas. The house was built on the bank of the creek and shaded by live-oaks with tops in the shape of umbrellas. The wild grapevines covered the trees and formed a nice, cool arbor the sun could not penetrate. Wild flowers of every variety and in the greatest profusion covered the plains as far as the eye could reach. To me it seemed like a miniature paradise. That summer was a very happy one, and the remembrance makes me love it better than anything on earth. My little sister Mary Ann, the only one left to share my joys and sorrows was now old enough to go around with me, and join in play. I would leave her on the bank of the creek while I would wade into the water to catch crabs and softshell turtles. At other times, we would go hunting turtle eggs along the sand of the creek, or out on the prairies after dewberries.[12]

Unhappily such great promise was unfulfilled. Despite raising a splendid crop, the two families were unable to harvest it and were forced by the fear of hostile Indians to leave the farm and return to Refugio. A feeling of abundance was also apparent in a surviving letter from Jemima and Mary Toll that described a safe arrival from New York via New Orleans to Matagorda before settling in San Patricio: "I found this country equal to what was said in the hand bills and better again, do not believe Martin M. or any person who went from here; poor lazy creatures having no inclinations to look after any prudence or industry, really I was astonished when I came amongst the colonists to see them all full of comfort, plenty of Corn, bread Mush Butter Milk and beef and what perhaps those who sent this false report never enjoyed before. As for pigs and fowls they are numerous as flees."[13] The letter acknowledged that some had given up on pioneer life and continued with sound, practical advice on what essentials would-be colonists should bring to Texas:

> John Parrot and Henry met me at the bar, is well, has a large stock of cattle of every description. The freight from Orleans here is 50 cents per foot, a Barrel from $2 to 2.50. Bring some boxes of glass, bars soap, plenty candle wicks, bring seeds of every kind, shallots; bring cross cut, whip and frame saws. Let Simon not delay to come as he will find everything according to your wishes. Bring good guns, and powder and shot

of every kind. . . . Bring as many cart wheels and cart mountings as you can, Chains for oxen; no timber, as this is the country for timber of every kind. Bring good Ploughs. Carts rate at $100, here. Bring a supply of sugar coffee and tea and flour for 8 or 9 months; if you have any to spare, you get your price. Gun locks and every thing belonging to locks, screws of every kind, plates for screws Your goods both small and large and every little article you can pack. Pots, pans with covers, ovens &, white muslin both white and brown in pieces. Bring tin cups. Porringers. Any man working 2 days in the week may take his gun and fishing rod the remainder and his horse. Bring your clean english blankets both second hand and new, as you'l get a horse for one fowl. Bring a candle mould. Bring Jerry a good long fowling piece. . . . You'll have no work, your daughters can milk 50 cows for you. . . . The healthiest country in the world. The richest land will show like Gentlemens domains in Ireland. Fine wood and water as in any part of the world. As for game and fowl and fish of every kind no man can believe, but those that see.[14]

The letter offered a contrast between a natural abundance providing a sense of well-being and the urgent need to provide basic necessities that were clearly unavailable on the frontier. This captures important features of what the pioneer colonists faced. Equally revealing is the aspiration among the colonists to have a life of relative ease, an unrealistic ambition, given the harsh conditions inherent in living in a wilderness. The reference to a man working only two days a week while enjoying the pleasures of hunting for game or fishing for the remainder of the week was obviously intended to appeal, but even more so was the enticing prospect of becoming like the gentry, the much-reviled landowners of Ireland. This would have represented a social transformation for the likes of small tenant farmers and artisans who could have had no such dreams realized at home.

To secure the fulfillment of such a grand and prosperous life in Texas, it was necessary to have a stable political situation with property protected by an established system of law and civil peace. For all the natural resources on hand and the possession of generous land grants, the colonists had to face the uncomfortable truth that they could not rely on any but their own resources to protect themselves from hostile Indian tribes, Mexican bandits, and assorted desperadoes.

The disturbances and destruction of property that drove out Rosalie Hart's family were a frequent hazard of early pioneer life. Indeed, wholesale destruction was the fate of both Irish settlements during the Texas

Revolution. Pat Burke recalled how his family returned after the battle of San Jacinto from New Orleans to San Patricio. They found their homes had been destroyed; the country was without supplies; and hard times stared them in the face. For the next ten years, the area was subject to both Mexican and Indian raids. They had to rebuild their homes:

> We soon constructed log house, made picket fashion, with dirt floors and thatched roofs, clapboards being used to stop the cracks between the pickets. Our pioneer architecture was simple and inexpensive, and did not require the outlay of large sums of money for plans, specifications, material and construction, but doubtless as much peace, contentment and real happiness was found dwelling in our quaint old homes as we now find in the palatial homes in our towns and cities. Our table fare, bread and meat, was also simple, but for our digestive organs were always good, and dyspepsia never interfered with the keen relish and fine appetites we always carried to the table with us. We drank water from the creeks, ponds barrels and cow tracks, enjoyed good health and never heard of microbes, germ theories and diseases of modern times.[15]

The accounts of Rosalie Hart and Pat Burke, while providing invaluable details of house construction, the simple daily fare on the frontier, and the delightful playground for young children living in a wilderness, possess an unmistakable tone of sentimentality conjured by memories of youth recalled in old age. Nostalgia and sentiment formed a powerful partnership in western writing. There was also a deep attachment to the beauty of the natural world. Independent, tough, and resourceful, the pioneers were also clearly at one with what they saw as God's creation.

By the 1850s frame houses were being built, reflecting the more settled times after the war between the United States and Mexico and the annexation of Texas by the United States. John Dunn recalled the house his newly arrived Irish grandfather built near Corpus Christi in 1852, which was still standing a century later.

> There were several smaller buildings detached from the main building, one was the dining-room and the kitchen. There was also a large circular underground cistern, made of material composed of sand and shell from the shores of the Bay. Beneath the house there was a basement or cellar, as it was called in those days – something that very few houses in this country had. The two front rooms were large. My child-

Family sitting in horse-drawn buggy in front of McGuill store. *Courtesy Anne McGuill Hawkins*

hood memory gives me this picture of the parlor: It was two steps lower than the Master's bedroom. A large fire-place in each room. Horse-hair upholstered furniture, marble top table-pictures of Daniel O'Connell, Robert Emmet, and a large picture of all the Popes from Pope Peter to Pope Leo XIII. A large posted bed with a canopy over it dominated Grandfather's room. In one corner there was a large book-case filled with books, a large wardrobe of mahogany, a sofa to match, and a center table and rocking chairs. The rest of the house consisted of a couple of smaller bedrooms and a large one in the attic, an entry hall between my Aunt's room and the pantry, a long front porch across the front– (gallery as we called it). The large yard was enclosed with a white picket fence. There was a long grape arbor, a number of plum trees and a peach tree, several shade trees and flowers, a vegetable garden, barn, stables, stock pens, sheds, chicken-house, pig pen, and a good well.[16]

This account points to the better accommodation and furnishings that became possible by the 1850s and also includes reference to the commemoration of Irish political heroes, Emmet and O'Connell, and the continued allegiance to the Catholic faith. In adapting to a new life as pioneer settlers and becoming citizens of the United States, the Dunn family characteristically retained their faith as part of their Irish identity. A staunch loyalty to the land they left was a common trait among western settlers and Irish migrants took an affection for Ireland with them.

To what extent the old values and identities that migrants brought with them from more settled communities in Europe or the United States were retained and how far life on the frontier shaped new values and customs is a matter of conjecture. Did the frontier act as a grindstone wearing down on old ways, as Walter Prescott Webb has argued? Or as Ray Billington has suggested, did some of the trappings of civilization in the form of religious faith, a reverence for learning, and an aspiration to respectability withstand the harsh struggle for survival among pioneer settlers? I suggest that the old and the new merged together to form a culture that still owed something both to the place of origin and to the place of new settlement. After all, frontier society itself was an amalgam of different peoples. In the case of the Irish settlements of San Patricio and Refugio, these were composed of two kinds of Irish migrants: those recruited from various parts of the United States who had come from Ireland some years or some months before coming to Texas and those who came directly from Ireland. Most of the San Patricio Irish came via the United States, but some came directly from Tipperary and other more westerly counties of Ireland. The Refugio Irish had mostly come directly from Wexford and other southeastern parts of Ireland but were joined by some who came with McMullen and McGloin and accepted grants in Refugio offered by James Power. To the Irish settlers were added significant numbers of Mexicans, among them high-born and sophisticated families of Spanish descent who were settled on the land already, and a smaller number of American and other European settlers who looked to take advantage of the land grants available under the empresario system.

When Nicholas Fagan's daughter Annie married Peter Teal in January, 1833, at the family ranch on the banks of the San Antonio River, the marriage services were conducted by a Mexican priest at the church in La Bahía. Among the guests were the Indian chief, Prudentia and his wife, Rosa Marie, who spoke Spanish. In her old age, Annie Fagan Teal recalled the splendor and style of the Spanish ladies:

This little town [La Bahía] was settled largely by wealthy, intelligent Spanish people. Among them was a family named Hernandez, who always invited the colonists to make their house a home whenever they came to the village to church. The lady of the house, though with hosts of servants at her command, would greet them in her own soft language say: "Pass on, ladies; I stay to serve you." Before going to church, she would replace their sunbonnets with silken crepe shawls. Mrs. Teal says she never in her life saw such handsomely dressed ladies as she once saw in this little village at La Bahía. It was Independence Day of the Indians of Mexico and was being celebrated on the 16th of September, 1832. Inside a gaily decorated carriage sat a little Indian girl, dressed in all the splendor of Indian royalty; long lines of white ribbons were fastened to the carriage and held by twelve elegantly dressed Spanish ladies who walked on either side, while the carriage was pushed forward by officers of high rank, and soldiers marched in front. . . . The Spanish ladies were dressed in silks that would stand alone, costly laces, jewels rich and rare of beautiful Mexican workmanship.[17]

This is a good example of the blending of cultures as a general characteristic of frontier life. This melting pot syndrome was recognized by Mary Austin Holley, writing on everyday life on the Texas frontier in 1831: "With regard to the state of society here, as natural to expect, there are many incongruities. It will take some time for people gathered from the north, and from the south, from the east, and from the west, to assimilate, and adapt themselves to new situations." But she observed that the commonality of their experience and their equal start had already given them certain attributes that could be ascribed to the conditions of frontier life.

The people are universally kind and hospitable, which are redeeming qualities. Everybody's house is open, and table spread, to accommodate the traveller. There are no poor people here, and none rich; that is, none who have much money. The poor and the rich, to use the correlatives, where distinction, there is none, get the same quantity of land on arrival, and if they do not continue equal, it is for want of good management on the one part, or superior industry or sagacity on the other. All are happy, because busy; and none meddle with the affairs of their neighbors, because they have enough to do to take care of their own. They are bound together, by a common interest, by the sameness of purpose, and hopes. As far as I could learn, they have no envyings, no jealousies, no bickerings, through politics or fanaticism. There is neither masonry, anti-masonry, nullification nor court intrigues.[18]

As a cousin of Stephen F. Austin, Holley might be expected to show a certain degree of special pleading for the contentment of Austin's colonists, but clearly discernible in this account is the easy affability and hospitality that was commonly found in frontier society. Furthermore, the old class distinctions, at least in the early years, were much less in evidence. Facing common dangers and the absolute necessity of relying on the cooperation of neighbors in emergencies must have developed a unity of purpose and outlook. Indeed, the friendship and loyalties of Irish and Mexican neighbors on the San Antonio River were often to transcend the barriers thrown up by war and revolution.

However, the evidence of other contemporary accounts relating the experience of the Irish colonists suggests that Mary Austin Holley's picture of everyday life in Texas was rather too wholesome and comfortable. Thomas Gunning, an Irish settler at San Patricio who returned to New York after finding pioneer life not to his taste, suggested that all was not sweetness and light in the relations between the empresarios and their fellow colonists:

> The magistrates are called Alcaldes they go often without shoes to their feet they are elected every two years and often not without a sharp contest, we were represented as slaves by McMullen & the McGs [McGloins] to the Authorities on account of the distance we were from the seat of Government,—located at Salta [Saltillo] 11 hundred miles from Texas, but the Revd. M. Doyle a R.C. Clergyman went to Salta it took him 9 weeks on horseback, and removed that obstacle. White People are never recognised slaves in the Republic, yet once going in, there is no leaving without a passport signed by the Magistrate which cost us no verey little trouble to obtain. Jerry Toole that was Brickmaker at Cloonasurra, & family together with many others are there yet, however we availed ourselves of the first opportunity of leaving & reached Burlington 300 miles W. of New Orleans where we got very Good encouragement but anxious to locate in a City at last for a time, we came within three miles of Orleans where Kitty took sick & died.[19]

HEALTH AND SICKNESS

Food shortages and killer diseases were common experiences that faced the colonists from their earliest days in Texas. Rosalie Hart Priour described how the Refugio colonists, who had already been decimated in number through many cholera deaths both in New Orleans and on their arrival on the Texas coast, were faced with a new outbreak of illness within six weeks, when they were almost all taken sick with flux:

> Mother and one more lady (I have forgotten her name) were the only ones left in the place to take care of the sick. The other lady would stay, and go from house to house doing what she could to relieve the suffering and mother had a block put in the middle of the river large enough to set her wash out on and she would wash twelve dozen pieces every day. She could not iron them, for it was all she could do to wash for so many sick, besides when it was too late for her to wash she would go around among the sick and help make them comfortable for the night. My share of the work was to cook, and keep the house clean, take care of my sister and carry mother's dinner to her so that she would lose no time from the washing, and as I was not quite eight years old and sister about a year and a half, I had all I could do and work hard. With all our exertions we could not save all, a great many died. It was dreadful to look at them after death, their eyes were always wide open and as clear as crystal and impossible to close them. As my mother always said, "God always fits the back for the burden." If He had not given her superhuman strength, she must have succumbed under the troubles of that year.[20]

In 1835 Rosalie's mother, whose husband had died on their arrival in Texas, married a fellow Power-Hewetson colonist, John James, who had lost his wife in the cholera epidemic in 1834. During the Texas Revolution, John James joined first Dimitt's and then Ira Westover's company before being captured by Karankawa auxiliaries of the Mexican army. He was surrendered to General Urrea and killed at the Goliad massacre in March, 1836. Mrs. Hart now had his two children and two of her own as well as several cows in the pen to look after. One evening she found the cows so contrary that

> she was as wet with sweat as if she had fallen in the river. She did not stop to change her clothes until she had finished milking the cows, and her work done up for the night. She did not feel the effect of the evening's work that night, but the next day she was taken down with pleurisy and remained speechless. There was no doctor in the place, ... and everyone had their houses fastened up and were afraid to leave their houses. My mother was speechless for two weeks and the

only thing I could do for her was to keep her mouth wet with tea. I had heard that certain herbs which grew across the river from our house were medicinal and I made it a rule to go over every day and gather what I thought I would need, with those herbs I made tea and wet her lips with it every few minutes.[21]

Imported diseases from Europe killed thousands of Indians and destroyed their way of life. But smallpox, cholera, and yellow fever could strike indiscriminately. Cholera had already decimated the numbers of would-be Irish colonists in New Orleans and on the Texas coast, and the survivors would have been weakened by the disease. The level of ignorance with regard to treatment meant that so-called cures may have done as much harm as the disease itself. The concept of germs and the dissemination of cholera by contaminated water was unknown, so any number of fanciful ideas were circulated as to its cause and cure. Pulverized black pepper mixed with opium made into pills and washed down with brandy and water; the old standby of "bleeding"; ten drops of laudanum repeated every three hours; and a prescription of calomel, peppermint, asafetida, tobacco, aloes, camphor, and garlic, some to be taken internally and others administered in poultices and injections – these were among the oddball ideas of the time. With unerring confidence, a Dr. A. G. Goodlet, late surgeon of the Seventh Regiment, could write in the *Nacogdoches Times* in 1849, "That the disease is conveyed in the atmosphere there seems to be no reason to doubt, or that it is wafted in currents."[22]

Cholera was a fatal digestive disorder with around half of the cases ending in death. Not diagnosed correctly until 1883, it was brought to the American continent from India in 1832, and three major outbreaks occurred before the Civil War between 1832 and 1854. To early settlers in Texas, cholera was the most feared of epidemic diseases. Death could occur within a few hours of the first symptoms. A graphic description of the progress of the disease was recorded in May, 1849, by a surgeon at Camp Salado near San Antonio:

The formal onset of the disease was preceded some twenty hours by a diarrhoea when profuse vomiting and purging of the characteristic discharge (having the appearance of water in which rice has been washed) commenced, attended by painful cramps in the stomach, calves of the legs, thighs, and arms – especially the flexor muscles of the fore-arms. The eyes had a dull, watery and muddy appearance, with a contracted, ill-defined pupil. The features became sharpened, and the entire body was blue, shrunken, shrivelled, cold, and clammy. The hands and fingers shrunken and sodden. The tongue gave to the finger a cold and disagreeable sensation. The patient complained of severe pain in the stomach, loins, and limbs; of insatiable thirst; and a burning heat in the stomach, and distressing heat of the surface of the body; although to the hand it had the cold feeling of a dead body.[23]

The 1849 cholera epidemic was the most devastating across both sides of the border. In San Antonio, 600 deaths occurred out of a population of 1,500. In Matamoros, 20 percent of the 5,000 inhabitants died.

Malaria, though less often lethal than cholera, was endemic, accounting for more than a quarter of cases of sickness among frontier soldiers in Texas. The widespread prevalence of malaria was an important deterrent to the settlement of Texas, posing a more serious problem than fears associated with Indian or Mexican attacks. Ignorance of the infected *Anopheles* mosquito as the cause of malaria led doctors to attribute miasmas to the exhalations from decaying animal and vegetable matter in marshy areas. Fortunately, quinine was recognized as a treatment that effectively limited fatalities.

Yellow fever was also a much-feared disease. Spread by the *Aedes aegypti* mosquito, it tended to be found on the coastal regions of Texas. Outbreaks occurred in 1839, 1847, 1848, 1853, 1854, 1858, and 1859. The outbreak of 1853 spread along the coast from New Orleans where it killed between 8,000 to 9,000 of the city's 150,000 population in a period of five months, making it the worst epidemic ever experienced in the city's history. Texas fared slightly better. While no civilian figures survive, 229 soldiers were affected with 50 fatalities. The 1858 epidemic was worse. It was introduced via an infected steamer from New Orleans. In Brownsville, 76 of the soldiers were attacked and half of them died. Doctors applied depletive remedies to little effect, general and local blood-letting, and calomel combined with quinine.[24]

A preoccupation with sickness and health emerges from the surviving correspondence of the Plummer family, American colonists who settled at Live Oak Point in the Power-Hewetson colony. Joseph Plummer, who became a customs official at Aransas, speculated on the land purchased in 1837 increasing in value. At first the tone of the letters to Alabama was upbeat: "I am in good health and much pleased with the country," he wrote to his son Frances.[25] A month later, he continued writing in a similarly optimistic vein: "the country is certainly the choice spot of this continent good land healthy and – sea coast and the most delightful climate peach trees in bloom 10 days ago and I have seen young sprouts a foot long some days past and with you the snow perhaps is now on the ground the swallows returned the 1st day of March and are as musical as in May."[26] By the end of the year, however, he was writing to his mother, complaining: "I have now been near three months here confined to my room," and he declared his intention to build a house at Live Oak Point: "it is a most beautiful spot no objections to it but muskitos in summer."[27] Almost two years later in November 1839, he was in further distress, explaining his neglect of writing for three months on account of a long spell of sickness, and in March, 1840, health was once again a perennial theme: "Grandmother I hope you have recovered your health by this time, I have myself been sick ever since I have been in the Country until last month with chills & fever & have been several times near dying but thank God I am now well again."[28] In November of the same year Joseph E. Plummer received a letter from William S. Hornburgh writing from Matagorda, Texas:

Esteemed Friend; I should have written to you before this time if my health would have admitted it – but such has been my unfortunate lot that have scarcely enjoyed one days health since Mr. Richardson left me, and the same day he left Matagorda we removed into the country – my wife had already all the premonitory symptoms of strong billious fever and it was with difficulty she could be carried in the wagon, were three days on the way – she was already down – the next morning after our arrival I was seized with one of the most violent shaking agues that I ever felt or witnessed – it was succeeded by as severe a fever as ever followed an ague. – I lay prostrate a week before it could be broken, during which time I also succeeded in breaking Jane's fever, – there were some twenty persons young and old sick in the settlement at the same time – so soon as I could walk I was called several places among the sick, and, but for the utmost exertion and attention some two or three must have died – This was more than my feeble state would admit of without rappidly declining – It has rained here regularly about every three days since the first of September, which in this deep rich soil and high timber, and other strong features of a very unhealthy country have no doubt been the cause of as much fever as we have been afflicted with during this fall – along the first of last month, Sarah, who had til then increased in health and flesh – and apparently no symptoms of fever, was taken violently and in a moment—hands and feet cold as if dead—and brain and vitals consuming with the heat of fever, to obtain an action on the bowels, by any means is almost an impossibility. She was so very fat and—that I was almost certain she would be another victim of this unrelenting disease which had already torn the most promising children from the neighborhood.[29]

In nursing her for ten days and nights, he succeeded in breaking her fever, only to find himself exposed to the same dreadful fever in which state he lay for three weeks: "I have felt or witnessed nothing in the course of my life so much resembling conjestion fever—my feet and hands are yet almost constantly cold and subject to sever[e] cramps—It has revived my old pulmonary symptoms and most of the time, I have to be pillowed strait up in the bed or strangle for want of breath and the difficulty of rasing matter from the lungs—my side and breast—gathered afresh and since that time (last Tuesday) it has regularly discharged nearly an ounce of matter every twenty four hours."[30]

The evidence of the Plummer correspondence suggests that frontier life held out considerable promise, but only the fittest and most fortunate survived to see that promise fulfilled. If little could be done to combat disease, the colonists proved inventive when it came to dealing with shortages of food, even though deficiencies in valuable nutrients from an unbalanced diet must have contributed to the incidence of sickness. Elizabeth McAnulty Owens was the daughter of McMullen-McGloin colonists who had come from Ireland in 1819 and settled in New York until moving to Texas in 1829. At Copano, Elizabeth's sister Mary Ann became the first death in the colony. Four more fatalities occurred while the party were at the Refugio mission before they had reached their destination of San Patricio. James and William Quinn, finding a shortage of supplies, walked to Matagorda to get a boat to New Orleans. For some months they remained in New Orleans sending provisions to Texas by boat. The winter after the 1836 war the colonists suffered from a shortage of bread:

neither army officials nor citizens could obtain it. The first pound of flour bought by Mr. Quinn cost seventy-five cents. Meal for bread was made from corn. As there were no steel mills the colonists made a mortar of a scooped-out log, put the corn into it and crushed the grain with a pounder worked by a windlass. There were plenty of milk and butter. Tender nettles and pokeweed were used as greens. Tea was made from goldenrod bay leaves and yaupon. Mrs. Quinn paid $6.00 for the first

Elizabeth McAnulty Owens, a San Patricio colonist, recorded her experiences of life on the frontier. *Courtesy Martha Elizabeth Owens Stanley Martin, UT Institute of Texan Cultures at San Antonio*

pound of tea she could obtain, being a great lover of the beverage. The only seed for crops planted this winter were obtained from Mr. Wilde. Elizabeth and Thomas rode horseback from Navidad to Carancahua to get the seed that Mr. Quinn planted. Money in circulation was Texas paper money.[31]

Thomas Gunning also went from New York to San Patricio but found he had been misled by "such extravagant expectations & promises" on the part of "a notorious pair of scoundrels," McMullen and McGloin. To his dismay, he found

everything wild & of course uncultivated, not a single house on it. Woods & prairie or land that never grew timber in abundance, we set about building huts & prepared for tilling, we provided ourselves with grain + seeds of every description, from appearances were not discouraged, vegetation went on luxuriantly in the month of November, the labor of our hands showed uncommonly well till the corn was going into ear, when to our mortification it literally got burn'd up for eleven weeks together we w'd not see a drop of corn, we could have land at a shilling an acre without limit, if we could grow anything we could do well enough.[32]

Gunning was also discomforted by the presence in Texas of dangerous neighbors, Spaniards, whom he described as "a faithless people and not to be confided in," and worse still, "the Indians, there were four tribes & one tribe the Comanches 15 thousand strong, war and hunting their zenith, they go naked except a piece of hair cloth or skin for a delicate purpose, on the head a sort of coif ornamented with feathers, ultimately their jealousy will be excited & they'l make war, woe to the colony then." He also reported that among the thirty-two families recruited by Mc-Mullen and McGloin, thirty-four family members died in the short period of thirteen months; some drowned, some were shot. Gunning returned to New York with some relief, and in writing to Major O'Hara in Sligo in Ireland he reported that his wife, Kitty, had died in New Orleans, and mused that if he had only stayed in New York, which is "the Garden yes the Emporium of all America we could be very happy & well off today." [33]

ENCOUNTERS WITH INDIANS

Gunning's alarm about the presence of the Comanches reflects the attitude of many of the pioneer settlers in Texas.[34] Reading contemporary accounts of Indian activity presents an ambivalent picture. To white men and women, Indians were feared, on the one hand, as uncivilized savages who were capable of cruel attacks on isolated homesteads, the capture or brutal killing of women and children, and even of alleged cannibalism. On the other hand, there was an undoubted fascination with Indian customs and habits, often incorporating an admiration for identified qualities of nobility, courage, and personal loyalty. For those who stayed as pioneer settlers, the threatening presence of Indian tribes served as a barometer of surviving Old World values and the new influences of frontier conditions. Those Europeans used to having servants and unused to hard physical work would have found the frontier a daunting place. Other more hardy folk among the pioneers, out of sheer necessity or through growing up in frontier conditions, found they were in some measure shaped by them.

Both the style and the ambivalence of pioneer writing on the Indians in Texas are exemplified in Noah Smithwick's memoirs.[35] An American with a clear sense of Anglo superiority over Indians and Mexicans and imbued with the philosophy of Manifest Destiny, he recalled with relish how Indian depredations were revenged and how he enjoyed pursuing and killing Indian braves, but he also spent three months living with a tribe of

Comanche Indians, befriended an old chief, and described with no little affection how the tribe lived. He was even sympathetic to their legitimate claim on their buffalo hunting grounds and the threat of the advancing white man. While he accepted that pride would not allow them to accept life on a reservation, he recognized that in the end they would die or be driven out of Texas. An enduring myth of the American West features the nobility of the native Indians in making a fatal last stand against the invasion of the white man. It serves to distract attention from the moral dilemma involved in the taking of land from a people who did not all disappear but remain as Native American citizens of the republic.

The stories that were told and retold before being recorded for posterity in personal memoirs retain these contradictory qualities of fear and affection with regard to the Indian tribes. For instance, a convention of kindness rewarded was commonly found in stories of individual encounters with Indians. The pioneer Irish colonist Michael Whelan, who built the first frame house in Refugio in the 1830s, recalled how he was coming down the road from Victoria one day and heard a sound of moaning.

When he went to investigate the odd noise he found a wounded youth lying in the tall grass. He took the boy home and nursed him back to health. When the boy was strong, Whelan returned him to his own people in the vicinity where he found him. Some years later Whelan was captured by Indians who had tied him to a stake and were preparing to burn him. Suddenly the same Indian whom he had cared for rode out of the brush, cut the ropes and kissed him. Seeing this, all the other Indians went up to Whelan and kissed him before letting him go free. Upon his return home, Whelan said, "Be gobbs! I'd rather be burned at the stake than be kissed by all those dirty Indians!" [36]

A blend of Irish and Texan humor was deployed to make light of a dangerous incident and convert it into a more memorable story. In a tradition of self-deprecating narrative, the joke was on the storyteller, as in this account of Indian raids. After a number of horses had been stolen by Indians, Michael Whelan and fellow Irish colonist Walter Lambert were determined they would not get Lambert's pet horse: "They, therefore, made their beds up on the front porch of the house and Lambert tied his horse's rope to his foot to make sure the Indians would not get him. Then they both went to sleep. Early the next morning Whelan raised from his pillow and called out, 'Faith and begorre! The rascals have cut the rope and your horse is gone.'" [37]

Michael Whelan, a colonist who built the first frame house in Refugio, wrote an account of his encounters with Indians. *Courtesy James Lambert Hynes Estate, UT Institute of Texan Cultures at San Antonio*

The convention of kindness rewarded also had its punitive side in the absence of kindness shown. Annie Fagan Teal, the daughter of Nicholas Fagan, a pioneer settler on the banks of the San Antonio river, recalled how "the Indians would test the friendship of the whites by sending one of their number, perhaps a young boy, to a house at nightfall; he would claim to be lost, and ask for a night's lodging. If he returned, the tribe would never harm that family, but say: 'He good white man; he no kill lone Indian.' But woe unto the house where one was killed. One went to the house of Don Juan Hernandez one night, and unknown to the family was killed by the Mexican hirelings on the place. Hernandez was compelled to flee the country, much of his property was destroyed, and two Mexicans killed."[38] A similar mixture of fear and affection was featured in Rosa Kleberg's reminiscences of early Texas days. Having arrived at Brazoria from Germany via New Orleans in 1834, her party were searching for their compatriots near Cat Spring:

> In the timber near Bostick's an Indian came toward them. My brother Louis was of course ready to shoot; but my husband restrained him. As it turned out the Indian was quite friendly and told them where they would find the people they were seeking. He belonged to a troop of Indians who were camping in the neighborhood and from whom our

relations had been in the habit of obtaining venison in exchange for ammunition. . . . As a matter of fact, the Indians were in the main quite amicable. They were constantly wishing to exchange skins for pots and other utensils. Quite a number of them was camping on Buffalo Bayou. I have often sewed clothes for them in exchange for moccasins. They were Coshattis, and big, strong men. There were also Kickapoos, who, however, were small.[39]

Conflict between the warlike Carancuhuas and the gentle Tarancuhuas also brought friendships with settler families. The De León family, an aristocratic and refined family in Victoria, had befriended the neighboring Tarancuhua tribe. Irish settler Elizabeth McAnulty Owens recalled:

For some reason the Carancuhuas bore Mrs. De Leon ill will. They had planned to make an attack on her and her family and invited the Tarancuhuas to join them. The two tribes met and made preparations for the war dance over the dead bodies of their intended victims. But the Tancahuas [sic], being friends to Mrs. De Leon, deceived the Carancuhuas. They cut their bow strings, killed thirteen of the tribe and took their scalps to Mrs. De Leon, dancing around her home with the scalps stuck upon their spears, as evidence of friendship and protection. Mrs. De Leon showed her gratitude to the Tancuhuas for having saved her life by giving them a great feast. Elizabeth witnessed this war dance in Market Square in Victoria, February, 1836.[40]

Reference was made to the Tonkawas in Rosalie Hart Priour's memoirs. Once again, conflicting impressions feature in a description of a first encounter at the homestead Rosalie's family shared with the surveyor Mr. Robinson: "The first time Mr. Robinson went out surveying he camped near where a tribe of Indians known as Tonkawas were having a dance, and as up to that time they had been on friendly terms with the whites he went to join them in their sports. He noticed that the women were eating human flesh, and enquired why they did so. They answered that it was 'to make them and their children savage,' and that the sweetest piece of meat they ever eat was a French man's heart or a white man's shoulder."[41] Friendly relations with the Tonkawas were qualified by the confirmation that they were still savages, although it should be recognized that Indians were happy to go along with Europeans' horror of cannibalism and provide the lurid details that fueled their fascination. Ironically, the Irish were past masters of such subversive humor in their own relations with

English authority figures in Ireland. Playing the part of "thick Paddy" was often the means of having a joke against landlords, agents, or magistrates, and so undermining their authority.[42]

However, it was less than a joke when Rosalie Hart and her mother had to abandon their home when they had news of a threatened attack on Mission Refugio:

> The next day the soldiers in Laberdee sent Tom Conners [O'Connor] and John O'Brien with their oxcarts to take all the women and children from the Mission to a place of safety, as they had proof that five hundred Mexicans and Indians were going to attack the town. We were ordered to take nothing but provisions for two days and one frying pan, one coffee pot and skillet. They would not tell us where we were going for fear the women and children would speak of it, and the consequences could be fatal to us, as the Mexicans and Indians would follow us and kill every one of us. We were allowed to take a change of clothing also. Besides mother, there were three others sick, my cousin, Col. Powers [James Power], and his nephew Martin Powers, who was a cripple. Everybody buried their valuables before leaving. Mrs. Synott [Sinott] tied some money in a handkerchief and putting the rest in a chest together with her tea service and other valuables, moved her bed, dug a hole and buried them under the bed, then removing as far as possible all trace of the ground having been disturbed, replaced the bed where it stood. She then tied up some of her husband's clothes, her own, and some for the baby, in a bundle to take with her. But in the confusion and hurry attending our departure, she made a mistake and carried off a bundle of rags.[43]

The threat of Indian raids, which continued after the Irish colonists had made their way back to their settlements after the "runaway scrape" and the end of the war in 1836, lasted until the 1850s. The aftermath of war also brought the threat of undisciplined troops stationed on the Nueces River seizing cattle and other goods, freebooters who stole from merchants, and a further threat from a renewed Mexican invasion. In the face of Indian raids, the colonists could organize themselves into a citizen militia in defense of their main settlements, but isolated homesteads remained vulnerable to attack. Some families, like the Corrigans on Aransas Creek, had to leave their home several times when threatened by Indians.[44] The most infamous massacre occurred in 1835 when the entire family of James Heffernan was wiped out in a surprise attack on their home in Poesta Creek. James, his brother John, and cousin Ryan were killed while working in the fields. Mrs. Heffernan and the children were then slaughtered in the house. The bodies of all of them were found a few days later.[45] Such incidents could only have added to the fear of Indians, even though they were mixed with examples of friendship and kindness.

Vivid memories of Indian raids have survived, to be recorded by Kathryn S. O'Connor in an unpublished history of the Fagan family. Between 1840 and 1855 the Karankawas and Comanches committed depredations on the white settlers:

Very close to the Fagan Ranch in 1842 occurred the Gilliland murders and the capture of the children. The night before the Indians descended upon the unsuspecting family Mr. Fagan's young daughter, Fanny, was invited and urged by little Rebecca Gilliland to spend the night with her, but Mrs. Fagan thought Fanny too young to sleep away from home and so refused to let her go. The next morning the band of Indians, without molesting the Fagans, attacked and killed Mr. Spins Gilliland and took the boy, William, about nine years old, and the girl, Rebecca, about twelve, captives. The Comanches headed for the river bottoms, and in keeping in the dense woods, made their way slowly and steadily up the river toward La Bahia. But the alarm was soon given and the Texas soldiers and men from the settlement were soon in pursuit. They came upon the band of Indians in the afternoon and a hot fight ensued. The Indians outnumbered and not wanting to be encumbered with the two children, speared the boy and knocked the little girl in the head and left them, as the red men thought, dead. But during the night both recovered consciousness and hid in the deep foliage of the brush under the trees. The soldiers had gone on after the Indians, not knowing the children had been left on the battle ground. But Fagan, Don Carlos, Tom O'Connor and the neighbors going over the ground found the children, as they heard Mr. Fagan's voice and called to him. They were taken to Carlos Ranch and cared for. Mr. Tom O'Connor was appointed by the court guardian of the children, but as they needed medical care he took them to Victoria and placed them with the Presbyterian minister's family.[46]

Understandably, stories involving the survival of children remain memorable, but what is also of interest is the way neighbors, Irish and Mexican, took up the challenge posed by Indian raids. Good neighbors were vital for survival. and times of distress brought families together in the face of common danger.

Pat Burke, whose mother, Ann Burke, had been assisted in suckling her infant son by an Indian squaw on arrival in Texas, recalled the perils of his boyhood from Indian raids:

> After we returned to our colonial homes Indian raids were still frequent. They invariable came on the full of every moon during the spring, summer and autumn months, and oxen coming home with arrows in their bodies often admonished us that Indians were lurking in the neighborhood, and ready to surprise us by swooping down upon us. They frequently swept the country of saddle ponies, not leaving mounts enough in the community on which men could pursue them. In making their escape when they were pursued they always had the advantage of their pursuers. They generally had already stolen the best horses and were returning with a large heard when discovered, and could change mounts whenever the horses they were riding became jaded, while our men usually had to take for mounts such animals as the Indians left behind or had failed to get. Whenever the Indians succeeded in crossing the Nueces river, about ten miles from Oakville, they were safe from further pursuit. In order to prevent the Indians from stealing our horses, the settlers usually made a thick, high brush fence around their back door without an entrance except through the house. About the full of the moon, or whenever an Indian raid was anticipated, the horses, oxen and milk cows were kept in this inclosure. One night the Indians stole Pat Corrigan's horse, which was tied to his gallery post. His wife heard them and told him the Indians were getting his horse. He picked up his gun, ran into the yard and snapped his old pistol at them three times. He just happened to see three Indians with their drawn bows and arrows hid in the grass in time for him to make a safe retreat into his house.[47]

Pat Burke also enjoyed the boyhood excitement of accompanying the men on revenge attacks on the Indians, but even here there was at least a hint of admiration for their prey:

> When a boy I [was] sent under the care of Major John Woods, with others in pursuit of the Indians. A man named Mandola, who had been captured when a boy, and reared to manhood by the Indians was our

guide. He was trained in all of their arts and cunning, and could even trail them by scent. It was hard sometimes for our men to distinguish between an Indian and a mustang trail, but Mandola was never at a loss to tell one from the other. We traveled that night until 12 o'clock and then slept till daylight. Next morning when we awoke, Mandola arose and sniffing the balmy atmosphere a time or two, he said he smelt the fumes of cooking meat and that our foes were not far away. We did not go further than five miles before we came upon and surprised our enemies while they were enjoying their breakfast of horse meat cooked on coals. Immediately a quick and spirited fight ensued. Major Woods kept me with him, the other men separating and taking advantageous positions in the scattering timber. One savage and ferocious old squaw attacked the major and myself. We tried as long as possible to avoid the necessity of shooting her, but she could handle her bow and arrows as well and as accurately as a trained warrior, and was hurling the missiles of death at us so rapidly that we were compelled to exchange shots with her in order to save our lives. Major Woods received an arrow wound in the fleshy part of the thigh, but this was the last raid and the last fight of this unfortunate squaw-warrior. Our force numbered fourteen. I do not know how many Indians there were. When the battle had ended we were the victors, with seven dead Indians streatched upon the field. A few old sore-back ponies and horse and the bows and arrows of the slain Indians were the spoils of our victory.[48]

The Indians were not always defeated and the blend of fear and admiration on the part of the settlers is evident in another of Pat Burke's boyhood scrapes:

Once I went with my stepfather [Pat Carroll] to Long Lake, carrying a jug with which to bring back some fresh drinking water. We were in no particular hurry, and while walking leisurely about the lake we discovered the Indians in some timber a short distance above us, cooking meat. While they did not seem to see us, we were suddenly inspired with St. Paul's injunction to lay aside every weight and run with swiftness the race set before us, so casting our jug aside, we pulled off the prettiest race you ever saw, going back into town, San Patricio, with the old man possibly leading me a neck or two. The sulking "redskins," who always seemed to need good horses in their business, made a call that night at the premises of several of the citizens, who found themselves without mounts and work animals next morning.[49]

Pat Burke's boyhood adventures were not confined to stories of Indian raids. He had to grow up quickly, support his mother, three little brothers and two half sisters, as well as a stepbrother who was nearly blind and unable to work. Apparently he lost his eye when a cork flew from a bottle of English porter while he was opening it. Pat Burke's boyhood on the frontier provided an education in self-reliance and courage, and a knowledge of useful, practical skills:

In those days the country was full of deer, panthers and other kinds of game and wild animals. On one occasion while I was a boy I went with Major Woods, Bill Clark and Martin O'Tool (the last named being a San Jacinto and Mexican war veteran) to cut a road through the bottom. While we were at work the dogs treed a large panther which we killed with an ax.

The country used to be full of wild mustang horses, and it was a sight to see them running when the settlers were trying to catch them. If we could manage to catch one of these old horses, we would tie an imitation man upon him and let him loose. Of course he would make for the herd, which would try to outrun him. This would start every mustang for miles around to running and the noise from these running horses, which sometimes numbered thousands, often sounded like the terrific roar of a passing cyclone. After they had run themselves down we could guide them into the pens with long wings which we had build for capturing them. It required strength and skill to rope and throw one of these old snorting, jumping, fighting horses. It looked like some of them could squeal, paw, kick and jump at the same time, and they could never be conquered until they were roped, thrown and tied down. We generally roached their manes and tails and used the hair for making ropes.

After annexation the United States sent troops to protect us against Indian raids, and though only a boy I drove an ox wagon three years carrying supplies for the troops from Corpus Christi to Fort Merrill. . . . I made $30 per month, and this was considered good wages for a boy in those times. When I commenced on this job I was scarcely large enough to put the yoke on the oxen. I wore hickory shirts and red shoes, and it usually took me eight days to make the round trip. Sometimes an axle would break and then I was two weeks making the round trip. There were only two blacksmiths accessible, one being at each end of the route. I made these trips alone, sleeping at night by the side of my wagon. Finally John Ross bought me a good wagon at a government sale, paying $30 for it. I worked it out.[50]

Pat Burke volunteered in Company F of Colonel Buchel's regiment during the Civil War. He had left between 500 to 600 head of cattle on the range but found he had lost cattle by the end of the war when he returned to his mother's headright land grant. The newspaper account of 1912 suggested that he was "perhaps one of the few sons of the Texas pioneers who now owns and lives upon his parent's head-right league. After all, the severe training in industry, self-reliance and economy to which he was subjected to in his youthful years may have taught him the value of hard-earned money, and in the end proved to be a blessing in disguise to him."[51]

The frontier experience also produced characters that embodied the pioneering spirit in abundance. Sally Skull, an American woman of Irish descent, was described "as fearless as any man who ever rode the range"; she was known by the old San Patricio people who encountered her en route to Mexico as a horse trader. Apparently, the settlement was shocked because "she wore bloomers of rawhide and rode astride a man's saddle," which was regarded as quite extraordinary in the 1850s and 1860s. She cut a daring and masculine figure "wearing two six guns, hanging from a cartridge belt," and she knew how to use them. Stories are told of some shooting scrapes with Mexicans in which Sally Skull came out with flying colors. Tradition also has it that "she always carried a long plaited rawhide horsewhip with her, whether walking or mounted," and "she could pick the flowers off bushes so accurate was she with her whip." On one occasion, "she is said to have publicly whipped a Mexican who had offended her." She was fearless enough to make long journeys of several weeks or months with her own outfit of Mexican cowboys who had the greatest respect for her prowess with the whip.[52]

Yet Sally was not shaped entirely by frontier values. She would not let her daughter come in contact with the hard life she had chosen. With the money made from horse-trading, she sent the girl off to college, ensuring that she received a splendid education. She remarked many times that she wanted her daughter to be a truly "ladylike lady." Sally met a tragic death at the hands of her last husband. The story of Sally Skull represents an embodiment of the tough virtues of frontier life applied admiringly to women as well as to men. Sally lived them out in an extreme form, but even in her case there was a yearning for a better, more civilized way of life in the aspirations she had for her daughter. Her aspirations can be interpreted as an example of Walter Prescott Webb's frontier "grindstone," existing alongside but not fully eroding the old European notions of gentility and refinement. Patricia Nelson Limerick, a new western historian, has argued that "we have by no means escaped the treachery of words." She has urged caution in accepting at face value western words as western actuality. The story of Sally Skull would appear to be a classic case that calls for a healthy dose of skepticism in translating oral traditions into written history.[53]

THE CONTRIBUTION OF IRISH COLONISTS

In recording the achievements of individual Irish pioneers in Texas, there is a danger in isolating them from the more typical experience of fellow settlers and according them a special status because of their Irish origins. Nonetheless the following examples demonstrate the importance of the cultural values, training, and skills that pioneer settlers brought with them from Ireland and from time spent in North America. A devotion to the Catholic faith, a belief in the value of education, a charitable concern for the poor, a retention of the portable elements of Irish culture, music, dancing, and storytelling, all remained important at least for the first generation of settlers. Perhaps more significant in terms of achieving prominent positions in politics and business were the education, venture capital, and commercial and professional skills they brought with them. Finally, in several cases that mirror the experience of the Irish empresarios, an ability to adapt to and integrate with the culture of prominent Mexican families through intermarriage proved to be an important avenue to wealth and status.

The importance the colonists accorded to education is further evidence of the survival and persistence of European values maintained by the leading colonists in the frontier conditions of Texas. Robert Dougherty, a highly educated emigrant from Donegal, taught school in San Patricio as well as working his land and looking after his livestock. From 1868 to 1874 he taught at Hidalgo Seminary in Corpus Christi before returning to San Patricio in 1876 where he established his own boarding school. The school still remains, well preserved, at Round Lake near the McGloin house west of San Patricio.[54]

Education remained something of a luxury while a general state of lawlessness was still evident in the Nueces River area, even after Texas joined the Union in 1846. The constant harassment and terrorizing of inhabitants, livestock driven off and homes destroyed, persuaded many San Patricio colonists to move to Corpus Christi. Among them was the Murphy family, who had their ranch plundered in 1846. John B. Murphy, following service in General Zachary Taylor's army during the U.S.-Mexico War, set up in business in Matamoros in 1848 and the following year married Margaret Mary Healy.[55] The Civil War left Corpus Christi impoverished and without proper schooling. Mrs. Murphy was concerned by the children roaming the streets and the obvious handicaps of the newly emancipated blacks. She wrote to Bishop Dubuis asking for sisters to be sent to educate the children. As a result of this request, three nuns from the Sisters of Mary in Belgium were sent to Waco in 1873, including Jane Healy, Mrs. Murphy's sister. After a hurricane in 1875 left many in Corpus Christi homeless, Mrs. Murphy established shelters out of three converted buildings on Antelope Street. What became known as "Mrs. Murphy's hospital for the poor" welcomed Anglos, Mexicans, and blacks.

After the death of her husband, Judge Murphy, in 1884, Mrs. Murphy went with two companions to Temple, Texas, to teach black children. The venture turned out to be a temporary prelude to a more lasting success with the black street children of San Antonio. In 1887, she rented some rooms in San Antonio on Commerce Street, sold off a portion of the family ranch in San Patricio, and bought property at Nolan and Live Oak Streets. Despite opposition from the exclusively white neighborhood, she built a church, convent, and school. Opened in 1888, the school enrolled day and boarding students but faced continual opposition from neighbors and problems with a shortage of dedicated staff. In 1892, on the advice of her sister, now mother superior of the Sacred Heart Academy in Waco, and Bishop Neraz, she established her own religious community, which became known as the Sisters of the Holy Ghost. She was then known as Mother Margaret Mary Healy-Murphy, the founder of the first religious order in Texas. More schools were eventually opened in Victoria, Mexico, and in Laredo, and she visited Ireland in 1896 and 1899 to recruit candidates for the order. When she died in 1907, she had set in motion an order that was to establish thirty-nine missions in Texas, Louisiana, and Mississippi. The Healy-Murphy Center still operates as a nondenominational center for school drop-outs on Nolan Street, San Antonio, where she started her first school. The career of Mother Margaret Mary formed part of a pioneering Irish contribution to the development of Texas communities in the nineteenth century. Many Irish-born individuals played

Mother Margaret Mary Healy-Murphy, a San Patricio colonist, was the wife of Judge Murphy. She cared for poor children in Corpus Christi, Temple, and San Antonio and founded the first religious order in Texas. *Courtesy Sisters of the Holy Spirit, UT Institute of Texan Cultures at San Antonio*

their part. In San Antonio, they were prominent in business and public life. John Brendan Flannery has recorded the activities of early settlers and shown that the presence of the quarter known as Irish Flats housed the new influx of Irish settlers in the 1840s.[56]

John Twohig, born in Cork, had established a mercantile business by 1830, took part in the Siege of Béxar in 1835, and by 1842 had become an alderman in the city. At the time of the Mexican invasion of San Antonio in 1842 he blew up his store to prevent the Mexican army from taking supplies and munitions. Taken prisoner and sent to a Mexican prison, he and nine others escaped in 1843 and returned to San Antonio. In 1869 he opened a banking firm that was to become widely known for its breadline provision made for the poor of the city. John Twohig, who personally financed the charity work, became known as San Antonio's Breadline Banker. Peter Gallagher, from County Westmeath, arrived in San Antonio in 1837 and worked initially as a stonemason. A member of the ill-fated Santa Fe Expedition, he was captured and imprisoned in Mexico. After his release in 1842, he served as a Texas Ranger with John C. Hays. From 1846 to 1850, he ran a mercantile business in San Antonio. He went home to Ireland to marry and returned to Texas to develop further business interests in Mexico. Gallagher served as a justice in Béxar County and made

John Twohig established a mercantile business in San Antonio in 1830. He was a city alderman in 1842 and, after 1869, a successful banker. He was known as the Breadline Banker for his financial assistance to the poor. *Courtesy Witte Museum, San Antonio, Texas*

a wider contribution by starting development in the Fort Stockton area and in the organization of Pecos County.

San Antonio's development in the late 1830s was influenced by several Irish-born settlers. Bryan V. Callaghan, a Cork man who opened a store on Main Plaza and rose through local politics to become mayor in 1845, founded a political dynasty, supported by marriage into the Ramon family. His son, a lawyer by profession, was first the city recorder and subsequently served nine times as mayor. The family tradition of public service continued into the twentieth century when Alfred Callaghan became mayor of the city. Edward Dwyer also married into one of the old Spanish San Antonio families and served with José Antonio Navarro on a land claim commission. He, too, served as mayor in 1845. He established a successful business partnership with William Elliott and owned extensive property in the city. Elliott himself had come to America in 1820 from a mercantile background in Dublin, and rather like the Irish empresarios, McMullen, McGloin, Power, and Hewetson, had mining and mercantile business interests in Mexico before joining with Dwyer as a merchant in San Antonio in 1839.

The Devine brothers, whose family came from County Waterford, arrived in the city, from Nova Scotia in the 1840s. Thomas J. Devine, an attorney, and James M. Devine, a doctor, were active in the political life of the city. James was treasurer of San Antonio from 1848 to 1849 and subsequently served as mayor on four occasions between 1849 and 1857. During the Civil War, he remained loyal to the Union; his brother was committed to the Confederate cause. James left to live in Connecticut at the start of the war. Thomas was city attorney and later district attorney; in 1851 he was elected as district judge of Béxar County. During the Civil War, he became Confederate state judge for the Western District of Texas and acted as Confederate emissary to Mexico. After the war he was indicted for treason by the federal government. Between 1873 and 1875 he was a Texas Supreme Court justice, and in 1881, he served as one of the regents of the University of Texas.

An Irish community presence also enabled the preservation of Irish traditions. In the Irish Flats district of San Antonio, old Irish customs were continued. The Saturday night dances, the traditional step-dancing, the jigs and reels were accompanied by fiddle and accordion. Memories of Irish history were preserved through the rendition of favorite pieces like "Emmet's Speech from the Dock," and the familiar practice of storytelling at social gatherings retained the link with Ireland's rich folk culture. The Irish wake, a traditional form of celebrating the life and rejoicing for the soul of the deceased, continued in San Antonio, accompanied by tobacco and whiskey for friends and family paying their respects.[57] The Irish were sufficiently numerous to form their own parish and to build Saint Mary's Catholic Church. As the community and the city expanded, Irish residents moved to a prosperous suburb on the northeast of the city centered on Saint Patrick's Church. The continuity of the Catholic faith remained an important element of Irish identity, but material success tended to lessen the importance of Irish roots.

Texas has few monuments that recall the contribution of Irishmen to the building of nineteenth-century communities, but one such is the McNamara House Museum at 502 North Liberty Street, Victoria, formerly William McNamara's home, which was built in 1876. A native of County Cork, he came to the United States during the 1850s, spent time in New York City and Pittsburgh, and in 1866 married Mary Ann Buckley who had been a fellow passenger when he sailed from Ireland. By 1870 the McNamaras had moved to Port Lavaca, Texas, before settling in Victoria with their four daughters. William McNamara quickly became a prosperous and influential citizen. He established a hide business in Victoria that was eventually extended to Austin, Dallas, and San Antonio. He also had a stake in the Texas Continental Meat Company, with packing houses in

Victoria and Fort Worth. It was entirely appropriate that a fellow investor in the company, Thomas Marion O'Connor, the son of the wealthy rancher Thomas O'Connor, should become his son-in-law. McNamara served for three years on the city council and helped finance Victoria's first electric lighting system, as well as playing a leading part in establishing the city's municipal water plant.[58]

These examples of individual achievement and public service have more than a local and Texan significance. They are part of a wider pattern of upward social, economic, and political mobility throughout the continents of North and South America. When Irishmen arrived in a frontier community at an early stage in its development, the professional, business, and political skills they brought with them from Ireland, or via Canada, America, Mexico, or Argentina, enabled them to take advantage of the great opportunities as lawyers and teachers, merchants, storekeepers, and ranchers, and rise to positions of wealth, prestige, and power. A similar pattern may be observed among the Irish in New Orleans in the period 1800 to 1830; in San Francisco and in Argentina in the 1830s and 1840s; and in Butte, Montana, from the 1870s.[59] Conversely, the Irish laborers who settled in Texas in the decades after the first Irish had come in the 1820s, 1830s, and 1840s, worked on the railroads or in the Houston docks and neither faced the dangers nor had the opportunities of the Irish pioneers in South Texas.[60] Timing was crucial in determining the possibility of triumph or disaster or the likelihood of mere survival.

In *Emigrants and Exiles: Ireland and the Irish Exodus to North America,* Kerby Miller argues that the Catholic Irish who migrated to America were handicapped by a worldview that was rooted in a fatalistic, passive, and dependent rural tradition, and so were ill equipped to cope in a society that was dynamic, entrepreneurial, and individualistic. For these allegedly reluctant emigrants driven into exile, the process of emigration posed severe psychological problems of adjustment in a rapidly urbanizing industrial society. The standard pattern of experience faced by the masses of poor, Catholic migrants on the East Coast cities like Boston and New York appeared to be one of unremitting struggle against the worst conditions in employment and housing.[61] Miller's cultural and psychological thesis explaining the difficulties the immigrants faced has been dubbed by Donald Akenson the Gaelic-Catholic-Disability Variable. In seeking to demolish Miller's argument, Akenson has pointed to the different conclusions reached by Ruth-Ann Harris in using the same source as Miller, the evidence drawn from emigrant letters. Akenson further points to the work of Darrock and Orstein on Canadian census data, which purports to show that Irish Catholics were not, in practice, disabled in the main entrepreneurial activity of farming in Canada. With Irish migration between Canada and the United States being so fluid, Akenson argues that Canadian data should be admissible evidence in the debate on the Irish in America.[62]

All-embracing explanations of emigration on the scale and time frame of Irish emigration are always difficult to sustain, but Kerby Miller has recognized that prefamine emigration should be distinguished from famine and postfamine emigration. More prosperous farmers, who could take their capital with them from prefamine Ireland, in taking advantage of lands opening up in Canada were more likely to do well than poor laborers who could only seek unskilled manual work. The successful Irish pioneer settlers in Texas did not lack entrepreneurial skills, so the cultural explanation of Irish Catholicism as a handicap to economic progress in the New World did not apply. What is more plausible is that the general prospect of making an independent fortune was much more likely with the support of capital, professional skills, or commercial know-how than without it. More specifically, entrepreneurial skills were rewarded where Irish pioneers settled early, where for instance, they established ranching empires in California, Texas, and Argentina.[63] *Where* people emigrated from and *when* they departed, as well as *where* they chose to settle, materially affected their chances of success in the New World.

Miller has advanced a more convincing case in the notion of a culture of exile among the Irish abroad. This rationalization of migration sought refuge in a retrospective oppression history in which migrants are depicted as unwilling victims of English rule. The open declaration of the motive of individual advancement was unacceptable in a traditional, rural environment where community and family loyalties were dominant. The culture of exile was a cloak to disguise individual aspirations. In reality, Miller has argued that Irish emigration was surrounded by conflicting pressures, and emigrants themselves possessed highly ambivalent attitudes. Many farmers and tradesmen believed emigration was essential for the process of modernization, a process synonymous with increasing bourgeois dominance and made possible only by a clearing out of the poor cottiers and landless laborers from Ireland. Emigration reduced the fear of potential agrarian violence in resistance to consolidation of holdings among the larger farmers. For parents on smallholdings, it also eased the way for the painful disinheritance of children without the prospect of unbearable family conflict.

Miller has suggested that the theme of emigration as exile, manifest in speeches, newspapers, and most especially the emigrant songs of the period, provided a way of reconciling tensions and anxieties. It did so by loading all the blame on England, whose continuing oppression and appalling neglect of Ireland had "forced" people to emigrate. This analysis was politically convenient in harnessing support for the nationalist cause and also supplied an emotional need in qualifying the sense of loss and defeat that emigration represented. More precisely, it diverted attention from the conflicting pressures within families and communities, and in the hearts and minds of emigrants themselves. The idea of enforced exile absolved the emigrant from the charge of desertion in the pursuit of personal gain and offered an external explanation of the personal agony that emigration commonly involved.[64] The culture of exile became incorporated into the mind-set of many Irish emigrants, serving as a rational explanation for their departure and continued absence, even long after they had prospered and had no realistic intention of returning to Ireland.

There is some evidence found in the surviving correspondence and oral testimony that Miller's notion of the "culture of exile" was internalized among the Irish pioneer settlers in Texas. The emphasis on oppression in Ireland, the notion of being driven into exile, and a strong identification with Catholic nationalism in Ireland all point in that direction. These sentiments found expression and endorsement in the published works of Oberste, Huson, and Flannery, which drew on the received opinion of emigrant families and were reinforced by standard histories of Ireland written in the nationalist tradition. When Irish pioneer families prospered in Texas and become part of a wealthy elite, they could still retain the fancy of returning one day from exile to Ireland.

The image of the rugged frontiersman leaving behind the cultural baggage of his European past, taming a wilderness, and enjoying the freedom of the open range remains a powerful and enduring one, not least in Hollywood Westerns. It is an image that reflects substantive truths but is nevertheless selective in representing the lived experience of pioneer settlers in Texas. For pioneer women conditions were especially tough. Judging by their own accounts, frontier life was a relentless struggle against disease, hardship, and the depredations of Indians who threatened remote

Town scene in front of Blanconia Post Office. *Courtesy Anne McGuill Hawkins*

homesteads. Nor was the pioneer experience simply the white man's conquest of native Indians and of Mexican inhabitants in a territory that had,
in turn, belonged to both peoples. The Irish colonists' relations with
Indian tribes were ambivalent—a mixture of fear and admiration. And
Mexican neighbors remained on friendly terms despite the conflict of
war. Irish newcomers were taught about crops, cattle, and climate, which
proved important in their survival on the frontier. Settlers had to adapt
to frontier conditions. The frontier did not simply wear down the trappings of European civilization. What emerged in the making of Texas was
a fusion not only of Anglo, Hispanic, and Irish cultures but also German,
Polish, and other national traditions that took root. Texas was spacious
enough to accommodate separate communities that preserved old European identities and adapted to a longer-term process of Americanization.
This created a profusion of dual identities—the hyphenated American. In
Corpus Christi, Victoria, and San Antonio, Irish men and women brought
from the Old World formal education, as well as commercial and professional experience. These qualities enabled them to flourish in the frontier towns of Texas.

One advantage the Irish enjoyed in Texas, in contrast with the Irish
in northeastern cities of the United States, was the experience of a shared
community and Catholic faith with their Mexican neighbors. This was
subject to a conflict of loyalties during the chaos and destruction of the

years 1835 to 1836, when Irish and Mexicans were found on both sides in the war to establish the independence of Texas. The relations between the Irish and the Mexicans also created surprising twists in the story, with individual friendships occasionally transcending political allegiances. Over the long term, an important cultural transfer occurred, with the Irish colonists learning from the Hispanic ranching tradition of their Mexican neighbors, as exemplified by the extraordinary career of Thomas O'Connor.

Ranching Culture and the Texas Cattle King: Thomas O'Connor of Refugio County

*Buy land and never sell. Land can't die and
it can't run away.*
—Louise S. O'Connor, *Cryin' for Daylight:
A Ranching Culture in the Texas Coastal Bend*

THE CULTURE OF TEXAS RANCHING

If the Alamo remains the most potent symbol of Texas, certainly its most marketable icon, cattle and ranching have continued to define the idea of Texas in the popular mind—long after most of the state's inhabitants had moved to the cities. Team names such as the Dallas Cowboys and the Texas Longhorns perpetuate the historic association between Texas and the romantic period of cattle drives and the Chisholm Trail. Yet the golden age of the cowboy, cattle raising, and trail driving lasted only some twenty years, from the mid-1860s to the mid-1880s, when disastrous droughts and blizzards brought it to an end. The main outlines of the history of cattle ranching in Texas are well known and require little amplification.[1] What is in dispute is the origin of Texas ranching, which, linked with the development of the stockyards and meatpacking industry centered in Chicago, was transformed into a major economic activity. A cultural transfer was evident in the relations between Tejano families, whose presence in south Texas endured for a generation or two after the independence of Texas, and their Irish neighbors, who inherited and acquired the Hispanic ranching tradition.

Central to the debate about the origins of the ranching industry are the links between Texas and Louisiana. Terry Jordan, in his book *Trails to Texas: Southern Roots of Western Cattle Ranching*, has argued that the most important influence on Texas ranching was the imported Anglo tradition from the southern states.[2] He challenges Walter Prescott Webb by arguing that the horsemanship required for herd control was used in Louisiana by Anglos, blacks, Indians, and French before it was introduced to Texas and that Hispanic roping techniques, the use of the lasso and the horned saddle, were also brought by Anglo settlers from Louisiana. Jordan's case also rests on the contention that the Hispanic ranching tradition more or less ceased with the decay of the Spanish missions at the end of the eighteenth century, thus making way for the new, predominantly Anglo settlers to establish their own ranching culture in Texas in the 1820s and 1830s. It is generally agreed that Austin's colonists brought only 5 to 10 cattle per family and were more likely to introduce their southern planter economy, based on cotton, than to concentrate on stock raising. However, the total number of cattle multiplied quickly. By 1826 there were 3,500 cattle or double the population and by 1831, some 26,000 cattle or four times the inhabitants of the colony.

Jordan looked to the roots of stock raising in Louisiana, subsequently imported into Texas, in an older tradition to be found in South Carolina. His argument in defense of the Anglo tradition is based on the techniques of cultural geography, which quantifies the origins and movement of people as a means of measuring cultural influences. While he acknowledged that Texas cattlemen had diverse origins, including Hispanic, German, Czech, and Irish, he asserts that the great majority were Anglos or Louisiana French. For instance, one of the earliest cattle kings of the southwest was Taylor White, born Leblanc, who came from Louisiana to Texas in the 1820s. On the other hand, Jordan conceded that Martín de León, the founder of the De León colony, who combined cattle and sheep on his coastal prairie range near Victoria, was an important link in maintaining the Hispanic tradition of ranching. The Irish who settled in the two colonies of Refugio and San Patricio were also prominent as major ranchers in the Coastal Bend. In 1836 no town possessed larger stocks of cattle than San Patricio, and Thomas O'Connor was to become the most successful cattleman in the region. By the time of the Civil War, he was the unchallenged cattle baron of Refugio County where a third of large-scale cattle raisers were Irish.[3]

The presence of the Irish colonists, some of whom came directly from a mixed farming tradition in southeast Ireland and others who came via the United States, pose an interesting question. How did they acquire the skills and knowledge to make a success of cattle raising in a climate that was quite different from their native land? The small farms of County Wexford, which combined a few stock with arable farming, were a world away from the cattle raising on open prairie. The Irish settlers in Refugio and San Patricio learned from the ranching practices of their Mexican neighbors and as early as 1835, the Texas Irish had adopted the Spanish word "ranch" to describe their activity.[4] The Irish empresarios spoke Spanish, married into high-born Hispanic families, and were well versed in Mexican ways from their time as merchants in Mexico. James Power in Refugio, in marrying into the Portilla family, was also able to learn from his father-in-law's experience both as an empresario and as a rancher in Texas. He, in turn, passed on the knowledge and culture of ranching to his nephew Thomas O'Connor, who spent some of his youth at the Carlos ranch. It was a process of cultural transfer. It worked through the example of neighbors and was facilitated by language and intermarriage.

Louise O'Connor, a direct descendant of Thomas O'Connor, confirms that the ranching culture of south Texas had its origins in the Hispanic tradition; the horses and cattle, the working equipment, saddles, bridles, clothing, and protective gear worn by cowhands all evolved from the Spanish equipment.

> Spanish is sprinkled all through our language and attitudes. The Span-
> ish essence is in all of us to varying degrees with the exception of the
> concept of time—we are very Anglo in that respect, but our concepts of
> the afterlife and our continuing relationship with our dead is very
> Spanish, Mexican and very non-Anglo. I am sure the old man [Thomas
> O'Connor] learned everything he knew from someone with an His-
> panic "vaquero" background. Louis Power, the illegitimate Black
> grandson of James Power, who was my father's teacher, learned from
> an Hispanic source and passed that down to my father. Then my fa-
> ther's way of running ranches had passed down to this generation and
> so many of these ways are strongly based in Hispanic tradition. We are
> far more Spanish than Anglo.[5]

In his book *Los Mesteños: Spanish Ranching in Texas, 1721–1821*, Jack Jackson took issue with Terry Jordan and argued that the Spanish influence on ranching did not end with the beginning of formal Anglo colonization in Texas but continued to be felt long after the institution passed to Anglo ownership.[6] Jackson claimed that Anglo cattlemen took over what was a going concern and incorporated the Hispanic tradition into their own way of doing things. Furthermore, he argued that what the

Anglos, as new settlers, brought with them from the southern states of America into Texas was a mingling of cultures from the Spanish borderlands that had taken place over several generations before the founding of the Austin colony. A rich mixture of ethnic diversity was evident that included French, Spanish, Irish, Scottish, black, Italian, English, German, and Indian rubbing shoulders with each other in a frontier society that lacked the restrictions of settled communities. Over time, they became a new breed of Americans, who looked for more elbow room, free of restrictions, and so were attracted to the opportunities for self-improvement that Texas offered. A cultural transfer followed the movement of cattle and people. In the final quarter of the eighteenth century, Texas livestock supported a flourishing industry in French Louisiana, which spread eastward. And with the cattle, there was a movement of what Jackson called "vaquero know-how" and the time-tested Spanish system that itself had already been subject to a process of "creolization" in the states bordering Texas. The transfer of knowledge was a gradual process that involved the blending of cultures. So when the early arrivals came to Texas from Louisiana and the Mississippi Valley before the empresario system, they were already well versed in the Hispanic ranching tradition. Some had married into old French and Spanish families, and they had lived in the midst of a polyglot of races and cultures.

Texas had been a cattle kingdom for a hundred years under Spanish rule, and when the Anglo-American colonists came in the 1820s and 1830s they marveled at the richness of the prairies surrounding the old Spanish missions along the San Antonio River. They proclaimed that Texas was ideally suited to cattle raising and that everywhere else man was obliged to work for his cattle but in Texas the cattle worked for him. The numbers of cattle had been depleted but remained significant in 1835; some 3 million head of cattle were found grazing between the Nueces and the Rio Grande. Jackson and Jordan agreed that what happened as a result of the Texas Revolution was the rapid decline of the Mexican rancheros of south Texas but, as Jackson saw it, this was not caused by "some kind of debilitating virus to which only Nordic peoples were immune" but by a brutal process whereby Mexicans' rights to the land were brushed aside because they were Mexican. This process was even extended to the Tejano ranchers who had sided with Texas during the war of 1835–36. The takeover of the cattle industry was perhaps "the greatest and most profitable of the spoils of the Texas Revolution and the Mexican War." The rapid decline of Hispanic cattlemen in subsequent years was due not to the "moribund nature of their livestock methods" but rather to "hot lead and cold steel, finished off by the stroke of a pen."[7]

What was lost in terms of the ownership of the land lived on in the form of a ranching culture inherited by the Anglo-Americans from the Hispanic and Mexican rancheros. Jackson pointed to the evidence of the survival of brand designs and cited Webb in endorsing the view that "no one can beat a Mexican" for ingenuity of design. It was the Spanish tradition to use initials in attractive configurations. He also interpreted the famous Running W brand of Richard King at the Rancho de Santa Gertrudis Ranch as a fast-moving snake *(la vibrita)* very well known to the Mexicans. Capt. Richard King, a former riverboat captain who had grown up in the slums of Brooklyn, removed a complete community from Mexico to set up his ranch and accepted that the Mexicans could teach him all there was to know about cattle, horsemanship, and ranching in the brush country. That Mexican influence remained strong as the same people stayed for generations on the King ranch.[8] The Hispanic tradition of ranching can also be traced in the survival of ranching terms. Texans emerged wearing sombreros, bandanas, ponchos, and silver-inlaid spurs. The essential tools of the branding iron and saddle rope were "bequeathed to the buckaroos of the nineteenth century by the vaqueros of the eighteenth century."[9]

More recently published Tejano history suggests that the decline of the Hispanic-Mexican ranching tradition may have been overstated by both Jordan and Jackson, and there is reason to postpone the decline until toward the end of the nineteenth century.[10] There is no doubt that south of the Nueces River and to the border of the Rio Grande, the Hispanic tradition was continued by Mexican rancheros who continued ranching alongside a strongly Mexican population. Their numbers were strengthened by other families who removed themselves by the 1880s from their ranches near Victoria and Goliad to the safer surroundings of south Texas. For instance, Manuel Flores, Seguín's brother-in-law, moved south to Atascosa County in the 1850s. How far the Hispanic tradition persisted north of the Nueces River is in dispute. By 1845 forty out of forty-nine Goliad Tejano ranches were in the hands of Anglos for a fraction of their value.[11] Mestizo vaqueros maintained a Hispanic presence in working for Anglo ranchers. Some Tejano rancheros lost out by being cast as disloyal by both sides in the Texas Revolution. Some retreated to Tamaulipas and to Nuevo León and others, to the old Spanish territory of Louisiana. Andrés Tijerina in *Tejanos and Texas Under the Mexican Flag, 1821–*

1836, has argued that many remained and strengthened their numbers to preserve an important and even dominant presence in south Texas. With 450 rancheros registered in the new Republic of Texas in March, 1837, and a further 175 who arrived by 1840, there was a significant number who represented a continuity with an Hispanic ranching tradition. Within the Béxar-Goliad region Tejanos qualified for first-class headrights but only a quarter of claimants patented their headrights. Along the San Antonio River many immigrant Tejanos lost their claims to Anglo ranchers. In an atmosphere of hostility to Mexicans, Tejanos, even those who had fought for the independence of Texas, were regarded as equally disloyal, and raids against Tejano property were condoned. Others were deprived of their land through ignorance of the procedures or a lack of documentation. Nevertheless, the war between the United States and Mexico had the effect of boosting the Mexican population in the disputed territory between the Nueces and the Rio Grande. The presence of General Taylor's army encouraged trade, established better order, and prompted the growth of new towns like Corpus Christ and Brownsville. As San Patricio became organized into several new counties, the new city governments included some of the old ranchero patriarchs. By the end of the war in 1848, the number of Tejanos had increased, and this was accompanied by the return of important families such as the De Leóns and the Benavides to Victoria. At the same time fifty other Tejano families were living at Goliad. The newcomers and the returnees more than made up for the losses sustained during the revolution, and Tijerina claims that by 1850 the Béxar-Goliad area had become unified with the region of the Rio Grande frontier into achieving a dominant Mexican character throughout south Texas.[12]

Tijerina's argument in support of a continuing Tejano presence and contribution to ranching culture in Texas received further confirmation in the work of Ana Caroline Castillo Crimm.[13] In studying the Mexican Americans of Victoria County from 1800 to 1880, Crimm searched through the deed, tax, marriage, and census records. She demonstrated that more than half of the elite rancheros survived the revolution period, returning to the area in the 1840s, and this number increased with migrants from Mexico in the 1850s. They were also able to reclaim their land and reap a profit from the boom in cattle prices in the 1870s. Through a process of intermarriage and godparenting, the Mexican Americans of Victoria preserved their honored position until the turn of the century when the system of partible inheritance, the division of estates between the members of the next generation, brought about a measurable decline in their fortunes.

Crimm cited a number of examples of elite ranchero families who survived the fallout from the Texas Revolution and maintained their presence on the land. Carlos de la Garza, who was responsible for the release of his Irish neighbors at Goliad in 1836 thus saving them from the subsequent massacre of prisoners, enjoyed, in turn, the protection of those Irish neighbors who controlled the Refugio government. When John J. Linn, an Irish merchant from Victoria, went into exile in Louisiana in 1836, he went with Mexican families, and on their return, John and Edward Linn acted as agents for the De León family in looking after their affairs. John J. Linn was a witness to Doña Patricia De León's will. Her son Fernando de León, returning from exile in Louisiana in 1849, petitioned the Texas legislature for the loss of his land, which in 1835 had been valued at fifty thousand dollars. He claimed that he had served with the Texas military, had been jailed by the enemy, and was entitled to compensation for his property, which had been left in the hands of the Texan army. Despite the fact that there were no written records on file, he was able to recover a good part of his land and went on to become both a successful rancher and a respected member of the Anglo and Mexican communities in Texas. While he lost something in the region of 50,000 acres through legal disputes and sheriff's sales, he retained another 50,000 acres, and although additional legal battles cost him further losses, he was able to leave almost 20,000 acres to his second wife and adopted son.[14] Another of the "old Spanish families" as they were called by Anglo settlers, out of respect for their status and wealth, the Carbajal family, sold 18 percent of their land to pay taxes, and others, like Miguel Aldrete of Goliad, offered a third of a league of land in exchange for the education of his two sons in New Orleans. The De León children were also educated at private schools in Victoria, Matamoros, and New Orleans and in universities in Europe. This investment in education allowed the second and third generations of these families to protect their interests in the legal battles of the 1840s and 1850s, which helped to sustain them as part of an Anglo-American elite through the end of the century. Survival was not confined to a few elite families. While the Mexican population of Victoria County fell from 36 percent in 1850 to 16.7 percent in 1870, there was an absolute increase in the number of families from 732 to 1,053 during the twenty-year period. Owners of land experienced mixed fortunes. Out of 27 families 17, or 63 percent, maintained their land and 10, or 37 percent, failed to hold on to it or to profit from ranching or farming.[15]

Crimm rejected the argument that the Tejanos were the victims of racist oppression. She points out that after the Texas Revolution Anglo-Americans, Irish, and Mexicans lost land to tax collectors. She contrasted the experience of Fernando de León, who was able to recover and hold on to a substantial share of his land, with that of the Irish empresario James Power. Power had bought the rights to 22 leagues of land from the Mexican government and a further 22 leagues from other purchases, which amounted to a total of approximately 200,000 acres. This land was located along the Gulf coast and included the potential for the development of ports that would have greatly added to its value. However, the grants were not surveyed by law, and in 1838 Joseph F. Smith, the nephew of the Texas governor Henry Smith, decreed that Power's titles were void without the consent of the supreme executive. Henry and Joseph Smith also questioned the empresario grants to Irish and Mexican settlers issued by the Mexican government on account of the lack of legal description of corner markers to their land. They persuaded the Texas Congress that all the Refugio and San Patricio settlers were required to resurvey their land, at their own expense, and to erect permanent markers at all the corners. Few of them had the resources to comply and were subsequently deprived of their land. James Power undertook to fight numerous costly court battles but by 1852, just before his death, he had lost the right to his claim on 200,000 acres.[16] A petition from the Refugio colonists in 1852 shows how indignant they felt about the challenge to their land from speculators and freebooters. They had signed agreements with the Mexican government, had fought and suffered during the Texas Revolution, and now felt they were being abandoned.[17]

A study by Armondo C. Alonzo, *Tejano Legacy: Rancheros and Settlers in South Texas, 1734–1900*, lends further support to the arguments advanced by Crimm. Alonzo's microstudy of land ownership in Hidalgo County showed that Tejanos remained a dominant force until the 1880s. He attributed the decline in land ownership to social and economic forces: the commercialization of ranching, the need for access to capital to withstand a period of adverse market conditions, and the imperative for scientific management of estates and livestock. All these put pressure on rancheros to divide their land among increased numbers of descendants or to sell it off to new settlers. His measured conclusion, after a careful analysis of landholding in south Texas, deserves to be accepted as part of a growing body of studies emphasizing the complexities of the conditions involved in the transfer of land: "Based on my study of land-grant adjudication of *Tejano* claims in south Texas and this brief comparative analysis of their jurisdictions in the Southwest, I believe that rancheros did not suffer as harsh a treatment as is commonly depicted in the popular literature, historical memory, and scholarly literature."[18]

Scholarly disagreement exists regarding the historic continuity of the Hispanic tradition through the continued presence of the old Spanish rancheros who survived after the Texas Revolution. Both Tijerina and Crimm point out that the Tejano families not only returned from exile but also added to their numbers, and some of the old elite families remained to make an important contribution to Texas ranching during the rest of the nineteenth century. However, where both Jordan and Jackson are surely correct and would not be seriously disputed by Tijerina and Crimm, is in establishing the significance of a cultural transfer from the old Hispanic ranching culture to be incorporated into the dominant Anglo-American presence.

Something of a mixed inheritance was introduced from the southern states into Texas with the Anglo-American colonists of the 1820s and 1830s in the Austin colony. A different case can be made for the more southern colonies centered on Victoria, Refugio, and San Patricio, which had their own mixed cultures of Mexican and Irish settlers. The close personal ties between Mexican and Irish neighbors survived the clash of loyalties of combatants in the war of 1835–36. In fact, the old settlers found a common cause when left unprotected by the empresarios; they united against the threats from land thieves, speculators, tax collectors, Indians, and Mexican troops. And the elite Spanish and Tejanos who stayed on had other bonds with the newly settled Irish: the Roman Catholic religion, the dangers and hardships of life on the frontier, and the threats to their respective land grants.

Donald Meinig in *Imperial Texas: An Interpretive Essay in Cultural Geography*, has pointed out that the region of east Texas was predominantly and culturally a planter economy, inhabited by migrants from the southern states. They brought with them their way of life built around southern ways. This meant growing cotton that was picked by their Negro slaves. South Texas was economically and culturally different, with cattle ranching predominating and the continuation of a Hispanic and Mexican presence. Meinig has argued that "because the Hispanos had long ago perfected the managing of large herds of half-wild cattle on semi-arid open ranges, their contribution was the more important and obvious, but the fact that the Anglos had for generations been working with smaller herds of half-wild cattle in the woods, canebrakes, and smaller prairies was also important and critical to the rapid acceptance and adaptation of Hispano methods to Anglo needs."[19] He also traced the expansion of the blending of livestock and traditions, not so much northward out of south Texas, but westward out of north Texas up the Brazos and Colorado Rivers across the Rolling Plains. The famous ranching names of the Nueces Valley, such as King and Kenedy, were matched by the famous pioneers, Goodnight, Loving, and Chisholm, who came out of the Cross Timbers after the Civil War. The cattle industry that developed on the plains was a mixture of two traditions, Hispanic and Anglo.

Meinig emphasized the importance of the mesquite borderlands along the San Antonio and Guadalupe Rivers "as the first point where a sustained contact between Anglo and Hispano produced the acculturation, the transfer of tools and techniques, which was obviously fundamental to the development of the industry."[20] What deserves greater recognition is the presence of Catholic Irish settlers who were taught the rudiments of Hispanic ranching culture, "vaquero know-how," by their coreligionists and fellow settlers. This facilitated a cultural transfer that allowed the persistence of a ranching tradition that has survived until the present day. Those among the original Irish colonists who prospered and created great ranching empires were the midwives of a cultural transfer and a cultural survival. While acquiring the skills and knowledge of their Mexican neighbors, the Irish also acquired business methods and knowledge of markets from the Anglo-Americans. In doing so, they mediated between the two cultures to achieve success. It is therefore fitting to reconstruct the story of the most successful of the original Irish colonists who embodied this cultural fusion. The life of Thomas O'Connor is presented not only in the broader context of Texas ranching but also as the culmination of the Power-Hewetson colony.

THOMAS O'CONNOR AND THE MAKING OF A RANCHING ESTATE

The little-known story of Thomas O'Connor contains the classic ingredients of Texas history: pioneer settler, soldier in the Texas Revolution, Indian fighter, and successful cattle rancher. The story also represents the culmination of the adventures of the Irish pioneer colonists who settled in Refugio and San Patricio between 1829 and 1834. A great part of the land granted originally to colonists by the Mexican government through the Irish empresarios Power and Hewetson was ultimately to form part of the immense estate left by Thomas O'Connor at his death in 1887. The central questions raised by his extraordinary career in Texas appear deceptively simple. How was he able to accumulate hundreds of thousands of acres within his lifetime? What persuaded him to pursue such a single-minded path, a life's work of investment in land? The wider significance of his story relates, first, to the development of Texas ranching during its golden age and, second, to the question of the cultural baggage the Irish colonists brought with them to the New World.

Surprisingly little has been published on the founder of the O'Connor estate. The most complete account was written as part of a graduate dissertation at Saint Mary's University, San Antonio, in 1939. As a member of the O'Connor family, Sister Margaret Rose Warburton had valuable access to family papers and to folk legends and was able to interview some of the hands on the O'Connor ranches who could remember events as far back as the 1870s and 1880s.[21]

Thomas O'Connor was baptized (probably within a few days of his birth) in County Wexford in Ireland on February 11, 1817. Legend, reproduced on a Texas historical marker at the old O'Connor ranch, has it that he was an orphan, but he was in fact, the younger son of a tenant farmer.[22] Like many a young man in his position, he had no prospect of inheriting the lease on the family mill farm and, in his own words, was "turned loos on the world on the day I became fifteen years of age."[23] He was more fortunate than most in having James Power, the Irish empresario, as his uncle. When Power returned to Ireland in the autumn of 1833, after an interval of twenty years, on a mission to recruit colonists for the Mexican province of Texas, he must have made a big impression on his nephew. Stories of adventures among Indians and Mexicans, and the prospect of big land grants for those willing to undertake life in the New World would surely have captivated a young man's imagination. It also seems likely that James Power, in looking for potential colonists who could stand up to the rigors of frontier life, was impressed with the young Thomas O'Connor. It has been suggested that Power arranged for Thomas O'Connor to make his way to Texas ahead of the main parties that sailed from Liverpool to New Orleans on the *Heroine* and the *Prudence*. And Thomas O'Connor stated that he had been in the country eight months before he received his land grant in Refugio from the Mexican commissioner Vidaurri on September 25, 1834. Nevertheless, he was listed as one of the passengers aboard the *Heroine*, accompanying James Power and his relatives, Martin Power and the O'Brien family, which arrived in New Orleans on May 7, 1834. In any case, James Power was present at the land grant ceremony; he testified as to Thomas's good character and to his allegiance to the Catholic faith. And it was through his offices as empresario that Thomas O'Connor was able to claim a family "composed of domestic servants" and receive a full league of land, 4,428 acres, and 177 acres of arable land rather than just the quarter of a league to which he was entitled as a single man.[24] James Power also gave his nephew the responsibility of aiding the surveyors in platting the site of Refugio; this was to be followed by later indications of Power's confidence in him.

Clearly, James Power was O'Connor's early guide and mentor. He was probably instrumental in encouraging his nephew to work breaking in horses for ten head of cattle and twenty-five cents a day, which he invested in buying cattle.[25] As the leader of the Refugio colony and colonel of the militia, Power inspired the young colonists to rally behind the Texan cause in the Texas Revolution in 1835–36. O'Connor was one of the signatories of the Goliad Declaration of Independence on December 10, 1835, and between October, 1835, and April, 1837, he enlisted for three periods of service, under three different commanders, Dimitt, Bingham, and the Tejano Flores, thus qualifying him for three grants of bounty land totaling 1,280 acres as a reward for military service on behalf of the Texas Republic.[26] He also fought in Captain Calder's company at the decisive battle of San Jacinto in April, 1836. Fighting for the Texan cause had a profound effect on changing his identity from an Irish colonist residing in a province of Mexico to a Texan supporting independence. It also provided material benefits that contributed to his financial independence.

During the war years, Thomas O'Connor, despite his youth, was able to advance his position by undertaking contracts for the army. He hauled goods and supplied horses to the military between San Antonio, Goliad, and the port of Copano, taking advantage of his location in a critical part of the war zone where there was a desperate shortage of supplies. Colonel Power was himself supplying military intelligence to the Texan army and could, no doubt, exercise his influence in directing where contracts for the military were placed. Power's friend John J. Linn, who was also a Power-Hewetson colonist although operating as a merchant in Victoria, was appointed as quartermaster for the Texan army, drawing on his mercantile experience and family relations living in Mexico. O'Connor's contracts were especially valuable to a young man intent on making his own way. From 1836 to 1842 he apparently earned at least $4,000 from supplying the military.[27]

In explaining how Thomas O'Connor was able to finance the buying of land and cattle, family legend has it that he learned the art of making saddletrees while spending time with young Mexicans at the Carlos ranch by the San Antonio River. The story goes that he walked the twenty miles to Victoria with his saddletrees on his back. He was able to trade them and purchase his first horse, and with the profits of his further efforts he was able to buy cattle, which formed the basis of his subsequent fortune. It is an attractive fable. Making and selling saddletrees may have occupied him for a short time but could not possibly have enabled him to buy land on the scale that he did. As early as October 3, 1836, Thomas O'Connor was buying a quarter of a league of land (1,107 acres) for $500 from his well-to-do neighbor and future father-in-law Nicholas Fagan.[28] He also borrowed $1,500 from Fagan, which with bounty land entitlement and his earnings from military service, enabled him to extend his land beyond the original land grant of 4,428 acres. By October, 1838, he had acquired an entitlement to 7,735 acres of land and was beginning to stock it with cattle and horses.

Thomas O'Connor served with distinction during the campaigns of 1835 and 1836 and was given significant responsibility by James Power. He and his cousin John O'Brien were put in charge of the evacuation of the families from Refugio and San Patricio in advance of the Mexican armies in the spring of 1836 during the "runaway scrape." It seems likely that the qualities that appealed to James Power would also have appealed to Nicholas Fagan, who acted in a timely way as an additional mentor. Here was a young man who may not originally have had much in the way of wealth and position but who had shown courage and ambition at an early stage of his life, and in his drive to build up his resources was promising much for the future.[29] At the time of his marriage in 1838, Thomas O'Connor had acquired 7,735 acres in his own right, and his bride's dowry brought him additional land and cattle. (Another story cherished by the O'Connor family can be verified. Thomas O'Connor and Mary Fagan made a journey of several days' ride on horseback to be married by the pastor of San Fernando in San Antonio. It was an important union between the two families that was duly solemnized by the Catholic church.[30])

Other opportunities presented themselves in the chaotic aftermath of the war. Many of the cattle ranches of the Mexican rancheros located beyond the Guadalupe and San Antonio Rivers were abandoned, and the stock was driven south beyond the Nueces. Consequently, large herds of cattle roamed freely in the territory between the Nueces and the Rio Grande. With the Texan army still in need of supplies, parties of soldiers were sent out to forage for meat to feed the troops. This was certainly the brief of Captain Flores's company in which Thomas O'Connor served. Once the army was disbanded, individuals were able to gather in herds on their own account. Sister Margaret Rose Warburton suggested it was more than likely that Thomas O'Connor, who was supplying the army with beef, corn, and other supplies, would have been well placed to add to his own stock in this way. It may also explain why he was not one of those who took part in the fateful Mier Expedition to Mexico.[31] In any case, the income he earned from military contacts was crucial in Thomas's early acquisition of land and cattle.

Military contracts were not always paid promptly, but Thomas O'Connor must have had faith in the Texas Republic. He even took a gamble on gaining from delayed payment. In July, 1840, he did fourteen days' work for a dollar a day for the military and took a promissory note that entitled him to a five-for-one payment. He was duly paid $70 by the quartermaster for his work.[32] He was also able to command the support of fellow colonists who could vouch for his character or act as his attorney-at-law and receive payment on his behalf. James Power, Martin Power, and John Dunn acted for him in dealings with the military authorities. By the time John Dunn was acting for him, in September and October, 1839, receiving $2,046 and $285 in those two months, he may have left the employment of James Power to become more of his own man at the young age of twenty-two. In 1842 Thomas O'Connor was supplying the military with eight head of beef for $100 and $5 for a yearling for the army stationed at Corpus Christi. A further four beefs for $50 and corn worth $120 were supplied to Texas volunteers in the same year. This was also the year of the first TC cattle brand, proof that Thomas O'Connor was making his mark in more ways than one.[33]

At this time, the fragile Republic of Texas was still threatened by invasion from Mexico. Live Oak Point, where James Power had his home, was captured by Mexicans in 1842. When a Mexican force attacked San Antonio, Thomas O'Connor volunteered as a member of Cameron's company to go to its relief and took part in the subsequent battle of Salado, which drove the enemy south without delivering a crushing blow against them.[34] O'Connor's active involvement with the military authorities in defense of his own property also proved to be an important source of profitable contracts.

A tailpiece to the story of the Gilliland family who were killed by a large band of Comanches in 1842 (see chapter 5) underlines the fragility of life and the lawless state of the frontier. "A posse of neighboring ranchmen, including Nicholas Fagan, Peter Teal, Thomas O'Connor and Anthony Sidick, pursued the Indians into Victoria County and overtook them," near the Murphy ranch. "There they engaged in a fierce battle with the savages. With their ammunition playing out and greatly outnumbered by the Indians, it seemed that the ranchmen were doomed. 'Connor, I guess we're done for,' remarked Teal to O'Connor, as he fired his last shot and pulled out his bowie knife for a hand to hand encounter with the redmen, when suddenly they heard the clatter of approaching horsemen and recognized 'Mustang' Gray and his 'cowboys' in the rear of the Comanches, who turned and fled, abandoning the boy and girl on the open prairie but not before they had run a lance through the body of the boy and dealt the girl a heavy blow on the head."[35] "Mustang" Gray was a legendary horse thief and murderer who was never brought to justice for his crimes. He may have enjoyed protection from the law as a favor for his rescue act.

In 1845 Thomas O'Connor was one of a group of settlers who drove out the Karankawa Indians after their attack at Kemper's Bluff on the lower Guadalupe River. Gradually, with the defeat of the Mexicans and the subjugation of the Indian tribes, the area achieved a more settled existence. In the spring of 1845, Irish colonists who had fled to Victoria were making preparations to return to their vacated lands situated on the Nueces River and at Copano Bay.[36] During their nine-year absence, Thomas O'Connor had stayed and built up his lands and herds of cattle and had survived the hazards of a lawless frontier.

Despite having come through battles with the Mexicans and Indians unscathed, Thomas O'Connor was confronted by the terrible uncertainty of frontier life when his young wife, Mary, died in 1843, a few days after giving birth to their third son. Mary's death and an alleged argument over the burial of one of Mary and Tom's children may have cast a shadow over the relations between her family and O'Connor. If there was a rift between

O'Connor and the Fagans, it was a temporary one. Good relations were restored by 1846–47, when both Fagans, father and son, entered into a bond with Thomas O'Connor for additional loans, his loan from ten years before having been paid off. In 1847 John Fagan sold O'Connor another quarter of a league of land for $500, which meant O'Connor now surpassed his father-in-law and mentor in terms of cattle and acres. Whereas Nicholas Fagan was assessed in 1848 for 4,426 acres and 150 cattle, his ambitious son-in-law was assessed for 5,853 acres and 600 head of cattle at a total value of $6,055.[37] With an enhanced cash flow, Thomas O'Connor continued to acquire more land, including a colonial grant for a full league of land, another 4,428 acres, in 1848.[38]

The same year brought an important move forward in his cattle enterprise. He changed his cattle brand to what was to become the famous O'Connor brand (T-C) in Refugio County, Texas, and sold his first shipment of beefs to be sent from the port of Indianola, on the Texas coast, to New Orleans. The contract with Foster, who was to dominate the New Orleans shipping trade, brought a healthy $10 per head and was to provide Thomas O'Connor with an all-important market in the antebellum period. The extent of the cattle shipments to New Orleans from south Texas was, in all probability, greater than has been understood and marks an important stage in the development of the O'Connor fortune.[39] Also in 1848 a sign of his standing in the community came with his election as commissioner for Refugio County.

The Republic of Texas was annexed by the United States in 1846, and the dispute over the Rio Grande border was finally settled in the Treaty of Guadalupe-Hidalgo at the end of the U.S.-Mexico War in 1848, but life on the frontier remained hazardous for pioneer settlers until the Indian tribes were pushed out of that part of Texas. As late as 1850, an Indian raid took place near the San Antonio River settlements. Two girls from the Taylor family, living near Lamar, were captured from land that later became part of the O'Connor pasture, and the same party of Indians attacked the Perry, O'Connor, and Welder ranches near the San Antonio River. In 1852 Thomas O'Connor was one of the group under Judge Hynes, sheriff of Refugio County, who took part in the last Indian fight at Hynes Spring where the Karankawas were driven from Texas into Mexico.[40]

At the time of the 1850 census, Thomas O'Connor was described as a herdsman with an estate valued at $4,000. This certainly underestimated the real value of his property. The Refugio tax rolls for 1850 record that

Thomas O'Connor had 7,495 acres, valued at $1,901, with thirteen hundred head of cattle worth $4,800. Including his town lot in Refugio, he was assessed at a total value of $7,211. His uncle, the empresario James Power, nominally held substantially more land through agents but only had five hundred head of cattle valued at $1,300.[41] With cattle becoming the major asset and much of the Power estate lost in legal disputes before the death of James Power in 1853, his nephew Thomas O'Connor was set to become Power's successor as a leading man in Refugio County.

The 1850 census recorded O'Connor as the owner of one black slave, age 15, and apart from his three children, Dennis (11), Martin (9), and James (7), he had five people in his employment and living in his household. His employees included a carpenter, a mason, and three herdsmen. Four of them, including all the herdsmen, were born in Ireland; the carpenter was born in Georgia. This suggests a policy at the time of hiring fellow Irishmen to work his cattle. More slaves were acquired during the 1850s; they lived in their own quarters adjoining the O'Connor log cabin and were employed to pick cotton on the estate. This turned out to be an unsuccessful venture. The failure of the cotton crop put an even greater emphasis on the rearing of cattle, but the employment of blacks continued even after the emancipation of slaves. Former slaves and their descendants were to prove themselves highly skilled and to play an important role working with horses and cattle on the O'Connor ranches.[42]

A traveler passing through the O'Connor place by the San Antonio River in 1855 offers a glimpse of the frugal conditions in which Thomas O'Connor lived while he was building up his estate:

It was built like an overseer's house, two cabins under one roof, a popular style in Texas, and one which gives a fine space under cover, yet open to the breezes, and there the table is set. This serves as a general assembly-room. Sometimes it has a floor, oftener not. The proprietor was an old Texan, [Thomas O'Connor] and his son, [Dennis] now seventeen years of age, was a native of the state. Cotton had been grown in a field adjoining the State [ranch], but it did not turn out a profitable crop, and his attention was directed exclusively to stock, of which he had about two thousand head. He was living with but few comforts, you would say with but few necessaries. In a cabin adjoining the one I mentioned, a wretched hovel, lived a large family of blacks, and in the evening the males danced a "break-down" for our amusement, while the females, made visible by the flame of a small fire on the heath, sat on the ground, not seemingly to take any interest in the "fun." When I rose the next morning a heavy fog enveloped the place. I saddled my horse, and waiting for breakfast, took a look at the premises. Two black pigs, a strutting turkey, and an old calico dress were in the yard, and some fine peach trees in the garden, with an acre or two of thrifty look-ing corn beyond. They had not attempted to raise garden vegetables.[43]

Increasingly, Thomas O'Connor concentrated on adding to his stock of cattle and extending his territory. One estimate reckons that he possessed 1,500 head in 1852 and the above account by Stillman records a figure of 2,000 head in 1855. It was a continual process of growth and expansion. In 1854 he purchased cattle in Refugio County: 132 from William Kuy-kendall for $1,450 and from William Clark, 1,000 head for $6,500. He acquired a league of prime land for $6,000 from the former empresario James Hewetson in 1855 and bought an adjoining league from the heirs of Keating, another colonist, in 1856.[44] Additional small parcels of land, typically 320 or 640 acres, were purchased from veterans of the Texas Revolution who preferred to redeem their bounty certificates for money rather than make use of the land. Thomas O'Connor, in coming from a country where the possession of land could mean literally the difference between life and death, had an Irishman's instinct for the value of land. During the decade of the 1850s alone, he may well have purchased many small parcels of land totaling 4,000 acres of bounty land in Refugio County.[45]

The availability of markets for beef cattle was crucial to the increased value of the land. Thomas O'Connor was early in the field with the ship-ment of beefs via Indianola to New Orleans, and he took personal charge of the cattle drives to Indianola. He was also directly involved in leading cattle drives to Rockport, where the meat was either processed or shipped on to New Orleans or Havana. Mrs. McCrea, an old citizen of Lamar, on the coast, recalled that Mr. O'Connor used to stop at her house on his re-turn from Rockport and that he always carried heavy money bags, which "he threw under the bed with his boots at night."[46] In addition to the Louisiana trade, there were early overland drives by Texas cattlemen to California, and a few attempted the long drives north to Chicago as early as 1856. This was to herald the postbellum golden age of the famous cattle drives on the Chisholm trail that contributed to making Texas cattle ranching into a prosperous industry and the so-called cattle kings into millionaires.

By 1860, on the eve of the American Civil War, Thomas O'Connor was the most successful cattleman in the region, "the unchallenged cattle baron of the Coastal Bend." Terry Jordan estimated that at least a third of large-scale cattle raisers in Refugio County were Irish, and significantly both the terminology and practices adopted in Refugio and San Patricio were shaped by those of the Mexicans and Coastal Prairie Anglos.[47] In the census of 1860, Thomas O'Connor was recorded as a farmer, age forty-one, with the value of his real estate assessed at $20,000 and his personal estate, largely his cattle and horses, assessed at $100,000. His eldest son, Dennis, twenty-four, and Martin, nineteen, were listed as farmers, working on the O'Connor ranch. Dennis had his own personal stock of cattle and horses, valued at $100.[48] He was obviously being trained as a stockman to follow in his father's footsteps, and he was given the responsibility of his own cattle. Thomas O'Connor had 40,000 head of cattle, branded about 12,000 calves annually, and was selling beef for about $80,000 annually.[49]

The conflict between the Union and the Confederacy brought great hardship to the South, and although Texas was not a main theater of the war, the usual markets for Texas cattle were suspended during the hostilities. Cattle ranchers found that the Confederate army offered lower prices for beef than the enemy in the North, and the superiority of the Union navy meant that the Confederate ports were blockaded. But considerable profits were to be made by Texas cattlemen driving herds to market in New Orleans and exchanging them for U.S. gold. In June, 1864, Texas beefs were bought for $40 to $60 a head in New Orleans. While Confederate leaders protested against dealing with the enemy, cattle continued to be sold throughout the war.[50]

The natural sympathies of most Texans lay with the Confederacy. Many of the colonists had come to Texas from the southern states and brought their plantation economy, with cotton and slaves, to their new home. A fierce spirit of independence had shaped the early history of the Republic of Texas, and resentment against interference from the industrial North could be harnessed to the defense of a predominantly rural way of life in the South. In this context, it is interesting that Thomas O'Connor remained opposed to the Civil War. He did not side with the Confederate cause and, as a result, risked being burned out of his property. However, his two surviving sons, Dennis and Martin, enlisted in the Confederate army. Martin did not survive the war, dying at the age of twenty-one. The O'Connor boys had been educated in Mobile, Alabama, which was another port of entry for cattle sent from Texas, and they had, in the process, acquired values and loyalties that set them apart from their father. Thomas O'Connor may not have worked out a philosophical position with regard to the rights or wrongs of the war ("I have no quarrel with either side"[51]), but he was a man of profound, practical intelligence who could foresee the economic damage that would be inflicted on the North and South. He had fought in the Texas Revolution (1835–36) and lived through the political uncertainty over the relations with Mexico that followed in the decade from 1836 to 1846 when the border remained in dispute. He had also seen how the state of Texas had flourished since its annexation by the United States in 1846, which coincided with a growth in population and a general expansion of the economy. His own prosperity had paralleled that of the state of Texas under the Union. More pertinently, he was involved in opening up markets for his cattle, which, he could surely envisage, depended for future prospects on the urban populations of the North. Put bluntly, it was not in his business interest to endorse the breaking up of the Union, and to a man of almost frightening single purpose that would have been a defining influence.

The war that caused such havoc for many of his neighbors was turned into another opportunity by Thomas O'Connor. Wisely, he did not invest in Confederate money. His preference for gold and for Mexican dollars protected him from the disastrous erosion of the currency as the war went on. He kept his wealth intact, almost certainly through investment, and was able to move swiftly after the war to buy more land from impoverished farmers who were forced to sell the only asset left to them. He maintained large herds that multiplied naturally over the war years, so that he was well placed to participate in the major cattle drives to the north that began in the spring of 1866. Folk tradition has it that he was opposed to the institution of slavery, which may have formed part of his opposition to the Civil War; nonetheless, he was a slave-owner. In May, 1864, more than a year after the Emancipation Proclamation issued by President Lincoln went into effect, Thomas O'Connor sold a thirty-year-old "Negro boy" called Thornton to Edward Perry for $850.[52] Whether the news of emancipation had reached Texas or whether people clung to the prospect of ultimate victory for the Confederacy, thereby preserving slavery, is not clear, but it was a clever move in terms of cutting his losses. O'Connor is said to have lost eighteen Negro men worth $18,000 through emancipation, but on the evidence of the Thornton sale, how much he actually lost remains in question.[53]

While O'Connor may have incurred some losses through emancipation, a source of additional income came with the growth of the tallow and hide industries in south Texas. Beef was not the only valuable product from cattle ranching, and with the establishment of W. S. Hall's tallow plant at Rockport in 1865, immense quantities were shipped out for candle making. Hides, which represented half the value of slaughtered cattle, were also sold as raw material for the leather and shoemaking industries, much of which was centered in the eastern cities of the United States.[54]

With the end of the Civil War, a new phase of the Texas cattle industry began. In the spring of 1866, the era of the long cattle drives to the north commenced, with an estimated 250,000 head crossing the Red River and moving on to Abilene and Kansas. Thomas O'Connor sent his foreman with herds up the trail to Chicago and later Montana. Over the next twenty years, during a period of general expansion, he took advantage of the growth of the industry and continued to develop the estate that had been built before the war. While he was selling cattle for profit, he was not depleting his herds, and he was buying more land as it came on the market. In Refugio County alone, Thomas O'Connor concluded six transactions involving land deeds between October, 1868, and October, 1869.[55]

By this time, he had become one of the wealthiest men in the Coastal Bend, but he continued to live frugally and remained modest and unassuming in his habits. Even in his later years, he rarely used a horse and carriage. Long days in the saddle and the tough conditions involved in working cattle on the range had given him a preference for riding horseback. His one concession to luxury, one that he shared with many cattlemen, was "the use of the finest handmade boots he could procure." To those who criticized his austere way of life, he would reply with a saying that reveals much of his character and desire to protect his family, "theirs will be walking when ours are riding."[56]

For a few years after the Civil War, Thomas O'Connor continued to live in the log cabin alongside the San Antonio River that he had built himself with the aid of a few friends in the 1830s. He was visited on June 10, 1869, by Mr. and Mrs. G. O. Stoner, who had been married that day at the home of Judge J. W. Rose, the bride's father in Victoria. The couple were traveling to the Stoner home at Saint Mary's in Refugio County and reached the O'Connor place at nightfall. He invited them in for supper and to stay the night. Thomas O'Connor, who was living alone, prepared the supper and the breakfast himself, and provided the couple with warm hospitality. One aspect of the visit was handed down as part of Stoner family folklore: both meals were exactly the same, consisting of bacon, corn cakes, and coffee.[57] What is significant here is not merely the frugality of Thomas O'Connor but the perceptions of a younger generation from a background of southern gentility used to more genteel standards of domesticity.

A year later, visitors to the O'Connor household would have found that he had acquired a housekeeper, Julia Hughes, age 30. Also resident on July 1, 1870, census night, were four men: 58-year-old Thomas Hilton, a stock raiser, who may have been a guest; Hugh and Ned Mitchel, 18 and 20, respectively; and Ned Rab, 30. Apart from Hilton, the others, employed by O'Connor either to work in the house or on the ranch, were illiterate, born in Texas, and black.[58] If the household had changed, the simple fare of bacon, corn cakes, and coffee, judging by the surviving grocery lists, almost certainly remained.[59] The census also revealed that Thomas O'Connor was assessed on the value of his real estate at $40,000 and his personal estate at $32,000, a decline from 1860 that may be accounted for by the loss of his slaves, but both figures almost certainly underestimated the extent of his total assets.

In 1876 Thomas O'Connor had a new ranch house built on Dry Bayou, probably at the time of his marriage to Ellen Shelly. She, no doubt, was not prepared to tolerate the primitive conditions of the log cabin. The house had five rooms and a hallway downstairs, and two large rooms above. A broad gallery extended across the front of the house. A dining room and kitchen were added in 1883. Surrounding the house was a three-acre yard with trees, shrubs, and flowers, and at the front a rose garden with native oaks, magnolias, wild peach, and banana trees. At the side of the house was an acre of ground for the vegetable garden. In 1884 a two-room servants' house was built. The new house may have been a symbol of Thomas O'Connor's wealth, but he had not abandoned his austere outlook. He insisted that the timber of the old house should be used in building the new one, and in surveying the contents of his new home, he used to say that the old rawhide-bottomed chair was the only thing that belonged to him—the house and all the rest belonged to "He-len" (his wife, Ellen, who died in 1878).[60]

Important economic changes in Texas during the 1870s facilitated the expansion of the O'Connor estate into one of the major ranches in the Coastal Bend. The state passed two homestead laws that encouraged further immigration, with new settlers entitled to a grant of 160 acres. The state's population grew from 604,215 in 1860 to more than 1 million by

1874, with an important increase in railroad mileage from a mere 392 in 1861 to 1,578 in 1873. Also by 1873 Texas had sufficiently recovered from the war and postwar reconstruction to exceed its prewar cotton production, with 487,771 bales compared with 431,463 bales in 1860. While cotton remained the main output of Texas agriculture, the state's economy was tied to a crop that experienced steadily declining profits.[61] Farmers, often occupying small acreages, were vulnerable to market conditions. If they had been forced to borrow money at rates of 10 to 12 percent per annum during the Civil War and Reconstruction, they were not able to survive through a period of low prices. On the other hand, Texas cattle ranching flourished during the 1870s, and Thomas O'Connor prospered mightily by exploiting the economic benefits of increased demand and improved transportation and by anticipating the changes effected by the enclosure of pasture through fencing and the use of barbed wire. These innovations had a damaging effect on many small farmers who lost their access to water in enclosed land and were compelled to sell to their larger and more powerful neighbors.

In the early 1870s Thomas O'Connor launched a massive program of buying, mostly small parcels of land of a few hundred acres each. For instance, 37 land transactions were completed in Refugio County alone between July, 1873, and January, 1875, where buying became almost the sole preserve of the O'Connor ranch.[62] Later in the decade, some larger acquisitions were made: 2,086 acres at Hynes Bay on the Gulf Coast in 1877; 3,396 acres on the Mission River in 1878; and 4,428 acres in 1879 on the San Antonio River.[63] Some of the prime lands that belonged to the Power family also began to be absorbed into the O'Connor estate. Into the 1880s O'Connor purchased thousands of acres of land, in some cases for as little as 31 cents an acre.[64]

A sinister explanation of the way the O'Connor lands were acquired in the 1870s is found in Abel G. Rubio's book *Stolen Heritage: A Mexican-American's Rediscovery of His Family's Lost Land Grant.*[65] The book is a family history in search of a lost land grant, originally conveyed to Rubio's ancestor Manuel Becerra in 1832. It is a trawl through surviving land records, maps, and deeds with the assistance of lawyers trying to bring a legal claim against the O'Connor family, and it relies heavily on the folk memory of members of the different branches of the family. The book reads more like a personal journey than a piece of history. The chronology of what happened to the land is sacrificed to a chronology of each piece of discovery. The labor of the search and the writing of the story are driven by a self-proclaimed obsession over an alleged injustice committed in 1875 when Antonio de la Garza, the descendant of Manuel Becerra, was forced to leave his land under a threat to his life by unnamed Americans. Rubio claims that Antonio de la Garza never conveyed or sold the land but was simply driven off it and therefore lost it through intimidation and force. This took place at a time of heightened tensions between the Anglos and the Mexicans in Refugio County following several murders and hangings that resulted in loss of life on both sides. As Thomas O'Connor and his son, Dennis M. O'Connor, were eventually to acquire the land of the original Becerra tract, the accusation of intimidation was leveled at the O'Connor family, although, as Rubio concedes, there was no tangible proof of their involvement. In the absence of firm evidence beyond the memory of family legends, descendants believe what they want to believe. Family legends are often unsustainable in the light of the surviving evidence.

In 1873, to the astonishment of his contemporaries and against the wishes of his eldest son, Dennis, Thomas O'Connor sold his cattle for the sum of $14,000, when their market value was low. He wanted to invest in more land. There appeared still to be an abundance of land on which cattle could roam freely, so why should anyone wish to buy more land? Contemporary wisdom did not anticipate events or understand the imperatives of a large-scale enterprise. With the purchases he had made by 1879, O'Connor had an enclosed pasture of 170,000 acres.[66] His policy of enclosure went along with the aggressive policy of land purchase and the consolidation of the estate. It began with plank fencing in 1873 and was extended to a huge purchase of barbed wire starting in 1876 that continued for the next thirty years. The barbed wire was stretched on the same posts that had held the planks, and the planks, brought in from Florida, were used in the construction of ranch buildings, including the barn floor of the River Ranch. Fencing the many miles of the O'Connor estate perimeter was a prolonged and expensive undertaking, but it was a shrewd investment. By 1907 when the D. M. O'Connor estate was divided, all the main pastures had been fenced with 100,000 pounds of barbed wire.[67] Within the first ten years of the period when fencing was being put in place, the price of land increased from $1 to $2 an acre, thus doubling the nominal value of the estate.

If Thomas O'Connor needed an example to follow, it was offered by the phenomenal success of the legendary Santa Gertrudis Ranch, founded in 1852 by the Irishman Richard King and located at the headwaters of

Baffin Bay near Corpus Christi. By the end of the Civil War, King and his partner Miflin Kenedy employed one hundred vaqueros and possessed thirty-three thousand longhorns and almost twice as many sheep, goats, and horses grazing almost five hundred thousand acres of unfenced land. However, neither King nor Kenedy were devoted to the open range, believing that an efficient operation demanded complete control of the grass and water on their pasture land. Enclosing the range supported the livestock breeding program. Fencing kept out strays, and in lawless times, it gave notice to trespassers, thieves, and squatters. Long before the introduction of barbed wire, huge tracts of land on the King Ranch were fenced.[68]

In the early 1870s, along with the selling his cattle, Thomas O'Connor negotiated for the sale of his cattle brand to Coleman, Mathis, and Fulton for thirty thousand dollars. The company went on to buy up the cattle of small owners and shipped them from Rockport to New Orleans and Havana. According to Frank Dobie, O'Connor doubted his ability to negotiate with the company, and he offered Jerry and Bob Driscoll either five thousand dollars or five thousand acres of land to make the trade. The Driscolls wisely chose the land while they were "secretly laughed at by some people."[69]

Clearly, Thomas O'Connor had thought out a strategy for taking his holdings into the top flight of cattle ranches in Texas. Buying land in exchange for cattle enabled him to consolidate his estate so that enclosure would give him a dominant position from the Gulf Coast inland, extending across several counties. He was able to achieve such a position by the late 1870s, but he had built up his estate by acquiring many small parcels of land in a host of beneficial deals. Examples of his land transactions illustrate his business acumen. In May, 1874, he sold to Louisa Welder his original colonial grant, situated on the southside of Sous Creek, for $4,428. This was pure profit: he had received the land grant at no cost in 1834. In December, 1876, he bought a league of land and one town lot from Martin Power's heirs in Ireland for the sum of 200 sterling or about $1,000. In February, 1887, he sold the same league of land to John Linney for $6,000, making a handy profit of 500 percent; he sold the town lot for 25 gold dollars.[70] He had acquired several thousand acres of bounty land in the 1850s, and by the 1880s he had amassed some 20,000 acres from donation and bounty land by buying up certificates to bail people out who desperately needed the money. He was also able to acquire land that was sold at the District Court Office to redeem tax debts at ridiculously little cost to himself. For instance, he paid the debts of $15.64, with $2.50 costs, for a total of $18.14, to Refugio County in 1877 for 2,086 acres near the coast in Hynes Bay that was owned by James Collier, an original Power-Hewetson colonist. Purchased at a fraction over one cent per acre, this was a considerable bargain.[71]

The availability of tax deeds and of bounty land brought opportunities that enabled O'Connor to add to his lands remarkably cheaply. The arrangement also benefited the county clerk, who was able to redeem his potential losses on unpaid taxes with the certain knowledge that in Refugio County, at least, O'Connor would be interested in paying the taxes and acquiring the land, if it was in the locality of his expanding estate. With the advantages to both parties so clearly conjoined, it seems highly likely that Thomas O'Connor was given advance notice of tax deeds that were due for sale and had first pick of what was available. Personal contacts would inevitably have played their part. Patrick Shelly, the clerk of Refugio County in the 1840s and 1850s, was a fellow Power-Hewetson colonist, neighbor, and brother-in-law of Thomas O'Connor. There is no evidence of anything illegal in such an arrangement, but when you look at the number of land transactions in the deed books held at the District Court Office in Refugio and see whole pages, including twenty or more consecutive entries in the 1870s, every single one involving Thomas O'Connor purchasing land, there would appear to be some form of advance notification involved.

If the 1870s saw the O'Connor holdings expand dramatically with a host of small parcels of land, the 1880s produced even greater expansion involving the purchase of major estates. In November, 1883, a mortgage was negotiated with the Shiner brothers of Béxar for $44,846, paid by Thomas O'Connor on tracts of land in La Salle and McMullen Counties.[72] Three years later, the 45,000-acre estate of the Shiner brothers was taken over by Thomas O'Connor in exchange for O'Connor cattle. The Shiner pasture was valued at $120,000.[73] This was a reversal of the situation when Thomas O'Connor started out in the 1830s, borrowing money from neighbors in order to purchase land. In the 1880s he was lending money at 12 percent per annum, with the condition that the land would revert to him if the payments were not maintained. He was also engaged in deals on selling cattle, allowing the purchaser loaned finance with the understanding that both the cattle and the land, used as collateral on the deal, could revert to the lender. In 1883, to facilitate this policy of lending money, Thomas O'Connor became the leading partner in the O'Connor and Sullivan Bank in San Antonio, putting his very considerable capital assets into financial diversification.[74] With cattle prices halving between 1882 and 1885, many Texas ranchers needed to borrow money to fatten up their stock for the market in Chicago.[75] The conditions that the O'Connor and Sullivan Bank were able to impose by specializing in the cattle business turned potential difficulties into commercial advantage.

Banking was merely one part of O'Connor's diversification. In 1877, the same year in which he moved his mansion to the suburbs of the town of Refugio, "to command a fine view," Thomas O'Connor went into the hotel business. A newspaper description of the time reported the O'Connor House "as a large, an elegantly fitted house . . . not surpassed by any hotel in the west in all of its arrangements." The opening was well timed to ensure a large share of patronage. "During court week the house was crowded to its utmost capacity. The landlord, Mr. Freeman, seems determined to spare no pains or expense to make his guests comfortable. The building was erected expressly for a hotel, the rooms are large and well furnished, while the table abounds in everything the market affords."[76]

A commercial venture of rather greater importance was made possible in the 1880s by the invention of refrigeration. In 1882 Mr. A. de Rollepot established an ice manufactory, and a number of the stockmen of Victoria and adjoining counties organized a joint stock company with $1 million capital. Thomas O'Connor, J. A. McFaddin, and other stockmen, and the banking firm of A. Levi and Company were foremost in the business of running refrigerator cars to eastern cities for the shipment of fresh meat, slaughtered in Victoria. There, the Texas Continental Beef Company, in which Thomas Marion O'Connor was involved, was slaughtering about 150 beefs per day, with varying numbers of sheep, hogs, and small cattle. The carcasses were then shipped over the NYT&M railroad to New Orleans where there was a ready sale for Texan beef. Victor Marion Rose, in characteristically florid style, reported this new technological development with unrestrained enthusiasm: "The giant possibilities in connection with this undertaking defies, for the present, even conjecture. The enterprise alone contains the germs of a commerce sufficient to found cities, run railways, and rival the magic powers of Aladdin's lamp."[77]

Thomas O'Connor did some service to the cattle industry in general by winning a legal battle over assessed taxes. He was in dispute with the sheriff of Aransas County in 1886 over taxes on his cattle; he claimed he had already paid taxes on the same cattle in Refugio County. With his large holdings, the cattle could not be confined within the boundary of a single county, but he argued he should be assessed in the county of his principal residence in Refugio. In the legal case that followed, it emerged that some branding of cattle took place in Aransas County on the land of Judge Hynes, but there was no O'Connor residence on the 18,191 acres with 4,000 cattle held within that county. The decision went in favor of Thomas O'Connor, thus preventing cattle ranchers having to pay taxes twice on the same herds of cattle. It also emerged that within Refugio County Thomas O'Connor had paid his assessed taxes in 1884 on 31,180 cattle valued at $374,160.[78]

Another legal dispute over the sale of cattle in 1887 reveals the way Thomas O'Connor used his strong financial position to his own advantage. On April 23, 1885, he signed a contact with Solomon Parks. Thomas O'Connor would deliver 8,000 head of cattle (mixed yearlings, steers, and heifers) all to be good merchantable cattle, to be delivered in three herds, the first herd on May 15, 1885, at the price of $8 per head. The contract stated that half the amount should be made available on loan at the O'Connor and Sullivan Bank in San Antonio, at any time on or before twelve months from the delivery of the first cattle, and the loan would draw an interest of 12 percent per annum. As collateral, a deed of trust was drawn up on the property of 12,709 acres of land owned by Parks, which was situated near the San Antonio River in Goliad County, and also on the entire stock of cattle.

After the delivery of some of the first herds, Mr. Parks declined to take the cattle, and a dispute arose as to their quality. The remaining cattle were then sold to the Shiner brothers and to Mr. Driscoll at $8 per head. The verdict found for the plaintiff, Thomas O'Connor. He was to receive $48,294.95, an aggregate amount in compensation for the cattle, including the 12 percent interest on the loan, together with the costs of the suit. In the event, not only were the cattle sold but O'Connor also obtained Parks's land on the San Antonio River as a result of the purchaser's default on the contract.[79]

By the 1880s the purchase of land necessitated the services of estate agents who specialized in the sale of ranch land. Thomas O'Connor, being well placed to purchase any lands that came up on the market, was given notice of upcoming sales before they became public knowledge. For instance, there is a letter dated August 5, 1888, addressed to T. M. O'Connor, the younger surviving son, from Naylor and Company Real Estate and Land Agents of San Antonio, which offered the services of the company in purchasing the San Antonio Viejo ranch.[80]

If selling cattle to purchase more land and enclosing the O'Connor pastures were important policies of the 1870s, purchasing major estates represented Thomas O'Connor's strategy in the 1880s, a decision that required the hazardous and expensive experiment of drilling for water. The idea of deep drilling had been talked about for some time, and in the last year of Thomas O'Connor's life, the explorations began. The O'Connor ranch was the first in the Gulf Coast region to attempt the boring of artesian wells.[81] Surviving correspondence from the American Well Works (A.W.W.) Company in Aurora, Illinois, provides a fascinating glimpse into the way business was conducted. It also highlights the respective roles of the father and his two sons, Dennis and Thomas Marion O'Connor, who continued to oversee the work after Thomas O'Connor died in October, 1887. The father made the initial enquiry, visiting the company in Aurora with his attendant. Initially, he did not contemplate making wells larger than six inches in diameter, and he wanted to purchase a four-horse-power machine. M. T. Chapman, the president of A.W.W., tried to persuade Thomas O'Connor to purchase a heavier rig and to use steam. He told him at what price he had sold a rig in Galveston, Texas, and what the work involved. A power rig was dispatched from Illinois to Texas in October, 1887, but the engine arrived without the trimmings, which had been stolen from the firebox. It also soon became clear that a six-inch pipe and a four-horsepower engine could not cope with drilling to a level of four hundred feet. By January, 1888, the O'Connor brothers were complaining to A.W.W. about equipment not being delivered and were, for their own part, obtaining patented articles from the Lee Foundry at Galveston. When A.W.W. found out about the O'Connors' buying their patented equipment at Galveston, they demanded royalty payments be made to them.

While Dennis O'Connor was accused by Chapman of "cursing and abuse" in his business correspondence over the well equipment, the latter remained eager to please and to keep a lucrative contract. Nevertheless, he had to admit to a number of unfortunate problems that had arisen over installing the drilling rig: "Now relative to our failure or success at Galveston I can answer those questions as I was there personally in finishing the work, unfortunately there was more whiskey used in sinking the well than was required for the oiling of the machinery and we had to suffer the unfortunate consequences in being slow to accomplish the work. Relative to the Duplex Pump we furnished there, we had never used salt wells and it was entirely overlooked or never thought of, that the salt would eat the pump, which it did and almost destroyed them for use, until brass parts could be secured to make them practical to handle salt water."[82]

Chapman argued that fitting up a horse-power rig and then adding to it did not work; he offered to bring new equipment and do the job at no additional cost. In February, Chapman was still trying to appease the O'Connors by sending $337 and asking them to withdraw legal claims made against his company. After some initial technical problems over the size of the well rig and a failure to deliver parts—plus difficulty over the brass fittings eroding in seawater and a dispute over the wages of $4 a day paid to Mr. King, the engineer on the site—the deep drilling went ahead.[83] Over the next few years, this proved to be an important step in providing a constant water supply for the O'Connor ranch.

The correspondence shows how the O'Connor family used its powerful position to demand that contracts be fulfilled to their requirements and the threat of legal action to drive a hard bargain. It also demonstrates that Thomas O'Connor always looked to secure the lowest price possible, that the tone of Dennis's correspondence could be aggressive, and that Thomas Marion, the steadier of the two brothers, was needed to resolve disagreements. A letter addressed to Thomas Marion from C. R. Johns & Austin reveals some differences between the brothers: "We are in receipt of your kind letter of the 7th inst. Relative to our resuming business relations as in the past. . . . We had some misunderstanding with your brother, and tried to justify our language as used in our letter to which he took offence. There was no need of any misunderstanding. As you say, let it be of the past, and we will do what we can in your interests, as we did in the interests of your esteemed father in the several difficult mat[t]ers we handled in his interest."[84]

Toward the end of his life, the esteemed father, Thomas O'Connor, was not able to maintain complete control over his affairs, and his sons increasingly took the initiative. In June, 1885, Thomas O'Connor had a serious fall from his carriage and was confined to bed for some time.[85] From May, 1886, until his death on October 16, 1887, he received constant medical treatment for the painful condition of cancer of the face; the purchase of wizard oil, saltpeter, and laudanum was recorded in the household accounts. During March, 1887, there were frequent visits to the doctor in town and in the last few days of his life, regular attendance by the doctor at his house.[86] He was nursed until the end by Dennis's wife, Mary Virginia Drake, and a faithful Mexican retainer, Cerillo Vasquez.[87]

The obituaries in the San Antonio newspapers that recorded his death proclaimed the qualities of the man and the scale of his achievement. The *San Antonio Daily Times* described Thomas O'Connor as "the millionaire stockman and senior partner of the banking house of O'Connor & Sullivan" and recalled that having been born in Ireland about seventy years ago, he had come to Texas in time to take part in the battle of San Jacinto. A brief report concluded with the statement: "He was a sterling citizen and by economy and perseverance amassed an immense fortune, all of which goes to his two sons, D. M. and Thos. O'Connor Jnr."[88] The *San Antonio Daily Express* described Thomas O'Connor as "probably the wealthiest man in Texas" and reported that he was without a penny when he landed in this country, "but by enterprise and economy amassed a very large fortune, and at the time of his death, was the largest individual land and cattle owner in Texas." In another piece in the same issue, it was claimed that "during his long life he is reputed to have amassed $6,000,000, and that he possessed the respect of all for his unimpeachable integrity." The legend of rags to riches was further strengthened with the account that the deceased "began life a good many years ago as a poor man, earning a scanty living by making saddletrees for ranchmen and cowboys. His spare money he invested in lands and cattle, until in a few years he became one of the richest men in the entire state, numbering his cattle by the thousands and his acres by the million. Three or four years ago Mr. O'Connor was offered $4,000,000 in cash for his Refugio County cattle ranch, but refused it. Though immensely wealthy, Mr. O'Connor was benevolent and charitable to his less fortunate fellowmen and his death will be regretted by all who knew him."[89]

The will of Thomas O'Connor had been drawn up in 1883 and came into full effect in 1890, three years after his death.[90] The terms of the will reflected the problem of the handover of the O'Connor estate to the next generation, a subject that clearly exercised Thomas O'Connor and to which he gave very careful attention. Thomas O'Connor had one surviving legitimate son and obvious heir to the estate, Dennis M. O'Connor, forty-seven years old at his father's death. The surviving correspondence between father and son reveals a strongly emotional and tempestuous relationship. The austere father who had lived frugally in building up his great estate, disapproved of his son's wayward behavior. The following letter is included nearly in its entirety because of its importance in understanding the father and his concern for his son.

Dear Sun,

it is in sorrow and downharted that I write to you not on my own account but on yours. I ain't angery with you for you are as deer to me as at any time in your life when your dear mother dide and you and your two little Brothers and my self was left alone my prares went up to God to grant me life to see you sixteen years of age, I thought then that you would have sense anofe to take Care of what I have and your two little Brothers. I offin told your unkle William and Judge Hynes those wordes. I had a good rite to think so as I was turned loos on the world on the day I became fifteen years of age and your dear mother had more sense than I had when you children was small and youse were nelt around me saying your prares you were my consolation sinse then till the present time day and night I praid for God to save you from harm. You will recollect that when the ware closd I went and hunted you up in Goliad I was afraid that you would get in bad Company, you spoke about some cottin, I told you to lave it alone that I had nof and if not that I could make anoufe for both of us it was only my duty towards you but whar was the outher father that done it.

Dinis for some time past I was in grate hopes that you had taking ferrim stand but all that was blasted. I dramed of you two nites that a horse had throwing you and run of with you and your feet fastened in the sturrip and bruised. . . . when I heard that you ware drinking in Goliad and Victory [Victoria], I had not felt so bad sinse the day that I saw your Dear Wife with her baby in her armes in Murphy's Store trying to get you home if you new the people talk about it like I doe I dont know what you would doe your friends and mine simpithise and feel sorry for you whilst others is Glad dinis your sertinly well informed and smart and intelligent and ought make diffirent mark in the wourld you think. Every man that spakes friendly to you is your friend but that false that what lave you unable to protect yourselfe now I will say to you in advise not to leave? the river nor go from home let those that want to see you come and see you or rite to you. Your unkle Peter [Fagan] and myself and a few friends on this side of the river is anofe for you to see there is nothing but severe sickness or death should take you across that river dinis, you will say that this is all infernal lie and that I am abusing you but that not so if any one has your intrust.

I remain as ever

T. O'Connor[91]

Dennis O'Connor was fond of a drink on a grand scale, took up with low company, and had many liaisons with women outside his marriage.[92] His own letters reveal him to be volatile and irascible. Correspondence from his physician reveals that he was suffering from ill health on several counts: malaria, arthritis, and almost certainly, some form of venereal disease.[93] From an inheritance point of view, his father must have feared that he was not completely fit and reliable to run the estate.

Thomas O'Connor also had two surviving illegitimate children, Thomas Marion and Mary O'Connor. Eighteen years younger than his brother, Thomas Marion O'Connor had been brought up to learn the business of ranching and had proved himself to be a steady and worthy successor to his father. The will divided the estate into four parts: Dennis to have three-quarters of the land and Thomas Marion to have the other quarter. A clause in the will asserted that if Dennis challenged the terms of the will, his share of the estate would be reduced from three-quarters to one half. Mary was left fifty thousand dollars, to be paid in three installments, a characteristically cautious action by the father. Finally, a donation of one thousand dollars was given to the Catholic convent in Refugio to support the church and education. This bequest began a tradition of philanthropy that continued into succeeding generations of the O'Connor family.

The terms of the will ensured that the estate would survive into the next generation and beyond. To their credit, Dennis and Thomas Marion got along together and until 1890 worked in partnership as the O'Connor brothers. The estate was then divided according to the terms of the will. Dennis received 276,203 acres; Thomas Marion received 92,264 acres. The sons continued the pioneering work begun by their father. Further land purchases, including railway land, took place in the 1890s, and a further consolidation of the estate was accomplished. Dennis sold the family interest in the O'Connor and Sullivan Bank in San Antonio and became active in the Republican Party in Texas. Thomas Marion, who had been the principal stockholder in the Texas Continental Meat Company in Victoria in 1883, made a success of slaughtering livestock, increasing production when the plant moved to Fort Worth in 1890.[94] He was one of the first to foresee the impact of the railways in transporting cattle and invested in railroad construction with a group of businessmen from Victoria to form the Guadalupe Railway Company in 1897. He was also aware of the importance of new breeds of cattle being imported from India. The

Brahma cattle were introduced in 1906, and the McFaddin and O'Connor Brahmas were soon attracting international attention. Cross-breeding experiments with English shorthorns and Hereford cattle began to replace the famous Texas longhorns. The importation of foreign breeds of cattle continued a policy begun by the first Thomas O'Connor.

The continuity of policy that accompanied the transfer of power from Thomas O'Connor to his sons, Dennis and Thomas Marion O'Connor, was fortunate for the long-term health of the O'Connor ranches, but the succession period that lasted until the death of Dennis in 1900 was not without its dangers. During the 1890s a combination of influences threatened the survival of Dennis O'Connor's inheritance. From 1893 to 1898 serious losses of cattle were encountered from severe drought, followed by further losses from frost. With cattle prices low and sales difficult, mounting financial losses occurred. Land was mortgaged on a short-term basis. Dennis O'Connor admitted in his family correspondence the seriousness of the situation, and the pressure he was under may have contributed to his continued ill health.

He was also beset by personal problems that compounded his business difficulties. Dennis had a stormy relationship with his wife, Mary Virginia, who apparently spent most of her time away from home. Rosalie McDuffy, the housekeeper, appeared to be holding things together, with Dennis suffering persistent ill health and two families living for free at the O'Connor ranch. Adding to the financial pressure was the second and third generations' habit of expensive travel and luxurious living. Mary Virginia and her daughter, Mary, spent time living in hotels, and all the family enjoyed the fashion for spa treatment in Arkansas. In contrast to the frugality of the senior Thomas O'Connor, those who followed him became gentrified and enjoyed their newfound wealth. They went away to boarding school and entered the more sophisticated society of Austin and New York City. In New York, Mary Virginia and Dennis's daughter became infatuated with Jack Hallinan, a charming but evil fortune hunter whom she eventually married despite the disapproval of her father. The tempestuous and brutal relationship was expensive and ultimately proved disastrous. (Mary and Jack Hallinan separated within three years, and she divorced him in 1908, after ten years of marriage. She died in 1910 at age thirty-nine.) Finally, Thomas O'Connor's nephew from Ireland (also named Thomas O'Connor) who had killed the foreman on a cattle drive and been convicted of manslaughter in 1871, was probably attempting to extract money from the family in 1892. He was put under surveillance while living in New Orleans, where he was observed drinking and bragging about the money he expected to claim.[95] The financial difficulties that faced Dennis O'Connor in the 1890s did not, in the end, damage the O'Connor estate, further testimony to the father's achievement in creating an estate that was sufficiently large to withstand the depredations of the next generation.

A number of key influences are identifiable in explaining the growth of the O'Connor estate from 1836 to 1887. By his own account, Thomas O'Connor was driven by the traumatic experience of being turned loose on the world at the age of fifteen, unable to share in the family farm in Ireland, which went to his twenty-one-year old brother, Dennis. Land hunger was a central obsession in prefamine Ireland. The pressure of population on the land created a desperate situation where 3 out of 8 million people were either critically dependent upon the staple crop of the potato for survival or struggled to exist in a state of endemic poverty on inadequate employment as landless laborers. The alternative of mass emigration was established in Ireland by the early 1830s, when Thomas O'Connor and the other Irish colonists left Ireland bound for Texas. They took their land hunger with them, and the offer of land grants under the Mexican empresario system was the major factor in their decision to emigrate.

Thomas O'Connor defended his newly acquired property during and immediately after the Texas Revolution by remaining on the land. Later he fought against the attempted Mexican invasion and defended his property against marauding Indians, freebooters, and Mexican bandits. He built up capital by borrowing from his father-in-law, establishing lucrative contracts with the army in the years 1836 to 1842, and investing shrewdly in the purchase of land. He took full advantage of opportunities to procure land from hard-pressed veterans selling bounty land, farmers struggling to pay tax debts, and colonists or their heirs who had no taste for pioneer life. Well before the American Civil War, Thomas O'Connor had acquired sizable herds of cattle and a burgeoning estate that he increased with each new small-scale purchase.

At each stage of the development of the Texas ranching industry, Thomas O'Connor anticipated events. In 1848 he was one of the first cattlemen to send beefs via Indianola to New Orleans. Immediately after the end of the Civil War, he was involved in sending herds on the long trails north. He diversified his business interests through involvement

Dennis O'Connor, who in 1887 inherited the bulk of his father's estate, which had been built up from Thomas O'Connor's 1834 land grant, sits with his sons *(from left to right)* Tom, Martin, and Joe. *Courtesy Louise O'Connor, Wexford Publishing*

with the tallow and hide industry in Rockport in the 1860s. In the early 1870s he shocked his contemporaries by selling his herd to purchase more land; he was, moreover, the first in Refugio County to begin fencing his land. He built the O'Connor House Hotel in 1877. With his son Thomas Marion he diversified into the meatpacking business. He also

Saint Denis Chapel on the O'Connor ranch, Victoria, Texas, was built in the Spanish Mission style. It reflects the Hispanic ranching culture that was taken up by Irish ranchers in the Coastal Bend. *Author's collection*

made a shrewd investment with other ranchers in the new refrigerated railway cars that allowed the transportation of freshly slaughtered beef to New Orleans. In the 1880s he used the O'Connor and Sullivan Bank to extend loans to fellow ranchers and acquired substantial estates when borrowers defaulted on the loans. He also initiated the attempt to drill for artesian wells, a decision that was ultimately to provide a constant supply of water on the O'Connor ranches. Finally, he was an early proponent of importing foreign breeds of cattle, a practice that would be fully developed by his sons after his death.

What personal traits drove Thomas O'Connor to acquire land and create a mighty estate—and allowed him to do so with such success? He was single-minded, farsighted, and independent in outlook, a man who anticipated events and turned them to his own advantage. While amassing great wealth he continued to live frugally to the point of austerity. These are classic characteristics of empire builders in any age. The evidence of surviving letters points to a very strong sense of family and the desire to create a safe haven for them in a hostile environment. Early in life, he had suffered exclusion from his own family in Ireland. Furthermore, the uncertainty and unpredictability of life was all around him. He had seen many would-be Irish colonists die of cholera or drown off the Texas coast. He had fought in the Texas Revolution and led the evacuation of women and children from Refugio and San Patricio in 1836. He had seen fellow colonists lose all their property and some their lives in the battle of Refugio and the massacre at Goliad. He had taken part in the savage butchery of the battle of San Jacinto, had seen his neighbors captured or killed by

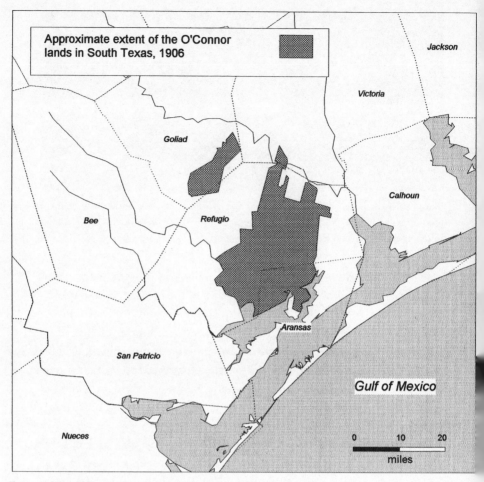

Extent of the O'Connor Lands in 1906

Indians, and later helped drive the Indians out of Texas. In one Indian fight, he was fortunate to escape with his life. As a young man, he experienced the heartache of losing his wife and youngest son. During the Civil War he lost his very promising second son, Martin, on the threshold of manhood. From the end of the Civil War until his death, he continued in an anxious state over the conduct of his wayward eldest son, Dennis. There remained a nagging doubt in his mind whether Dennis would be reliable enough or even live long enough because of ill health to succeed his father and maintain the estate for the benefit of his grandchildren.[96] After a long interval, he married again, but Ellen Shelly died not long after they were married. By his own account, the consolation for losing his first wife rested with his young children, and he offered daily prayers to God to keep them from harm. He had them privately educated, and when they were grown, he wanted and expected them to make a mark in the world. But his eldest son, whom he dearly loved, was a cause of worry and a disappointment to him. He took some consolation in recognizing his illegitimate son, Thomas Marion O'Connor, whom he raised to understand the ranching business. He gave him further experience operating as a merchant and in the meatpacking industry, and included him in his will. Well before his death, Thomas O'Connor had included Thomas Marion as part of the family and given him full responsibility in running the business of the estate.

Beset by the insecurity of his own circumstances, Thomas O'Connor was driven by a desire to safeguard his family. He wanted to protect his children, even against their own self-destructive behavior as adults. And he wanted to provide for his daughter-in-law and grandchildren, who showed him great affection in his old age.[97]

The wider significance of the O'Connor story as a cultural journey by Irish immigrants, first as citizens of Mexico in the province of Texas and later as citizens of the United States, mirrors the experience of many European settlers during the nineteenth century. Through an extraordinarily revealing letter written by Dennis O'Connor, prompted by an article in the *Galveston News*, we can trace a journey that encompassed the first two generations of settlers in Texas. It is quite clear that Thomas O'Connor remained loyal to Ireland, the land of his birth, and brought up his sons in the same belief and in the Roman Catholic faith. Throughout his life Thomas spoke and wrote with a trace of the Irish brogue of his youth. His son Dennis wrote of his own affection for the Emerald Isle and of his sympathy for Irish tenants wanting their own and their nation's freedom from British rule:

> Yes Sir, I decend from the Emerald Gem of the ocean and am proud of that decent next in point of esteem to my citizenship of the United States, the Galveston News to the contrary notwithstanding. I can spread out the tail of my coat widely and most defiantly under these suns and your Queen's police dare not tread theron lest they also tramp upon Uncle Sam's striped and starry handkerchief not so safe an undertaking as collecting rents in the land of the shamrock. It is scarcely worthwhile to say republicans are not dynamite advocates. But I must

presume to suggest that you dealt in that commodity superfluously. . . .
I will concur with you by answering you that if I were compelled to
choose between the occupation of using dynamite on English landlords in Ireland or elsewhere by word or insinnuation deride and slan-
der a downtrodden people I would certainly prefer the former especially if it would terrify one of the oppressors of mankind but for one
single moment.[98]

Through Thomas O'Connor's involvement in the defense of Texas independence, it is clear that he became a Texan, as well as an Irishman, and
when the Republic of Texas was annexed by the United States in 1846, all
the evidence suggests he accepted his role as a citizen of the American
Republic. He remained loyal to the union during the Civil War, and some
of that allegiance influenced Dennis, who had fought in the Confederate
army. By his own account, Dennis, was so moved by the generous terms
offered by General Grant to General Lee at Appomattox, that he pledged
his loyalty to the unity of the United States and became a Republican, the
party of Abraham Lincoln bitterly opposed by southern Democrats.

I was born in this Refugio County in the Republic of Texas in 1839 of
Irish parents of the colony of Power and Hewitson. Enlisted and served
as a Confederate Soldier throughout the rebellion. When in military
camp I read Gen. Grant's terms of surrender to Gen. Lee + army I expressed myself thus—I believe it not, for the history of man gives no
record of such magnanimity but if it be true then I intend to become a
loyal citizen of the great nation whose servants met such acts. We dis-
bandoned [disbanded] I went home and dispassionately watched the
proceedings of my southern brethren. All my political schooling was
democratic, had voted once for S. A. Douglas. My father was a slave
owner. I registered as a voter, took the amnesty oath and had as I expressed it, a country again.[99]

Dennis was also appalled by the attitude of some of the old southern
slave owners who planned to exploit their emancipated slaves to their political advantage, forcing them to register and vote for the Democratic
Party and the interests of their white landowners on pain of eviction from
the land. He claimed that intimidation of Negro tenants was widespread
in Texas and Louisiana, and he saw this practice as an affront to the ideals
that had been fought for in the Texas Revolution:

In my county and Goliad the Anglo Saxon outposts of 1835 and 1836, these counties consecrated to human liberty by the blood of Fannin + King + their brave followers witnessed at this election what they perhaps never saw nor could have seen under the semi-barbarous people + govt. of Santa Anna. I will exemplify most of this Southwest Texas is taken up by immense pastures the small streams + rivers therein are pretty freely dotted with habitations of tenants who have built up little places under verbal pledges to be allowed to remain as long as general good conduct + honesty on their part were exercised paying rent — on these grounds they tilled the soil on shares or worked after stock. The fruit of their life's toil consisted mostly of humble cabbins, gardens + general domestic provision which were made under faith in the landlords agreement, accumulations of half a life. From ten days before until the hour of polling their votes, they were informed that if they voted the Republican ticket, their term of lease would end from the date of such voting. Some of these immense pasture owners thusly controlled hundreds of votes.[100]

The early ideals of the infant republic of the United States in 1776 still appealed to immigrant Irish Texans a hundred years later, reinforced by the war to establish the Republic of Texas. There is also a curious circularity about the experience of the O'Connor family and a continuity of cultural identity despite the huge change that occurred in their fortunes. Having left Ireland, where they had been held back by an agrarian system dominated by English landlords, the O'Connors found themselves becoming great landlords in Texas. They continued to identify with the struggle of tenant farmers in Ireland and opposed the worst excesses of landlord power by landowners in Texas and other southern states. They viewed such antidemocratic practices as an affront to the men who had fought and died for the freedom of Texas against the brutal autocracy of Santa Anna.

This important theme of identification between the O'Connor family and what might be called the "blood sacrifice" of the Irish pioneers in the Texas Revolution continued to exercise its power as late as the 1940s. This was evident in the Krause and Harris legal disputes with the O'Connor family, after the discovery of oil on the O'Connor estate in the 1930s. Both cases contested the claim of the Power-Hewetson lands that were originally granted in 1834 and subsequently transferred to Thomas O'Connor in 1874, approximately nine thousand acres in Copano and Melon Creek.

Opportunistic lawyers were looking to exploit the crude definition of boundaries in the original land titles and under the terms of the vacancy land laws of Texas to reclaim the mineral rights ostensibly for the public free school system of Texas. The text of the lawyer's defense on behalf of the O'Connor estate presented at the supreme court in Texas in October, 1945, proved crucial in achieving victory for the O'Connor family. It concluded with this statement:

> As is not uncommonly the case in suits brought by virtue of the "vacancy" statute, the vacancy applicants here profess less concern for their own special interests than for preserving the "sacred school fund," and the attorney general of Texas echoes that plea. It is truly a sacred fund; so sacred indeed, that the sources from which it springs should remain pure and uncontaminated. The state of Texas should be able to train and educate its future citizens without robbing the descendants of a colonial pioneer and soldier of San Jacinto of their birthright; and without appropriating that which rightfully belongs to others, and which has come to them by reason of years of vision, thrift and honest labor; or of their will to work, spend and risk. It would hardly be inspiring to the children of Texas nor tend to strengthen their moral fiber to have them know that the funds which afford them an education are being acquired, in part, in violation of a Commandment that "Thou shalt not covet thy neighbor's goods." [101]

Thomas O'Connor had fought and suffered for the land. The O'Connor family believe they belong to it as it belongs to them. From beginning to end, it is a story of a people and their deep affinity with the land—land they occupy to this day as cattle ranchers and oil producers.

The story of the Irish colonists in Texas began with visions of a New World paradise, free of the restrictions that prevailed in prefamine Ireland. As the story unfolded, the hopes of many would-be colonists were dashed by shipwreck, cholera, massacre, and loss of property in the Texas Revolution. Some survived to build new lives as farmers and ranchers. Others settled in Victoria, San Antonio, and Corpus Christi and made important contributions to the business and professional life of their communities. The O'Connor family emerged from the original Power-Hewetson colony to take over the holdings of fellow colonists and dominate the landscape of the Coastal Bend.

Conclusion

The gift of hindsight allows us to see the past from a long perspective. We can observe the immense changes that have occurred in Texas since the days of the pioneer settlers in the 1820s and 1830s. What they would have made of modern Texas can only be imagined. The small, scattered homesteads of a frontier society set in a vast wilderness represented an entirely different world to the modern state where most people live in cities that are sustained by sophisticated technology. Houston did not exist when the Irish colonists first came to Texas; now it is the fifth largest city in the United States, the administrative center of the oil and gas industries, and home to the famous space agency. The capital, Austin, is a rapidly growing center of information technology and home to the University of Texas, with a student population greater than the whole Texas population in 1834. San Antonio, where Santa Anna laid siege to the Alamo in 1836, is now the leading tourist center in Texas, with thousands of visitors each year who experience the river walk, the Spanish Fiesta, and the shrine of the Alamo. Refugio, situated on a main route (Highway 77) between Kingsville and Victoria has some fine, historic houses, a museum, and the newly discovered site of the old Spanish mission to appeal to visitors. San Patricio is now a virtual ghost town located off Highway 37, north of Corpus Christi. Once the county seat, it was bypassed by the railroad in 1886, then lost its courthouse, school, and county government to the town of Sinton. The hurricane of 1919 destroyed much of its historic property and sealed its decline.

Retrospectively, we can appreciate the vision and courage of pioneers who settled the country and helped to build communities, schools, businesses, and the political and economic structures that were essential to the successful development of Texas during the nineteenth-century. Among those who saw the potential of Texas were the American political leaders Stephen F. Austin and Sam Houston; the empresarios De León, a Mexican, James Power and John McMullen, both of Irish birth; and the Mexican government officials Tadeo Ortiz de Ayala and Juan Nepomuceno Almonte. Among the adventurers who settled in Texas or fought in the war of independence were Americans, Irish, Mexicans, Germans,

French, Swiss, Poles, English, and Scots. Mexican Texas developed with a mix of cultures and diverse national origins and evolved into the republic then the state of Texas—with contributions from not only the leaders but also general population of Texas. They have left their mark in place-names on the map of Texas, and all have their own story to tell. Equally important is the interaction between them. This story of the Irish pioneer settlers is set in a broader and more inclusive history of Texas, allowing the significance of cultural influence to be identified. It is tempting in writing on the Irish pioneer settlers to isolate their story and to laud only their achievements. Such an approach distorts the Irish experience by suggesting a privileged contribution history. Perhaps, more important, it ignores the presence of Mexican and Irish colonists as neighbors and the cultural transfer of the Hispanic ranching tradition to Irish settlers. This produced the most far-reaching development of all—the building of great ranching estates like the O'Connor's.

What runs throughout the story of the Irish pioneer settlers is the theme of land. The Mexican government, in wishing to populate its vulnerable northern frontier, decided on the allocation of very sizable land grants to entice Americans, Mexicans, and Europeans to settle in what was still a relative wilderness. Americans from the southern states, Irish immigrants in New York, Kentucky, and Philadelphia, and Irish emigrants recruited directly from Wexford, Waterford, and Tipperary came to Texas on the promise of empresario land grants and a new life in an earthly paradise. Behind the idea of Texas depicted as a garden of Eden was an abundance of virgin land and the hope of prosperity for all. The central issue in pre-famine Ireland was a shortage of land under the pressure of overpopulation and poverty. The Irish who left for Texas were among the better-off tenant farmers who despaired of conditions improving in Ireland and who looked for a better prospect of acquiring their own land in the New World.

The story of the Irish empresarios is essentially about the acquisition of large tracts of land as an investment, which formed only part of a wider, entrepreneurial activity. The successful recruitment of colonists brought the empresarios entitlement to many thousands of acres that would increase in value with annexation to the United States and the growth of coastal trade. McMullen and McGloin and Power and Hewetson were all engaged in land purchases beyond their empresario grants. All four were also involved in subsequent litigation over title to land. In the United States, land speculators and volunteers fighting for land and liberty in the

Texas Revolution formed part of what was known as Texas fever, which was, in reality, land fever. Beneath the high-flown rhetoric of the war years was a conflict over territory, between the state of Texas, the interested nations of Mexico, and the United States and between the colonists themselves. As a result of the war, the Irish and Mexican settlers of San Patricio and Refugio suffered a disproportionate loss of property, and many were forced to abandon their land for a period of ten years. The end of the war did not end the fight to preserve the colonists' land. It had to be continuously defended from further Indian depredations, Mexican attacks, and from American freebooters challenging the original claims. Life on the frontier was also a constant battle against disease and harsh conditions. Many of the original colonists did not succeed in retaining their land, whereas others gained from land forfeited to tax demands, farming losses, or descendants being willing to sell out to neighbors. Those who stayed and survived on their homesteads were shaped by the conditions of frontier life and incorporated into family lore some of the myths associated with the taming of a wilderness. The Irish also brought their professional and commercial skills from Europe, which contributed to the growth of towns on the frontier. Finally, land in abundance such as Thomas O'Connor's estate took up a sizable part of the original Power and Hewetson claim, as well as land that had belonged to fellow colonists, stretching inland from the Gulf coast across several counties.

The story of the Irish pioneer colonists has a wider significance in the context of the Irish diaspora. As a prefamine migration, it compares with the Irish who settled as farmers in British North America, who cleared forests, built communities, tamed a wilderness, and demonstrated entrepreneurial skills in the process. An even more direct comparison may be made with territories in Spanish America; in California and Argentina, Irish settlers enjoyed equally spectacular success in cattle ranching and sheep farming. What may be termed the Hispanic dimension of the Irish diaspora, the long historic connections between Ireland and Spain through trade, politics, and military involvement, plus the common allegiance to the Catholic faith and the support of the Catholic network, deserve further study and research.

The Irish pioneer settlers in Texas might also be best understood not so much as a hapless and oppressed people of British colonial policy in Ireland but rather as heroic entrepreneurs who when presented with a unique life-chance to make an independent fortune, weighed up the hazards and risked all. They were not so much victims as opportunists. A further parallel presents itself with Irish colonists who settled in the far-flung parts of the British Empire: Canada, South Africa, Australia, and New Zealand. Occasionally, land grants or assisted or free passage were inducements to settle in British colonies, where settlers became, unwittingly or not, part of the British imperial mission developing new frontier territories and subjugating the aboriginal people who inhabited them. The Irish in Texas, in accepting their land grants, took on the burden of developing frontier territories and subjugating or driving out the native people, the American Indians, as part of the Spanish imperial mission inherited by the newly independent republic of Mexico.

Finally, there was something distinctive in the system of land grants allocated under the Mexican colonization law. Apart from the empresarios themselves, each family was to receive an equal share of a league of land, with single men entitled to a quarter of a league. Everyone started life on the frontier on an equal basis, but within a generation, a few had prospered while many had given up the struggle. Of those who set out from Ireland, perhaps a third never reached Texas, having died from cholera or shipwreck on the way. Others were killed in the Texas Revolution or at the hands of Indians, or were the victims of epidemic disease. Some returned to the United States even before accepting their land grants; others sold out or gave up under pressure of hard times, tax bills, or legal disputes. The whole story of the Irish pioneer settlers in Texas could be viewed as a Darwinian experiment in the survival of the fittest, and for what constituted "fittest," no doubt good fortune played its part in the endurance of the descendants of the first settlers who remain on the land to this day.

APPENDIX 1   *Passenger Lists*

A list of the passengers aboard the *Albion* and the *New Packet* from New York introduced by McMullen and McGloin into the colony of San Patricio.

Edward J. McGloin
Patrick Levan
Patrick Kevlin
John McMullen
James McGloin
Patrick Brennan
Patrick McGloin
John Carroll
John Hearth [Hart]
Dennis McGowan
Bridget Hafey (widow)
John Heffernan
John McGloin
John McGloin II
Martin McGloin
John Conway
Rev. Henry Doyle
Thomas Henesy
Walter Henesy
Ellen Jourdan
Peter McCann

A. (Felix) P. McGloin
James Conway
John Cunnings
H. I. Cullen, M.D.
James O'Connor
William Wallace
John Wallace
Charles Golden
Wm. Ryan
James O'Connor II
Wm. Quinn
John Lambe
John Gunning
John Ganley
James Brown
William Quinn II
Felix Hearth [Hart]
Timothy Hearth [Hart]
John Scott
James Keveney [?]
Peter Golden

Mark Kelly
James Quinn
Jeremia Tool
Joseph Coleman
James Byrnes
Mary Hearth [Hart]
(widow)
Patrick O'Boyle
Daniel O'Boyle
Nathan Safford
James Duke Hearth
[Hart]
James Carson

Source: Affidavit of
Robert Carlisle,
November 7, 1851,
Texas State Library and
Archives, Austin, Texas.

"The following named persons I have also known to be admitted as colonists by the same empresarios [McMullen and McGloin] the greatest part of which obtained patents for their lands from 1830 to 1835 in San Patricio Colony."

Miguel Delgado
Pedro Delgado
Juan Delgado
Tomeseno Delgado
William O'Docharty
John Houghilan
Catherine Hoye
Edward O'Boyle
Richard Everett
Thomas Adams

Mark Kellelia
John Turner
Michael Heley
James Gardner
Louis Ayres
Simon Ryan
George Pettick
Patrick Faddin
Jeremia Scanlan
Christopher Scanlan

John W. Bowers
Mathew Byrns
Benjamin Oslum
Rodrick O'Boyle
I. M. O'Boyle
James Pettick
Edsward Gardner
Daniel O'Boyle
John Faddin
Marcelo Sejuro

Mary Carroll (widow)   Thomas Murphy   William Dundas
Ann Burk (widow)   James Anderson   J. Sargent
Bridget Haffy   Thomas Pugh   John Clark
John Cummings   Carmen Molino   William Hallett
William Hill   Teodor Molino   Robert Carlisle
Edward Scrugham   Torivo Molino   Hugh O'Brien
William Benham   Juan Molino   Francis Trenor
Thomas Henesy   Juan Molino Jr.   Benjamin Dale
John T. Molloy   Victoriano Suares   Jo Carpenter (blacksmith)
Patrick Carroll   Juan de la Garza   Isack Robinson
James Heffernan   Louiciano Resendez   John Duncan
John Ryan   Alexandro Gonzales   Edward McCaferty
Edward Ryan   Franciso Leal   William Thompson
Stephen Hayes   Louis Leal
Thomas Duty   John Williams   *Source:* Harbert
James C. Boyde   James Duglas   Davenport Papers, State
                                                      Archives, Austin, Texas.

"List of all passengers in vessels from foreign ports which have arrived at the port of New Orleans during the second quarter of the year 1834."

The *Prudence* arrived at New Orleans from Liverpool, April 20, 1834. All the listed passengers were from Ireland. No deaths were recorded during the voyage.

	Name	Age	Sex	Occupation
1.	W. O'Connell	46	Male	Farmer
2.	M. O'Connell	40	Female	None
3.	J. O'Connell	19	Male	Farmer
4.	E. O'Connell	14	Male	None
5.	B. O'Connell	9	Female	None
6.	W. O'Connell	2	Male	None
7.	M. O'Connell	23	Male	Farmer
8.	J. O'Connell	22	Male	Farmer
9.	M. O'Connell	24	Male	Farmer
10.	P. Hartagan	30	Female	None
11.	C. O'Connell	23	Female	None
12.	J. Connoly	35	Male	Farmer
13.	M. Conolly	19	Female	None
14.	A. Connolly	22	Female	None
15.	C. Kenty [?]	22	Female	None
16.	C. Daujan	32	Female	None
17.	P. Daujan	40	Male	Farmer
18.	M. Daujan	12	Male	Farmer
19.	C. Daujan	10	Female	None

20.	P. Daujan	3	Male	None
21.	C. Daujan	2	Female	None
22.	W. Butler	36	Male	Farmer
23.	W. Butler	40	Female	None
24.	P. Butler	15	Male	None
25.	C. Butler	15	Male	None
26.	J. Butler	11	Male	None
27.	C. Butler	9	Female	None
28.	W. Butler	7	Male	None
29.	P. Butler	3	Male	None
30.	B. Butler	23	Female	None
31.	P. Butler	46	Male	Farmer
32.	J. Hynes	40	Male	Farmer
33.	A. Hynes	28	Female	None
34.	M. Hynes	35	Male	Farmer
35.	M. Hynes	30	Female	None
36.	P. Hynes	6	Female	None
37.	J. Hynes	3	Male	None
38.	M. Hynes	1	Female	None
39.	A. O'Connell	35	Male	Mechanic
40.	C. O'Connell	35	Female	None
41.	M. O'Connell	11	Female	None
42.	J. O'Connell	9	Male	None
43.	J. O'Connell	7	Female	None
44.	E. O'Connell	5	Female	None
45.	P. O'Connell	4	Male	None
46.	E. O'Connell	2	Female	None
47.	P. Allen	25	Male	Farmer
48.	W. O'Connell	27	Male	Farmer
49.	M. Connell	20	Female	None
50.	P. Connell	24	Male	Farmer
51.	J. Senaye	35	Male	Farmer
52.	M. Senaye	29	Female	None
53.	C. Senaye	6	Female	None
54.	P. Senaye	3	Male	None
55.	J. Senaye	24	Female	None
56.	M. Griffin	24	Female	None
57.	W. Lavory	36	Male	Mechanic
58.	E. Lavory	28	Female	None
59.	M. Lavory	5	Female	None
60.	A. Lavory	3	Female	None
61.	M. Lavory	2	Female	None
62.	J. Magran	29	Male	Farmer
63.	M. Magran	25	Female	None

64.	W. Magran	8	Male	None
65.	M. Magran	5	Female	None
66.	M. Magran	1	Female	None
67.	P. Foley	25	Male	Farmer
68.	M. Foley	23	Female	None
69.	E. Foley	15	Female	None
70.	J. Tlary [?]	16	Male	None
71.	R. Looby	36	Male	Farmer
72.	C. Looby	30	Female	None
73.	J. Looby	1	Male	None
74.	E. Looby	3	Female	None
75.	E. Flinn	20	Female	None

Source: Quarterly Abstracts of Passenger Lists of Vessels Arriving at New Orleans, January 1, 1820–December 30, 1837, Louisiana State Historical Society Archives, Louisiana State Museum, New Orleans.

The *Heroine* arrived in New Orleans from Liverpool on May 7, 1834. All the passengers listed were from Ireland.

	Name	Age	Sex	Occupation
1.	P. Fitsimons	46	Male	Farmer
2.	M. Fitsimons	37	Female	None
3.	P. Roach [Roche]	55	Male	Farmer
4.	M. Roch [Roche]	50	Female	None
5.	T. Bryan	50	Male	Farmer
6.	M. Bryan	40	Female	None
7.	T. Hart	36	Male	Farmer
8.	M. Hart	35	Female	None
9.	J. Burn	34	Male	Farmer
10.	M. Burn	28	Female	None
11.	St. John	40	Male	Farmer
12.	M. St. John	32	Female	None
13.	J. Shelly	40	Male	Farmer
14.	M. Shelly	32	Female	None
15.	J. James	46	Male	Farmer
16.	M. James	40	Female	None
17.	J. Bray	38	Male	Farmer
18.	M. Bray	30	Female	None
19.	W. Bourke	41	Male	Farmer
20.	M. Bourke	28	Female	None
21.	W. Hughes	23	Male	Farmer
22.	M. Hughes	26	Female	None
23.	W. Flannagan	30	Male	Farmer
24.	J. Sinnot	26	Male	Farmer

25.	M. Sinnot	20	Female	None
26.	J. Sinnot	24	Male	Farmer
27.	T. King	24	Male	Farmer
28.	J. Toole	19	Male	Farmer
29.	J. Kehoe	20	Male	Farmer
30.	J. Caughlin	24	Male	Farmer
31.	P. Dunsey	23	Male	Farmer
32.	W. Redmond	32	Male	Farmer
33.	T. Redmond	20	Male	Farmer
34.	W. Magille	25	Male	Farmer
35.	M. Riely	23	Male	Farmer
36.	P. Kilhoe	25	Male	Mechanic
37.	R. Roche	24	Male	Mechanic
38.	S. Kilhoe	24	Male	Farmer
39.	W. Lambert	22	Male	Farmer
40.	E. Rigley	24	Female	None
41.	E. Byrn	18	Female	None
42.	P. Donahoe	25	Male	Farmer
43.	M. Walshe	25	Female	None
44.	T. Connores	16	Male	None
45.	M. Powers	22	Male	Farmer
46.	M. Cavanagh	25	Female	None
47.	C. Kelly	25	Male	Farmer
48.	J. Doylc	21	Male	Farmer
49.	M. Fox	25	Male	Farmer
50.	M. Fox	23	Female	None
51.	J. Cavanah	26	Male	Farmer
52.	M. Cavanah	21	Female	None
53.	J. Brown	20	Male	Farmer
54.	R. Brown	25	Female	None
55.	T. Blake	21	Female	None
56.	P. Byrne	26	Male	Farmer
57.	C. Kinsale	23	Female	None
58.	T. Redmond	25	Male	Farmer
59.	T. Consey	20	Male	Farmer
60.	M. Conway	24	Male	Farmer
61.	M. Dolan	19	Male	Farmer
62.	J. Neile	22	Male	Farmer
63.	J. Cushion	20	Male	Farmer
64.	C. Linigan	12	Male	Farmer
65.	C. Quitt [?]	17	Female	None
66.	M. Kehoe	22	Female	None
67.	C. Dray	28	Female	None
68.	T. Henry	48	Male	Farmer

69.	P. Kinsella	27	Male	Farmer
70.	J. Powers [Power]	50	Male	Farmer
71.	J. Kavanah	20	Male	Mechanic

Source: Quarterly Abstracts of Passenger Lists of Vessels Arriving at New Orleans, January 1, 1820–December 30, 1837, Louisiana State Historical Society Archives, Louisiana State Museum, New Orleans.

Land Grantees in San Patricio and Refugio

Grantees in the Colony of McMullen and McGloin (San Patricio)

Name of Grantee(s)	Date of Title	Quantity of Land	
		Leagues	Labors
1. Thomas Adams	July 30, 1835	1	1
2. Lewis Ayers	June 25, 1835	1	1
3. William D. Benham	July 30, 1835	—	
4. John Bower	July 20, 1835	—	
5. Maria Brennan	Dec. 2, 1835	1	
6. Anna Burke	June 25, 1835	1	1
7. Matthew Byrne	July 12, 1835	—	
8. John Carroll	Dec. 3, 1835	1	
9. Mary Carroll	June 25, 1835	1	1
10. John Conway	July 5, 1835	—	
11. Juan Delgado and sons Miguel, Nepo, and Pedro	Nov. 26, 1831	4	
12. Festus Doyle	June 28, 1835	1	1
13. Thomas Duty	Aug. 3, 1835	—	
14. Simon Dwyer	June 25, 1835	1	1
15. Richard Everitt	July 30, 1835	1	1
16. John Fadden	July 14, 1835	—	
17. Patrick Fadden	July 30, 1835	1	1
18. Edward Garner	Aug. 3, 1835	—	
19. James Garner	June 30, 1835	1	1
20. Joaquin de la Garza	March 24, 1834	—	1
21. Juan de la Garza	July 4, 1835	1	1
22. John Hart	Dec. 3, 1831	1	
23. Bridget Haughy	June 25, 1835	1	1
24. Stephen Hayes	July 8, 1835	1	1
25. James Heffernan	June 30, 1835	1	1
26. John Heffernan	June 25, 1835	1	1
27. Michael Hely	July 30, 1835	1	1
28. Thomas Hennessy	July 30, 1835	—	
29. Patrick Henry	July 10, 1835	—	
30. Thomas Henry	July 30, 1835	1	1
31. Walter Henry	July 20, 1835	—	
32. Ignacio Herrera	March 20, 1834	1	1

33.	John Houlihan	June 25, 1835	1	1
34.	Catalina Hoye	July 20, 1835	—	
35.	Elizabeth Jourdin	July 4, 1835	1	1
36.	Victoriano Juarez	July 4, 1835	1	1
37.	Mark Killely	July 30, 1835	1	1
38.	Maria Brigida Kivlin	Dec. 3, 1835	1	
39.	Francisco Leal	July 20, 1835	1	1
40.	Luis Leal	July 30, 1835	—	
41.	Domingo Losoya	March 20, 1834	1	
42.	Manual de la Luna	March 20, 1834	1	
43.	Dionisio Martinez	March 20, 1834	1	
44.	Carmen Molina	Aug. 3, 1835	1	1
45.	Juan de Dios Molina	Aug. 3, 1835	1	1
46.	Teodoro Molina	Aug. 3, 1835	1	1
47.	Toribio Molina	Aug. 3, 1835	1	1
48.	John Thomas Molloy	July 15, 1835	1	1
49.	Edward J. McGloin	Dec. 5, 1831	1	
50.	James McGloin	Dec. 2, 1831	1	
51.	James McGloin	Dec. 22, 1831	2,295,000 sq. varas	
52.	James McGloin	Dec. 18, 1831	1	
53.	John McGloin	July 5, 1835	—	
54.	Patrick McGloin	Dec. 3, 1831	1	
55.	Dennis McGowan	Dec. 3, 1831	1	
56.	John McMullen	Nov. 30, 1831	1	
57.	John McMullen	Nov. 30, 1831	? leagues	
58.	Patrick Nevin	Dec. 2, 1831	1	
59.	Daniel O'Boyle	July 20, 1835	—	
60.	Edward O'Boyle	July 30, 1835	1	1
61.	Michael O'Boyle	July 14, 1835	—	
62.	Patrick O'Boyle	June 25, 1835	1	1
63.	Roderick O'Boyle	July 13, 1835	—	
64.	Benjamin Odlum	July 12, 1835	—	
65.	George O'Docharty	June 25, 1835	1	1
66.	William O'Docharty	Dec. 3, 1831	2	
67.	Rosalio Pena	Aug. 3, 1835	1	1
68.	George Pittick	July 14, 1835	—	
69.	Thomas Pugh	June 30, 1835	1	1
70.	Luciano Resendes	Aug. 3, 1835	1	1
71.	Edward Ryan	Aug. 3, 1835	—	
72.	John Ryan	June 25, 1835	1	1
73.	Simon Ryan	July 5, 1835	1	1
74.	Jose Maria Salinas	March 20, 1834	1	
75.	Town of San Patricio	Oct. 24, 1831	4	
76.	Town of San Patricio	June 26, 1835	Sale of town lots	
77.	Christopher Scanlan	July 13, 1835	—	

78.	Jerry Scanlan	July 5, 1835	1	1
79.	Edward W. B. Scrugham	June 25, 1835	1	1
80.	Marcelino Segura	July 30, 1835	1	1
81.	John Turner	June 30, 1835	1	1
82.	Julian Zavala	Aug. 3, 1835	1	1

Grantees in the Colony of Power and Hewetson (Refugio)

	Name of Grantee(s)	*Date of Titles*	*Quantity of Land Leagues*
1.	Jose Miguel Aldrete	Sept. 10, 1834	1
2.	Jose Miguel Aldrete	Sept 22, 1834	4
3.	Jose Miguel Aldrete	Sept. 22, 1834	1
4.	Jose Ma. Aldrete	Sept. 22, 1834	¼
5.	William Anderson	Dec. 27, 1834	¼
6.	Samuel Blair	Aug. 4, 1834	¼
7.	Isabella Brien	Aug. 10, 1834	1
8.	William Burk	Aug. 16, 1834	1
9.	Rosa Brown	Sept. 25, 1834	1
10.	Mary Byrne	Oct. 8, 1834	1
11.	James Bray	Oct. 12, 1834	1
12.	Elkanah Brush and his sons, Gilbert, Russell, and Bradford	Oct. 31, 1834 Oct. 1, 1834	1 ¼
13.	Solon Bartlett	Oct. 30, 1834	¼
14.	Caleb Bennet	Nov. 13, 1834	1
15.	John Bowin	Nov. 15, 1834	1
16.	James Brown, for himself and for L. Brown and Wm. Hews	Nov. 15, 1834 Nov. 15, 1834	1 1
17.	William Bartels	Nov. 20, 1834	¼
18.	Jose Manuel Blanco	Nov. 21, 1834	1
19.	James Burk	Nov. 25, 1834	¼
20.	Thomas Banuelos and his two sons-in-law	Nov. 24, 1834	1½
21.	Joseph Bartlett	Nov. 20, 1834	¼
22.	John Coughlin	Sept. 2, 1834	1
23.	John Clarke	Sept. 5, 1834	1
24.	James Colleyer	Sept. 26, 1834	1½
25.	Thomas Connor	Sept. 28, 1834	1
26.	Robert Carlisle, for his two sons	Sept. 30, 1834	½

27.	Jose Maria Cobarrubias	Oct. 28, 1834	1
28.	Jose Maria Cobian,	Oct. 30, 1834	¼
	and Gegoren and Andrew		
	Devereux	Oct. 30, 1834	½
29.	Robert Carlisle	Oct. 31, 1834	1
30.	Juan Cameron	Oct. 31, 1834	2
31.	Ignatio Castro,		
	for himself and	Nov. 12, 1834	1 Renounced
	orphans of		in favor of
	Jerome Huizar		1 Dona Iginia
			Estrade
32.	John Cassidy and		
	James H. Mullen	Nov. 24, 1834	½
33.	Phebe Crain	Nov. 29, 1834	1
34.	Dolores Carbajal	Dec. 17, 1834	1
35.	Jose Maria Castilla	Dec. 25, 1834	1 Transferred
			to P. Scott
36.	Joseph Coffin	Oct. 7, 1834	¼
37.	Andrew Devereux	Oct. 30, 1834	¼ Concession
			to J. V. Campos
38.	Joshua Davis	Aug. 9, 1834	5¼
39.	John Dunn	Oct. 8, 1834	1
40.	Guad. Careaga de Cobian	Oct. 25, 1834	¼
	and her two sons	Oct. 25, 1834	1¼
41.	Catalina Dugan	Oct. 21, 1834	1
42.	Benjamin Dale	Oct. 30, 1834	1
43.	Patrick Downey		
	for his sons, Richard,		
	John, and Patrick	Nov. 25, 1834	¾
44.	James Douglas	Nov. 28, 1834	1
45.	John Daly	Nov. 20, 1834	¼
46.	Patrick Downey	Sept. 15, 1834	1
47.	Francis Dieterich,		
	Juan Andres Baumacker,		
	and William Langenheim	Nov. 24, 1834	¾
48.	Robert Eyles	Nov. 20, 1834	1
49.	Patrick Fitzsimmons	Sept. 26, 1834	1½
50.	Miguel Fox	Nov. 25, 1834	
51.	Nicholas Fagan, for		
	himself	Sept. 22, 1834	1
	for his son James	Sept. 22, 1834	¼
	for his son John	Sept. 22, 1834	¼
52.	Thomas Galan	Oct. 4, 1834	1¼
53.	Juan Gonzales	Oct. 15, 1834	1

54.	Jacinto de la Garza,	Oct. 23, 1834	1
55.	Carlos de la Garza, for himself and his son Rafael	Oct. 28, 1834	$1\frac{1}{4}$
56.	Pedro Gallardo	Oct. 30, 1834	1
57.	Julian de la Garza, for himself,	Nov. 15, 1834	$2\frac{3}{4}$
	and for his daughter and 3 sons	Nov. 15, 1834	1
58.	Cayetano Garza	Nov. 15, 1834	1
59.	Maximo Gomes	Dec. 20, 1834	1
60.	Jose Maria Galban	Oct. 30, 1834	1
61.	Francisco Gonzales	Oct. 13, 1834	1
62.	John Haynes and Peter Haynes	Sept. 9, 1834	$1\frac{1}{4}$
63.	Robert Patrick Hearn, for himself and son James	Oct. 24, 1834	$1\frac{1}{4}$
64.	Sarah Hall	Oct. 31, 1834	1
65.	John Hart, for himself and his 3 sons	Oct. 10, 1834	$1\frac{3}{4}$
66.	Timothy Hart as heir for his mother	Nov. 20, 1834	1
	and himself	Nov. 20, 1834	$\frac{1}{4}$
67.	James Hewetson	Nov. 19, 1834	$\frac{1}{4}$
	James Hewetson	Nov. 19, 1834	1
68.	Thomas Holden	Nov. 22, 1834	1
69.	Felix Hart, for himself	Nov. 22, 1834	1
	and his son Timothy	Nov. 22, 1834	$\frac{1}{4}$
70.	Thomas Hay, for himself, and his son Cornelius	Nov. 27, 1834	$1\frac{1}{4}$
71.	Manuel Hernandes	Nov. 28, 1834	2
72.	Elizabeth Hart	Dec. 29, 1834	1
73.	George H. Hall, William Holly, Wm. D. Crane, and Edward Townsend	Nov. 20, 1834	1
74.	John James	Oct. 25, 1834	1
75.	Peter Kehoe	Dec. 29, 1834	1
76.	Charles Kelly	Sept. 27, 1834	$\frac{1}{4}$
77.	John Kelly	Sept. 27, 1834	$\frac{1}{4}$
78.	John Keating	Oct. 10, 1834	1
	John Keating	Oct. 2, 1834	$\frac{1}{2}$
79.	Estavan Lopes	Sept. 3, 1834	1
80.	Martin Lawlor	Nov. 20, 1834	$\frac{1}{4}$

81.	Victor Loupy	Nov. 26, 1834	1
82.	Walter Lambert	Nov. 27, 1834	1
83.	William Lavery	Nov. 25, 1834	1
84.	John Malone	Sept. 6, 1834	1
85.	Michael and Martin Tool	Sept. 12, 1834	¾
86.	Thomas Mullen	Sept. 18, 1834	1
87.	James McGeehans	Sept. 21, 1834	1
88.	Edward McDonough	Sept. 15, 1834	1
89.	Miguel Musques	Sept. 23, 1834	1
90.	George McKnight	Sept. 18, 1834	¼
91.	George Morris	Sept. 27, 1834	1
92.	Edward Murphy and		
	his sons William and James	Oct. 28, 1834	1½
93.	Malcolm McAuly	Oct. 30, 1834	1
94.	James Henry Mullen	Nov. 24, 1834	¼
95.	Sam. W. M'Camley	Nov. 30, 1834	1
96.	James M'Cune	Nov. 30, 1834	1
97.	Juan Moya	Sept. 20, 1834	1¼
98.	Augustin Moya	Nov. 30, 1834	¼
99.	Marcos Marchand	Dec. 30, 1834	1¼
100.	Domingo Morris	Oct. 30, 1834	1¼
101.	James O'Reilly	Sept. 11, 1834	1
102.	Miguel O'Donnell	Oct. 15, 1834	1
103.	James O'Connor	Nov. 15, 1834	¼
104.	Hugh O'Brien	Nov. 22, 1834	1
105.	Danl. and John O'Boyle	Nov. 24, 1834	1¼
106.	Michael O'Donnel	Sept. 26, 1834	1
107.	James Power	Sept. 5, 1834	1
108.	Martin Power	Sept. 29, 1834	1
109.	Edward Perry	Sept. 22, 1834	1
110.	James Power and James		
	Hewetson as empresarios	Sept. 15, 1834	7¼
111.	John Pollan	Oct. 30, 1834	1
112.	James Power and		
	James Hewetson	Oct. 12, 1834	4¼
113.	Rouge Felipe Portilla	Oct. 23, 1834	1
	and for his 4 sons	Oct. 23, 1834	1
114.	Juan Caliste Francisco		
	and Encarnacion	Oct. 23, 1834	4
	same for his sons,		
	Jose, Maria, and Felipe	Oct. 23, 1834	¼
115.	James Power and James		
	Hewetson as empresarios	Oct. 30, 1834	10
116.	Juan Pobedano	Sept. 10, 1834	1

117. James Power and his
son James   Oct. 20, 1834   1
118. James Power for himself
and James Hewetson   Nov. 22, 1834   4¾
119. James Power   Nov. 28, 1834   11
120. James Power and James
Hewetson as empresarios   Dec. 5, 1834   5
121. James Power and partner
James Hewetson   Nov. 20, 1834   11
122. Bridget Quinn   Oct. 12, 1834   1
123. Edmund Quirk and sons   Oct. 30, 1834   1¼
124. William and Patrick Quinn   Nov. 20, 1834   ½
125. William Quinn   Nov. 22, 1834   ¼
126. Thomas Quirk   Oct. 25, 1834   ¼
127. William Quinn   Dec. 25, 1834   1
128. Anastacia Reojas   Sept. 1, 1834   1
129. Garret Roache   Sept. 13, 1834   1
130. John Roache   Sept. 16, 1834   ¼
131. William Redmond and
William M'Gill   Sept. 16, 1834   ½
132. Maria and Ann Roache   Sept. 16, 1834   1
133. Florentino Rios   Aug. 28, 1834   1
134. Michael Reiley   Sept. 10, 1834   1
135. William Robertson   Sept. 24, 1834   1
136. Leonardo Rodrigues
and D. Nira   Oct. 15, 1834   2
137. Maria Josefa Rios   Oct. 12, 1834   1
138. Francisco Ramon   Oct. 20, 1834   1
139. Juan Rener and his son   Oct. 28, 1834   1¼
140. Y. Nes Rene   Sept. 16, 1834   1
141. Isaac Robinson   Nov. 20, 1834   1
142. James Reynolds   Nov. 30, 1834   ¼
143. Leonardo Rodrigues,
for his sons Francisco
and Jose Maria   Dec. 4, 1834   ½
144. John Sinnott   Aug. 6, 1834   1
145. Thomas Scott   Sept. 2, 1834   ¼
146. John Scott   Sept. 2, 1834   1
147. Edmund St. John   Sept. 3, 1834   1
148. Patrick Shelly   Sept. 13, 1834   ¼
149. John Shelly   Sept. 13, 1834   1
150. John Scott   Sept. 16, 1834   ¼
151. James and William St. John   Sept. 29, 1834   ¼
152. Santiago Serna   Oct. 29, 1834   1

153. Santiago Serna	Oct. 16, 1834	3
154. Santiago Serna, as agent for Juan Flores and M. Menchaca	Oct. 20, 1834	2
155. Anthony Sideck	Oct. 27, 1834	1
156. John B. Sideck	Oct. 28, 1834	1
157. Charles Smith	Oct. 30, 1834	¼
James Walmesley	Oct. 30, 1834	¼
John Smiley	Oct. 30, 1834	¼
H. Winchester	Oct. 30, 1834	¼
158. John M. Sherry, for his son Joseph Lewis Sherry	Oct. 28, 1834	¼
159. Charles Shearn, for himself	Oct. 31, 1834	1
and his son John	Oct. 31, 1834	¼
160. Miguel de los Santos	Dec. 20, 1834	1
161. Jeremiah Tool	Sept. 11, 1834	1
162. Josefa Maria Traviezo	Oct. 8, 1834	1
163. Peter Teal	Oct. 13, 1834	1
164. John Toole	Nov. 24, 1834	¼
165. Victoriano Tares and P. Villareal	Nov. 26, 1834	2
166. Antonio de la Vina	Sept. 9, 1834	1
167. Jose Maria Valdez	Oct. 8, 1834	1¼
168. T. Vairin and Augustin L. Fernet	Oct. 29, 1834	1
169. Pedro Villa, for himself	Oct. 14, 1834	1
and his son	Oct. 14, 1834	½
170. Sacarias Villarreal	Nov. 26, 1834	¼
171. Ira Westover	Sept. 22, 1834	1
172. Elliott Ward	Sept. 14, 1834	1

Source: Land Grantees, McMullen-McGloin Colony and Power-Hewetson Colony, General Land Office, Austin, Texas.

APPENDIX 3
Signers of the Goliad Declaration of Independence

The Goliad Declaration, signed December 20, 1835, was transmitted to the General Council at San Felipe by a committee consisting of Thomas H. Bell, Benjamin J. White Sr., William J. Hill, William S. Brown, J. Dodd Kirkpatrick, and John Dunn. Names of Refugio colonists are in **boldface** type.

Miguel Aldrete
J. W. Baylor
J. T. Bell
John Bowen
John J. Bowman
Joseph Bowman
Wiliam S. Brown
Elkanah Brush
Joseph Cadle
Gustavus Chalwell
   [Caldwell]
H. F. Dale
Joseph Benjamin Dale
Jeremiah Day
Thomas Mason Dennis
C. M. Despalier
Andrew Devereux
Philip Dimitt
Spirse Dooley
James Duncan
John Dunn
James Elder
E. B. W. Fitzgerald
David George
H. George
William Gould
William Haddon
Thomas Hanson
Timothy Hart
William G. Hill
Nathaniel Holbrook
Wm. E. Howth
J. C. Hutchins

Peter Hynes
Ira Ingram
John James
John Johnson
D. M. Jones
Francis Jones
Michael Kelly
J. D. Kirkpatrick
Walter Lambert
William H. Living
Victor Loupy
Alexander Lynch
Charles Malone
Robert McClure
Edward McDonough
Dugald McFarlane
Hugh McMinn
Charles Messer
Henry J. Morris
William Newland
Benjamin Noble
Morgan O'Brien
C. J. O'Connor
James O'Connor
Thomas O'Connor
Michael O'Donnell
Patrick O'Leary
G. W. Paine
C. A. Parker
D. H. Peeks
P. H. Perkins
John Pollan
Lewis Powell

Albert Pratt
William Quinn
Edmund Quirk
R. L. Redding
W. Redfield
Wm. Robertson
Isaac Robinson
Antoine Sayle
James W. Scott
Charles Shearn
John Shelly
Albert Silsbee
Francis P. Smith
Horace Stamans
Edward St. John
James St. John
Thomas Todd
Jefferson Ware
Geo. W. Welch
Allen White
Benj. J. White
Benj. J. White Jr.
David Wilson
Alvin Woodward

Sources: John Henry Brown, *History of Texas from 1685 to 1892*, 1:376-379; Souvenir Program, Refugio County Centennial Celebration, Refugio, Texas, 1936, 12.

APPENDIX 4

Irish Colonists in the Texan Armies

SAN PATRICIO
COLONISTS ENLISTED
IN THE TEXAN
REGULAR ARMY

_____

Matthew Byrne
John Fadden
Edward Garner
John McGloin
Dennis McGowan
Patrick Nevan
Michael O'Boyle
George Pettock
Edward Ryan

Source: Harbert Davenport Papers, Center for American History, University of Texas at Austin.

MUSTER ROLL
OF CAPT. PHILIP
DIMITT'S COMPANY
STATIONED AT FORT
GOLIAD, JANUARY 10,
1836

_____

Officers
Philip Dimitt, Captain
B. Noble, 1st Lieutenant
J. P. Borden,
    2d Lieutenant
Ira Ingram, Adjutant
B .J. White, Commissary
R. Redding,
    Assistant Commissary

Alexander Lynch,
    Surgeon
Dugald McFrland,
    1st Sergeant
John Hancock,
    3d Sergeant
Francis Jones, Musician
John J. Bowman,
    2d Sergeant
**Edward St. John,
    4th Sergeant**
**C. J. O'Connor,
    Armorer**

Privates
Thomas J. Adams
J. W. Baylor
Thomas M. Blake
John Bowen
John Bracken
Elkanah Brush
William Burke
Mariano Carbajal
G. W. Cash
Gustavus Cholwell
William Cummins
Benjamin Dale
Tatum Davis
Jeremiah Day
Andrew Devereaux
Spirse Dooley
James Duncan
John Dunn
James Elder
John Fagan
David George
H. George
William Gould

Henry Haddon
William Haddon
Thomas Hanson
Timothy Hart
Robert Patrick Hearne
John James
F. Keller
Daniel Kincheloe
Walter Lambert
[?] Lightfoot
William H. Living
Victor Loupy
Charles Malone
Robert McClure
Edward McDonough
Charles Meser
Thomas S. Mitchell
George Morris
[?] O'Baker
Daniel O'Boyle
Morgan O'Brien
James O'Connor
Thomas O'Connor
Michael O'Donnell
Patrick O'Leary
George Payne
John Pollan
John Quinn
Patrick Quinn
William Quinn
Edmund Quirk
Benj. Rawls
James Rawls
W. Redfield
Michael Riley
Isaac Robinson
Antoine Sayle
G. W. Scott

James O. Sharp **Antonio Sydick** Benjamin White
Charles Shearn **Peter Teal** *Note:* Names of Refugio
John Shelly Thomas Todd colonists are in **boldface**
A. Silsbee **B. Williams** type.
Charles Smith **H. Williams**
James St. John Allen White

Volunteers from Refugio under Ira Westover arrived at Goliad the morning after its capture by Captain Collinsworth and a number of Refugio colonists were in the garrison at Goliad from time to time between October 10, 1835 and January 16, 1836. Among them were Ira Westover, adjutant, John Fagan, Nicholas Fagan, John Dunn, George McKnight, Martin Lawlor, Thomas O'Brien, William Redmond, and Anthony [Antonio] Sydick.

James Power, Nicholas Fagan, John Fagan, George McKnight, John J. Linn, Peter Teal, Walter Lambert, Francis Dietrich, James Kerr, Augustus N. Jones, and George Morris were among those who were with Westover in the Lipantitlan expedition. The young Irishmen John O'Toole and John Williams were sent by Dimitt to San Patricio as messengers. Their capture provoked the Lipantitlan expedition.

Practically all signers of the Goliad Declaration were soldiers at one time or another at Goliad.

Sources: Capt. Dimitt's Muster Roll (Goliad), 1835, Adjutant General Military Rolls, Texas Revolution, 1835–36, Texas State Archives, Austin, Texas; Souvenir Program, Refugio County Centennial Celebration, Refugio, Texas, 1935, 13.

REFUGIO COLONISTS WHO DIED AT THE ALAMO

Samuel Blair
Edward McCafferty

Source: Souvenir Program, Refugio County Centennial Celebration, 1936, 14.

REFUGIO COLONISTS WHO SERVED IN GEN. SAM HOUSTON'S ARMY
AT THE BATTLE OF SAN JACINTO

Walter Lambert
William McGuill
George Morris
James O'Connor
Thomas O'Connor
Daniel O'Driscoll

Source: Souvenir Program, Refugio County Centennial Celebration, 1936, 14.

Notes

Chapter 1. The Province of Texas in Newly Independent Mexico

1. John J. Linn, *Reminiscences of Fifty Years in Texas*, 23. For a fuller review of attitudes about the land, see Robin W. Doughty, *At Home in Texas: Early Views of the Land*. Throughout this book, unless orthographical anomalies in a citation are open to misinterpretation, I have reproduced the original spelling without comment.
2. David B. Edward, ed., *The History of Texas*, 41.
3. Quoted in *Texas in 1837: An Anonymous Contemporary Narrative*, ed. Andrew Forest Muir, 131.
4. William Shakespeare, *The Complete Works*, 311.
5. Mrs. T. C. Allen, "Reminiscences of Mrs. Annie Fagan Teal," *Southwestern Historical Quarterly* 34 (April, 1931):327.
6. Rosalie Hart Priour, "The Adventures of a Family of Emmigrants [*sic*] Who Emmigrated to Texas in 1834," 49.
7. Nettie Lee Benson, "Texas Viewed from Mexico, 1820–1834," *Southwestern Historical Quarterly* 90, no. 3 (1987):225.
8. Jack Jackson, ed., *Texas by Terán: The Diary Kept by Manuel de Mier y Terán on His 1828 Inspection of Texas*, trans. John Wheat; Juan N. Almonte, "Statistical Report on Texas, 1835," trans. C. E. Castañeda, *Southwestern Historical Quarterly* 38, no. 3 (January, 1925):177–222.
9. William Kennedy, *Texas: The Rise, Progress, and Prospects of the Republic of Texas*; Mary Austin Holley, *Texas*.
10. W. Kennedy, *Texas*, 14–15.
11. Solis, *Diary of a Visit*, 42–43, quoted in Marilyn McAdam Aibley, *Travellers in Texas 1761–1860*, 78. For an authoritative view of the Karankawas, see *The New Handbook of Texas*, 3:1031–33.
12. Quoted in *Texas in 1837*, 38, from *Telegraph and Texas Register*, May 16, 1837. A later account reported that one of the parties had declared that "the affair was not settled as above stated," *Telegraph and Texas Register*, March 3, 1838.
13. Stephen Stagner, "Epics, Science, and the Last Frontier: Texas Historical Writing, 1836–1936," *Western Historical Quarterly* (April, 1981):166.
14. For a discussion of racial theories on both sides of the Atlantic, see L. Perry Curtis Jr., *Apes and Angels: The Irishman in Victorian Caricature*.
15. For the continuing influence of John Foxe's, *Book of Martyrs*, first published in 1563, see Linda Colley, *Britons: Forging the Nation, 1707–1837*, 27–28.
16. David J. Weber, "Scarce More Than Apes," in *Myth and History of the Hispanic Southwest*, 153–67; see also Arnoldo De León, *They Called Them Greasers: Anglo–Attitudes towards Mexicans in Texas, 1821–1900*.

17. Philip Wayne Powell, *Tree of Hate*, 118, quoted in Weber, "Scarce More Than Apes," 160.
18. Quoted in Weber, "Scarce More than Apes," 162. Weber offers a useful discussion of the influences that contributed to the Black Legend, 159–61.
19. David Roediger, *The Wages of Whiteness: Race and the Making of the American Working Class*, 133–63; see also Noel Ignatiev, *How the Irish Became White*.
20. Allport, *Nature of Prejudice*, 199, quoted in Weber, "Scarce More than Apes," 164.
21. *Texas in 1837*, 101–102.
22. Ibid., 102.. Among the Spanish laborers who came to Mexico were natives of southern Spain who did not speak the same Spanish as the Castilian Spanish of the administrative elite who governed imperial Spain. I am indebted to Professor Malcolm Mclean for this information.
23. *Texas in 1837*, 104.
24. "Deep, indeed, has the canker eaten. Not into the core of a precarious and suspected root—but into the very hearts of the people, corrupting them with a fatal lethargy, and debasing them with a fatuous dependence! . . . Thus the plow rusts, the spade lies idle, and the fields fallow," *Times* (London), March 26, 1847.
25. *Texas in 1837*, 107–109.
26. David J. Weber, *The Mexican Frontier, 1821-1846: The American Southwest Under Mexico*, 159.
27. Andreas V. Reichstein, *Rise of the Lone Star State: The Making of Texas*, trans. Jeanne R. Wilson, 53.
28. Linn, *Reminiscences of Fifty Years in Texas*.
29. See chapter 5 for a fuller discussion of the idea of the frontier.
30. Mark E. Nackman, "Anglo-American Migrants to the West: Men of Broken Fortunes? The Case of Texas, 1821–1846," *Western Historical Quarterly* (October, 1974):442–55.
31. D. W. Meinig, *Imperial Texas: An Interpretive Essay in Cultural Geography*, 35.
32. Quoted in Weber, *The Mexican Frontier*, 167.
33. Quoted in Jackson, *Texas by Terán*, 100–101.
34. Ibid., 98.
35. Edith Louise Kelly and Mattie Austin Hatcher, eds., "Tadeo Ortiz de Ayala and the Colonization of Texas, 1822–1833," *Southwestern Historical Quarterly* 32 (October, 1928):223–24.
36. Ibid., 225.
37. Ibid., 226.
38. Ibid., 241.
39. Ibid., 229.
40. Lists of Land Grantees, San Patricio and Refugio Counties, General Land Office, Austin; see app. 2.
41. Benson, "Texas Viewed from Mexico," 227.
42. Weber, *The Mexican Frontier*, 177.
43. Almonte, "Statistical Report on Texas," 178.
44. Ibid.

45. Weber, *The Mexican Frontier*, 176.

46. Edward, *History of Texas*, 279; emphasis in original.

47. Ibid., 279–80.

Chapter 2. The Context of Emigration: Prefamine Ireland

1. Kerby A. Miller, *Emigrants and Exiles: Ireland and the Irish Exodus to North America;* see app., table 1 "Number of Overseas Emigrants from Ireland Classified by Destination, 1851–1921." 3,794,852 went to the United States out of a total of 4,514,017. In addition, 313,622 went initially to British North America (Canada) from where an unknown proportion migrated across the border to the United States.

2. Ibid., 169, 197–200, 292.

3. Donald Harman Akenson, *The Irish Diaspora: A Primer*, 39.

4. British Parliamentary Papers, Emigration 2, First, Second, and Third Reports from the Select Committee on Emigration from the United Kingdom, 1826–27 (Shannon: Irish University Press, 1968), Abstracts of All Petitions and Memorials Received at the Colonial Department from Persons Desirous of Emigrating from the United Kingdom–Irish Applicants, 484–99.

5. Patrick McKenna, "Irish Migration to Argentina," in *The Irish World Wide*, ed. Patrick O'Sullivan, 1:63–83.

6. Earl F. Niehaus, *The Irish in New Orleans 1800–1860*.

7. Ruth-Ann Harris, *The Nearest Place That Wasn't Ireland: Early Nineteenth-Century Labor Migration*, 185.

8. For collections of emigrant letters from Australia and Canada, see Patrick O'Farrell, *Letters from Irish Australia, 1825–1929;* C .J. Houston and W. J. Smyth, *Irish Emigration and Canadian Settlement: Patterns, Links, and Settlers;* David Fitzpatrick, ed., *Oceans of Consolation: Personal Accounts of Irish Migration to Australia*.

9. Hobart Huson, *Refugio: A Comprehensive History of Refugio from Aboriginal Times to 1953;* William H. Oberste, *Texas Irish Empresarios and Their Colonies: Power and Hewetson, McMullen and McGloin. Refugio-San Patricio;* Rachel Bluntzer Hébert, *The Forgotten Colony: San Patricio de Hibernia: The History, the People, and the Legends of the Irish Colony of McMullen-McGloin;* John Brendan Flannery, *The Irish Texans;* Richard Roche, *The Texas Connection: The Story of the Wexford Colony in Refugio*.

10. Oberste, *Texas Irish Empresarios*, 101.

11. William H. Oberste Papers, Box 1, Correspondence, Rev. Owen Kavanagh, 1943–45, Catholic Archives, Austin.

12. Ibid., letter, February 4, 1943.

13. Oberste, *Texas Irish Empresarios*, 98.

14. Alexis de Tocqueville, *Alexis de Tocqueville's Journey in Ireland, July–August, 1835*, trans. and ed. Emmet J. Larkin, 64.

15. Kevin Whelan, "The Catholic Community in Eighteenth-Century County Wexford," in *Endurance and Emergence: Catholics in Ireland in the Eighteenth Century*, ed. T. P. Power and Kevin Whelan, 130–70.

16. L. J. Proudfoot, "Property, Society, and Improvement, c.1700 to c.1900," in *An Historical Geography of Ireland*, ed. B. J. Graham and L. J. Proudfoot, 219–357.

17. Flannery, *The Irish Texans*, 16.

18. Whelan, "The Religious Factor in the 1798 Rebellion in County Wexford," in *Rural Ireland, 1600–1900: Modernisation and Change*, ed. Patrick O'Flanagan, Paul Ferguson, and Kevin Whelan, 62–85. A townland is a small unit of administration below the level of counties and baronies.

19. Ibid.

20. Flannery, *The Irish Texans*, 13

21. Ibid., 43.

22. Akenson, *The Irish Diaspora*, 273.

23. Deposition of Rosalie Hart Priour, District Court, Refugio County, *Welder vs. Lambert*, cited in Huson, *Refugio: A Comprehensive History*, 1:165.

24. Martin Power to his father in Ireland, June 23, 1839, Power Papers, Library of the Institute of Texan Cultures, University of Texas, San Antonio; my emphasis.

25. Roche, *The Texas Connection*, 9.

26. Deposition of William St. John, District Court, Refugio County, *Welder vs. Lambert*, 1891 and 1892, Refugio County District Court, Corpus Christi.

27. William Makepeace Thackeray, *The Irish Sketch Book, 1842*, 265–66; J. C. Curwen, "Observations on the State of Ireland in 1818," in *The English Travellers into Ireland*, ed. John P. Harrington, 214–15.

28. Census of Ireland, 1841, xiv (504), H.C. 1843, xxiv, 14, University of Bath.

29. Cormac O'Grada, "Poverty, Population, and Agriculture, 1801–1845," in *A New History of Ireland: V. Ireland Under the Union, I. 1801–1870*, ed. W. E. Vaughan, 114.

30. British Parliamentary Papers, Devon Commission Report (Occupation of Land), 1845, digest, 398–99.

31. John Mitchel, the foremost critic of the British government over the famine deaths in Ireland, saw a sinister intent in the establishment of the Devon Commission and concluded that the proposed consolidation of small holdings amounted to a deliberate policy of genocide. Mitchel's view has long held sway over Irish American popular opinion even though historians have largely discounted the charge of genocide. For a discussion of the importance of John Mitchel's writing on the famine, see Graham Davis, "Making History: John Mitchel and the Great Famine," in *Irish Writing and Exile*, ed. Neil Sammells and Paul Hyland, 98–115.

   For a review of recent interpretations of the famine, see Davis, "The Historiography of the Famine," in *The Irish World Wide*, ed. Patrick O'Sullivan, 6:15–39.

32. T. W. Freeman, "Land and People, c 1841," in *A New History of Ireland: V. Ireland Under the Union, I. 1801–1870*, ed. W. E. Vaughan, 264.

33. The term "conacre" applies both to a plot of land allowed to rural laborers to cultivate, usually with potatoes, and to the system of labor service given up in return for it.

34. O'Grada, "Poverty, Population, and Agriculture," 111.

35. Ibid., 108.

36. F. B. Smith, *The People's Health, 1830–1910*, 91.

37. Fitzpatrick, *Irish Emigration, 1801–1921*, 17, 23. For the importance of Irish female servants in the United States in providing remittances to Ireland, see Hasia R. Diner, *Erin's Daughters in America: Irish Immigrant Women in the Nineteenth Century*, 71.

38. Freeman, "Land and People," 251.

39. Eion O'Malley, "The Decline of Irish Industry in the Nineteenth Century," *Economic and Social Review* 13, no. 1 (1981):22.

40. Brenda Collins, "Proto-industrialisation and Pre-Famine Emigration," *Social History* 7, no. 2 (1982):127–46.

41. O'Grada, "Poverty, Population, and Agriculture," 114.

42. Freeman, "Land and People," 264.

43. O'Grada, "Poverty, Population, and Agriculture," 117.

44. Joel Mokyr, *Why Ireland Starved: A Quantitative and Analytical History of the Irish Economy, 1800–1850*, 12; O'Grada, *Ireland: A New Economic History*, 81.

45. R. Harris, *The Nearest Place That Wasn't Ireland*, 97.

46. S. Lewis, *A Topographical Dictionary of Ireland*, London, 1837, 2:153.

47. O'Grada, *Ireland: A New Economic History*, 119–20.

48. Ibid., 120–21.

49. Tape-recorded interview by Eugenia Landes with descendants of Irish settlers in Refugio in which a reference was made to the "Royal Irish" in Refugio, Refugio Museum, 1993.

50. Oscar Handlin, *Boston's Immigrants: A Study of Acculturation*; Robert Ernst, *Immigrant Life in New York City, 1825–1863*; Dennis Clark, *The Irish in Philadelphia: Ten Generations of Urban Experience*. For a more recent study of the New York Irish, see Ronald H. Baynor and Timothy Meagher, eds., *The New York Irish*.

51. Cecil J. Houston and W. J. Smyth, "The Irish Diaspora: Emigration to the New World, 1720–1920," in *An Historical Geography of Ireland*, ed. B. J. Graham and L. J. Proudfoot, 343.

52. James H. Johnston, "The Distribution of Irish Emigration in the Decade before the Great Famine," *Irish Geography* 21 (1988):78–87.

53. All preceding excerpts taken from British Parliamentary Papers, Commissioners of Inquiry into the Condition of the Poorer Classes in Ireland, 1836, Reports and Supplement, app. F 33, 133–41.

54. Houston and Smyth, "The Irish Diaspora," 343.

55. Bruce S. Elliott, *Irish Migrants in the Canadas: A New Approach*, 6, 134.

56. British Parliamentary Papers, Emigration 2, 1826–27, Minutes of Evidence, Testimony of Peter Robinson, May 10, 1827, 344–57.

57. British Parliamentary Papers, Emigration 2, 1826–27, Report, 6–10.

58. British Parliamentary Papers, Emigration 2, 1826–27, Minutes of Evidence, Testimony of Rev. T. R. Malthus, May 5, 1827, 327. The apparent success of the Robinson scheme was endorsed by a number of collectively signed letters sent to

Earl Bathurst, secretary of state for the colonies. The emigrant letters invariably expressed gratitude for the attention and support they had received through the emigration scheme, and countered the negative reports that surrounded emigration from Ireland. Ultimately, the scheme proved to be less successful than the early optimism of settlers suggested. The quality of the land proved to be poor and many colonists moved across the border to the United States in search of alternative opportunities.

59. British Parliamentary Papers, Emigration 2, Minutes of Evidence, Testimony of Peter Robinson, May 10, 1827, 355–56.

60. British Parliamentary Papers, Commissioners of Inquiry into the Condition of the Poorer Classes in Ireland, 1836, (40) xxx, iv, 432; the statement of Samuel Holme, builder of Liverpool, cites the testimony of Christopher Shields, an Irish laborer from County Wexford who was earning 6s (30 pence) a week before he came to Britain.

61. Roche, *The Texas Connection*, 3.

62. "The Tithe Applotment Books," Donaghmore Parish, County Wexford, December, 1834, National Archives, Dublin, Ireland; Griffith Land Valuation, 1841, National Archives, Dublin, Ireland.

63. British Parliamentary Papers, Devon Report (Occupation of Land in Ireland), Evidence, 1845, 3 :478.

64. Priour, "The Adventures of a Family of Emmigrants,"18.

65. "Tithe Applotment Books," Donaghmore Parish, County Wexford, 1834. Louise O'Connor in researching her family history has located her cousin Martin O'Connor and his family who still live in the same farmhouse from which the young Thomas O'Connor left for Texas in 1834.

66. Priour, "The Adventures of a Family of Emmigrants," 17.

67. *Freeman's Journal* (Dublin), June 19, 1833.

68. K. Miller, *Emigrants and Exiles*, 218–19.

69. Ibid., 224.

70. O'Grada, *Ireland: A New Economic History*, 121.

Chapter 3. Irish Recruitment and the Settlements of San Patricio and Refugio

1. *New Handbook of Texas*, "James Power," 5 :306; "James Hewetson," 3 :383; "John McMullen and James McGloin," 4 :436–37. Kate S. O'Connor believed that Power and Hewetson were related in some way. Further research in Ireland is needed to verify their relationship.

2. Oberste, *Texas Irish Empresarios*, 86.

3. Reichstein, *Rise of the Lone Star State*.

4. See the agreement between James Power and D. S. Walker of Johnsburgh, June 6, 1837, to sell a quarter of Power's interest in a half league of land on Aransas Bay at Live Oak Point for $12,500. Power retained a special mortgage on the land for

the sale of up to one hundred town lots, Power Papers 1, Hobart Huson Library, Refugio, Texas.

5. J. McMullen to M. B. Lamar, in Mirabeau Buonaparte Lamar, *The Papers of Mirabeau Buonaparte Lamar*, ed. Charles Adams Gulick, vol. 1, no. 523 (1836).

6. Empresario Contract, John McMullen and James McGloin, August 16, 1828, State of Coahuila and Texas, English translation by Thomas G. Western, General Land Office, 1840, 3:157–58. Subsequent references to the articles are from the same source.

7. Huson, *Refugio: A Comprehensive History*, 1:140.

8. Stephen F. Austin to Governor, June 5, 1826, *The Austin Papers*, ed. Eugene C. Barker, 1353.

9. Empresario Contract, James Power and James Hewetson, June 11, 1828, General Land Office.

10. Huson, *Refugio: A Comprehensive History*, 1:145.

11. Kelly and Hatcher, "Tadeo Ortiz de Ayala," 222–51.

12. Ibid. Ortiz was also petitioning for ten leagues of land for his retirement, so he had his own reasons for opposing the settlement of foreign colonists.

13. Oberste, *The History of Refugio Mission*, 324.

14. Huson, *Refugio: A Comprehensive History*, 1:154.

15. Thomas Gunning, New York, January 26, 1832, to Major O'Hara, Sligo, Ireland, Gunning Letters, MS 20328, National Library of Ireland, Dublin. I am indebted to Professor Kerby Miller for the location of these previously unpublished letters.

16. Ibid.

17. Oberste, *Texas Irish Empresarios*, 478.

18. Ibid., 50. Pedro de Oro, his wife, and two children were on board the *Albion*, and John Carzol and his wife were on board the *New Packet*.

19. Hébert, *The Forgotten Colony*, 17.

20. Oberste, *Texas Irish Empresarios*, 53.

21. Ibid., 57.

22. Ibid., 58.

23. Huson, *Refugio: A Comprehensive History*, 1:125–27, 171.

24. Oberste, *Texas Irish Empresarios*, 60.

25. Martin Toole testified that the following were among those who transferred from San Patricio to the Power-Hewetson Colony: Robert Carlisle; James Carlisle; Bridget Quirk; Mary Felix; Luke, Pat, and Timothy Hart; Daniel O' Boyle; Martin, Michael, and John Toole; Patrick and William Quinn, *Welder vs. Power*, Refugio County, cited in Oberste, *Texas Irish Empresarios*, 129.

26. Reminiscences of Pat Burke, *Beeville (Texas) Bee*, January 12, 1912, Oberste Papers, Box F15.

27. For a list of San Patricio land grants, see app. 2.

28. Thomas Gunning's letter refers disparagingly to his Mexican neighbors as Roman Catholics: "there are numbers of Spaniards, they are a faithless people & not to be confided in." Thomas Gunning to Major O'Hara, January 26, 1832, Gunning Letters.

29. Oberste, *Texas Irish Empresarios*, 93.

30. Deposition of Dolores Welder, daughter of James Power, in *Agnes E. and Jas. Power vs. Mary F. Swift et al.*, no. 449, District Court, Refugio County, cited in Oberste, *Texas Irish Empresarios*, 95.

31. Lamar, *Papers of Mirabeau Buonaparte Lamar*, 5:239–42.

32. Ibid., 240.

33. Priour, "The Adventures of a Family of Emmigrants," 27.

34. Rosalie B. Hart Priour deposition in *Welder et al. vs. Lambert*, District Court, Refugio County, Texas. This is confirmed in the quarterly passenger list for the *Heroine*, arriving in New Orleans from Liverpool, May 7, 1834, Quarterly Abstracts of Passenger Lists of Vessels Arriving at New Orleans, January 1, 1820–December 30, 1837, NARS MF 272 Roll 1, Louisiana State Historical Society Archives, Louisiana State Museum, New Orleans. I am indebted to Mary White for locating this source in New Orleans. The passenger lists were previously thought not to have survived as they are missing from the WPA abstracts of the originals.

35. Priour, "The Adventures of a Family of Emmigrants," 29.

36. It may be significant, in terms of the subsequent loss of life, that the *Prudence* changed owners in 1808, from J. Kelso of Londonderry in Ireland to Thomas Elmes, a New Orleans merchant, after condemnation in the U.S. District Court in New Orleans for a breach of the revenue laws on March 19, 1805, the Liverpool Papers, Manuscript Room, British Library, London, cited in Oberste, *Texas Irish Empresarios*, 102–103.

37. Quarterly Abstracts of Passenger Lists of Vessels Arriving at New Orleans, January 1, 1820–December 30, 1837, passenger list of the *Heroine*, May 7, 1834, Louisiana State Historical Society (see app. 1). The *Heroine* was a relatively new ship built at New Brunswick in 1827 and registered with owners Roy and Co. in Liverpool. Its later sailing from Liverpool on March 11 or 12, 1834, can be explained by the need to negotiate a charter deal on unfamiliar territory, the advisability of sailing in better weather, and the need to coincide with the second sailing of the *Prudence*, with the intention that the two ships would arrive at New Orleans at about the same time.

38. For instance, see Terry Coleman, *Passage to America*, and Edward Laxton, *The Famine Ships*.

39. Priour, "The Adventures of a Family of Emmigrants," 29.

40. Ibid., 30.

41. Ibid.

42. Ibid., 32.

43. Oberste, *Texas Irish Empresarios*, 103.

44. "Very Late from England," *Louisiana Courier*, New Orleans, April 21, 1834, Louisiana State Historical Society Archives, Louisiana State Museum, New Orleans. I am indebted to Mary White for recovering newspaper references in New Orleans.

45. Quarterly Abstracts of Passenger Lists of Vessels Arriving at New Orleans, January 1, 1820–December 30, 1837, passenger list of the *Prudence*, April 30, 1834; *Louisiana Courier*, New Orleans, April 22, 1834, Louisiana State Historical Society.

46. Admission Books, vol. 5, November, 1833–July, 1834, recorded cholera cases April 29 to May 26, 1834, Charity Hospital, New Orleans. I am indebted to Mary White for finding this information.

47. Priour, "The Adventures of a Family of Emmigrants," 34.

48. Theodore Clapp, *Autobiographical Sketches and Reflections during a Thirty-Five Years' Residence in New Orleans*, 120–29.

49. Priour, "The Adventures of a Family of Emmigrants," 35.

50. Linn, *Reminiscences of Fifty Years in Texas*, 30–31.

51. Deposition of Rosalie B. Hart Priour, completed February 7, 1896, before J. C. Crisp, cited in Oberste, *Texas Irish Empresarios*, 43.

52. Ibid.

53. Priour, "The Adventures of a Family of Emmigrants," 40–41.

54. Ibid., 45.

55. Ibid., 46.

56. Cited in Oberste, *Texas Irish Empresarios*, 110–12.

57. Deposition of William St. John, in *Welder vs. Lambert*, September 10, 1892, District Court, Refugio County.

58. Ramón Músquiz to Santiago Power, Béjar, May 28, 1834, Letter 33, Oberste Papers.

59. Libero Becerro, 1834, General Land Office.

60. Oberste, *Texas Irish Empresarios*, 123.

61. *Texas in 1837*, 164–65.

62. Daniel Power to Martin Power, Ballinhash, August 24, 1835, Power Papers, Library of the Institute of Texan Cultures.

63. Ibid.

64. Ibid.

65. Martin Power to Col. James Power and to his parents in Ireland, Guadalupe, June 23, 1839, Power Papers, Library of the Institute of Texan Cultures.

66. James Power to Peter Keogh, New Orleans, April 20, 1836, copied from the original by Joe O'Connor and given to Kate Stoner O'Connor, Box 2R745, Personal Correspondence File, Mrs. Kate Stoner O'Connor, O'Connor Family Papers, Center for American History, University of Texas, Austin.

67. Santiago Hewetson petition, Refugio, September 9, 1834, Nixon Papers, General Land Office. I am indebted to Galen Greaser of the GLO for directing me to this collection.

68. James Hewetson to James Power, Monterrey, September 22, 1845, Power Papers 1, quoted in Oberste, *Texas Irish Empresarios*, 281.

69. James Hewetson to Patrick Hoyne, Saltillo, April 27, 1847, Hewetson Papers, Library of the Institute of Texan Cultures.
      Another example of Hewetson's humor is in his description of an Irish relative: "I shall never forget the druidical phis of cousin Pat Cullen. I wish you to anoint the muscles of his face with oil of olives so as to soften his countenance. He appears to me as fierce as a rat with one ear the last time I saw him. Do not tell him anything, of my prescription as, it might ruffle his temper," James Hewetson to Margaret Hewetson, Saltillo, January 28, 1837, Hewetson Papers.

70. The will of James Hewetson, signed April 6, 1870, Monterrey, Mexico, Hewetson Papers.

71. Resolution of the citizens of Refugio and San Patricio seeking a law of relief, to the legislature of Texas, Refugio, October 10, 1853.

72. Joseph F Smith to the Hon. D. M. Stapp, Refugio, November 1, 1853, Memorial 184, Box 78, Texas State Library and Archives, Austin.

73. Citizens of Refugio County to the Hon. President of the Senate, n.d., Texas State Library and Archives. Capt. Philip Dimitt's surname is sometimes spelled Dimitt and sometimes Dimmitt, depending on the source consulted. I have used Dimitt except when citing a source that uses the alternate spelling.

74. For a fuller account of McMullen's death, see Hébert, *The Forgotten Colony*, 51–60; for an account drawing on family memories of James McGloin, see 61–107.

Chapter 4. The Irish and the Texas Revolution, 1835–36

1. T. R. Fehrenbach, *Lone Star: A History of Texas and the Texans*.

2. President Lyndon Johnson, a Texan, in justifying U.S. policy in Vietnam and American invulnerability was reported to have said, "Remember the Alamo," see David J. Weber, *Myth and History of the Hispanic Southwest*, 150–51.

3. Paul D. Lack, *The Texas Revolutionary Experience: A Political and Social History, 1835–1836*; Stephen L. Hardin, *Texian Iliad: A Military History of the Texas Revolution, 1835–1836*; Andrés Tijerina, *Tejanos and Texas Under the Mexican Flag, 1821–1836*.

4. Flannery, *The Irish Texans*, 77; see also Huson, *Refugio: A Comprehensive History*, and Oberste, *Texas Irish Empresarios*.

5. Oberste, *Texas Irish Empresarios*, 280.

6. Daniel W. Cloud to his brother in Kentucky, December 26, 1835, Daughters of the Republic of Texas Library, San Antonio; hereafter DRTL.

7. Anglo-Americans, or Anglos, may be generally defined as white, English-speaking people but there were a number of other Europeans (Irish, Germans, and Poles, for instance) who fought on the Texan side. Mexicans may include people from Mexico or of Mexican descent, and *Tejanos* were Mexican residents of Texas. Mestizos are considered people of mixed Spanish and Indian ancestry. The Irish include those born in Ireland who arrived in Texas via the United States and those who came to Texas directly from Ireland.

8. Weber, *Myth and History*, 146.

9. Nackman, "Anglo-American Migrants," 441–55.

10. Daniel W. Cloud, letter, December 26, 1835, DRTL.

11. Daniel W. Cloud to a young friend in Kentucky, *Jackson Mississipian*, May 6, 1836, printed in the *Russelville Advisor*, Kentucky, DRTL.

12. Daniel W. Cloud to his brother, December 26, 1835, DRTL.

13. William B. Travis, letter, February 24, 1836, DRTL.

14. Lack, *The Texas Revolutionary Experience*, 10.

15. Fehrenbach, *Lone Star*, 152–73.

16. *Telegraph and Texas Register*, February 27, 1836.

17. Ibid., March 12, 1836.

18. Lack, *The Texas Revolutionary Experience*, 12.

19. Meinig, *Imperial Texas*.

20. *Telegraph and Texas Register*, October 25, 1835.

21. Lack, *The Texas Revolutionary Experience*, 14.

22. P. Dimmitt to Stephen F. Austin, October 17, 19, 1835, in *The Papers of the Texas Revolution*, ed. John H. Jenkins, 2:146.

23. Martín Perfecto de Cos to José María Turnel, November 2, 1835, in *Papers of the Texas Revolution*, 2:165–67, 299.

24. Souvenir Program, Refugio County Centennial Celebration, 1936, 13.

25. James Power to Peter Keogh, New Orleans, April 20, 1836, Box 2R745, Correspondence of Mrs. Kate S. O'Connor, O'Connor Family Papers.

26. Details of supplies to the military are discussed later in the chapter.

27. Lack, *The Texas Revolutionary Experience*, 15.

28. Margaret Swett Henson, "Tory Sentiment in Anglo-Texan Public Opinion, 1832–1836," *Southwestern Historical Quarterly* 40 (July, 1986):1–34.

29. Fehrenbach, *Lone Star*, 190; for an account of the Alamo, see Walter Lord, *A Time to Stand*.

30. Hardin, *Texian Iliad*.

31. Mary Agnes Mitchell Simmons, *The First Flag of Texas Independence*.

32. Goliad Declaration, December 20, 1835, in *Papers of the Texas Revolution*, 2:265–69. The two Mexican signatories were Miguel Aldrete and M. Carbajal.

33. Souvenir Program, Refugio County Centennial Celebration, 1936, 14.

34. Goliad Declaration, in *Papers of the Texas Revolution*, 2:266.

35. Ibid., 2:267.

36. Ibid.

37. John Turner to Capt. Dimmitt, November 30, 1835, Harbert Davenport Papers, Box 2N205, vol. 24, Center for American History, University of Texas at Austin.

38. Wyatt Hanks, Report to Council, December 15, 1835, ibid.

39. D. C. Barrett to Captain Hall, Proceedings of the General Council, January 4, 1836, ibid.

40. J. C. Neill to Maj. Gen. Sam Houston, January 14, 1836, Army Papers, Texas State Library and Archives.

41. W. H. Wharton to Governor Henry Smith, February 7, 1836, Harbert Davenport Papers, Box 2N204, vol. 12, Center for American History.

42. W. H. Wharton to Governor Henry Smith, February 13, 1836, ibid.

43. Col. James Fannin to Governor Smith, February 14, 1836, Harbert Davenport Papers, Box 2N205, vol. 21, Center for American History.

44. James McGloin to J. W. Bowers [Bower], San Patricio, February 22, 1836, quoted in Oberste, *Texas Irish Empresarios*, 179; also in Power Papers 2, Library of the Institute of Texan Cultures.

45. Col. James Fannin to Acting-Governor Robinson to Council, February 22, 1836, Harbert Davenport Papers, Box 2N204, vol. 12, Center for American History.

46. Sarah Wharton to Henry Smith, March 26, 1836, Harbert Davenport Papers, Box 2N205, vol. 21, Center for American History.

47. *Telegraph and Texas Register*, April 14, 1836.

48. Wm. Parker to Ira Ingram, Matagorda, June 30, 1836, in *Free Trader and Natchez (Mississippi) Gazette*, July 29, 1838, Harbert Davenport Papers, Box 2N205, vol. 21, Center for American History.

49. David G. Burnet to officers in the Army of Texas, September 20, 1836, ibid.

50. David G. Burnet, letter, October 11, 1836, ibid.

51. Ibid.

52. David G. Burnet to Congress, October 25, 1836, Harbert Davenport Papers, Box 2N205, vol. 21, Center for American History.

53. W. H. Wharton, 1st Congress, 1st session of the Senate, November 10, 1836, ibid.

54. For a more detailed account of the activity of Thomas O'Connor during the war see chapter 6.

55. Reichstein, *Rise of the Lone Star State*.

56. Joseph E. Plummer to his son Frances, February 14, 1837, Plummer File, Library of the Institute of Texan Cultures.

57. "An Honest Man," *Telegraph and Texas Register*, December 6, 1836.

58. Harbert Davenport, "Refugio and the Paducah Volunteers," Harbert Davenport Papers, File 2-23/181, Texas State Library and Archives.

59. Ira Westover, Adjt., to Genl. Sam Houston, Goliad, November 15, 1835, *Telegraph and Texas Register*, December 2, 1835.

60. James Power's report concerning General Mexía, Council Proceedings, December 17, 1835, Harbert Davenport Papers, Box 2N205, vol. 28, Center for American History.

61. Petition to Stephen F. Austin, Commander in Chief of the Army of the People of Texas, November 21, 1835, Harbert Davenport Papers, Box 2N205, vol. 12, ibid.

62. Petitions for compensation, Mary Byrne, November 28, 1839, Texas State Library and Archives.

63. Petitions for compensation, Thomas Pew and Michael Hely of San Patricio, September 23, 1841; Patrick McGloin of San Patricio, September 23, 1841, both in Texas State Library and Archives.

64. Dilue Rose Harris, "The Reminiscences of Mrs. Dilue Harris," *Quarterly of the Texas State Historical Association* 4 (January, 1901):155–89.

65. Charles H. Ayers, "Lewis Ayers," *Quarterly of the Texas State Historical Association* 9, no. 4 (April, 1906):272.

66. Ibid., 274.

67. José Urrea, "Diario Militar, 1838," in *The Mexican Side of the Texas Revolution*, trans. Carlos E. Castañeda, 223–37.

68. Sabina Brown, "Sabina Brown's Mournful Story of the War at the Mission," Texas State Library and Archives. Sabina Brown was the wife of James Brown who was killed at Goliad. She then married fellow colonist Michael Fox.

69. Ibid.

70. Ibid.

71. E. N. Hill, "Galveston, the Siege of the Mission of Refugio, and the Slaughter of Capt. King's Men, May 21, 1836," 189, Harbert Davenport Papers, Texas State Library and Archives.

72. Herman Ehrenberg, *With Milam and Fannin: Adventures of a German Boy in the Texas Revolution*, trans. Charlotte Churchill, 163.

73. Col. Francisco Garay, "The Battle of Refugio," trans. Harbert Davenport from Filisola's *Memorias Para La Guerra de Tejas*, 2:410–14, Harbert Davenport Papers, Texas State Library and Archives.

74. Mexican general to his wife, Goliad, March 25, 1836, reprinted in *New Orleans Bee*, June 15, 1836.

75. Ehrenberg, *With Milam and Fannin*, 138–39.

76. Joseph Milton Nance, "Abel Morgan and His Account of the Battle of Goliad," *Southwestern Historical Quarterly* 100, no. 2 (October, 1996):211–13.

77. Ehrenberg, *With Milam and Fannin*, 174.

78. Andrew A. Boyle, Pension Application, p. 6, Genealogy Library, Texas State Library and Archives.

79. Linn, *Reminiscences of Fifty Years in Texas*, 161.

80. Andrew A. Boyle, Pension Application, p. 7, Genealogy Library.

81. Linn, *Reminiscences of Fifty Years in Texas*, 163.

82. Andrew A. Boyle, Pension Application, p. 7, Genealogy Library.

83. Ehrenberg, *With Milam and Fannin*, 200–201. An undated claim for compensation survives from Irish colonist Ellen Cash. In a letter to Anson Jones, president pro tem of the Senate, she stated that she and her husband were citizens of Goliad when that town was "invaded" by the Mexicans. Her husband joined Fannin's command, was wounded in action, and was carried to Goliad where he was shot. All her property was destroyed by the Mexican army except for one wagon and one yoke of oxen, which were taken by General Rusk. She put the value of the wagon and oxen at eight hundred dollars and asked for appropriate compensation. Ellen Cash also stated that she performed "much service in Camp in attendance on the sick and wounded being the only female there, for this she claims no compensation having as she believes only done her duty." She ended her letter, "throwing herself entirely upon the Justice of the Congress and relies upon their Magnanimity to award her relief. . . . to which she may seem entitled in Justice and Equity," Petitions for Compensation, Ellen Cash, undated, Texas State Library and Archives.

84. Jack Shackelford, "Some Few Notes upon a Part of the Texan War," in *Documents of Texas History*, 110.

85. For the names of Irish colonists who were killed at Goliad, see Souvenir Program, Refugio County Centennial Celebration, 1936, 14.

86. Andrew A. Boyle, Pension Application, p. 10; see also Boyle, "Reminiscences of the Texas Revolution," *Quarterly of the Texas State Historical Association* 13 (April, 1910).

87. Mrs. Tom O'Connor Sr., "Nicholas Fagan, Texas Patriot," typescript, 1958, Box 2R745, Personal Correspondence File, O'Connor Family Papers.

88. Hardin, *Texian Iliad*, 174.

89. Ibid.

90. "Mexican Account of the Battle of San Jacinto," *Texas Almanac* (Galveston, 1870), 41–53.

91. Hardin, *Texian Iliad*, 250.

92. Audited Military Claims, Received of James Power supplying clothing to the Army of Texas, Victoria, June 19, 1836, $532.20, signed John Forbes, Commissary General; James Power supplying mules, oxen, and beef for Gov. use in 1835 and 1842, $312, certificate issued October 6, 1853; James Power, Commandant Texas Spying Company, October 5, 1836; John J. Linn supplying flour, coffee, rice, etc. valued at $2,258.86; Refugio, Thomas O'Connor for hauling goods to Copano, $120, February 19, 1836, approved March 1, 1836; Nicholas Fagan, supplied one cart load of corn, eight barrels delivered to the Mission Refugio, February 1, 1836, and one beef valued at $33 for the troops under Maj. Wallace, February 18, 1836, all in Texas State Library and Archives. Fort Goliad, J. J. Linn supplying corn to Col. Fannin, February 14, 1836, in John J. Linn, *Reminiscences of Fifty Years in Texas*, 125–26.

93. Kate S. O'Connor, speech, "The Part the Irish Had in the Settling of Victoria and Vicinity," Box no. T976, 411, O'Connor Family Papers.

94. Hardin, "The Texas Revolution in South Texas: A Reassessment," *South Texas Studies* 1 (1990):68–87; James W. Pohl and Stephen L. Hardin, "The Military History of the Texas Revolution," *Southwestern Historical Quarterly* 89 (January, 1986): 269–308.

95. Pohl and Hardin, "Military History," 248–50.

96. Lack, *The Texas Revolutionary Experience*, 158–59, 132–34.

97. Martin Power to Dan Power, 1839, Power Papers 1, Huson Library; Public Meeting, October 10, 1853, Refugio, Texas, Library of the Institute of Texan Cultures. See also Memorial no. 164, Power's and McGloin's Colonists, Protest of Power's and McGloin's Colonists with reference to locating land certificates on colonial titles, October 10, 1852, Box 101, Texas State Library and Archives.

98. Souvenir Program, Refugio County Centennial Celebration, 1936, 14. See app. 4 for details of Irish colonists in the war.

Chapter 5. The Life of Pioneer Settlers in Texas

1. Ray A. Billington, "Cowboys, Indians, and the Land of Promise: The World Image of the American Frontier," *Proceedings of the Fourteenth International Congress of the Historical Sciences*, 69–70.

2. F. J. Turner, "The Significance of the Frontier in American History," in *The Frontier in American History*, 3–4.

3. Walter Prescott Webb, *The Great Frontier*, 34.

4. Ibid., 34–35.

5. Billington, *America's Frontier Culture: Three Essays*, 52–54. For a broader narrative, see Ray A. Billington and Martin Ridge, *Westward Expansion: A History of the American Frontier*.

6. Walter Cronon, George Miles, Jay Gitlin, "Becoming West: Toward a New Meaning for Western History," in *Under an Open Sky: Rethinking America's Western Past*, ed. Cronon, Miles, and Gitlin, 4. See also *The Oxford History of the American West*, ed. Clyde A. Milner II, Carol A. O'Connor, and Martha A. Sandweiss.

7. Patricia Nelson Limerick, "Making the Most of Words: Verbal Activity and Western America," in *Under an Open Sky: Rethinking America's Western Past*, ed. Cronon, Miles, and Gitlin, 167–84.

8. Address of Wm. H. Wharton, in *Papers of Mirabeau Buonaparte Lamar*, vol. 2, no. 357, April 26, 1836.

9. Mrs. Kate Dougherty Bluntzer, "Biographies and Memoirs of Pioneers," 1958, 3–4, Kilgore Collection, Texas A&M University, Corpus Christi State University. For a contrasting view see the account of Jack Duval, a Kentucky soldier in the Texan army who, in passing by the vicinity of Refugio, asked for milk from an Irishwoman. She led him to an outhouse where there were a number of pans filled with milk. Duval was dismayed by the lack of hygiene when "she rolled up her sleeve and deliberately proceeded to skim it with her open hand, which looked to me to have been unacquainted with soap and water for some time past. When she had finished skimming the milk in this primitive fashion, she poured the contents of the pan into my camp kettle, at the same time saying: 'There, my little mon, there's a pan of milk for yez that's fit for the Pope of Room, Heaven protect his Holiness.'" Duval paid for the milk, took it back to camp but preferred to drink coffee in preference to such "nice new milk" while his companions were much less squeamish about it. J. C. Duval, *Early Times in Texas*, 25.

10. Priour, "The Adventures of a Family of Emmigrants," 45.

11. Ibid., 46.

12. Ibid., 49–50.

13. Jemima and Mary Toll, letter, New York, reprinted in David Woodman Jr., *Guide to Texas Emigrants*, 168–69.

14. Ibid.

15. Reminiscences of Patrick Burke, *Beeville (Texas) Bee*, January 12, 1912, Oberste Papers, Box F15.

16. John H. Dunn, "My Family as I Remember Them," November 15, 1952, typescript, 2–3, Kilgore Collection 4589.

17. Allen, "Reminiscences of Mrs. Annie Fagan Teal," 320–22.

18. Holley, *Texas*, 115.

19. Thomas Gunning to Major O'Hara, New York, January 26, 1832, Gunning Letters, MS 20328. I am indebted to Professor Kerby Miller for referring me to this collection.

20. Priour, "The Adventures of a Family of Emmigrants," 46–47.

21. Ibid., 57–58.

22. James O. Breeden, "Health of Early Texas: The Military Frontier," *Southwestern Historical Quarterly* 80, no. 4 (April, 1977):380–81.

23. Ibid., 379.

24. Ibid., 376–79.

25. Letter dated February 14, 1837, Plummer File. I am indebted to Tom Shelton, the librarian at the institute, for directing me to this collection of letters.

26. Ibid., letter dated March 9, 1837.

27. Ibid., letter dated December 24, 1837.

28. Ibid., letter dated March 19, 1840.

29. Ibid., letter dated November 11, 1840.

30. Ibid.

31. Elizabeth McAnulty Owens, *The Story of Her Life*, 16–17, Center for American History, University of Texas, Austin.

32. Thomas Gunning to Major O'Hara, January 26, 1832, Gunning Letters.

33. Ibid.

34. The term "Indians" reflects the language employed at the time by the pioneer settlers. The modern term "Native Americans," altogether more acceptable today, was not part of the vocabulary of either Mexican or independent Texas.

35. Noah Smithwick, *The Evolution of a State, or, Recollections of Old Texas Days*.

36. "Whelan Tales Told of Texas Irishman," undated newspaper clipping (probably *Refugio County Press*), Press Cuttings, Library of the Institute of Texan Cultures.

37. Ibid.

38. Allen, "Reminiscences of Mrs Annie Fagan Teal," 321–22.

39. Rosa Kleberg, "Some of My Early Experiences in Texas," *Texas Historical Quarterly* 1 (April, 1898): 297–98.

40. Owens, *The Story of Her Life*, 5–7.

41. Priour, "The Adventures of a Family of Emmigrants," 51.

42. See Curtis, *Apes and Angels*; Roy Foster, *Paddy and Mr. Punch: Connections in Irish and English History*.

43. Priour, "The Adventures of a Family of Emmigrants," 61. Mexicans and Indians were lumped together as equally threatening to the colonists during the fight at Matagorda (73).

44. Flannery, *The Irish Texans*, 81.

45. Ibid., 80.

46. Mrs. Tom O'Connor Sr., "Nicholas Fagan, Texas Patriot," typescript, 1958, Box 2R 936, Personal Records, File 18, Literary Productions, O'Connor Family Papers. I am indebted to Margaret Eakin for directing me to this source. Mrs. Kathryn O'Connor (1883–1979), preservationist, philanthropist, and historian, married Thomas O'Connor, son of Denis O'Connor and grandson of Thomas O'Connor who came to Texas in 1836.

47. *Beeville (Texas) Bee*, January 12, 1912.

48. Ibid.

49. Ibid.

50. Ibid.

51. Ibid.

52. Article on San Patricio, *San Antonio Express*, February 11, 1984.

53. Limerick, "Making the Most of Words," 167–68.

54. Flannery, *The Irish Texans*, 115.
55. Ibid., 130–32.
56. Ibid., 103–108.
57. Ibid., 107–108.
58. Richard Demeter, *Irish America: The Historical Travel Guide*, 2:506–507.
59. Niehaus, *The Irish in New Orleans*; R. A. Burchell, *The San Francisco Irish, 1848–1880*; McKenna, "Irish Migration to Argentina," 1:63–83; David Emmons, *The Butte Irish: Class and Ethnicity in an American Mining Town, 1875–1925*.
60. Flannery, *The Irish Texans*, 123–28.
61. K. Miller, *Emigrants and Exiles*.
62. Akenson, *The Irish Diaspora*, 58.
63. Joseph A. King, "The Murphys and the Breens of the Overland Parties to California, 1844 and 1846," in *The Irish World Wide*, ed. Patrick O'Sullivan, 1:84–109.
64. K. Miller, *Emigrants and Exiles*, 125–26.

Chapter 6. Ranching Culture and the Texas Cattle King: Thomas O'Connor of Refugio County

1. For the origins of cattle ranching in Texas, see J. F. Dobie, "The First Cattle in Texas and the South West Progenitors of the Longhorns," *Southwestern Historical Quarterly* 42, no. 3 (January, 1939):171.
2. Terry Jordan, *Trails to Texas: Southern Roots of Western Cattle Ranching.*
3. Ibid., 81.
4. Ibid.
5. Personal communication, Louise O'Connor, November 18, 1997.
6. Jack Jackson, *Los Mesteños: Spanish Ranching in Texas, 1721–1821.*
7. Ibid., 601.
8. Ibid., 595.
9. Ibid., 612.
10. Tijerina, *Tejanos and Texas*; Anna Caroline Crimm, "Success in Adversity: The Mexican Americans of Victoria County, Texas, 1800–1880," Ph.D. diss., University of Texas, Austin, 1994.
11. Tijerina, *Tejanos and Texas*, 138.
12. Ibid., 137–44.
13. Crimm, "Success in Adversity."
14. Ibid., 174–75.
15. Ibid., 207–208.
16. Ibid., 187.
17. Memorial no. 164, Power's and McGloin's colonists, October 10, 1852, Box 101, Texas State Library and Archives.
18. Armondo C. Alonzo, *Tejano Legacy: Rancheros and Settlers in South Texas, 1734–1900*, 270.
19. Meinig, *Imperial Texas*, 68.
20. Ibid., 66.

21. Sister Margaret Rose Warburton, "A History of the Thomas O'Connor Ranch," Ph.D. diss., Catholic University of America, San Antonio, 1939. This is an absorbing account of the building up of the ranch, but it does not explore how it was achieved or assess the significance of O'Connor's achievement. My own study fills a number of gaps in the story and offers an analysis beyond a broadly pietistic biography. This has been made possible through privileged access to the O'Connor Family Papers at the Center for American History at the University of Texas at Austin. These have been supplemented by reference to land deeds at the Refugio County Courthouse, to legal records at the Texas State Library and Archives, and to newspapers in Victoria and San Antonio. See also Louise S. O'Connor, *Cryin' for Daylight: A Ranching Culture in the Coastal Bend.*

22. Louise O'Connor, a direct descendant of Thomas O'Connor, in researching her own family history, has discovered a branch of the O'Connor family still living at the old farmhouse in County Wexford, Ireland. Farmer, Martin O'Connor is a descendant of the older brother of Thomas O'Connor who went to Texas in 1834.

23. Thomas O'Connor to Dennis O'Connor, c. 1880, Box 2R739, File 2, Personal Records, Correspondence of Dennis Martin O'Connor, 1877–1900, O'Connor Family Papers.

24. Translation by Professor Malcolm Mclean from the original petition of Thomas O'Connor, 1834, Title Book no. 17, Spanish Archives, General Land Office. Martin Power, also a nephew of James Power, similarly claimed a family of domestic servants as an entitlement to a full league of land.

25. *Historical and Biographical Record of the Cattle Industry and Cattlemen of Texas and Adjacent Territory*, entry on D. M. O'Connor also refers to Thomas O'Connor, 2:637.

26. Thomas O'Connor's military service: joined Philip Dimitt's Company at Goliad, October 10, 1835; a private in Captain Bingham's Company of Citizen Volunteers, February 25, 1836; a private in R. J. Calder's Company at San Jacinto, April, 1836; a private in Captain Flores's Company 1st Regiment of Cavalry, October 7, 1836, to April 11, 1837, Box 2R772, Legal Records, O'Connor Family Papers.

27. Thomas O'Connor's military contracts, 1836–42: hauling goods to Goliad and Copano, approved by Martin Power, $120, February 19, 1836; military services, draft signed by James Power, $120, March 3, 1836; military services, $120, March 7, 1836; supply of horses, $285, May 10, 1837; military supplies, $129.32, April 19, 1838; military supplies, $285.61, April 15, 1839; payment from Paymaster-General, $2,046, September 20, 1839; military supplies, $285, November 15, 1839; 14 days' work for the military, $70, June 18, 1840; supplying 8 head of beef for the army at Corpus Christi, $100, 1 yearling for Texian Army, brand TC, $5, May 13, 1842; corn delivered , $120, and 4 beefs for the army under J. Coleman, Texan Volunteers, $50, June 25, 1842; corn and beef supplied to the army, $275, in May–July, 1842; supplies to Texian Army, $285, September, 1849, all in Public Debt Claims, Genealogy Library, Texas State Library and Archives.

28. Title Deed, October 3, 1836, Refugio County, Texas, Box 2R767, Legal Records, File 2, O'Connor Family Papers.

29. There is a legend connecting Thomas O'Connor and Nicholas Fagan. When young Thomas presented himself at the Fagan ranch in 1838, in a new suit bought for the occasion, to propose marriage to Mary Fagan, the family's younger daughter and the second niece of the Duke of Wellington, he was disapproved of by the Fagan family. The only thing Nicholas Fagan approved of was the suit, not the young man of twenty who was wearing it. It is a good story in terms of the subsequent history of the O'Connor family and only makes sense in retrospection, but it is difficult to reconcile with the chronology of events. If Nicholas Fagan disapproved of Thomas O'Connor, he would not have lent him money and sold him land in October, 1836, two years before the marriage took place. Also, Fagan and O'Connor were together on December 20, 1835, unfurling the flag of independence at Goliad, so they shared a common bond, as fellow Irishmen, in supporting the Texan cause.

When he was discharged from the army in 1837, his worldly possessions were described in true legendary style as few: "a Spanish pony, a saddle and bridle, two old bell pistols, one of which was broken off at the breach, and one rifle gun, all of which were much worse for having been in constant use in obtaining our independence," W. G. Kingsbury, "Cattle Raising in Texas," 41, quoted in Warburton, "A History of the Thomas O'Connor Ranch," 110.

30. Marriage Records, Bexar County Court House, San Antonio, vol. A, 13, license no. 29, issued October 13, 1838.

31. Warburton, "A History of the Thomas O'Connor Ranch," 113.

32. Thomas O'Connor for 14 days' work, 70 dollars paid in full, Public Debt Claims, Genealogy Library.

33. See n. 27, this chapter, military contracts.

34. For details of the battle of Salado, see *New Handbook of Texas*, 5:772–73.

35. "Why Gray Went Unpunished for Heinous Crime," typescript, Box 2R889, File 5, Historical Material, Victoria, Texas, Mabry B. (Mustang) Gray, undated, O'Connor Family Papers; see also Frank J. Dobie, "Mustang Gray," *Texas Folk-Lore Society*, 1932.

36. Victor Bracht, *Texas, 1848*, 89.

37. Refugio County Tax Rolls, 1848, Genealogy Library.

38. Title Deeds, Refugio County, Title Bond, grantor Nicholas Fagan, October 3, 1846; Book C, 90-1; Title bond, grantor John Fagan, October 3, 1846, Book C 92-3; fee, grantor, John Fagan, March 6, 1847, Book C, 176-7.

39. David G. Surdam, "The Antebellum Texas Cattle Trade across the Gulf of Mexico," *Southwestern Historical Quarterly*, 100, no. 4 (April, 1977):477–92.

40. Warburton, "A History of the Thomas O'Connor Ranch," 113.

41. Refugio County Tax Rolls, 1850, and Seventh Texas Census, 1850, Refugio County, both in Genealogy Library.

42. O'Connor, *Cryin' for Daylight*, 65–124.

43. J. D. B. Stillman, "Wanderings in the Southwest," edited with introduction by Ron Tyler, undated (c. 1855), 27, photostat in Box 2R894, Literary Productions, File 6, O'Connor Family Papers.

44. Transcribed Record of Deed, Refugio County, Book D, 508, Book E, 394; see also Warburton, "A History of the Thomas O'Connor Ranch," 79.

45. Abstracts of Land Records, 1885, Box 2R807, O'Connor Family Papers.

46. Warburton, "A History of the Thomas O'Connor Ranch," 80.

47. Jordan, *Trails to Texas*, 81.

48. Eighth Texas Census, 1860, Refugio County, Genealogy Library.

49. C. M. Love, "History of the Cattle Industry in the South West," *Southwestern Historical Quarterly* vol. 19 (April, 1916):384, quoted in Warburton, "A History of the Thomas O'Connor Ranch," 80.

50. David G. Sturdam, "The Antebellum Texas Cattle Trade across the Gulf of Mexico," *Southwestern Historical Quarterly* 100, no. 4 (April, 1977); Wayne Gard, *The Chisholm Trail*, quoted in Jimmy M. Skaggs, *Prime Cut: Livestock Raising and Meatpacking in the United States, 1607–1983*, 27.

51. I am indebted to Louise O'Connor for this piece of family folklore recalled from her grandmother Katherine O'Connor.

52. Bill of sale of the Negro, Thornton, between Thomas O'Connor and Edward Perry, May 3, 1864, Box 2R778, File 1, Papers of George Overton Stoner, File 1, O'Connor Family Papers.

53. Warburton, "A History of the Thomas O'Connor Ranch," 115.

54. For details of the hide and tallow trade, see *New Handbook of Texas*, 3:593–94.

55. General Index of Deeds, Refugio County, District Court Office, Refugio, Texas.

56. Warburton, "A History of the Thomas O'Connor Ranch," 114.

57. Ibid., 115–16.

58. Ninth Texas Census, 1870, Refugio County, Genealogy Library.

59. Grocery lists, A. Goldman, Victoria, October 13, 1887; A Levi and Co., November 3, 1887, December 30, 1887, Box 2R 773, File 3, O'Connor Family Papers.

60. Warburton, "A History of the Thomas O'Connor Ranch," 116.

61. *New Handbook of Texas*, "Reconstruction," 5:474–81.

62. General Index of Deeds, Refugio County; thirty-seven transactions out of forty-two involving Thomas O'Connor are listed on a single page.

63. Deed Register, Refugio County, Book M, 155-7, Book K, 253; Book M, 459.

64. District Court Refugio County, Case No. 2435, filed March 27, 1939, *Abraham Krause et al. vs. Thomas O'Connor et al.*; Jack Keever's report on legal disputes claims that Thomas O'Connor paid three cents an acre for the Power-Hewetson headrights, making the final purchase in 1888, Box 2R769, File 8, Legal Records, June 15, 1976, O'Connor Family Papers.

65. Abel G. Rubio, *Stolen Heritage: A Mexican-American's Rediscovery of His Family's Lost Land Grant*. In support of the charge made against the O'Connors, a broad picture of events is presented showing how Mexicans were generally deprived of their lands by unscrupulous Anglo-Americans. Yet the book contains many examples that contradict the idea of wholesale, anti-Mexican discrimination. Rubio cites the friendship between the de la Garzas and their neighbors the Fagans, which endured through the Texas Revolution and the U.S.-Mexico War (177). Henry Scott and other neighbors came to Goliad County in 1879 to implore Antonio de la Garza to return to his land (143). The basis of Rubio's case, the Becerra tract, was not registered at the General Land Office, and despite Rubio's claim of earlier validity conveyed by the Mexican government, this was a fatal

weakness in the legal case that was filed unsuccessfully against the O'Connor family. The illustration in the book purporting to be the basis of the claim is not a land grant at all but merely an application for one and was worthless without supporting documentation.

66. *Victoria Advocate*, October 11, 1879.

67. Warburton, "A History of the Thomas O'Connor Ranch," 68.

68. Skaggs, *Prime Cut*, 27.

69. Dobie, *A Vaquero in the Brush Country*, 120.

70. Sale of colonial land grant, Thomas O'Connor to Louisa Welder, original land grant situated on the south side of Sous Creek, adjoining the land of Martin Power, May 8, 1874, 4,428 acres for $4,428; December 23, 1876, 1 league of land and town lot bought by Thomas O'Connor for 200. The league of land was subsequently sold to John Linney on February 23, 1887 for $6,000 and Lot No 2 Federacion St., Refugio was sold for twenty-five gold dollars, all in Box 2R767, File 2, Legal Records, Deed Record, O'Connor Family Papers.

71. Deed Record, Refugio County, Book M, 155-7.

72. Deed of sale, November 1, 1883, "Mortgage to M. M., J. V., and M. C. Shiner, firm of Shiner Bros. of Co. Bexar for the sum of $44,846 to us in hand paid by Thomas O'Connor," Box 2R767, File 2, Legal Records, O'Connor Family Papers. All the tracts of land were situated in La Salle and McMullen Counties.

73. *Victoria Advocate*, June 27, 1886, quoted in Warburton, "A History of the Thomas O'Connor Ranch," 26

74. *San Antonio Daily Times*, October 18, 1887.

75. *Historical and Biographical Record of the Cattle Industry*, 2:137.

76. *Victoria Advocate*, April 7, 14, 1877, Newspaper Clippings File, Library of the Institute of Texan Cultures. I am indebted to Tom Shelton, the librarian at the institute, for this reference.

77. Victor M. Rose, *A History of Victoria County*, 75–76.

78. Thomas O'Connor versus the Sheriff of Aransas County, 1886, *Southwestern Reporter*.

79. *Southwestern Reporter*, Supreme Court Decisions and Court of Appeals of Texas, May 28–July 30, 1888, 8:104–109; *Parks vs. O'Connor*, Supreme Court of Texas, March 27, 1888. Appeal from District Court, Goliad County. Action by Thomas O'Connor appellee against the appellant, Solomon Parks, to recover the price of cattle sold appellant. The ranch was purchased by the O'Connor family in the mid-1980s.

80. Naylor and Co., Real Estate and Land Agents of San Antonio to T. M. O'Connor over land available in the San Antonio Viejo Ranch, 19,940 acres in all, plus cattle and horses, Box 2R773, Financial Records, Folder 1, Correspondence A-H, 1887–88, O'Connor Family Papers.

81. J. Allhands, *Gringo Builders*, 188.

82. American Well Works to D. M. O'Connor, January 21, 1888, Box 2R773, Financial Records, Folder 1 Correspondence A-H, 1887–88, O'Connor Family Papers. A gentler and more considerate side of Dennis M. O'Connor's character was revealed in a personal letter to Mrs. Rosa Lambert, December 22, 1894, offering to gather

her cattle for her. Dennis also paid $6,000 for the building of Saint Anthony's Chapel for the Mexican ranch hands, as reported in the *Southern Messenger,* July 12, 1900.

83. Box 2R773, Financial Records, Folder 1, Correspondence A–H, 1887–88, O'Connor Family Papers.

84. C. R. Johns and Austin to T. O'Connor, November 22, 1888, Box 2R773, Financial Records, Folder 2, Correspondence 1887–88, O'Connor Family Papers.

85. *Victoria Advocate,* June, 1885, quoted in Warburton, "A History of the Thomas O'Connor Ranch," 28.

86. Medical bills from S. Ragland May, 1886–October, 1887, Box 2R773, Financial Records, 1886–87, O'Connor Family Papers.

87. Interview with Alonzo Edwards, September 5, 1938, cited in Warburton, "A History of the Thomas O'Connor Ranch," 28.

88. *San Antonio Daily Times,* October 18, 1887.

89. *San Antonio Daily Express,* October 18, 1887.

90. Will of Thomas O'Connor, County Court, Refugio County, Texas, November 3, 1883.

91. Box 2R739, Personal Records, File 5, D. M. O'Connor Correspondence, O'Connor Family Papers.

92. Ibid., File 3, records of illness, 3/8/95, March to April, Hotel Salge, Austin. These included regular quantities of brandy ordered every hour of the day together with cough medicine, digitalis, and "carb. ammon." (ammonium carbonate, or smelling salts).

93. Ibid., letter from his physician to D. M O'Connor (incomplete), Victoria, August 18, 1898. For the darker side of life in the river bottoms, see Louise S. O'Connor, *Tales of the Santone River Bottom,* chapter 7, 173–201.

94. Warburton, "A History of the Thomas O'Connor Ranch," 33; William McNamara, Thomas Marion O'Connor's father-in-law, was forced to mortgage his house to his son-in-law following a lost shipment of cotton in a hurricane, probably in 1886, see Demeter, *Irish America,* 2:506–507.

95. D. M. O'Connor to his wife, January 17, 1892, records drought affecting the crop, land mortgaged for $220,000 with interest for four years or be sold out. Letter January 23, 1893, reports gossip about Dennis and his wife falling out and a public row in the hall of the Driskell Hotel in Austin, and a reference to cattle dying. Letter March 31, 1893, lists beefs offered at $16.50 but no buyers. Thomas Marion O'Connor suggested selling old cows at $7.50 per head to which Dennis responds "that beats all . . . beeves can't be sold, price going down every week—no rain." Letter January 31, 1894, 350 cattle lost in 12,000 acre pasture, 215 in Duke pasture, 250 in big pasture. Letter, February 1, 1894, cattle losses of 14,000, all in Box 2R739, personal correspondence of D. M. O'Connor, File 9, O'Connor Family Papers.

Box 2R740, File 2, letter from New Orleans, 1889, describing the behavior of the nephew, Thomas O'Connor, and another, dated June 25, 1892, referring to him not paying his way. "Only the kind old heart of Thomas O'Connor had kept him from serving his sentence for the conviction of murder against the trail boss,

Dees," Letter January 27, 1894, from Rosalie McDuffy, housekeeper at the O'Connor ranch, to Mrs. D. M. O'Connor, refers to cattle losses and the cold weather: "I do not know what will become of us all times is hard now and will be worse." Letter February 22, 1894, McDuffy to Mrs. D. M., reports how Mr. O'Connor was pushed out of his quarters into the servants' house as the Duncan and Sidley families were staying. Further reference to cattle dying, "he should close the ranch for a while."

Box 2R740, File 6, correspondence of Mary O'Connor Hallinan, letters from Jack Hallinan, 1896–98.

Box 2R741, File 1, correspondence of Mary O'Connor Hallinan, letters from Jack Hallinan, 1899–1900.

96. The terms of Thomas O'Connor's will included the clause, "in case of the death of either of said sons during my lifetime leaving children or descendants, the devise and bequest to such son shall not lapse, but shall descend and vest in his children or descendants." His black, illegitimate daughter was not mentioned in the will; personal communication, Louise O'Connor.

97. Box 2R740, Personal Records, Mary Virginia Drake O'Connor, File 5, Personal Correspondence, 1888–1910, and undated letters from cousin Elly, O'Connor Family Papers.

98. Draft letter to editor of *Galveston News*, December 22, 1888, Box 2R739, Personal Records of D. M. O'Connor, File 6, Correspondence, 1884–96, O'Connor Family Papers.

99. Ibid.

100. Ibid.

101. Decision of Supreme Court of Texas, El Paso, October 24, 1945, Box 2R769, Legal Records 1, O'Connor Family Papers.

Bibliography

Adjutant General Army Papers. Texas State Library and Archives. Austin.

Aibley, Marilyn McAdam. *Travellers in Texas, 1761–1860.* Austin: University of Texas Press, 1967.

Akenson, Donald Harman. *The Irish Diaspora: A Primer.* Belfast: Institute of Irish Studies, Q.U.B., 1993.

Allen, (Mrs.) T. C. "Reminiscences of Mrs. Annie Fagan Teal." *Southwestern Historical Quarterly* 34 (April, 1931).

Allhands, J. *Gringo Builders.* Joplin, Mo., and Dallas: Privately printed, 1931.

Almonte, Juan. "Statistical Report on Texas, 1835." Trans. C. E. Castañeda. *Southwestern Historical Quarterly* 38, no. 3 (January, 1925):177–222.

Alonzo, Armondo C. *Tejano Legacy: Rancheros and Settlers in South Texas, 1734–1900.* Albuquerque: University of New Mexico Press, 1998.

The Austin Papers. Ed. Eugene C. Barker. 2 vols. Washington, D.C.: Government Printing Office, 1924–28.

Ayers, Charles H. "Lewis Ayers." *Quarterly of the Texas State Historical Association* 9, no. 4 (April, 1906).

Barker, Eugene C., ed. *Readings in Texas History for High Schools and Colleges.* Dallas: Southwest Press, 1929.

Baynor, Ronald H., and Timothy Meagher, eds. *The New York Irish.* Baltimore and London: Johns Hopkins University Press, 1996.

Beeville (Tex.) Bee, January 12, 1912.

Benson, Nettie Lee. "Texas Viewed from Mexico, 1820–1834." *Southwestern Historical Quarterly* 90, no. 3 (1987).

Béxar Archives. Center for American History. University of Texas, Austin.

Billington, Ray A. *America's Frontier Culture: Three Essays* College Station: Texas A&M University Press, 1977.

———. "Cowboys, Indians, and the Land of Promise: The World Image of the American Frontier." *Proceedings of the Fourteenth International Congress of the Historical Sciences.* New York, 1976.

Billington, Ray A., and Martin Ridge. *Westward Expansion: A History of the American Frontier.* 5th ed. New York: Macmillan, 1982.

Bollaert, William. *William Bollaert's Texas.* Ed. W. Eugene Hollon and Ruth Lapham Butler. Norman: University of Oklahoma Press, 1956.

Bolton, Herbert Eugene, and Eugene C. Barker. *With the Makers of Texas.* Austin: Gammel-Statesman, 1904.

Boyce, George D., and Alan O'Day. *The Making of Modern Irish History.* London and New York: Routledge, 1996.

Boyle, Andrew. "Reminiscences of the Texas Revolution." *Quarterly of the Texas State Historical Association* 13 (April, 1910).

Bracht, Victor. *Texas, 1848*. Trans. Charles Frank Schmidt. San Antonio: Naylor Printing, 1931.

Breeden, James O. "Health of Early Texas: The Military Frontier." *Southwestern Historical Quarterly* 80, no. 4 (April, 1977).

British Parliamentary Papers. Commissioners of Inquiry into the Condition of the Poorer Classes in Ireland, 1836. University of Bath.

———. Devon Report (Occupation of Land in Ireland). Vol. 3, Evidence, 1845.

———. Emigration 2. First, Second, and Third Reports from the Select Committee on Emigration from the United Kingdom, 1826–27.

———. Emigration 3. Third Report from the Select Committee on Emigration from the United Kingdom, 1834.

Brown, John Henry. *History of Texas from 1685 to 1892*. 2 vols. 1892–93. Reprint, Austin and New York: Pemberton Press, 1970.

Buenger, Walter E., and Robert A. Calvert, eds. *Texas through Time: Evolving Interpretations*. College Station: Texas A&M University Press, 1991.

Burchell, R. A. *The San Francisco Irish, 1848–1880*. Manchester: Manchester University Press, 1980.

Campbell, Randolph B. *An Empire for Slavery: The Peculiar Institution in Texas, 1821–1865*. Baton Rouge: Louisiana State University Press,1989.

Castañeda, Carlos E. *The Mexican Side of the Texas Revolution*. Dallas: P. L. Turner, 1928.

———. *Our Catholic Heritage in Texas, 1519–1936*. 7 vols. Austin: Von Boeckmann-Jones,1931–58.

Census of Ireland. Report of the Commissioners Appointed to Take the Census of Ireland for the Year 1841. Dublin, 1843. University of Bath.

Charity Hospital. Admission Books. Vol. 5, November, 1833–July, 1834. New Orleans.

Clapp, Theodore. *Autobiographical Sketches and Reflections during a Thirty-Five Years' Residence in New Orleans*. Boston: Philips, Sampson, 1857.

Clark, Dennis. *The Irish in Philadelphia: Ten Generations of Urban Experience*. Philadelphia: Temple University Press, 1993.

Cloud, Daniel W. Letters. Daughters of the Republic of Texas Library. San Antonio.

Comptroller of Public Accounts Collection. Audited Military Claims. Texas State Library and Archives. Austin.

Comptroller of Public Accounts Collection. Republic Pension Applications. Genealogy Library. Texas State Library and Archives. Austin.

———. Petitions for Compensation.

———. Refugio County Tax Tolls, 1848–76.

———. San Patricio County Tax Rolls, 1848–76.

———. Seventh Texas Census, 1850.

———. Eighth Texas Census, 1860.

———. Ninth Texas Census, 1870.

———. Tenth Texas Census, 1880.

Coleman, Terry. *Passage to America*. London: Bloomsbury, 1972.

Colley, Linda. *Britons: Forging the Nation, 1707–1837*. London: Vintage Press, 1996.

Collins, Brenda. "Proto-industrialisation and Pre-Famine Emigration." *Social History* 7, no. 2 (1982).

Connor, Seymour V. *Texas: A History*. New York: Crowell, 1971.

Cork (Ireland) Examiner, 1846–48.

Crimm, Anna Caroline. "Success in Adversity: The Mexican Americans of Victoria County, Texas, 1800–1880." Ph.D. diss., University of Texas, Austin, 1994.

Cronon, Walter, George Miles, and Jay Gitlin. "Becoming West: Toward a New Meaning for Western History." In *Under an Open Sky: Rethinking America's Western Past*, ed. Cronon, Miles, and Gitlin. New York and London: W. W. Norton, 1992.

——, eds. *Under an Open Sky: Rethinking America's Western Past*. New York and London: W. W. Norton, 1992.

Curtis, L. Perry, Jr. *Apes and Angels: The Irishman in Victorian Caricature*. Rev. ed. Washington, D.C.: Smithsonian Institution Press, 1997.

Curwen, J. C. "Observations on the State of Ireland in 1818." In *The English Travellers into Ireland*, ed. John P. Harrington. Dublin: Wolfhound Press, 1991.

Daily Mississippian (Jackson), 1836.

Davenport, Harbert. "The Men of Goliad." *Southwestern Historical Quarterly* 43 (1939).

Davenport, Harbert. Papers. Center for American History. University of Texas. Austin.

Davenport, Harbert. Papers. Texas State Library and Archives. Austin.

Davis, Graham. "The Historiography of the Famine." In *The Irish World Wide*, ed. Patrick O'Sullivan. Vol. 6. Leicester: Leicester University Press, 1997.

——. *The Irish in Britain, 1815–1914*. Dublin: Gill and Macmillan, 1991.

——. "The Irish in Britain, 1815–1939." In *The Irish Diaspora*, ed. Andy Bielenberg. Harlow, Eng., and New York: Longman, 2000.

——. "Making History: John Mitchel and the Great Famine." In *Irish Writing and Exile*, ed. Neil Sammells and Paul Hyland. Basingstoke, Eng.: Macmillan, 1991.

——. "Models of Migration: The Historiography of the Irish Pioneers in South Texas." *Southwestern Historical Quarterly* 94, no. 3 (January, 1996).

——. "Talking Freedom: The Irish in the Texas Revolution." *Irish Studies Review* no. 8 (autumn 1994).

Davis, Graham, and Eugenia Landes. "Talking of Paradise: Irish Pioneer Settlers in South Texas." *Irish Studies Review* no. 5 (winter 1993).

De León, Arnoldo. *The Tejano Community, 1836–1900*. Albuquerque: University of New Mexico Press, 1982.

——. *They Called Them Greasers: Anglo Attitudes toward Mexicans in Texans, 1821–1900*. Austin: University of Texas Press, 1983.

Demeter, Richard. *Irish America: The Historical Travel Guide*. 2 vols. Pasadena: Cranford Press, 1996.

Diner, Hasia R. *Erin's Daughters in America: Irish Immigrant Women in the Nineteenth Century*. Baltimore and London: Johns Hopkins University Press, 1983.

Dobie, J. F. "The First Cattle in Texas and the South West Progenitors of the Longhorns." *Southwestern Historical Quarterly* 42, no. 3 (January, 1939).

———. *The Longhorn.* Boston, Austin: University of Texas Press, 1980.

———. "Mustang Gray." *Texas Folk-Lore Society,* 1932.

———. *A Vaquero in the Brush Country.* Dallas, 1929. Reprint, Austin: University of Texas Press, 1981.

Documents of Texas History. Ed. Ernest Wallace and David M. Vigness. Lubbock: Texas Technological College, 1960.

Doughty, Robin W. *At Home in Texas: Early Views of the Land.* College Station: Texas A&M University Press, 1987.

Duval, J. C. *Early Times in Texas.* Austin: Gammel, 1892.

Edward, David B., ed. *The History of Texas.* 1836. Reprint, Austin: Texas State Historical Assoc., 1990.

Ehrenberg, Herman. *With Milam and Fannin: Adventures of a German Boy in the Texas Revolution.* Trans. Charlotte Churchill. Dallas: Tardy Publishing, 1935.

Elliott, Bruce S. *Irish Migrants in the Canadas: A New Approach.* Kingston and Montreal: McGill University Press, 1988.

Emmons, David. *The Butte Irish: Class and Ethnicity in an American Mining Town, 1875–1925.* Urbana: University of Illinois Press, 1989.

Ernst, Robert. *Immigrant Life in New York City, 1825–1863.* New York: Columbia University Press, 1949.

Fehrenbach, T. R. *Lone Star: A History of Texas and the Texans.* New York: Macmillan,1968.

Fitzpatrick, David. *Irish Emigration, 1801–1921.* Dublin: Economic and Social History Society of Ireland, 1985.

———, ed. *Oceans of Consolation: Personal Accounts of Irish Migration to Australia.* Cork: Cork University Press, 1994.

Flannery, John Brendan. *The Irish Texans.* San Antonio: University of Texas Institute of Texan Cultures, 1995.

Foster, Roy. *Paddy and Mr. Punch: Connections in Irish and English History.* London: Allen Lane, 1993.

Freeman, T. W. "Land and People c. 1841." In *A New History of Ireland: V. Ireland Under the Union, I. 1801–1870,* ed. W. E. Vaughan. Oxford: Clarendon Press, 1989.

Freeman's Journal (Dublin), 1833–34.

Free Trader and Natchez (Miss.) Gazette, July 29, 1838.

Gammel, Hans Peter Nielson, comp. *The Laws of Texas, 1822–1897.* 10 vols. Austin: Gammel Book Co., 1898.

General Index of Deeds. District Court Office. Refugio County. Refugio, Texas.

General Land Office. Land Grants. McMullen-McGloin Colony and Power-Hewetson Colony. Austin.

———. Libero Becerro, 1834. Austin.

Goodwyn, Frank. *Life on the King Ranch.* New York: Crowell, 1951.

Graham, B. J., and L. J. Proudfoot, eds. *An Historical Geography of Ireland.* London and San Diego: Academic Press, 1993.

Gunning, Thomas. Letters. MS20328, 1831–36. National Library of Ireland. Dublin, Ireland.

Haley, J. Evetts. *Charles Goodnight: Cowman and Plainsman.* Norman: University of Oklahoma Press, 1949.

Hammett, A. B. J. *The Empresario: Don Martín de León* Waco, 1973.

Handlin, Oscar. *Boston's Immigrants: A Study of Acculturation.* Rev. ed. Cambridge, Mass.: Harvard University Press, 1959.

Hardin, Stephen L. *Texian Iliad: A Military History of the Texas Revolution, 1835–1836.* Austin: University of Texas Press, 1994.

——. "The Texas Revolution in South Texas." *South Texas Studies* vol. 1 (1990).

Harris, Dilue Rose. "The Reminiscences of Mrs. Dilue Harris." *Quarterly of the Texas State Historical Association* 4 (January, 1901).

Harris, Ruth-Ann. *The Nearest Place That Wasn't Ireland: Early Nineteenth-Century Labor Migration.* Ames: Iowa State University Press, 1994.

Hébert, Rachel Bluntzer. Papers. Corpus Christi Library. Corpus Christi, Texas.

Hébert, Rachel Bluntzer. *The Forgotten Colony: San Patricio de Hibernia: The History, the People, and the Legends of the Irish Colony of McMullen-McGloin.* Burnet, Tex.: Eakin Press, 1981.

Henderson, H. M. "Minor Empresario Contracts for the Colonization of Texas, 1825–1834." *Southwestern Historical Quarterly* 31 and 32 (1928).

Henson, Margaret Swett. "Tory Sentiment in Anglo-Texan Public Opinion, 1832–1836." *Southwestern Historical Quarterly* 40 (July, 1986):1–34.

Hewetson, James. Papers. Library of the Institute of Texan Cultures. University of Texas. San Antonio.

Historical and Biographical Record of the Cattle Industry and Cattlemen of Texas and Adjacent Territory. Vol. 2. 1894. Reprint New York: Antiquarian Press, 1959.

Holley, Mary Austin. *Texas.* 1833. Reprint, Austin: Steck, 1935.

Houston, Cecil J., and W. J. Smyth. "The Irish Diaspora: Emigration to the New World, 1720–1920." In *An Historical Geography of Ireland*, ed. B. J. Graham and L. J. Proudfoot. London: Academic Press, 1993.

——. *Irish Emigration and Canadian Settlement: Patterns, Links, and Settlers.* Toronto: University of Toronto Press, 1990.

Hurley Family. Letters. Cork Archives Council, Cork, Ireland.

Huson, Hobart. *Refugio: A Comprehensive History of Refugio from Aboriginal Times to 1953.* 2 vols. Woodsboro, Tex.: Rooke Foundation, 1953–55.

——, ed. *Journal: A Composite of Known Versions of the Journal of Dr. James H. Barnard.* Refugio, Tex., 1950.

Hyland, Paul, and Neil Sammells, eds. *Irish Writing: Exile and Subversion.* Basingstoke and London: Macmillan, 1991.

Ignatiev, Noel. *How the Irish Became White.* London and New York: Routledge, 1995.

Ikin, Arthur. *Texas: Its History, Topography, Agriculture, Commerce, and General Statistics.* London, 1841.

Jackson, Jack. *Los Mesteños: Spanish Ranching in Texas, 1721–1821* College Station: Texas A&M University Press, 1986.

Johnston, James H. "The Distribution of Irish Emigration in the Decade before the Great Famine." *Irish Geography* 21 (1988).

Jordan, Terry. *Trails to Texas: Southern Roots of Western Cattle Ranching*. Lincoln: University of Nebraska Press, 1981.

Kleberg, Rosa. "Some of My Early Experiences in Texas." *Texas Historical Quarterly* 1 (April, 1898).

Kennedy, Liam, and David S. Johnson. "The Union of Ireland and Britain, 1800–1921." In *The Making of Modern Irish History*, by George D. Boyce and Alan O'Day. London: Routledge, 1996.

Kennedy, William. *Texas: The Rise, Progress, and Prospects of the Republic of Texas*. 1841. Reprint, Fort Worth: Molyneaux Craftsmen, 1925.

Kilgore Collection. Texas A&M University. Corpus Christi State University. Corpus Christi, Texas.

King, Joseph A. "The Murphys and the Breens of the Overland Parties to California, 1844 and 1846." In *The Irish World Wide*, ed. Patrick O'Sullivan. Vol.1. Leicester: Leicester University Press, 1992.

Lack, Paul D. "Slavery and the Texas Revolution." *Southwestern Historical Quarterly* 89 (1985).

——. *The Texas Revolutionary Experience: A Political and Social History, 1835–1836*. College Station: Texas A&M University Press, 1992.

Lamar, Howard Roberts. *Texas Crossings: The Lone Star State and the American Far West, 1836–1986*. Austin: University of Texas Press, 1991.

Lamar, Mirabeau Buonaparte. *The Papers of Mirabeau Buonaparte Lamar*. Ed. Charles Adams Gulick. 6 vols. 1921–27. Reprint, New York: AMS Press, 1973.

Laxton, Edward. *The Famine Ships*. London: Bloomsbury, 1997.

Lewis, S. *A Topographical Dictionary of Ireland*. 2 vols. London, 1837.

Limerick, Patricia Nelson. "Making the Most of Words: Verbal Activity and Western America." In *Under an Open Sky: Rethinking America's Western Past*, ed. William Cronon, George Miles, and Jay Gitlin, 167–84. New York and London: W. W. Norton, 1992.

Linn, John J. *Reminiscences of Fifty Years in Texas*. 1883. Reprint, Austin: State House Press, 1986.

Liverpool Papers. Manuscript Room Collection. British Library, London.

Lord, Walter. *A Time to Stand*. Lincoln: University of Nebraska Press, 1978.

Louisiana Courier (New Orleans), 1834.

Louisiana State Historical Society. Archives. Quarterly Abstracts of Passenger Lists of Vessels Arriving at New Orleans, January 1, 1820–December 30, 1837. Louisiana State Museum. New Orleans.

Love, C. M. "History of the Cattle Industry in the South West." *Southwestern Historical Quarterly* 19 (April, 1916).

Matovina, Timothy M., ed. *The Alamo Remembered: Tejano Accounts and Perspectives*. Austin: University of Texas Press, 1995.

McKenna, Patrick. "Irish Migration to Argentina." In *The Irish World Wide*, ed. Patrick O'Sullivan. Vol. 1. Leicester: Leicester University Press, 1992.

Meinig, D. W. *Imperial Texas: An Interpretative Essay in Cultural Geography.* Austin: University of Texas Press,1988.

Miller, Kerby A. *Emigrants and Exiles: Ireland and the Irish Exodus to North America.* Oxford: Oxford University Press, 1985.

Miller, Thomas L. *Bounty and Donation Land Grants, 1835–1888.* Austin: University of Texas Press, 1967.

——. *The Public Lands of Texas, 1519–1970.* Norman: University of Oklahoma Press, 1971.

Mitchell, Mary Agnes. *The First Flag of Texas Independence.* San Antonio: Standard Printing, 1937.

Mokyr, Joel. *Why Ireland Starved: A Quantitative and Analytical History of the Irish Economy, 1800–1850.* London: Allen and Unwin, 1983.

Montejano, David. *Anglos and Mexicans in the Making of Texas, 1836–1886.* Austin: University of Texas Press, 1987.

Nackman, Mark E. "Anglo-American Migrants to the West: Men of Broken Fortunes? The Case of Texas, 1821–1846." *Western Historical Quarterly* (October, 1974).

Nance, Joseph Milton. "Abel Morgan and His Account of the Battle of Goliad." *Southwestern Historical Quarterly* 100, no. 2 (October, 1996).

Nation (Ireland), 1845–48.

The New Handbook of Texas. 6 vols. Austin: Texas State Historical Society, 1996.

Niehaus, Earl F. *The Irish in New Orleans, 1800–1860.* Baton Rouge: Louisiana State University Press, 1965.

Nixon Papers. General Land Office. Austin.

Oberste, William H. Papers. Catholic Archives. Austin.

Oberste, William H. *History of Refugio Mission.* Refugio, Tex.: Timely Remarks, 1942.

——. *Texas Irish Empresarios and Their Colonies: Power and Hewetson, McMullen and McGloin. Refugio-San Patricio.* Austin: Von Boeckmann-Jones, 1953.

O'Connor Family. Papers. Center for American History. University of Texas. Austin.

O'Connor, Katherine S. *The Presidio la Bahía del Espiritu Santo de Zuniga, 1721 to 1846.* Austin: Von Boeckmann-Jones, 1966.

O'Connor, Louise S. *Cryin' for Daylight: A Ranching Culture in the Coastal Bend.* Victoria, Tex.: Wexford Publishing, 1989.

——. *Tales from the Santone River Bottom: A Cultural History.* Victoria, Tex.: Wexford Publishing, 1999.

O'Farrell, Patrick. *Letters from Irish Australia, 1825–1929.* Sydney: New South Wales University Press; Belfast: Ulster Historical Foundation, 1984.

O'Flanagan, Patrick, Paul Ferguson. Kevin Whelan, eds. *Rural Ireland, 1600–1900: Modernisation and Change.* Cork: Cork University Press, 1987.

O'Grada, Cormac. *Ireland: A New Economic History.* Oxford: Clarendon Press, 1994.

——. "Poverty, Population, and Agriculture, 1801–1845." In *A New History of Ireland: V. Ireland Under the Union, I. 1801–1870,* ed. W. E. Vaughan. Oxford: Clarendon Press, 1989.

Olmsted, Frederick Law. *A Journey through Texas; or, A Saddle-Trip on the Southwestern Frontier.* New York, 1857. Reprint, Austin: University of Texas Press, 1978.

O'Malley, Eoin. "The Decline of Irish Industry in the Nineteenth Century." *Economic and Social Review* 13, no. 1 (1981).

O'Sullivan, Patrick, ed. *The Irish World Wide.* 6 vols. Leicester: Leicester University Press, 1992–97.

Owens, Elizabeth McAnulty. *The Story of Her Life.* San Antonio: Naylor, 1936. Center for American History. University of Texas. Austin.

The Oxford History of the American West. Ed. Clyde A. Milner II, Carol A. O'Connor, and Martha A. Sandweiss. Oxford: Oxford University Press, 1994.

The Papers of the Texas Revolution. Ed. John H. Jenkins. Vol. 2. Austin: Presidial Press, 1973.

Peña, José Enrique de la. *With Santa Anna in Texas: A Personal Narrative of the Revolution.* Trans. and ed. Carmen Perry. College Station, Tex.: Texas A&M University Press, 1975.

Plummer File. Library of the Institute of Texan Cultures. University of Texas. San Antonio.

Pohl, James W., and Stephen L. Hardin. "The Military History of the Texas Revolution." *Southwestern Historical Quarterly* 89 (January, 1986).

Power Papers. Library of the Institute of Texan Cultures. University of Texas. San Antonio.

Power, Philip. Memoirs. Hobart Huson Library. Refugio, Texas.

Power, T. P., and Kevin Whelan, eds. *Endurance and Emergence: Catholics in Ireland in the Eighteenth Century.* Dublin: Irish Academic Press, 1990.

Priour, Rosalie Hart. "The Adventures of a Family of Emmigrants Who Emmigrated to Texas in 1834." Corpus Christi Museum. Corpus Christi, Texas.

Proudfoot, L. J. "Property, Society, and Improvement, c. 1700 to c. 1900." In *An Historical Geography of Ireland,* ed. B. J. Graham and L. J. Proudfoot. London: Academic Press, 1993.

Public Debt Claims. Genealogy Library. Texas State Library and Archives. Austin.

Refugio County District Court . Depositions before the District Court, Refugio County, Texas. Rosalie Priour, William St. John, Patrick Quinn, no. 449, *Mrs. Dolores Welder vs. Philip Lambert et al.,* September 10, 1892; Felipe Roque de la Portilla, *Agnes and Jas. Power by their guardian Phil Power et al. vs. Mary Swift et al.,* September 7, 1892. Corpus Christi, Texas.

———. Title Deeds. Refugio County, Corpus Christi, Texas.

Reichstein, Andreas V. *Rise of the Lone Star State: The Making of Texas.* Trans. Jeanne R. Wilson. College Station: Texas A&M University Press, 1989.

Robinson, Peter. Papers. Cork City Library. Cork, Ireland.

Roche, Richard. *The Texas Connection: The Story of the Wexford Colony in Refugio.* Wexford, Tex.: County Heritage Committee, 1989.

Roediger, David. *The Wages of Whiteness: Race and the Making of the American Working Class.* London and New York: Routledge, 1995.

Rose, Victor M. *A History of Victoria County.* Ed. J. W. Petty Jr. 1883. Victoria, Tex.: Bookmart, 1961.

Rubio, Abel G. *Stolen Heritage: A Mexican-American's Rediscovery of His Family's Lost Land Grant.* Austin: Eakin Press, 1998.

Russelville (Ky.) Advisor, n.d.

San Antonio Daily Express, 1887.

San Antonio Daily Times, 1887.

San Antonio Express, 1984.

Shakespeare, William. *The Complete Works.* Stanley Wells and Gary Taylor, gen. eds. Oxford, 1988.

Skaggs, Jimmy M. *Prime Cut: Livestock Raising and Meatpacking in the United States, 1607–1983.* College Station: Texas A&M University Press, 1986.

Smith, F. B. *The People's Health, 1830–1910.* London: Croom Helm, 1979.

Smithwick, Noah. *The Evolution of a State, or, Recollections of Old Texas Days.* 1900. Austin: University of Texas Press, 1983.

Southwestern Reporter. Vol. 8. St. Paul, Minn.: West Publishing, 1888.

Souvenir Program. Refugio County Centennial Celebration. Refugio, Texas, 1936. Hobart Huson Library. Refugio, Tex.

Stagner, Stephen. "Epics, Science, and the Lost Frontier: Texas Historical Writing, 1836–1936." *Western Historical Quarterly* (April, 1981):164–81.

Stillman, J. D. B. *Wanderings in the Southwest in 1855.* Ed. and intro. Ron Tyler. Spokane, Wash.: A. H. Clark, 1990.

Sturdam, David G. "The Antebellum Texas Cattle Trade across the Gulf of Mexico." *Southwestern Historical Quarterly* 100, no. 4 (April, 1977).

"Tadeo Ortiz de Ayala and the Colonization of Texas, 1822–1833." Ed. Edith Louise Kelly and Mattie Austin Hatcher. *Southwestern Historical Quarterly* 32 (October, 1928).

Takaki, Ronald. *A Different Mirror: A History of Multicultural America.* Boston: Little, Brown, 1993.

——*Texas by Terán: The Diary Kept by General Manuel de Mier y Terán on His 1828 Inspection of Texas.* Ed. Jack Jackson. Trans. John Wheat. Austin: University of Texas Press, 2000.

Telegraph and Texas Register (San Felipe), 1835–38.

Texan Almanac. Galveston, 1870.

Texas in 1837: An Anonymous Contemporary Narrative Ed. Andrew Forest Muir. Austin: University of Texas Press, 1988.

Thackeray, William Makepeace. *The Irish Sketch Book, 1842.* 1843. Belfast: Blackstaff Press, 1985.

Tijerina, Andrés. *Tejanos and Texas Under the Mexican Flag, 1821–1836.* College Station: Texas A&M University Press, 1994.

Times (London), 1847.

Timmons, Wilbert H. "Robert Owen's Texas Project." *Southwestern Historical Quarterly* 52 (1949).

——. "Tadeo Ortiz and Texas." *Southwestern Historical Quarterly* 72 (1968).

Tithe Applotment Books. Donaghmore Parish, County Wexford, 1834. National
  Archives. Dublin, Ireland.
Tocqueville, Alexis de. *Alexis de Tocqueville's Journey in Ireland, July–August,
  1835*. Trans. and ed. Emmet J. Larkin. Washington D.C.: Catholic University of
  America Press, 1990.
Turner, F. J. "The Significance of the Frontier in American History." In *The
  Frontier in American History*. 1920. Reprint, New York: Holt, Rinehart and
  Winston, 1962.
Urrea, José. "Diario Militar, 1838." In *The Mexican Side of the Texas Revolution*,
  trans. Carlos E. Castañeda. Dallas: P. L. Turner, 1928.
Vaughan, W. E., ed. *A New History of Ireland: V. Ireland Under the Union, I. 1801–
  1870*. Oxford: Clarendon Press, 1989.
Victoria (Texas) Advocate, 1877, 1879, 1885–86.
Warburton, Sister Margaret Rose. "A History of the Thomas O'Connor Ranch."
  Ph.D. diss., Catholic University of America, San Antonio, 1939.
Webb, Walter Prescott. *The Great Frontier*. Austin: University of Texas Press, 1964.
———. *The Great Plains*. Lincoln: University of Nebraska Press, 1981.
———. *The Texas Rangers: A Century of Frontier Defense*. Boston: Houghton Mifflin,
  1935.
Weber, David J. *The Mexican Frontier, 1821–1846: The American Southwest Under
  Mexico*. Albuquerque: University of New Mexico Press, 1982.
———. *Myth and History of the Hispanic Southwest*. Albuquerque: University of New
  Mexico Press, 1988.
———. "Scarce More than Apes." In *Myth and History of the Hispanic Southwest*.
  Albuquerque: University of New Mexico Press, 1988.
Whelan, Kevin. "The Catholic Community in Eighteenth-Century County Wexford."
  In *Endurance and Emergence: Catholics in Ireland in the Eighteenth Century*,
  ed. T. P. Power and Kevin Whelan. Dublin: Irish Academic Press, 1990.
———. "The Religious Factor in the 1798 Rebellion in County Wexford." In *Rural
  Ireland, 1600–1900: Modernisation and Change*, ed. Patrick O'Flanagan, Paul
  Ferguson, and Kevin Whelan. Cork: Cork University Press, 1987.
Woodman, David, Jr. *Guide to Texas Emigrants*. 1835. Reprint, Waco: Texian Press,
  1974.

Index

Page numbers in *italics* indicate illustrations.

interests, 188; and support of the military, 147, 150; and Texas Revolution, 126, 132. *See also* McMullen-McGloin colony

McGloin, Patrick, 133

McGrath, John, 67

McKenna, Patrick, 41

McKnight, George, 257

Mclean, Malcolm, 260n.22

McMullen, John, 115, 238; background of, 73, 75; as businessman, 42, 104; death of, 104; as empresario, 6, 76–77, 113, 173–74; and establishment of San Patricio, 32, 61, 83–88; as council member, 117, 126, 150; and land acquisition, 104, 238; and mining interests, 188; and the Texas Revolution, 132. *See also* McMullen-McGloin colony

McMullen-McGloin colony: delays in colonization, 88; discontent within, 84–86, 166, 168, 173–75; land boundary issues, 77–79; and land grant issues, 86–87; recruitment of colonists for, 82, 113. *See also* McGloin, James; McMullen, John

McNamara, William, 189, 280n.94

McNamara House Museum (Victoria), 189

Malone, John, 117

Malthus, Rev. Thomas, 53, 65

Manifest Destiny, 3, 13, 175

Martinéz, Antonio, 22

Matagorda (port), 79, 83, 172, 274n.43

Matagorda Bay, 83

Matamoros (Mexican port), 35, 42, 73, 74, 82, 115, 121, 124, 186; cholera deaths in, 171; during the Texas Revolution, 131, 132, 132

Medina River, 104

Meinig, Donald W., 26, 112; *Imperial Texas: An interpretive Essay in Cultural Geography*, 203–204

Mendoza, Pedro, 41

Mesquite Landing, 83

Mexía, Gen. José Antonio, 132

Mexico: Anglo-American hostility toward, 13, 15–19; Catholic settlers in, 78; and centralists, 108, 132; and Colonization Law of 1825, 78, 89, colonization policy of, 22–23, 36; Committee on Foreign Relations of, 12; Constitution of 1824, 108, 112, 124, 130; and emancipation of slaves, 36, 112; and empresario system, 5, 8, 23, 29, 38, 73; and European migrants, 32, 42; and federalists, 108, 132; and General Colonization Law of Mexico, 78; and immigration law of 1830, 28–32, 36, 86; and independence from Spain, 19–20, 108; and land grants, 5, 7, 73, 77, 80–81, 113, 129, 151, 152, 159; immigrant loyalty to, 73, 77, 114; and settlement requirements, 96–97; *See also* Coahuila y Texas (Mexican state); United States

Mexico City: as seat of government, 31

Mier Expedition, 208

Mier y Terán, Manuel de, 14, 27–29, 31, 33, 79, 81

Milam, Ben, 120

Miller's troops, 142

Miller, Kerby, 69, 70, 82, 191–92, 273n.19; *Emigrants and Exiles: Ireland and the Irish Exodus to North America*, 190

Mission Espíritu Santo, 80

Mission River, 97

Mitchel, Hugh, 216

Mitchel, John, 262n.31

Mitchel, Ned, 216

Mokyr, Joel, 58

Molloy, Father T. J., 86

Monahan, William, 99

Monclova (town), 86

Morgan, Abel, 139

Morris, George, 257

Mount Calvary Cemetery (Refugio), 103

Murphy, Judge John B., 105, 186, *187*

ISBN 1-58544-189-9

90000